WALKING IN THE SPIRIT

A REFLECTION ON JERÓNIMO NADAL'S PHRASE "CONTEMPLATIVE LIKEWISE IN ACTION"

JOSEPH F. CONWELL, S. J.

THE INSTITUTE OF
JESUIT SOURCES
SAINT LOUIS

No. 17 in Series 3: Original Studies Composed in English

© 2003 by The Institute of Jesuit Sources
3601 Lindell Blvd.
St. Louis, MO 63108
tel: [314] 966-7257
fax: [314] 977-7263
e-mail: ijs@slu.edu

Library of Congress Control Number: 2003113473
ISBN: 1-880810-52-2

To

Cecilia, my long-time co-worker,
who breathed prayer like air

Acknowledgments

Words of thanks fall short when I think of all the love and labor my Jesuit brother, Father Pat Howell of Seattle University, expended in supporting me from the beginning and in tirelessly critiquing the many versions of the manuscript. I am also grateful to Sister Phylis Taufen, S.N.J.M., who read the manuscript meticulously and made valuable suggestions regarding style and punctuation. I am grateful also to the Manresa Jesuit community, where I live, and the Regis Community, where I write, for their support and patient endurance, to Denis Donoghue, S.J., also of Seattle University, for his thorough critique of the manuscript and enlightening comments in private conversations, to John Padberg, S.J., of the Institute of Jesuit Sources, for accepting the manuscript in the first place and making perceptive observations regarding its content.

I owe special thanks to Dr. Michael Downey for writing the Foreword as well as making valuable comments regarding the text. I am grateful for the mainly anonymous assistance given by the library staff of the Foley Center at Gonzaga University, especially Connie Som for her help with interlibrary loans, and David Kingma, Stephanie Plowman and Sharon Prendergast in Archives and Special Collections.

Little would have been accomplished without the prayerful support of many friends, particularly of two who read the manuscript, Ann Kramp and Sister Mary Ann McGee, S.N.J.M. Finally, the patience, editing skill, and good humor of John L. McCarthy, S.J., of the Institute of Jesuit Sources, sustained me in the final months, for which I thank him gratefully.

CONTENTS

FOREWORD

C hristian prayer is a way of speaking in the Word and breathing in the Spirit. This can only come as gift. But the gift is always and everywhere an offer. One who has learned how to receive the gift is contemplative, as is one who lives freely and responsibly with, in, and from the gift. Contemplation is a way of beholding in wonder and in gratitude the presence of God in human life, history, the world, and the Church. Whether at prayer or immersed in activity, the contemplative is seized and saturated by gift.

Every page of this work, indeed each word, has been steeped in a gift given. For nearly fifty years Joseph F. Conwell has quietly undertaken the task of painstaking, thorough, careful, meticulous scholarship. From the time of his doctoral dissertation completed at the Gregorian University in 1957, Father Conwell has mined the veins of the Jesuit sources, narrowing in on the gem-laden legacy of Jerónimo Nadal. In so doing, he has rendered an inestimable contribution to the Society of Jesus. But it is especially in the present volume that he unearths the rich reserves of a Jesuit approach to prayer for the benefit of anyone of any tradition who is drawn by way of the paths of prayer into communion with the living God.

Walking in the Spirit is the *chef d'oeuvre* of a true master in the ways of Ignatian prayer and spirituality. Clearly delineating the contours of the kind of prayer proper to the Society of Jesus, Conwell is unwavering in his conviction that this prayer is not exclusive to the members of the Society. What has been received as a gift is given as a gift. And the gift is this: to be contemplative in prayer, contemplative likewise in action. Whether at prayer or while buzzing about the seemingly insurmountable tasks of the daily grind, it is the call of some *to be contemplative all the time.*

In the course of a life of study, research, and teaching, during which he also directed retreats, worked with Jesuit novices and scholastics, offered spiritual direction to priests, religious, and laypeople, over a lengthy period of time Joseph Conwell collaborated with Cecilia Wilms, a religious hermit who died on May 13, 1998. This encounter deepened his conviction that the prayer proper to the Society is not exclusive to it. Formed in the monastic tradition, Cecilia lived in strict solitude at the Hermitage of Our Lady of the City—a simple, stark, and spare second-floor apartment—in Spokane, Washington. Her life was given in its entirety to breathing in the Spirit and speaking in the Word. She lived the truth that Conwell conveys in his own life and writing: Whatever our way or walk in life, it is our gift and task to listen long and lovingly to the beating of the heart of God, becoming contemplative in prayer, contemplative likewise in action.

A gift of such magnitude overspills such designations as Jesuit, Ignatian, Cistercian, monastic, or lay. It is given to anyone who knows—from the inside out—that all we are and have, and all we ever shall be, is given by the One who is, above all, faithful. But this knowing is itself a gift freely given to those who, in living and dying, know how to receive.

Receive, now, the gift being offered in and through these pages.

Michael Downey

Professor of Systematic Theology and Spirituality
Saint John's Seminary, Camarillo, Cal.
Cardinal's Theologian, Archdiocese of Los Angeles

FREQUENTLY USED ABBREVIATIONS

AdhortRom	=	"Adhortationes in Collegio Romano"
AHSI	=	*Archivum historicum Societatis Iesu*
CIS	=	*Centrum Ignatianum Spiritualitatis*
CommInst	=	*P. Hieronymi Nadal commentarii de Instituto Societatis Iesu*
Cons.	=	*Saint Ignatius of Loyola: The Constitutions of the Society of Jesus* (Ganss)
ConsCN	=	*Constitutions of the Society of Jesus and Their Complementary Norms*
Constitutiones	=	*Constitutiones Societatis Jesu*
CSEL	=	*Corpus scriptorum ecclesiasticorum latinorum*
DocsGC3132	=	*Documents of the 31st and 32nd General Congregations of the Society of Jesus*
DocsGC34	=	*Documents of the Thirty-Fourth General Congregation of the Society of Jesus*
DocsVatII	=	*Vatican Council II: The Conciliar and Post-Conciliar Documents*
DSAM	=	*Dictionnaire de spiritualité ascétique et mystique*
Epist.mixt	=	*Epistolæ mixtæ ex variis Europæ locis ab anno 1537 ad 1556 scriptæ*
EpistBorg	=	*Sanctus Franciscus Borgia, quartus Gandiæ dux et Societatis Iesu præpositus generalis tertius*
EpistBroët	=	*Epistolæ PP. Paschasii Broëti, Claudii Jaji, Joannis Codurii, et Simonis Rodericii Societatis Iesu*
EpistFab	=	*Beati Petri Fabri, primi sacerdotis e Societate Iesu epistolæ*
EpistIgn	=	*Sancti Ignatii de Loyola Societatis Iesu fundatoris epistolæ et instructiones*
EpistLain	=	*Lainii monumenta: Epistolæ et acta Patris Jacobi Lainii secundi præpositi generalis Societatis Iesu*
EpistNadal	=	*Epistolæ et monumenta P. Hieronymi Nadal*
Exhort. 1554 Hisp.	=	"Exhortationes in Hispania"
Font.narr	=	*Fontes narrativi de Loyola et de Societatis Iesu initiis*
IHSI	=	Institutum historicum Societatis Iesu
MattGM	=	*For Matters of Greater Moment: The First Thirty Jesuit General Congregations*

PREFACE

A Bit of History

Walking in the Spirit is written for everyone interested in prayer. It invites Jesuits and others in the Ignatian tradition to feast on some of the earliest expositions of its spirituality; it invites and challenges those who are not Jesuits to "taste and see." Taste the piquancy of the Society of Jesus. If you are a Jesuit, see how profoundly you enjoy its spicy tang; if you are not a Jesuit, taste Loyola's cuisine. See the subtle differences in bouquet and flavor, so that you can savor even more your own call to serve God. John Dunne, C.S.C., of the University of Notre Dame, has excelled in helping Christians cross over for a moment to Buddhism or Hinduism or Islam, come to a deeper appreciation of that religious experience, and return with a better understanding and love of Christianity.[1] Taste and see, savor the flavor, and recognize that nothing can match your own mother's cooking.

Over fifty years ago I had a conversation about prayer in St. John of the Cross with a Jesuit friend, Ed McDermott, as we walked around a small lake at Alma College in California, where we were studying theology. "It's great for Carmelites," I said. "I wonder, is there anything special about Jesuit prayer?" I found the answer in the writings of Jerónimo Nadal, the man Ignatius of Loyola chose to promulgate the newly written Constitutions of the Society of Jesus throughout Europe. From that conversation about John of the Cross grew an idea for a licentiate paper in theology, which both expanded and contracted into a doctoral dissertation,

---

[1] For example, John S. Dunne, C.S.C., The Way of All the Earth: Experiments in Truth and Religion (Notre Dame: University of Notre Dame Press, 1978). Others have drawn fruitful comparisons between Ignatian spirituality and other spiritualities; for example, Ovey N. Mohammed, S.J., "Hinduism and Ignatian Spirituality," The Way, Supplement 68 (1990): 112–24; Donald Moore, S.J., "An Ignatian Perspective on Contemporary Jewish Spirituality," Thought 67 (1992): 420–29; Aloysius Pieris, S.J., "Ignatian Exercises against a Buddhist Background," The Way, Supplement 68 (1990): 98–111.

Contemplation in Action.[2] That study has now transformed itself into the present work, new in scope and intent.

Hints of subtleties that I could safely ignore in the 1950s haunted me at the end of the old and the beginning of the new millennium. What is, after all, *proper* to Carmelites, and what *proper* to Jesuits? Almost fifty years of directing retreats and serving as spiritual director for Jesuits and diocesan priests, lay men and women, and religious sisters of various congregations made me realize their differences; but if pricked a little, I saw, they all bled crimson Christian blood. They used the same words, but applied different concrete meanings. Along the way, I exposed myself in 1968–69 to eleven months of Asian religions, savoring the sameness and the differences; and that fall I arranged a seminar on Buddhism and Ignatian Spirituality. The best student in the seminar was a Cistercian nun to whom this book is dedicated, Sister Cecilia W. Wilms, a Belgian and a founding member of the Abbey of Our Lady of Redwoods in California. Thus began an almost thirty-year association that culminated in our working together for the last fifteen years of her life, even writing one book together, *Impelling Spirit,* and starting on this one.[3] She was clearly a nun and I was clearly a Jesuit with no temptation to be a monk. She helped me understand monasticism better; she aided me to see what is and what is not monastic, and how profoundly different our charisms are. For thirty days I directed her in the Spiritual Exercises and helped her understand Ignatius and the Society better. She came to love the early companions as well as individual living Jesuits she met, and some of these she helped to grow through her superb skill in listening and directing. Tasting and respecting what is *peculiar* or *proper* to another's spirituality make one appreciate what is *peculiar* or *proper* to one's own.

The differences were sometimes startling. Fairly early in my relationship with Cecilia, and long before we became co-workers in common enterprises like this book, we discussed the norms for choosing the work she needed for support while on leave from her Cistercian monastery. She was employed as secretary in a health program conducted by a secular university, and I proposed that apostolic impact might be one criterion—a normal suggestion for a Jesuit. She prayed over the matter, and decided next day that the primary criterion should be the extent to which the work

---

[2] Originally entitled *Prayer Proper to the Society of Jesus according to Jerome Nadal, S.J. (1507–1580),* Ph.D. dissertation presented at the Pontifical Gregorian University (Rome, 1957); with a change of cover and title to appear more reader friendly, it was also published under the title *Contemplation in Action: A Study in Ignatian Praye* (Spokane: Gonzaga University, 1957).

[3] Joseph F. Conwell, S.J., *Impelling Spirit: Revisiting a Founding Experience, 1539: Ignatius of Loyola and His Companions: An Exploration into the Spirit and Aims of the Society of Jesus as Revealed in the Founders' Proposed Papal Letter Approving the Society* (Chicago: Loyola Press, 1997).

would support her life of prayer. In view of the life to which she was called, she was, of course, correct.

Years later, after answering her call to be a hermit in the desert of the city, while cooperating with me on this book, Cecilia shocked me one day when she casually said, "For you this book is part of your mission; for me it is a job that earns money for my support." For a long moment the old prejudice arose of seeing matters from my limited Jesuit point of view, and I was shattered. Was all her effort just for money—her total dedication, her creativity in research, the demands she made on herself and her equally demanding critique of my writing, her search for truth that would impact others, her invariable dissatisfaction with the less than perfect? Didn't she really care? Then I realized that she was speaking as a hermit, that her calling was to pray, and that anything she did in partnership with me or for me was literally in support of her life of prayer. She wished to earn her living expenses so that she could pray, and all that she did she did with love as part of her prayer. Her heart was in her work because it opened avenues to prayer; but a question always remained for further discernment: Was it too absorbing in its breadth, too stimulating in its depth, too much like dulling drudgery in its demands for precision at times, and would her prayer be better if she were sweeping floors? I had always known that the more I made it possible for her to be a solitary hermit in the work, the more her work would be of profit to me. God calls us all in different ways.

Despite the fact that *Walking in the Spirit* has some roots in the past, its content makes it a sequel to *Impelling Spirit,* which tells how the Society of Jesus came into being; *Walking in the Spirit* tells how it continues in being, or to use the title of Part X of the *Constitutions,* How the Whole Body of the Society Is to Be Preserved and Increased in Its Well-Being. The earlier book centers on the persons, events, and spirituality surrounding the writing of the extremely brief Jesuit rule of life called the *Formula of the Institute.* Only the pope can change the *Formula. Walking in the Spirit* concerns the Jesuit *Constitutions* and a prior document called the *General Examen* (designed for candidates and their examiners), both the work of Ignatius of Loyola. Jesuit general congregations can modify these. *Impelling Spirit* is about founding the Society; *Walking in the Spirit* is about creative fidelity to its spirit, daily living out in community the "fifth week" of the Spiritual Exercises. *Impelling Spirit* touches on matters basic to any Christian spirituality; *Walking in the Spirit* tries to be a mirror in which all can salute their own charism.

Both books recognize the universal call to holiness expressed in Vatican II and respond to the council's invitation for religious to return to the sources of the whole of the Christian life and to the primitive inspiration of their own institute. It invites religious to taste and see the common source, the wellspring, of all religious life: the Holy Spirit living and working in the Church today. In and through the Spirit, each institute witnesses in a special way to something found in all. It invites their members to taste and see something that belongs to you and to others as well. Each Christian way of life is a gift to the Church and to every other Christian way of living. The council invites religious to taste and see the similarities and the delicate shades of difference between their institutes; it calls upon them to enjoy these and return more enthusiastically than ever to the old and familiar that is just right for each one.

After the publication of *Impelling Spirit* in 1997, people asked me if I intended to prepare a new edition of *Contemplation in Action*. Since I had learned a fair amount over forty years, the idea seemed good. Many manuscripts not easily accessible in the 1950s had been edited. Jesuits had written innumerable articles on Nadal and Jesuit prayer or published books on Jesuit spirituality, and over forty years of ministry, both the Society's and my own, had gone by.[4] A new vision had come to the Church through Vatican II, and to the Society through four general congregations (selected Jesuits gathered from around the world as the Society's chief legislative body): the Thirty-First General Congregation, meeting from 1965 to 1966, the Thirty-Second (1974–75), the Thirty-Third (1983), and the Thirty-Fourth (1995), inciting through their decrees a new outlook, a new purpose, a new energy. As I tried to make it up to date, inserting it into the larger context of the contemporary and future Society, absorbing insights from the newer books and articles, and paying attention to an Ignatian phrase, "walking in the spirit," that I had ignored in the 1950s, it took on a life of its own. After reading an early version of the new manuscript, a Jesuit friend from Seattle University, Pat Howell, said, "Let's face it. This is a new book. Why don't you call it *Walking in the Spirit*"? I already knew it was a new book and found the Ignatian phrase intriguing. It reminded me of the Navaho phrase "walking in beauty," living in harmony with nature and all of life, to which Tony Hillerman refers in his mystery novels of the American Southwest.[5] And so it was.

General Congregation 34, meeting in Rome in 1995, pointed out both what was obsolete and what was relevant in the decrees of earlier congregations and the writings of the generals of the Society. It clearly determined what the governing norms of the Society are, and hoped for a renewal in the understanding of the Constitutions comparable to what had already occurred in the understanding of the Exercises. This new book, *Walking in the Spirit,* approaches the Constitutions and General Examen,

---

[4] For a listing of books relevant to this topic, see appendix 1, pp. 271 f.

[5] "With beauty before me may I walk, / With beauty behind me may I walk, / With beauty above me may I walk, / With beauty all around me may I walk" (*Pocket Prayers,* ed. Gertrud Mueller Nelson and Christopher Witt [New York: Doubleday Books, 1995]), 48.

not as a commentator analyzing every word and statement, but as a treasure seeker searching out works of art buried in the sand at the bottom of the sea. *Walking in the Spirit* points in general directions and rejoices in specific finds. The treasure is vast.

Writing *Contemplation in Action* in the 1950s, I was already aware of paying insufficient attention to the chronological sequence of texts I chose for comment, the possibility of growth in Nadal, and especially in his understanding and presentation of the implications of the Constitutions. Some forty years later, while writing *Impelling Spirit,* about the foundational experience of Ignatius and his companions, I realized the need to include more of the actual context in which Nadal worked and spoke and wrote. Working on that book made those men come alive for me: they became real people with all their virtues and all their faults; it also made Nadal more alive and real, his times more vivid, his dreams more vibrant, his disappointments more painful. After forty years of dreams and disappointments of my own, I understood better what he was talking about and trying to do.[6]

In view of the revival of interest in Trinitarian studies, and especially in view of Pedro Arrupe's talks and letters to the Society on the Trinity and Ignatian spirituality, I have been more careful than I was in the 1950s to emphasize the Trinitarian foundations of Ignatian spirituality and prayer.[7] As I was giving the book its final touches, a gift to aid me in that task came in the form of Dr. Michael Downey's *Altogether Gift: A Trinitarian Spirituality.*[8]

Regarding the fundamental role of the Trinity in Ignatian spirituality, it would be too much to say that Ignatius (or Nadal) was untainted by the distractions and abstractions introduced into theology through the Trinitarian controversies of the early Church. Those controversies belong to a long historical moment that is coming to an end only in our own

---

[6] I owe an apology to Dr. Pedro Ortiz, although he probably took no offense when I mistakenly called him a layman in *Contemplation in Action.* He was a doctor of theology, not of medicine, a priest (see Ignacio Iparraguirre, S.J., *Práctica de los ejercicios de San Ignacio de Loyola en vida de su autor [1522–1556],* 124, 196) who taught at the university when Ignatius and his companions were in Paris, preceding them to Rome as Charles V's negotiator in the matter of Henry VIII's divorce from Catherine of Aragon. He made the Exercises under Ignatius at Monte Cassino, and would have become a Jesuit if his girth had not made him an unlikely candidate for the Society's ministries (Juan de Polanco, S.J., *Vita Ignatii Loiolæ et rerum Societatis Iesu historia,* 6 vols., vols. 1, 3, 5, 7, 9, and 11 of the series Monumenta historica Societatis Iesu [Rome: Institutum Historicum Societatis Iesu (IHSI), 1:64]). This source is collectively known as the *Chronicon* of Polanco and hereafter will be cited as POLCHRON. The Monumenta series will be designated MHSI.

[7] For a list of readings relevant to this material, see appendix 2, pp. 272 f.

[8] Maryknoll, N.Y.: Orbis Books, 2000.

times, a moment caricatured in phrases such as "one nature, two processions, three persons, four relations, and five properties." The Trinity is not an arithmetical conundrum in the minds of Ignatius and Nadal. Neither do they represent a return to the simplicity of the New Testament, in which the Father is God, the Son is Lord, and the Holy Spirit is the Spirit of the Father and the Son; the simplicity in which the Father is creator, the Son is redeemer who pleads for us at God's right hand, and the Holy Spirit is sanctifier and our advocate before the Father and the Son. Only after careful study of Ignatian texts can the reader determine the divine Person to whom the name "God" refers, an ambiguity unknown in the New Testament. Ignatius, for example, frequently uses the phrase "God our Creator and Lord" when referring to the Son. In any case, I must be faithful to the texts and cannot place a contemporary Trinitarian grid over passages of Ignatius and Nadal and read into the texts what is not there. On the other hand, the contemporary theologian of the Trinity might find much place for dialog with Ignatius, the alert reflective pray-er, whose theology, imbibed fresh from the source, is spontaneous, and even with the reflective theologian, Jerónimo Nadal, whose thought on occasion muddies the spring.

Nadal coined the phrase "simul in actione contemplativus" (contemplative likewise in the midst of action), which inspired the title of my book *Contemplation in Action*. In a provocative study, *Karl Rahner and Ignatian Spirituality*, Philip Endean makes the statement that

> what became the standard Jesuit reading of Nadal's phrase may have no basis in Nadal's own thinking. Only once does the expression "contemplative in action" appear in Nadal's published writings, and Nadal never systematically developed it. . . . The strong contrast between *contemplata aliis tradere* and *in actione contemplativus* found in Nadal's twentieth-century Jesuit interpreters . . . is probably foreign to his thought.[9]

He argues that Thomas equates "contemplata aliis tradere" with "vita activa superior" and, moreover, that Nadal talks about "vita activa superior" frequently and systematically. The twentieth-century interpretation "moves beyond Thomas in suggesting that one finds God actually in activity, including the so-called corporal works of mercy. . . . However edifying and valid this thought may be, it is probably absent from Nadal's text."[10]

I freely admit that Nadal used the phrase only once, and perhaps it can be said that he "never systematically developed it"; but before and after coining the phrase, he used equivalent language whenever he talked

---

[9] Philip Endean, S.J., *Karl Rahner and Ignatian Spirituality* (Oxford: Oxford University Press, 2001), 74.

[10] *Ibid.*, 74 f.

to Jesuits about prayer. As you read, count the ways. If he was not particularly taken by his own phrase, he was genuinely sold on the idea that contemplation leads to action and that the action to which it leads should be contemplative action.

Some persons lead profoundly contemplative lives, lives of quiet prayer and seclusion; they do not engage in action beyond the ordinary actions of eating and drinking and reading and writing and performing the manual labor or exercise needed to remain in good health. Others are persons of action engaged in enterprises of greater or lesser importance— even prayerfully engaged—who would in no way consider themselves contemplative. Still others regularly and often engage in contemplation, but also find themselves busily performing good works for the sake of other people. They may be sometimes contemplative, sometimes active. Or they may be contemplative all the time, contemplative in prayer, contemplative likewise in action. Strictly speaking, *Walking in the Spirit* is about the third group of people, and about those who desire to become like them. Since persons, however, tend to break the bonds of categories, anyone interested in prayer and contemplation can learn much by reflecting through these pages on what it means to be not only contemplative in prayer but "contemplative likewise in action," for all Christians are called to that in some way.

My definition of contemplation is rather broad, certainly not limited to that kind of prayer which is described as non-discursive to distinguish it from discursive meditation. Contemplation suggests a certain awareness, attentiveness, a being in touch with mystery, being caught up with delight in what is going on in life, or in a gospel story, or in the mysterious depths of God. To be contemplative suggests watching, and also receiving, and being present. On a sunny day one is aware of the sunshine even when not adverting to the sunshine; just so, a contemplative person can be aware of God, or of being on a search for God, or of being about God's work when not actually thinking of God. The old person in the nursing home reciting the rosary may be thinking about home and family and years gone by, but is aware of being at prayer. Paying attention to what is going on embraces wide differences and degrees, and so does contemplation. To be contemplative suggests an attitude, a way of being, and has something to do with mystery.

Regarding the kind of prayer proper to the Society of Jesus, while studying Nadal's remarks one must keep in mind that the Society in the time of Nadal was brand new. Ignatian innovations that were startling then are ordinary things today. During the past 450 years, many religious communities have come into existence whose institutes owe much to the rule and spirit of Ignatius. In addition, many lay people find that God is impelling them along a path similar to that of the Society. Even the older orders and the diocesan clergy have felt the impact of the Society, just as

Ignatius and his companions felt the lasting impact of the Carthusians, Franciscans, and Dominicans. How much they have been affected and modified by its influence would make, in fact, an intriguing study. To the extent that any or all of these paths to God may be similar to that of the Society, the prayer practiced on these paths will also be similar to that of the Society. At times the shades and tones of difference will be too delicate to define.

Bear with me, then, if following my most effusive witness, Jerónimo Nadal, I often speak in terms of Jesuit prayer. Whatever Nadal may have intended at the time, I do not believe that prayer *proper* to the Society of Jesus is *exclusive* to the Society of Jesus. Be prepared to hear yourself protest, "But we do that too!" I am convinced that many who are not members of the Society of Jesus will find described in these pages a kind of prayer that they not only find attractive but have been practicing for a long time—indeed, a kind of prayer that will clarify their own struggles and their own experiences in prayer. In any case, just as musing over the prayer of the Carmelite John of the Cross stimulated me to learn more about the prayer proper to a Jesuit, so I hope studying the kind of prayer practiced in the Society of Jesus will stir every reader to search for and find the kind of prayer that is appropriate to the vocation to which, in that old impelling way, the Holy Spirit has called the reader.

Way of Proceeding

At the start of a new millennium we are more conscious of the need for new beginnings. The recent general congregations of the Society of Jesus have responded to this need, and the Society has both struggled and rejoiced to reincarnate in its own time the vision of St. Ignatius. The challenge is great, something like that of the new Society in 1540, when it was born into a culture that had rigid views of what a religious order was, rigid expectations of the religious way of life, rigid norms for holiness. Even in the midst of cries for reform, no established society, secular or ecclesiastical, has ever wanted anyone to rock the boat. The Spiritual Exercises of St. Ignatius, the General Examen, and the Constitutions are all designed to rock the boat, to do what John the Baptist and Jesus did; they all call out, "Change your lives and believe the Good News!"

The Good News is that Jesus is alive and his Spirit is moving in our times, in us, impelling us toward that quiet death that sprouts forth into new life, "first the blade, then the ear, then the full grain in the ear" (Mark. 4:28). That is why Dominique Bertrand can write of the Constitutions:

> The Constitutions . . . do not evoke nostalgia for a bygone heroic epoch, . . . are not a guide to living the way some giants might have lived by way of example in the beginning. . . . In the Constitutions the institute

is proposed for all, first companions and new companions, as the future; there is one continuing end to be realized by all the companions in the line of the end of every human being, an end both ultimate and primary: God who works for the salvation of the human race.[11]

The goal of the Constitutions is not the goal of Jesuits alone; it is the goal of the Church, the goal of the human race as intended by God. Anyone, therefore, can learn about his or her own goal in life by studying the experience of the Society. This book is not for Jesuits only, but for any person of goodwill who wishes to learn something about serving God in daily life.

Chapter 1 of *Walking in the Spirit* sets the stage and introduces Jerónimo Nadal as the man Ignatius chose to promulgate the newly written *General Examen* and *Constitutions* throughout the Society. Nadal talks about the grace proper to the Society, and begins to reflect on the *General Examen* (chapter 2), and on the *Constitutions,* including chastity and obedience (chapter 3). In his exhortations he presents different ways of knowing the grace of the Society: (1) the imitation of Jesus and the primitive Church (chapter 4); (2) the considerations in the *Spiritual Exercises* on the Kingdom and the Two Standards (chapter 5); (3) the end of the Society (chapter 6); (4) the life of Ignatius as it illumines the life of novices (chapter 7), of scholastics (chapter 8), of those with final vows (chapter 9), and his own prayer life (chapter 10). The final chapter looks to the future as seen in the present life of elderly Jesuits (chapter 11).

This book is not a collection of meditations on the *General Examen* and the *Constitutions;* but it *is* a book for reflection. To provide some sense of the life of this prodigious traveler and pilgrim, I present a comment before each chapter on or from Nadal and part of the chronology of his life (not necessarily coextensive with the content of the chapter). So that it is not an exercise in reflection on the past only, I open each chapter with a quotation from Vatican II's decree *Perfectæ Caritatis (On the Up-to-Date Renewal of Religious Life),* as well as a passage from a decree of one of the more recent general congregations of the Society of Jesus. Taking a cue from Ignatius, I also introduce into each chapter (1) a short history to provide at least a partial setting or background for the chapter, (2) a brief passage from the *Spiritual Exercises* of St. Ignatius, and (3) a prayer for the grace we desire from our reflection—since I also hope that the experience of reading the book will be a prayerful one for each reader.

Feast of the Conversion of St. Paul, January 25, 2003

---

[11] Dominique Bertrand, S.J., *Un Corps pour l'Esprit* (Paris: Desclée de Brouwer, 1974), 57 f.

PROLOG: 1572

The startling originality of the new Society of Jesus had from the beginning caused problems in the Church. In spite of the enthusiastic support demonstrated by Pope Paul III when he approved the Society in 1540, and in spite of the Society's success and growth, dark clouds continued to hover just above the horizon. In 1558 Pope Paul IV had imposed a three-year term of office upon the general of the Society and commanded Jesuits to chant the office in common, a mandate they carried out until the Pope's death the following year. Pope St. Pius V (1566–72) again ordered the Society to chant the office in common in a modified form, and also required Jesuit scholastics to pronounce solemn vows before ordination, thereby fundamentally changing the Society's Institute, its way of proceeding. In 1571, while Fr. General Francis Borgia left Rome on a mission assigned him by Pius V, the former appointed a vicar-general to govern the Society in his absence. After the Pope's death, the vicar-general appealed to the new pope, Gregory XIII, to restore the Institute to its original design. The new pope appointed Cardinal Borromeo to preside over a commission charged with studying the matter. While Borgia was still out of the country, the vicar-general wrote a lengthy letter to Borromeo defending the Society's traditions and asking the Pope to restore them. Part of that letter (two out of its sixteen printed pages) will make much that is contained in this book easier to understand.

Following a tradition stemming from Bonaventure or an unknown writer now called Pseudo-Bonaventure, the vicar-general used terminology likely to be unfamiliar to many modern readers.[1] After explaining that the Society's field of endeavor embraced an incredible variety of works among heretics and infidels as well as among the faithful, he remarked as follows:

> Wherefore, ours is not a monastic order, nor should it be judged in terms of other orders of clerics with a rule, but according to its own end and the means necessary for that end.

---

[1] "Meditationes vitæ Christi," chap. 45, in *S. Bonaventuræ Opera*, ed. A. Peltier (Paris, 1868), 12:569–70. See *Dictionnaire de spiritualité ascétique et mystique (DSAM)*, s.vv. "Vie active, contemplative, mixte," by Aimé Solignac.

Hence the Society is substantially and of its very Institute a religious order that is contemplative as well as active.

We practice the contemplative life in meditation, prayer, and in the diligent and ongoing use of all the spiritual exercises. For, without the spiritual vitality that prayer preserves, the Society could not practice the active life with proper dignity.

The active life in the Society is multiplex. It consists primarily in the more excellent action of preaching, lecturing, and other spiritual ministries proper to simple priests, and of studying for scholastics, and secondarily in the ministry of the corporal works of mercy.

Wherefore, the Society as a religious order is multiplex, as if to say many religious orders rolled into one through the divine goodness. For the Society was instituted for contemplation, for preaching and hearing confessions, for other spiritual ministries, for the corporal works of mercy, and finally for study: for the teaching of theologians is that religious orders can be instituted for all these purposes.

For these reasons (that our way of living is so broad, our ministries so multiple, so difficult, and so exhausting), it follows that our times of probation, or novitiate, should be very lengthy and carefully done, our obedience most demanding, and every aspect of the religious life perfect as far as possible. Then also, since we have so many difficult and necessary occupations—mind you—lest souls be lost for whom Christ Jesus was crucified and died, we judge that certain rituals are not proper for us since they can impede our ministries, just as certain things are suitable for other religious orders and other things are not. Besides, we also take care that those to be professed have not only been proved in the practice of living after the manner of religious, but have also been sufficiently trained in the ministries that they have to undertake. Whence it follows that they should first be priests before they are professed. Other religious orders train their novices in choir and in other ceremonies; we train ours in the ministries proper to our Institute, those that prepare our men to undertake those ministries of the Society for the salvation of souls.[2]

The vicar-general argued convincingly. Borromeo's commission gave its approval, and Pope Gregory XIII restored the Society to its earlier form.

The name of the vicar-general who persuaded both cardinal and pope was Jerónimo Nadal.

---

[2] "De professione et choro," in *Epistolæ et monumenta P. Hieronymi Nadal*, ed. Miguel Nicolau, S.J., vols. 13, 15, 21, and 27 of MHSI (Rome: Institutum historicum Societatis Iesu, 1962) 4:174f. Hereafter these first four volumes of *Epistolæ Nadal* will be abbreviated to *EpistNadal*, and the Institutum historicum Societatis Iesu TO IHSI.

Chronicle for Chapter 1

Father Nadal's virtues were very great, especially his esteem and zeal for our Institute and the well-being of the Society for which he worked hard. Our blessed Father spoke to me in high praise of him frequently, and from the tasks given him by Ignatius and the other generals can be seen the confidence and esteem they had of his religious commitment, prudence, and learning.

—Pedro Ribadeneira, S.J., Letter to Fr. Antonio Moranta

Nadal's Life and Travels (1507–1553)

1507: Born, Palma in Majorca, August 11

1526–32: Studies in Alcalá; sees Ignatius from afar

1532–36: Studies in Paris; comes to know Ignatius and companions; will not join them

1536–38: Studies in Avignon; doctorate in theology; ordained

1538–45: Returns to Majorca; lives in constant anxiety with headaches and stomach pains; greatly influenced by prayers, life, and death of Isabel Cifra; general confession; discusses prayer with local hermit, Antonio; reads Pseudo-Dionysius the Areopagite; stirred by reading copy of letter from Francis Xavier

1545: Goes to Rome; admitted into the Society of Jesus; stays in Rome

1548–51: Messina, Sicily; founds college and establishes novitiate, visits Trapani, establishes novitiate in Palermo, preaches, founds house for penitent women; presents self as chaplain to navy assembled to fight Turks, is shipwrecked, stranded in Africa at Aphrodisium (formerly Hippo, later Bône or Annaba[h]), teaches

1552

Establishes orphanage in Catania; goes to Rome for final vows; stops in Naples on return to Messina; promulgates the *Constitutions* in Messina and then in Palermo; teaches Hebrew, preaches; leaves Palermo via Naples for Rome

1553

April 11: Leaves Rome for Spain

April 18: Sails from Genoa; storm; Nice

May 5–17: Barcelona; establishes "order" in college

May 24–June 7: Valencia

June 11–16: Cuenca

June 19–24: Alcalá, consults with Araoz

Heads for Lisbon via Madrid, Villaviciosa, Évora

The chronology at the beginning of each chapter is based primarily on "Cronologia de la vida del P. Jerônimo Nadal, S.I. (1507–1580)," by Manuel Ruiz Jurado, S.J., *Archivum historicum Societatis Iesu* 46 (1979): 248-76.

Chapter One

GROWING PAINS AND HEALING PRESENCE

> From the very beginning of the Church, there were men and women who set out to follow Christ with greater liberty and to imitate him more closely by practicing the evangelical counsels. They led lives dedicated to God, each in his own way. Many of them under the inspiration of the Holy Spirit, became hermits or founded religious families. These the Church, by virtue of her authority, gladly accepted and approved.
>
> —Vatican II, *Decree on the Appropriate Renewal of the Religious Life*

Renewing a religious order or congregation, like founding one, is an enterprise filled with joy suffused with pain. Like Abraham, one sets out into the unknown, departing from the familiar, setting a new course different from those of others, different from one's present and one's past, yet rooted in the past and called forth from the past by God to fulfill the past in a manner new, surprising, and unexpected. Just as Christ calls all Christians "to put away your former way of life, your old self, corrupt and deluded by its lusts, . . . and to clothe yourselves with the new self, created according to the likeness of God" (Eph. 4:22, 24), so he calls each religious community. The early Society of Jesus answered the call, wavered, stumbled, flailed about, righted itself with God's grace, and went on. So, too, the Society of Jesus in the third millennium:

> In our review of the state of the Society, we faced our limitations and weaknesses. . . . But we also found much that was wise and good, especially the powerful and pervasive effort to pursue the service of faith and that struggle for justice which it includes. In the review of our graces over these years, we found again "the omnipotent hand of Christ, God and our Lord."[1] In gratitude for so much good accomplished and for so much forgiven, we follow this Christ, the Crucified and Risen Lord, in pilgrimage

---

[1] *The Constitutions of the Society of Jesus and Their Complementary Norms* (St. Louis: The Institute of Jesuit Sources, 1996), *C:* 812 (p. 400). This source will hereafter be abbreviated to *ConsCN*, followed by the marginal number of the text and, for convenience, the page number. When necessary to avoid confusion, *C:* will indicate citations taken from the *Constitutions; CN:* those taken from the *Complementary Norms*.

and labor. We see our renewal of the law and our review of our life and apostolic labor as one reality, the confirmation of our union as servants of Christ's mission.[2]

The task of this chapter is to introduce the Society of Jesus in the first decade and a half of its "infancy and adolescence," as well as the man who had the formidable task of promulgating the Society's *Constitutions* to hundreds of its energetic and sometimes bewildered members.

History

Bursting suddenly into the consciousness of the mid-sixteenth century, Ignatius of Loyola (as though anticipating Vatican II) "set out to follow Christ with greater liberty, and to imitate him more closely" in creative continuity with the first fifteen Christian centuries, but *in his own way*. *Liberty* meant putting off the old self and putting on the new, the true self, free to serve God in joy and generosity. So completely original was his new religious family, the Society of Jesus, that it transcended the limits of the common paradigm of religious institutes, upsetting early critics, yet "the Church gladly accepted and approved" this new way of living: without habit, without choir, without regular penances obligatory on all, with works multiple and varied and a general elected for life, requiring two years of novitiate when most others were satisfied with one.[3] With profession not the same as taking vows, the Society at first admitted as members only those who were priests or desired to become priests, who at the end of the novitiate pronounced three *simple* but perpetual vows of poverty, chastity, and obedience, adding to them a promise to enter the Society. Some years after ordination they were invited to take three *solemn* vows of poverty, chastity, and obedience, and usually a fourth solemn vow to go wherever the pope might send them. When the first few years showed that these "professed" could make good use of assistance in both their spiritual and temporal activities, the Society admitted priests who had more limited skills, who could help with the sacraments and other spiritual works, and laymen, who assisted in tasks not requiring priestly ordination. These priests were known as spiritual coadjutors and the laymen as temporal coadjutors. Like the scholastics preparing for profession after ordination, these spiritual and temporal coadjutors took simple vows of poverty,

---

[2] General Congregation 34, Decree 1, "United with Christ in Mission," in *Documents of the Thirty-Fourth General Congregation of the Society of Jesus* (St. Louis: The Institute of Jesuit Sources, 1995), no. 3. Hereafter this source will be abbreviated to *DocsGC34*.

[3] See Rafael M.ª Sanz de Diego, S.J., "La novedad de Ignacio de Loyola ante un mundo nuevo," in *Ignacio de Loyola y su tiempo: Congreso internacional de historia (9–13 Setiembre 1991)*, ed. Juan Plazaola (Bilbao: Mensajero—Universidad de Deusto, 1992), 909–30 (hereafter this volume will be cited as Plazaola, *Ignacio y su tiempo*).

chastity, and obedience, and were not eligible for the highest offices in the Society.[4]

In failing thus to meet accustomed expectations, the Society puzzled some, confused others, and disturbed many. Some theologians considered the order dangerous, scripturally unsound, a threat to the life of the Church. It was so out of tune with the climate and expectations of the times that some of the young men who eagerly joined the Society's ranks in the beginning failed to grasp its spirit; others found its spirituality woefully lacking. Even some of its more committed members were blinded by its brilliance and its spiritual freedom. To paraphrase Josef Stierli, in a revolutionary break from a thousand years of Western monastic tradition, in which contemplation held the central place, the Society regarded everything as pointing toward ministry, embracing not one work only but a ministry universal in its scope. Moreover, in abandoning many monastic practices, like regular penances, Ignatius introduced a new ideal as the central principle of religious life, "seeking or finding God in all things," and thus opened a path for new religious communities and gave lay people a way to integrate faith and their daily lives.[5]

A Pause for Prayer

Ignatius spent over ten months in prayer at Manresa, an experience that gave birth to the book called the *Spiritual Exercises,* containing directions on how to lead someone else through a similar experience in the space of about thirty days.[6] All the other men who joined him in Paris made these

---

[4] One day a young Jesuit student complained that someone had called him a "baby Jesuit." "In the Society," he said, "we are all peers." "Baby Jesuit" is condescending at best; in the Society no one should lord it over anyone else. But as to "We are all peers," yes and no. Ignatius says yes when he writes in the *Constitutions* that the Society in its broadest sense includes all who live under obedience to the superior general, even novices; he says no when he states that in its most proper sense the Society comprises only the professed. The *Complementary Norms* explain the matter well: Yes, insofar as all members participate in the same vocation and mission, but no, insofar as they do so "each according to the proper mode of his vocation" (*ConstCN C:* 511 [p. 192]; *CN:* 6, §1 [p. 62 f.]).

[5] Josef Stierli, S.J., "Ignatian Prayer: Seeking God in All Things," in *Ignatius of Loyola: His Personality and Spiritual Heritage, 1556–1956: Studies on the 400th Anniversary of His Death,* ed. Friedrich Wulf, S.J. (St. Louis: The Institute of Jesuit Sources, 1977), 135–63, esp. 135–37. This is also found with some slight differences in *Woodstock Letters* 90 (1961): 135–66, trans. Morton J. Hill, S.J., from the original, *Ignatius von Loyola: Seine Gestalt und sein Vermächtnis* (Würzburg, 1956).

[6] See, for example, *The Spiritual Exercises of Saint Ignatius,* trans. and commentary by George E. Ganss, S.J. (St. Louis: The Institute of Jesuit Sources, 1992). Hereafter, this source will be abbreviated to *SpEx,* followed by the marginal number and, for

Exercises under his direction or that of Pierre Favre. They asked the Holy Spirit to set them free, so that they might be fully available to God. Nadal wrote one day:

> Through our Lord's favor each of us draws from the Exercises a very special grace which allows us to know and be interiorly aware of our own special vocation, bringing special peace and union with God in spiritual obedience and in the particular fulfillment of the way each of us has to go to God.[7]

"Exercises to overcome oneself and to order one's life, without reaching a decision through some disordered affection" (*SpEx* 21).

After the usage of the Spiritual Exercises of St. Ignatius, we ask for what we desire in this chapter, an open heart longing to be set free so that God may breathe the Holy Spirit into us, drawing us to follow Christ with greater liberty, and to imitate him more closely, teaching us how to embrace the "flesh" of God's world and become effective instruments to do the work of God in our own times, depending always on God's transforming power and goodness and love.

The Task of Ignatius

Ignatius of Loyola prayed for years about his role in the life of the Church before he actually found that role. He had desired to go on pilgrimage to the Holy Land as a layman and there work for "the good of souls"; but once there he found that ecclesiastical authorities would not allow him to remain. He began to realize the need for study, for priestly ordination, for working together with other priests. After some years he was ready to lead a group of priests to the Holy Land to help in the work of the Church; but Pope Paul III said to them: "Why this great desire to go to Jerusalem? Italy is a bona fide Jerusalem if you want to produce fruit for God's Church."[8] When war with the Turks made Jerusalem an impossible dream, they enthusiastically embraced Italy and the rest of the world as the place where Christ lived and breathed and walked the earth in God's people.

---

convenience, the page number.

[7] *EpistNadal* 4:673.

[8] Reported by Nicolás Bobadilla, one of the Paris companions, in his autobiography (*Fontes narrativi de Loyola et de Societatis Iesu initiis [Font.narr.],* ed. Cándido de Dalmases, 4 vols., vols. 66, 73, 85, and 93 of MHSI [Rome: IHSI, 1943–65], 3:327).

They offered themselves to the Pope to work wherever he wished. When he began to send them singly or in twos to various places, they asked themselves whether they wanted to separate from one another or preserve their unity in some fashion. Eventually they decided to establish a religious body whose members would be available to be sent anywhere in the world.

In 1539 Pope Paul III orally approved the *Formula of the Institute,* a brief summary of the Jesuit way of life that would serve as its rule. Some murmurings came from Girolamo Cardinal Ghinucci, the Pope's secretary for papal briefs, when he was asked to create a papal letter solemnizing the oral approbation of the new Society. Some of the wording in the *Formula* troubled him. He was apprehensive that forbidding organ music or singing at Mass and other liturgical ceremonies played into the hands of the Lutherans. He was disquieted that the companions ruled out common fasts, common penances, and a common habit. The vow to go anywhere the pope might send the Society's members struck him as unnecessary. After consulting Ignatius and his companions, however, he accepted the vow as appropriate; the companions agreed to omit the passages he found inopportune and received solemn approbation in 1540.[9]

From 1540 to 1550 Ignatius worked on the *Constitutions,* spelling out in detail the Jesuit way of living. His first helper, Jean Codure, died in 1541. When Juan de Polanco took office as secretary of the Society in 1547, serious work on the *Constitutions* began. During these early years the members of the Society had little guidance beyond letters from Ignatius and the general principles laid down in the *Formula.* As he was writing the *Constitutions,* Ignatius himself was learning from both the successes and the shortcomings of the Society. He kept in touch with provincial and local superiors and others by letter and insisted that they keep in touch with him. Nothing was lost; nothing went to waste. The *Constitutions* echo over and over again with reverberations from the houses and missions: instances of excessive zeal, excessive generosity, excessive fear, lack of trust in the presence of the Holy Spirit—the attempts of men to create themselves. In the prayerful writing of the *Constitutions,* which are Ignatius's own yes to the Holy Spirit, God broke into that attempt of men to create themselves and through Ignatius outlined how the Society is to say yes to God. Julius III confirmed the *Formula* in 1550, including changes that the experiences of ten years showed were needed or helpful. After "finishing" the *Constitutions* that year, Ignatius

---

[9]Letter of Ghinucci's nephew, Lattanzio Tolomeo, September 28, 1539, to Cardinal Contarini, who had presented the petition of the companions to the Pope. This letter is found in *Regesten und Briefe des Cardinals Gasparo Contarini (1483–1542),* by Franz Dittrich (Braunsberg: 1881), 379–80; parts of the letter are in *Storia della Compagnia di Gesù in Italia,* by Pietro Tacchi Venturi, 2nd ed. (Rome, 1950), vol. 2, pt. 1: 277 nn. 1 and 3, 278.

invited a group of talented Jesuits from all over Europe to a conference to reflect on what he had composed and to give him feedback. The fruit of the consultation was a document in 1552 containing their suggestions for improvements.[10]

Ignatius now needed a man who had a profound knowledge of the Society and loved it, who knew the heart of Ignatius as well as his own heart, who by his manner of living and by his understanding of the mind of Ignatius could make clear to the rest of the Society what was new and what was different about the Society they had joined, and in what new and different way the Society mirrored Jesus, whose name it bore. Ignatius needed a healing presence, someone to strengthen the faltering, bind the wounds, mend the gaps, check the overzealous, and encourage both the healthy and the fainthearted.

In those early days the original companions, on whose wisdom and experience local superiors might have drawn, were scattered or had passed on to the next life. Of the six young men Ignatius had gathered around him in Paris, Pierre Favre, from the diocese of Geneva in Savoy, was dead by 1546, after he had tramped around much of Europe; Francis Xavier, from the diocese of Pamplona in Navarre, had been provincial in India but died at the threshold of China in 1552; Diego Laínez, from Sigüenza in Spain, was currently a papal theologian at the Council of Trent, along with Alfonso Salmerón, from Toledo in Spain; Nicholás Bobadilla, from a village of the diocese of Palencia in Spain, was busy preaching in Italy, founding a college in Naples, and investigating heresy in Calabria; Simón Rodrigues, from Vizeu in Portugal, had been sidetracked on the way to India to become provincial in Portugal, where he was attracting numerous recruits but not governing them well. Of the three companions Favre had attracted after Ignatius left Paris for Spain and Venice, Paschase Broët, a priest from Geneva, had spent a harrowing time with Salmerón on a mission to Thomas Cromwell's Ireland and then went to work in Italy, becoming provincial there before being named provincial of France; Claude Jay,

---

[10] "Observata patrum," in *Monumenta Constitutionum prævia,* vol. 1 of *Constitutiones Societatis Jesu* (hereafter *Constitutiones*), 3 vols., vols. 63, 64, and 65 of MHSI (Rome: IHSI, 1934), 1:390–96, written in Spanish. Ignatius and Polanco had produced a rather prolix text α of the *Constitutions* in Spanish between 1547 and 1550, which they revised into text A (1550), the text discussed at the meeting in Rome. They revised text A into text B, called the autograph. Nadal's copy of text B is called B[1]. Ignatius continued making revisions and marginal notations on the autograph manuscript until his death in 1556. Text C depends largely on the autograph copy of Ignatius and includes all his corrections. The First General Congregation approved text C and Polanco's Latin translation in 1558, and General Congregation 5 approved a new version in Spanish in 1594. For a full discussion in Latin, see *Constitutiones,* 2:v-cclxxii; for a shorter but adequate presentation in English, see *Saint Ignatius of Loyola: The Constitutions of the Society of Jesus,* trans. and annot. by George E. Ganss, S.J. (St. Louis: The Institute of Jesuit Sources, 1970), 35–59, especially pp. 49–54.

another Savoyard, spent four years in Germany, then participated in the Council of Trent, and finally died in Vienna in 1552; Jean Codure, a gentle Frenchman from Embrun, died in 1541 while helping Ignatius with the *Constitutions*. Even if those who were alive had been free, none of them had spent much time recently at the side of Ignatius in the heart of the Society in Rome.

Therefore, instead of turning to one of his first companions, Ignatius preferred to rely on a man whom he had invited to join them in the beginning, only to have his invitation clearly and deliberately rejected. Jerónimo Nadal's experience in making a life decision during the Spiritual Exercises some years later illustrated the transforming power of God's grace that freed him from his old false self and set his new true self at liberty to follow Christ.

The Early Years

Chronicle of Nadal (*EpistNadal* 1:1–25, nos. 1–92)
Commentary on the Life and Virtues of Fr. Nadal (*EpistNadal* 1:26–46, nos. 1–42)

The story line of Nadal's *Chronicle* traces the ups and downs of his vocation to the Society of Jesus. Beginning in Paris, it takes us to Avignon, Majorca, and Rome. Diego Jiménez, a later companion on some of Nadal's journeys, wrote his *Commentary* on Nadal's life, though he was not witness to the events Nadal relates about his vocation.[11]

Jerónimo Nadal was born on August 11, 1507, at Majorca, an island off the coast of Spain. "More medium than short in height, unassuming in appearance, vigorously religious, indefatigable in spirit, a hard worker, passionate, very bright," in 1526 he began studying in Alcalá, where he came to know Ignatius only from afar.[12] He did not like what he saw: a

---

[11] My brief account of Nadal's background is drawn from the summary in *Jerome Nadal, S.J., 1507–1580: Tracking the First Generation of Jesuits*, by William V. Bangert, S.J., ed. Thomas M. McCoog, S.J. (Chicago: Loyola University Press, 1992), checked against the narrative in Nadal's own chronicle, found in *EpistNadal* 1:1–25 (hereafter abbreviated to *NadChron*); Martin E. Palmer, S.J., "Jerónimo Nadal, S.J., 'The Chronicle: The Beginning of His Vocation,'" *Studies in the Spirituality of Jesuits* 24, no. 3 (1992): 31–37, and 24, no. 5 (1992): 37–45; and Diego Jiménez, S.J., "Commentarium de vita et virtutibus Patris Nadal," in *EpistNadal* 1:26–46. Like others, the name of Diego Jiménez enjoys a wide variety of forms. He became socius to Nadal in 1560. See also *EpistNadal* 2:67.

[12] Franciscus Sacchinus, S.J., *Historiæ Societatis Iesu pars quarta* (Rome, 1652), 8, no. 28, cited by Georg Schurhammer, S. J., *Francis Xavier: His Life, His Times*, ed. and trans. M. Joseph Costelloe, S.J. (Rome: IHSI, 1973), 1:241 n. 149. For the significance of Alcalá in the life of Ignatius, see Rafael Mª Sanz de Diego, S.J., "Ignacio de Loyola en

beggar in pilgrim garb, attracting women while incurring the criticism of ecclesiastical authorities. Ignatius left for the University of Salamanca a little over a year later and then went on to the University of Paris in 1528.[13] In 1532 Nadal also enrolled in the University of Paris, where he found two former students from Alcalá, Diego Laínez and Alfonso Salmerón, joined a few months later by a third, Nicolás Bobadilla. All accompanied Ignatius and some other students every Sunday to the Carthusian church for confession and Communion; and there Nadal met Pierre Favre and Francis Xavier. Even then, sharing the same friends and even the same confessor, Nadal rejected all overtures to be part of the new movement. Laínez visited him, Favre talked to him, and his confessor, Manuel Miona, who was also Ignatius's confessor, urged him (*NadChron* pp. 1–3; the following quotations are from this same source). To his confessor he equivalently said, "If you will not join them, why should I?" (2, no. 7). Ignatius tried to persuade him by taking him to the baptismal font of a church and reading him a letter about leaving the world and seeking perfection; "but the devil recognized the power of the letter and of Ignatius, and violently alienated me from the Spirit who was passionately seeking me" (3, no. 9). Outside the church, at its very door, Nadal held a New Testament in his hand and said to Ignatius: "I want to follow this book. I have no idea where you are going. Leave me alone. Forget about me" (3, no. 9). In his *Chronicle,* the story of his vocation, he wrote: "This is how I felt: I do not want to join these people. Who knows whether they will one day fall into the hands of the inquisitors? . . . I saw them no more in Paris, neither Ignatius nor anyone else" (3, no. 10). Jerónimo experienced too much group pressure and had no desire to be linked with unorthodoxy. He lived in his head and his heart was divided. He needed to be set free.

Nadal left Paris in 1535 and went to Avignon. In a one-sentence paragraph he makes a confession: "I heard absolutely nothing about them, I did not think about them, I did not inquire about them." In another one-sentence paragraph he passes judgment: "A dangerous cure for a disease, and in it not a spiritual thought; I was never farther from devotion" (4, no

---

Alcalá de Henares (1526–1527): Andanzas de un universitario atípico," in Plazaola, *Ignacio y su tiempo,* 883–900.

[13] For some idea of what the University of Paris was like in those days, see James K. Farge, "The University of Paris in the Time of Ignatius of Loyola," in Plazaola, *Ignacio y su tiempo,* 221–43.

12 f.).[14] The old false self gripped his heart. He fled from the Spirit who passionately sought him.

He studied Hebrew in the Jewish community in Avignon, showing so much philosophical and theological learning and making such progress in Hebrew that a group of rabbis wanted to make him the chief rabbi and spiritual leader of the community; whereupon he denounced them vigorously in their own language. In turn, they denounced him for disobeying a law of the French king that all Spaniards should leave France because of the war with Spain. He was actually condemned to death, had a rope around his neck, and was about to be hanged and his body burned, when he again denounced in Hebrew the Jews who were now taunting him. Confused by this turn of events, the official in charge let him go free (4 f., no. 15; 29–31, nos, 5–9).

Nadal was ordained a priest in Avignon in 1538, a few days later received his doctor's degree in theology (5, no. 15), and a month later returned to Majorca, where his three benefices provided him with financial security. Soon he fell into a deep depression (5, nos. 16 f.; 31, no. 10). Interiorly lost, suffering from headaches, plagued by poor health, for seven years he wandered listlessly through life. One day he received a letter from a friend containing a copy of a letter from Francis Xavier to Ignatius that narrated the progress of the Church in his three years in India and expressing joy that the Society had been solemnly approved by the Pope. Nadal was deeply moved, "as though awaking from a long sleep" (11, no. 31). His true self began to stir. A few days later a Majorcan priest in the Roman Curia invited him to Rome to assist in preparing a general council of the Church, later to be known as the Council of Trent (32 f., no. 13). After due deliberation he set out, arriving in Rome in October 1545, fully determined to remain a secular priest. He visited the Jesuits, however, and Father Jerónimo Doménech suggested that he make the Exercises; "but the fish slipped off his hook that time" (14, no. 39). Laínez and Doménech tried again. He agreed, temporized, and spent a restless and troubled month as a tourist; finally he told the story of his life, stressing why he would not fit into the Jesuit way of life. Smiling, Ignatius said that if God called him, the Society could find some use for him (15, no. 42). He began the Exercises in November under Doménech's direction (16, no. 43).

All went well until he had to choose: retain his benefices or become a Jesuit? His false self moved in and days of impasse followed: agitation, darkness, a balky will, headaches, stomach aches, fever. He had written

---

[14] Martin Palmer, S.J., a careful and scrupulous translator, translates "Cura morbi periculosa" as "During a hazardous recovery from an illness," and does not connect the one-sentence para. 12 with the one-sentence para. 13, as I have. He may be correct, but the juxtaposition of the two paragraphs is striking, and Nadal's story admits his own lack of openness, his deception by the evil spirit, and God's relentless pursuit.

out the reasons for and against, but he could make no decision, and his despairing director wanted to move on. "One more night," begged Nadal; "I'll work hard" (17, no. 47). But God broke into Nadal's attempt to create himself, and created a yes instead:

> As I did so, a special grace of God came to my help. I took up my pen and wrote as I was moved by Christ's Spirit, with extraordinary consolation: "So far I have examined both courses as best I could, and see that the reasons against are so insubstantial that there is no need to refute them one by one. Even more: the very obstacles seem rather to be confirmations. But what moves me most is my not finding any opposing arguments that would move me at all, just sheer repugnance, which is a great and convincing sign that this is God's will; consequent upon this repugnance there are those feelings—a perverse will, the world, prestige, a kind of lack of faith by thinking too much of difficulties—that cannot receive the Kingdom of God and are opposed to the Spirit. And so, despite whatever hosts of difficulties—even beyond those I have experienced or the devil can instill— may come, assail, obstruct, oppose, or terrify, nevertheless,
>
> "In the name of the Most Holy Trinity—Father, Jesus Christ, and Holy Spirit—I determine and resolve to follow the evangelical counsels with vows in the Society of Jesus. I am ready to do everything pertaining to that Society, even should they want me to take the vows immediately. With great fear and trembling before our God and Lord Jesus Christ and through the sovereign mercy he has exercised towards me, I make this vow with my whole soul, my whole will, and my whole strength. Glory be. Amen." (18 f., nos. 49 f.)

There followed incredible spiritual consolation as well as physical relief (18, no. 50).[15]

Doménech later told Nadal that Ignatius had warned him: "He'll be a tough one for us. He is full of melancholy; you can see it in his eyes. I am afraid that if the Lord does not call him, he will be overcome by melancholy and lose his mind. Right now he wants to serve God, but he can't" (21, no. 72). His false self had stood against him, revealing his lack of authenticity, but through divine grace his true self was set at liberty and put order into his life.[16]

Nadal's experience that night affected the way he thought of vocation throughout his life. Sometime later he wrote in his spiritual journal that when God calls a man to the Society, a star arises within him which leads him to seek Christ recently born in him, and to offer gifts to

---

[15] As translated in Palmer, "Jerónimo Nadal," 40.

[16] On Nadal's story of the decision, see Roger Cantin, S.J., "L'Élection de Jérôme Nadal," *Cahiers de spiritualité ignatienne* 4 (1980): 263–73. A summary of the story line of Nadal's *Chronicle* is in "Autobiografie di Gesuiti in Italia (1540–1640): storia e interpretazione," by Lorenzo M. Gilardi, S.J., *Archivum historicum Societatis Iesu* (*AHSI*) 64 (1995): 11–17.

Christ, first of all his own will and then the gifts of gold (poverty), frank-incense (obedience), and myrrh (chastity); let him follow that light and seek the Child, not inquiring from Herod, from the worldly and unfriendly, but from those God has given the task to illumine that grace in the Church.[17]

Those words describe every call from God, a creative act in which the Holy Spirit, or Holy Breath *(ruah)* of God, hovers over the waters of chaos, and God, breathing in and breathing out, communicates his own divine life to a human being and brings forth in that person light and life, order and purpose. Vocation is the breathing-in, and mission is the breath-ing-out. In every call from God, in God's own in-breathing of the Holy Spirit, God draws a human being into his own divine self, his own life; and for that human being a star bursts, illumining the sky and filling the one called with light and life and a desire to serve. Mission is the out-breath of God, God breathing out the Holy Spirit on the world in the sending of the Son, and sharing the mission of the Son with the one called, so that through the Son in union with the Father the one called breathes forth the Holy Spirit upon the human race and the rest of God's universe. In every call from God, the yes of the out-breath uncovers wondrous gifts of gold, frankincense, and myrrh appropriate to that particular call—all within the framework of the Church, not the world.[18]

On November 29, 1545, Nadal became a novice of the Society of Jesus (*NadChron* 19, no. 56). One of his fellow novices was Manuel Miona, the confessor he had shared with Ignatius in Paris, a Portuguese of whom someone wrote a few days later, "He is like the moon among the stars on a clear and quiet night, like a lily among flowers, like a giant among locusts, or Saul among the children of Israel because he stood out above all the rest."[19] United once more with their former friends, they, too, "set out to follow Christ with greater liberty," free of self, free to hear Christ's voice, free to respond, "and to imitate him more closely."

Nadal's Life in the Society

Jerónimo Nadal was a man of great talent, facile in languages both ancient and modern, a theologian familiar with Scripture and the Fathers

---

[17] *P. Hieronymi Nadal orationis observationes (Orat.observ.)*, ed. Michael Nicolau, S.J., vol. 90a of MHSI (Rome: IHSI, 1964), 198, no. 654.

[18] For vocation as in-breath and mission as out-breath, I am indebted to a conversation with Gretel Buchmann. See John of the Cross, *The Spiritual Canticle*, can. 39, 3–5, for the intimate way human beings share in breathing the Holy Spirit.

[19] *Font.narr.*, 1:585 n. 49. Letter of Antonio Araoz to Bartholomew Ferrão, December 22, 1545 (*Epistolæ mixtæ ex variis Europæ locis ab anno 1537 ad 1556 scriptæ [Epist.mixt]*, 5 vols., vols. 12, 14, 17, 18, and 20 of MHSI [Madrid, 1898–1901], 1:243).

of the Church, an educator and organizer who became a wise and prudent administrator, even though sometimes he was inclined to melancholy, manifesting a proclivity toward impatience and a temper not always under control. His limitations underlined that "greater liberty" is a gift. From the moment Nadal entered the novitiate in Rome, Ignatius began to train him in the Institute of the Society, its spirit and aims, its way of proceeding. Ignatius, once rejected as suspect, became Nadal's father in Christ.

Almost at once Ignatius put him in the kitchen to help the cook. In April he made him minister of the house (the one in charge of temporal affairs). Nadal commented later that Ignatius often tested a new member by giving him the office of minister, "a position in which he could not hide: his character emerged at once."[20] Then Ignatius employed him in assisting with the correspondence that kept the Society running and united. Daily he witnessed the dialog between Ignatius and Polanco as they struggled with the *Constitutions*. The training was long, careful, and very demanding. He wrote in his spiritual diary, *Orationis observationes:*

> Whenever you enter into prayer, always prepare yourself so that you may understand in spirit what Paul said: "The Spirit helps us in our weakness. For we do not know how to pray as we ought, but the Spirit himself begs for us with unutterable groans." And also, "We have received the spirit of sons by which we cry out, Abba, Father. For the Spirit himself testifies to our spirit that we are sons of God." If you feel these words in your heart as you go to prayer, they will have a profound effect. The first passage stirs up a sense of our own lowliness and the working of the Spirit within us. The second blossoms into hope, unites us with Christ, inclines us to confidence in the Son and intimacy with the Father. (52, no. 72)

And then he went on to write: "When seeking God, you have come at times to the nub of every difficulty: come now, acknowledge your weakness at last: do not run ahead of the Spirit, but allow yourself to be led and guided by the Spirit in truth, and learn to cooperate with grace" (52, no. 73). The relationship grew over the months and years until Juan de Polanco, the secretary of the Society, could write to Diego Miró, the provincial of Portugal, that Nadal was "one of those who had consistently showed themselves to be true sons of the Society."[21]

---

[20] "Exhortationes in Hispania," in *Commentarii de Instituto S.I. (CommInst)*, vol. 90 of MHSI (Rome: MHSI 1962), 75, no. 93. Hereafter this first source will be abbreviated to "Exhort. 1554 Hisp."

[21] *Sancti Ignatii de Loyola Societatis Iesu fundatoris epistolæ et instructiones (EpistIgn)*, 12 vols., vols. 22, 26, 28, 29, 31, 33, 34, 36, 37, 38, 40, and 42 of MHSI (Madrid, 1903–11; reprinted in Rome, 1964–68), 5:109. For Nadal's filial relationship to the Society and to Ignatius, see Pierre-Antoine Fabre, "Ignace de Loyola et Jérôme Nadal: Paternité et filiation chez les premiers jésuites," in Plazaola, *Ignacio y su tiempo*, 617–35.

This man's talent was not to go to waste. In 1548 Ignatius sent him to found and govern the college in Messina, the first Jesuit college for laymen. He made friends with Juan de Vega, the viceroy, established a novitiate as well as a college, organized a program of lectures and sermons and theological disputations, even joined the royal navy as chaplain when the Turks threatened the city, as we shall see more in detail in chapter 5.[22] He structured a program of studies based on the method followed at the University of Paris, which embraced and put into practice the highest humanistic ideals of the Renaissance. His work and that of Hannibal du Coudret, one of his cadre of Jesuits, laid the foundation for what would become the Society's *Ratio studiorum*, or program of studies.[23] As we shall see later, however, not all the members of the Jesuit community in Messina were happy with his style of governing.

Ignatius recalled Nadal to Rome toward the end of 1551 to join the group reviewing the *Constitutions,* or as Nadal himself put it, "to see the *Constitutions* and to make final profession."[24] During that short time in Rome, Ignatius drew on Nadal's experience in Messina to establish norms for his own pet project, the Roman College. Through the influence of the Roman College, Nadal's work in Messina affected every school the Society established down to the present day. After two months in Rome, Nadal went back to Sicily to promulgate the *Constitutions,* returning to Rome in March 1553.

Sometime, probably in 1552, Nadal noted in his spiritual journal that he experienced within himself a profound attraction "to the Constitutions and rules of the Society, to obedience, and to the whole Institute."[25] He wrote that when praying in the catacomb of San Sebastian, he received an uncommon consolation regarding the Institute because of the fruit it could bring to the Church, and understood that "he could do nothing more useful than devote his energy to the *Constitutions* and rules so as to

---

[22] Letters of Nadal to Ignatius: December 18, 1548; May 7, 1549; May 14, 1549; May 20, 1549; June 1549; July 1, 1549 (*EpistNadal* 1:53–63).

[23] See George E. Ganss, S.J., *Saint Ignatius' Idea of a Jesuit University: A Study in the History of Catholic Education* (Milwaukee: Marquette University Press, 1954), 107–11; see also *The Jesuit* Ratio Studiorum: *400th Anniversary Perspective,* ed. Vincent J. Duminuco, S.J. (New York: Fordham University Press, 2000).

[24] *EpistIgn* 3:233, 237. Also see *Constitutiones* 1:lxxx. and "Natalis Ephemerides" (*NadEphem*), in *EpistNadal* 2:6, no. 52.

[25] *Orat.observ.,* 97 f., no. 223. Nadal began his spiritual journal in Rome in November 1545 and polished and revised it in Hall near Innsbruck in 1574–77 (ibid., 23). As editor, Nicolau divides the total text into seventeen sections and attempts to date them.

promulgate them as precisely as possible, clarify them with scholia [explanatory comments], and fully reveal the entire scope of the Institute."[26]

No record remains of Nadal's experiences in promulgating the *Constitutions* in Sicily in 1552. A few notes of his, however, from late 1551 or early 1552, while he was serving as rector in Messina, reveal some of his ideas on prayer, which in subsequent years grew into major themes as Nadal talked to his brothers scattered throughout Spain and Portugal:

- The Society is open to vocal as well as mental prayer.
- One prays according to one's own capacity and the movement of the Holy Spirit.
- The rector (or spiritual director) has a guiding role in the prayer of his subjects.
- We should pray for ourselves, for the Church, for the Society, and for the world.
- Pure love should rule in everything; meditation and contemplation perish if they do not lead to prayer and affectivity, to doing and accomplishing God's holy will.[27]

By 1553 Ignatius needed someone to put order into the burgeoning Society in Spain and Portugal, someone who knew how things were done in Rome, who knew the mind of Ignatius; someone who could establish in the newer colleges the order used in the new and successful Roman College; someone who could explain the office of rector and the office of minister and all the other offices in a house. Only eight years a member of the Society, Nadal had been minister in Rome, founding rector and administrator of the school in Messina, and adaptor for the Roman College of the norms established in Messina. Furthermore, he had already promulgated the Constitutions in Messina the year before. The job and the man were a perfect fit.

---

[26] Ibid., 100, no. 232. At the First General Congregation doubtful points regarding the *Constitutions* were referred to Nadal and Polanco (d. 17 after the election of the general). Ignatius had empowered three priests to make changes in the wording of the *Constitutions* without changing the meaning (d. 53 after the election). Persuasive reasons argue that Polanco and Nadal were two of the three, and Cristóbal de Madrid was probably the third (*Constitutiones*, 2:cciii–cciv). For the First General Congregation, see *Institutum Societatis Iesu*, 3 vols. (Florence: SS. Conception, 1893), 2:162 (d. 17), 168 (d. 53); for an English translation of these decrees, see *For Matters of Greater Moment: The First Thirty Jesuit General Congregations: A Brief History and a Translation of the Decrees (MattGM)*, ed., John W. Padberg, S.J., Martin D. O'Keefe, S.J., John L. McCarthy, S.J. (St. Louis: The Institute of Jesuit Sources, 1994), 76, d. 17; 83, d. 53.

[27] "De oratione" (*CommInst* 26–30), delivered in Messina, about 1551. Study and prayer go hand in hand. Study and planning produce *effective* action; prayer transforms it into *affective* action, action done with spiritual zest and love. The two should be one.

The task was formidable. The cadence of the *Formula of the Institute* was out of step with the opinions prevailing in the Iberian Peninsula regarding prayer and penance, even regarding the very nature of religious life. Nonetheless, the time for a strong, more immediate healing action had come. It was time to instruct the Society more clearly and more forcefully about its true spirit and charism. The time was ripe to send Jerónimo Nadal to Portugal and Spain.

Healer in Action

Recalled from Sicily, Nadal arrived in Rome on April 3, 1553. Ignatius said to him, "Get ready immediately; you have to go to Spain." Nadal replied, "Can I expect some instructions regarding what I have to do?" "No," said Ignatius. "You know enough already, and if something comes up, it will be given to you in writing and you can read it on the way to Genoa." With that Nadal set out, and on the way he began to read some instructions and papers Ignatius had dispatched to him. One was a letter appointing him vicar-general with full authority over the whole Society, an appointment that struck him as so extravagant that in his humility he felt torn apart. He sent the letter back from Bracciano (a ride of a day or two from Rome), saying that such a letter of introduction was not for him and requesting Ignatius to send something else. The latter immediately sent another document appointing Nadal commissary-general, limiting his authority to Spain and Portugal. Under this title he made his first visit:[28]

> Since after long and frequent observation and testing we have the greatest confidence in the integrity of your life, your learning, and your prudence, which is in Christ Jesus, and since in the Spanish kingdoms there are many matters regarding persons, places, local living norms, the *Constitutions* of the Society, and other concerns that need our presence or that of someone who knows our mind thoroughly and can exercise our authority, it has seemed right in the Lord to impose on you this task for the glory of God and the spiritual good of our Society. We, therefore, appoint you commissary-general in these kingdoms, with all of our authority that through the graciousness of the Apostolic See we can communicate to you, and we enjoin and command that all who owe us obedience will be obedient to you in the same way as to us, and that you freely proceed to act in accordance with our mind, which you know, and by all means according to what you think right in the Lord, with all our authority in all matters, in the name of the Father and of the Son and of the Holy Spirit, and we pray that the eternal wisdom may deign to illumine and guide you in all things.[29]

---

[28] The story is in Jiménez, "Commentarium," 36 f.

[29] Dated April 10, 1553, the letter is in *EpistIgn* 5:7 f., and also in *EpistNadal* 1:143–45, in which the editors include a footnote providing a letter of April 5 to Diego

His instructions were to promulgate the *Constitutions,* adapt the schools to the norms of the Roman College, and resolve other problems.[30]

Nadal left Genoa aboard a galley on April 18 and arrived in Barcelona on May 5, "very badly treated by the sailing."[31] His main objective at this time was to go to Portugal as soon as possible. Ignatius had appointed Diego Miró provincial there and called Simón Rodrigues back to Rome. Polanco wrote to the new Portuguese provincial that Nadal was coming to explain the *Constitutions* of the Society, "which he knows well how to do as a person who has understood and penetrated the mind of our father Master Ignatius."[32] Miró welcomed the news.

Nadal knew that he was walking into a volatile situation. Simón Rodrigues, reluctant, unhappy, and somewhat in disgrace as he made his way to Rome, turned back when he heard that Nadal (formerly the reluctant one) was coming to Lisbon. Nadal attacked Simón's problem with obedience by exercising him in it. He wrote to Melchor Carneiro, whom Miró had appointed as Simón's superior on the trip to Rome, that he was not to let Simón return to Lisbon even if he had to order him under holy obedience to proceed to Rome.[33] Without success Nadal tried to repair the damage Simón's manner of governing had caused, visiting disaffected former Jesuits, offering to forget their faults, remember their good works, and restore them to their place in the Society.[34]

Nadal stayed in the Iberian peninsula for sixteen months. He visited all the Jesuit colleges, adapted the rules of the Roman College to the circumstances of each college, adding some rules that appeared necessary or useful.[35] On July 15 he wrote to Ignatius from Lisbon that he had begun to explain the *General Examen* for an hour each day, and that the Jesuits there had received his remarks with great joy, consolation, and fervor. The Society in Portugal was beginning to experience a renewal of spirit.[36] Two months later he was greatly consoled to receive a copy of the *Constitutions* Ignatius had sent from Rome. He finished his exhortations on the *Examen* and started to explain the *Constitutions,* to the great consola-

---

Miró, the Portuguese provincial, announcing Nadal's coming, explaining his powers, and providing as well a list of other letters Nadal brought with him. The same catalog is in *EpistIgn* 5:18 f.

[30] Letter of Ignatius to Nadal, April 12, 1553 (*EpistIgn* 5:13–15); *NadEphem,* in *EpistNadal* 2:7 f.; *PolChron* 3:439.

[31] Letters to Ignatius, *EpistNadal* 1:146–48.

[32] *EpistIgn* 5:108.

[33] *EpistNadal* 1:156–59, letter of about July 12, 1553.

[34] Letter to Ignatius, December 13, 1553, ibid., 194 f.

[35] *NadEphem,* in *EpistNadal* 2:8.

[36] *EpistNadal* 1:176, no. 9.

tion of all.[37] Although he was primarily addressing younger Jesuits, both the younger ones and the "senior" Jesuits (few, indeed, in number in 1553 and 1554) still had much to learn about the Jesuit vocation and its special graces.

Miguel de Torres wrote to Ignatius in September:

> We have all been greatly consoled by what we have learned of the *Constitutions,* especially from the living voice of Fr. Nadal. Believe me, it has been needed, for everyone was going his own way, each fixed a course according to his own fancy, and very few of us hit the mark. Since Spain and Portugal are not the smallest part of the Society, nor the most sterile area for the service of God and the growth of the Society, it would be good for this true spirit of the Society to be deeply rooted right here, for talking about it is not enough if it is not established by an experienced person who can communicate it with authority.[38]

The result of Nadal's visit was that, in spite of the "purging" (Polanco's word), the number of scholastics soon increased to more than 330, and in 1553 the Society grew in the esteem both of Jesuits and of others, even of some earlier opponents.[39] The Ignatian vision of an apostolic order, however, was so radically original that, in spite of Nadal's efforts, many in the Society could not throw off their fascination with the practices of monasticism.

That fascination lies hidden in the judgment of Francesco Sacchini, a famous historian of the Society in the middle of the seventeenth century, who averred that Nadal was "without doubt the most skilled in the Institute after the Generals and Polanco."[40] A more modern Jesuit historian gently corrects that judgment in suggesting that Nadal should be placed before Polanco and the generals who immediately succeeded Ignatius, taking into account all that Nadal accomplished in word and deed through most of Europe, studying, promulgating, and putting into practice the *Constitutions,* chosen for this work by Ignatius himself.[41] In more recent times Paul Begheyn has been explicitly critical of the generals immediately after Ignatius and Laínez: Borgia, Mercurian, and Aquaviva.[42] Ignatius,

---

[37] Ibid., 1:186, nos. 7 f.

[38] Ibid., 1:774.

[39] *PolChron* 3:402, no. 885; 3:399, no. 876; 401, no. 884.

[40] Sacchinus, *Historiæ Societatis Jesu,* lib. 8, no. 25.

[41] *EpistNadal* 1:xi n. 1. For Nadal's impact on the Society lasting until the present day, see the dissertation abstract of *Jeronimo Nadal and the Early Development of the Society of Jesus, 1545–1573,* by Dennis Edmond Pate, presented at the University of California, Los Angeles, 1980, in *Dissertation Abstracts,* A41 (1980–81) 353A.

[42] Paul Begheyn, S.J., "The Controversies on Prayer after the Death of Ignatius and Their Effect on the Concept of Jesuit Mission," *Centrum Ignatianum Spiritualitatis*

saint and mystic, found prayer wherever he found God—everywhere, that is. Francis Borgia, saint and mystic, preferred prayer and solitude, and increased the time explicitly given to prayer. Everard Mercurian, as we shall see in more detail, was suspicious of mysticism and affective prayer; and Aquaviva organized everything perhaps to the point of sterility, leaving little room for the innovative spirit of Ignatius.

Nonetheless, all these men, to return to the words of Vatican II at the beginning of the chapter, "set out to follow Christ with greater liberty and to imitate him more closely. . . . They led lives dedicated to God, each in his own way." In spite of our contemporary reluctance to identify the Society in military terms, we invite you to join us in reviewing the troops and in hearing what Father General Ignatius has to say through his lieutenant and vicar-general, Jerónimo Nadal. Just as the early Society had difficulty in establishing its original spirit, so five hundred years later the Society has struggled in trying to recover that original spirit, as General Congregation 34 remarked at the beginning of this chapter:

> In our review of the state of the Society, we faced our limitations and weaknesses. . . . But we also found much that was wise and good, especially the powerful and pervasive effort to pursue the service of faith and that struggle for justice which it includes. In the review of our graces over these years, we found again "the omnipotent hand of Christ, God and our Lord." In gratitude for so much good accomplished and for so much forgiven, we follow this Christ, the Crucified and Risen Lord, in pilgrimage and labor. We see our renewal of the law and our review of our life and apostolic labor as one reality, the confirmation of our union as servants of Christ's mission.[43]

This chapter has introduced the Society of Jesus and some of its struggles in its earlier years, as well as the man who was given the task of promulgating its *Constitutions* to an ever increasing multitude of eager but inexperienced members. The next chapter will reflect on his explanation of the grace proper to the Society of Jesus, one that distinguishes it from other religious orders and congregations.

(*CIS*) 24, no. 1 [1993]: 78–93). He quotes Michael Campbell-Johnston, S.J.: "Ignatius set up the Society of Jesus as light cavalry; Borgia turned us into infantry; Aquaviva put us into barracks; Roothaan canceled all leave; Ledóchowski set up a concentration camp; and Pedro Arrupe said, 'Break ranks'" ("How I Pray: Being and Doing," *The Tablet* 246 [1992]: 434); see also Frank J. Houdek, S.J., "Jesuit Prayer and Jesuit Ministry: Context and Possibilities," *Studies in the Spirituality of Jesuits* 24, no. 1 (1992): 1–37.

[43] *DocsGC34*, d. 1, no. 3.

Chronicle for Chapter 2

Nadal understands well the mind of our Father Ignatius, for he has dealt with him extensively, and seems to have grasped his spirit, and has penetrated the Institute as thoroughly as any man I know in the Society.

—Polanco to Diego Miró

Nadal's Life and Travels (1553)

1553

July 7-August 16: Lisbon; visits King, begins exhortations

August 19-Sept. 4: Évora; Constitutions, rules for college

Sept 8-Oct. 9: Lisbon; meets Francis Borgia, founds college and professed house at San Roque; exhortations

Until end of October: Coimbra, Constitutions, rules; Sans Fins, San Juan de Longavares (3 days)

Nov. 2: St. James of Compostela (one and a half days)

9–18: Nov. Coimbra; Constitutions

Nov. 23-Dec. 13: Lisbon, Évora

Dec. 24: Cordoba; Constitutions (about a month)

Chapter Two

GRACE PROPER TO THE SOCIETY OF JESUS

> Thus, in keeping with the divine purpose, a wonderful variety of
> religious communities came into existence. This has considerably
> contributed to enabling the Church not only to be equipped for
> every good work (cf. 2 Tim. 3:17) and to be prepared for the work
> of the ministry unto the building-up of the Body of Christ (cf. Eph.
> 4:12), but also to appear adorned with the manifold gifts of her
> children, like a bride adorned for her husband (cf. Apoc. 21:2), and
> to manifest in herself the multiform wisdom of God (cf. Eph. 3:10).
>
> Vatican II, *On the Up-to-Date Renewal of the Religious Life*

This chapter reveals how the Society of Jesus fits into that "wonderful variety of religious communities" that God has brought into existence; it shows how from its beginning it "contributed to enabling the Church" to fulfill its own purpose and "to appear adorned . . . like a bride adorned for her husband."[1] General Congregation 34 indicated how the Society helps to enable the Church in her mission in the present day:

> As the Society of Jesus, we are servants of Christ's mission. . . . The
> Society has also become a body more diverse than ever before, engaged in
> a variety of ministries at the crossroads of cultural conflict, social and
> economic struggles, religious revivalism and new opportunities for bringing
> the Good News to people all over the world.[2]

This chapter considers Jerónimo Nadal as a theologian reflecting on the special grace of the Society of Jesus that sets it apart from other religious orders. Its objective is to stir appreciation for and esteem not only of the Society's charism but of the distinctive charisms of others as well.

---

[1] "Decree on the Up-to-Date Renewal of Religious Life," in *Vatican Council II: The Conciliar and Post-Conciliar Documents,* ed. Austin Flannery, O.P. (Collegeville, Minn.: The Liturgical Press, 1975), no. 1 (p. 611).

[2] *DocsGC34* d. 2, nos. 1 5f. (pp. 25 f.).

History

The year 1547 marked the end of an epoch in Europe. Henry VIII of England died in February, one year after Martin Luther. Francis I of France followed Henry at the end of March, freeing the emperor Charles V of his chief antagonist. In April Charles defeated the Lutheran princes at Mühlberg. Charles asked his son Philip, who was in charge of the government in Spain, to join him; but Philip did not leave Spain until November 1548, when he sailed with Admiral Andrea Doria.[3] In 1547 Ivan the Terrible assumed power in Russia, John Knox was preaching reform in England and Scotland, and the Council of Trent moved temporarily to Bologna.[4]

By that time the immense success of the infant Society of Jesus became also the measure of its vulnerability, expanding as it did in the first half dozen years from Rome into Germany, the Low Countries, France, Portugal, Spain, and as far as India. How many hundreds joined the original ten in those first six years we do not know.[5] Houses of study, eventually called colleges—that is, residences for the Society's young recruits pursuing an education at a university—opened in Paris (1540), Louvain (1542), Coimbra (1542), Valencia (1544), and Alcalá (1545).[6] The next six years saw the Society expand to Malacca and the Moluccas, Sicily, the Congo, Brazil, Austria, and Japan; and colleges for Jesuits were established in Gandía, Salamanca, Saragossa, Barcelona, Valladolid, Padua, and Bologna.

By 1553, when Ignatius sent Jerónimo Nadal to Spain, that country was embroiled in a long war with France; it was also busy making Prince Philip king of Naples and arranging his marriage with Mary Tudor of England.[7] The Spanish Inquisition was also guarding against heretical writings coming into the country from outside and carefully inspecting works of literature and devotional works written in the vernacular.[8] When Nadal reached Lisbon and found a copy of the *Constitutions* Ignatius had sent him, was it also under suspicion, coming as it did from outside Spain and written in Spanish?

---

[3] Henry Kamen, *Philip of Spain* (New Haven: Yale University Press, 1997), 34–36.

[4] André Ravier, S.J., *Les Chroniques: Saint Ignace de Loyola* (Paris: Nouvelle Librairie de France, 1973), 93.

[5] See the discussion by the editors in *Font.narr* 1:63*; Fathers Zapico and Dalmases feel safe in saying that by the time Ignatius died in 1556 at the age of sixty-five, the Society numbered about one thousand. Of those only some forty were professed.

[6] *Synopsis historiæ Societatis Jesu* (Ratisbon: Pustet, 1914), 13–15.

[7] Kamen, *Philip of Spain*, 52–57.

[8] Henry Kamen, *The Spanish Inquisition: A Historical Revision* (London: Weidenfeld and Nicolson, 1997), 109 f.

Meanwhile, Ignatius spent more energy meeting internal criticisms of the Society than he did warding off attacks from outside the Society. "A wonderful variety of religious communities" had, indeed, come "into existence"; but in a garden of flowers the unusual can appear to be a weed.

A Pause for Prayer

Nadal prayed that, through Jesus' merits, Mary's intercession, and that of all the angels and saints, he might receive the grace of "a greater knowledge of this Institute and its proper grace."[9]

> **Principle and Foundation: "Human beings are created to praise, reverence, and serve God our Lord"** (*SpEx* 23).
>
> As we seek in this chapter the call and the grace proper to the Society of Jesus, so that it may praise, reverence, and serve God our Lord in its own unique way, we join Nadal in imploring God "for a greater knowledge of this Institute and its proper grace," so that through reflecting on the Society's special call and grace we may know our own better, and enable the Church to be equipped for every good work, and also to appear adorned with the manifold gifts of her children, like a bride adorned for her husband.

Crisis in Portugal

The common expectations of the day that made some persons consider the Society a weed in the garden of the Church set a high priority upon prayer and penance. So did Simón Rodrigues, the only Portuguese among the original ten companions and the first choice of Ignatius for the Portuguese mission to India (1540). While awaiting a ship in Lisbon for a year, Rodrigues quickly became a favorite of the royal court.[10] The King started talking about a Jesuit college (residence) in

---

[9] "Capita quædam, quibus in spiritu adiuuari possumus", in "Instructiones" (*EpistNadal* 4:580). The title "Instructiones" represents a collection of ninety instructions dating from 1568 to 1575, including corrections that Nadal completed in 1576. Also see Miguel Nicolau, S.J., *Jerónimo Nadal, S.I. (1507-1580): Sus obras y doctrinas espirituales* (Madrid: Consejo superior de investigaciones cientificas, 1949), 109.

[10] *PolChron* 1:86 f, no. 20; see also letter of Martin Santacruz to Ignatius from

Coimbra, a town centrally located, where young Jesuits could live and attend the University of Coimbra. Ignatius decided to keep Rodrigues in Portugal and sent Xavier on to India (1541). Scholastics from Paris and Rome formed the backbone of the new college.[11] Beginning with a dozen scholastics in 1542, Coimbra could boast more than sixty in 1545, and ninety-five in 1546.[12] Meanwhile not all reports about Portugal were encouraging.[13] Ignatius tried to recall Rodrigues to Rome, but the King would not allow him to go.[14]

Rodrigues's easy method of governing won all hearts and the province prospered; Coimbra, with 115 students in 1547, including 92 scholastics, had no room for all who wanted to come (*PolChron* 1:252, no. 214). His method of governing also created chaos. The story of the young community at Coimbra in this first house of studies in the Society is one of boundless generosity and unchecked mortification. An eager and attractive but inconstant man himself, Rodrigues urged the young members to the generosity of the Third Degree of Humility as found in the Spiritual Exercises—the longing to be humiliated with Christ in his humiliations—but neglected to contextualize it in obedience: doing God's will with love. He imposed bizarre penances on the scholastics: they were instructed to go to class in odds and ends of clothing, to incense the community at dinner, or to sprinkle them with holy water. With or without his permission, the scholastics invented creatively: bringing a skull to class and gazing at it throughout a two-hour lecture, stripping and chaining oneself to a column in the public square, sallying forth in torn and tattered clothing carrying water pots through the market place, begging from door to door, crying out in the middle of the night to arouse sinners to repentance, entering the refectory barefoot with bare shoulders and a discipline in the hand and a rope around the neck.[15] The purpose of exterior asceti-

---

Lisbon, August 26, 1542, in *Epist.mixt* 1:105 f.

[11] *PolChron* 1:94 f., nos. 31 f.

[12] Ibid., 104, no. 45; 157, no. 99. "Eighty students and fifteen who serve the needs of the others" (*Epistolæ PP. Paschasii Broëti, Claudii Jaji, Joannis Codurii, et Simonis Rodericii Societatis Iesu [EpistBroët]*, vol. 24 of MHSI [Madrid, 1903; reprinted 1971], 545). Polanco adds that another fifteen were employed hearing confessions (*PolChron* 1:192, no. 150).

[13] John W. O'Malley, *The First Jesuits* (Cambridge, Mass.: Harvard Univ. Press, 1993), 330.

[14] Ignatius to King John, March 15, 1545 (*EpistIgn* 1:296–98); Ignatius to Marcello Cervini (ibid., 1:300–302); Ignatius to Rodrigues, May 6, 1545, calling him to Rome (ibid., 1:302 f.); Ignatius to Rodrigues, December 14, 1545, commenting that the King would not grant permission (ibid., 1:346).

[15] Letter of Hermes Poen, to Pierre Favre on July 31, 1545 (*Fabri Monumenta: Beati Petri Fabri, primi sacerdotis e Societate Iesu epistolæ [EpistFab]*, vol. 48 of MHSI [Madrid, 1914; reprinted 1972], 339–42; letter of the rector, Martin Santacruz, to

cal practices is to develop an interior asceticism of openness to God: to hear God's voice and do God's will, to let God set one free. Apparently without regard to purpose, Rodrigues had vigorously taught the scholastics the foundation of the Society: being despised and regarded as of little worth by the world, made fools for Christ. They responded equally vigorously. Near the beginning of 1547 Rodrigues wrote to Ignatius: "The fervor that existed in the house cannot be described; it was like the fervor that Christ gave his apostles on Pentecost. . . . They are like lions, and I have to work every day through the grace of God to restrain their fervor."[16] They had gone overboard in their public display of penance. Would Ignatius, pleaded Rodrigues, please set them on the right course?

Ignatius replied to the crisis in religious life in a masterful display of diplomacy and psychology. First of all, he spurred the community to greater fervor in the pursuit of virtue and of learning for God's honor and glory, their own salvation, and the help of their neighbor. Then he cautioned against extremes in fervor, advised discretion, balance, moderation, while indicating some of the inappropriate consequences of excess. He quoted St. Bernard, "Good will must not always be trusted, but reined in, restrained, especially in a beginner." The middle way between tepidity and excessive fervor is through self-revelation to the superior, always staying within the bounds of obedience.[17] A crisis in obedience was not something an infant organization could afford. After hinting at the root of their

---

Pierre Favre in August 1545 [ibid., 342–50]). See Ricardo Garcia-Villoslada, S.J., *San Ignacio de Loyola: Nueva Biografía* (Madrid: Biblioteca de Autores Cristianos, 1986), 649–53. Later one of the more creative and harmless penitential humiliations was the 1550 decision of a former nobleman to drive hogs through the city to a distant market instead of taking an easy side route where no one would have noticed him (*PolChron* 2:135). Later, in 1552, the whole community marched through the streets taking the discipline (ibid., 2:699f.). Ignatius advanced from seeking humiliations for ascetic reasons to seeking them for apostolic reasons; see J. Peter Schineller, S.J., "The Pilgrim Journey of Ignatius: From Soldier to Laborer in the Lord's Vineyard and Its Implications for Apostolic Lay Spirituality," *Studies in the Spirituality of Jesuits* 31, no. 4 (1999): 1–41, referring in n. 68 to Roger Cantin, S.J., "Le Troisieme Degré d'humilité et la gloire de Dieu," *Science Ecclésiastique* 8 (1956): 237–66. For contemporary, more humane reflections on being a fool for Christ in contemporary times, see Peter-Hans Kolvenbach, S.J., "'Fools for Christ's Sake,'" in *The Road from La Storta* (St. Louis: The Institute of Jesuit Sources, 2000), 87–105; also, id., "'Anguish with Christ in Anguish': Ignatian Spirituality and the Cross," *Theology Digest* 44, no. 1 (1997): 35–4; Philip Sheldrake, S.J., "Theology of the Cross and the Third Week," *The Way*, Supplement no. 58 (1987): 21–34.

[16] *EpistBroët* 547–53.

[17] *EpistIgn* 1:504–7. For St. Bernard, see ibid., n. 23, where the editors indicate that the ideas are attributed to a variety of sources and are found here and there in Bernard's letter on the solitary life *(De vita solitaria)*, but not precisely in those words.

problems in 1547, Ignatius wrote a letter in 1548 devoted entirely to obedience.[18]

Rodrigues visited Rome for the consultation on the *Constitutions* in 1551. At the end of year, Ignatius wrote to Diego Miró, naming him provincial of Portugal, and on the next day he wrote to Simón Rodrigues informing him that because of "age and poor health" he was being relieved of the burden of the office of provincial.[19] On January 1, 1552, Ignatius drew a very rough line north and south dividing Spain into two provinces, leaving Araoz as provincial of Castille in the west and appointing Rodrigues provincial of the new province of Aragon (including four colleges in Saragossa, Valencia, Gandía, and Barcelona) because of "your prudence and experience in governing."[20] Either his age (forty-one!) and poor health had improved remarkably during the week between letters, or the new office held far less responsibility; or, more likely, Ignatius's principal objective was to remove Rodrigues from Portugal without humiliating him in any way. On the same day, Ignatius named Miguel de Torres visitor to Portugal, granting him the full authority of the general, even the power to remove the provincial from office.[21] The next day he sent letters to Torres telling him to remove Rodrigues from office as provincial of Portugal and then to send him to Aragon or Brazil.[22] Rodrigues, indeed, had once dreamed not only of going to India but also to Ethiopia and to Brazil.[23]

On hearing from Ignatius, Rodrigues at first rejoiced, kissing the letter and calling it a precious relic. Later he began to raise questions: he was uncertain that the order was valid without the approval of the King; he even wondered whether he was obliged to obey the command. These reactions suggest that the exterior ascetical activity of the community was not forming the proper docility of obedience. He also appealed to certain points in the Constitutions, and said he would study the matter to see if he was obliged to obey. When the King approved the documents, Rodrigues capitulated. Even so, he asked for some time in the country, pleading

---

[18] Letters of May 7, 1547, and January 14, 1548 (*EpistIgn* 1:495–510 and 687–93); for an English translation see *Letters of St. Ignatius of Loyola,* trans. William J. Young, S.J. (Chicago: Loyola University Press, 1959), 120–130 and 159–62. Young calls the second letter a preliminary draft of the famous letter on obedience written on March 26, 1553.

[19] *EpistIgn* 4:48 f., 49 f.

[20] Ibid., 4:53 f.

[21] Ibid., 4:56.

[22] Ibid., 4:72.

[23] About India: 1541 (*EpistBroët* 525); 1546 (ibid., 541); 1547 (ibid., 571); 1548 (ibid., 607, 609–11); about Ethiopia: 1548 (ibid., 590, 601, 607 f.); 1552 (ibid., 636); about Brazil: 1549 (ibid., 2:88, 114); 1552 (ibid., 636).

ill health that would prevent him from going to either Aragon or Brazil.[24]
Not until September did Rodrigues reach Barcelona, where in a letter to
Ignatius he asserted that he would be happy to stay in that city for the
rest of his life unless Ignatius wanted to send him to Ethiopia or to Brazil.
Still, he was not enthusiastic about the latter assignment, because the
people there were "barbaric and quite irrational."[25] A month later he wrote
that he was depressed, the food was different and so were the people, and
he would like to go back to Portugal.[26] In December Ignatius removed
from him the burden of governing the new province of Aragon and let him
return to Portugal, instructing him, however, that he was not to occupy his
former residence and that he was to obey the provincial as he would
Ignatius himself.[27] When he learned, however, that Rodrigues had gone to
Lisbon (not exactly a place of rest in a rural setting), Ignatius recalled him
to Rome.[28] Even the King thought Rodrigues should leave Portugal; and
this time Simón set out for Rome, only to hear that Nadal was on his way
to Portugal, as narrated in the first chapter.[29]

Meanwhile, Jesuit religious life continued to deteriorate. Some
openly criticized Ignatius, preferring obedience to Rodrigues over obedience to Ignatius or Miró.[30] Some had grown accustomed to a greater
delicacy in matters of food, living quarters, and the like.[31] In January 1553
the visitor Torres reported to Ignatius from Lisbon that the vineyard was
so decayed from within that many of the vines seemed to have nothing
but leaves; since the beginning, 318 vines had been planted, but more
than 127 of them were now outside the vineyard, causing harm to those
who remained. Torres thought the apostolic nuncio had dispensed some
from their vows, but Polanco states that the nuncio, who was friendly to
the Society, denied that he had dispened anyone.[32] Many of these former
Jesuits became malcontents and criticized the Society bitterly.[33]

---

[24] Letter of Emmanuel Godinho, rector at Coimbra, to Ignatius, May, 29, 1552
(*Epist.mixt* 2:721–27).

[25] *EpistBroët* 634–37.

[26] Ibid., 637–40.

[27] *EpistIgn* 4:557 f.

[28] Ignatius to Simon Rodrigues, May 20, 1553 (ibid., 5:73–74); *PolChron* 3:13,
no. 16.

[29] *PolChron* 3:393, no. 859. Miró to Ignatius, June 27, 1553 (*Epist.mixt* 3:361–69).

[30] Luis Gonçalves da Câmara to Ignatius, October 15, 1552 (*Epist.mixt* 2:807–12).

[31] *PolChron* 2:700, no. 621.

[32] *Epist.mixt* 3:25. *PolChron* 3:390, no. 854. To attempt to discover the whole
truth about the matter would take us too far afield.

[33] *PolChron* 390, no. 854; 393, no. 860; 401 f., no. 885; Luis Gonçalves da
Câmara to Ignatius, October 15, 1552 (*Epist.mixt* 2:807–12); Francis Anriques to

The Grace of the Society of Jesus

Exhortations in Spain, 1554

"Exhort. 1554 Hisp." (*CommInst* 36–105, nos. 1–187)

In his exhortations on the General Examen and the Constitutions, Nadal approaches the problems and questions his listeners face each day, exploring especially what makes the Society of Jesus different from other religious orders, a flower, not a weed, in the Church's garden, with its own special gifts that "contribute to enabling the Church . . . to be equipped for every good work . . . to be prepared for the work of ministry . . . but also to be adorned with manifold gifts." Members need to be clear on the end of the Society, Nadal insisted, on the Jesuit way of proceeding. They must understand how to fit work and prayer together. He himself had been wary of the Society, reluctant to throw in his lot with Ignatius, suspicious, attracted, confused. Overwhelmed by the eventual gift of his call to the Society, he enthusiastically explains what that call means, reducing a vast body of material into eight exhortations: one introductory, four on the General Examen, and three on the Constitutions.[34] His opening words provide deep insight into how he and Ignatius envisioned their call and understood the documents outlining their way of living. His reflections on the General Examen and the Constitutions are an extension of the contemplation in the Spiritual Exercises on the Incarnation, in which Ignatius imagines the Holy Trinity pondering over the sinful human race, deciding that the Second Person should become man for our salvation, and sending the angel Gabriel to the Virgin of Nazareth, who, overshadowed by the Holy Spirit, said, "Here am I, the servant of the Lord." The initiative in the life of the spirit comes from the Trinity, Nadal reminded his hearers. The missions of the Son and of the Holy Spirit continue in the mission of the Church, drawing men and women according to their own vocation to share in this Trinitarian initiative of salvific activity.[35] Today General Congregation 34 insists on our participation in the mission of the Son.[36]

Polanco, June 1553 (ibid., 3:355–61); *PolChron* 3:393, no. 860.

[34] "Exhortationes 1554 in Hispania," in *CommInst* 35–105, with explanatory preface, 31–35. In Alcalá he acquired Emmanuel de Sa as a companion, who is credited with preserving the talks by taking notes that were later emended by Nadal.

[35] On the way Ignatius envisions the world, see Jean Daniélou, S.J., "La Vision ignatienne du monde et de l'homme," RAM 26 (1950): 5–17; Thomas R. Royce, S.J., "The Ignatian Vision of the Universe and of Man," *Cross Currents* 4 (1953/1954): 357–66, and Manuel Ruiz-Jurado, S.J., "La perspectiva de San Ignacio en su visión del mundo y su influjo en el modo de ser de la Compañía," *Manresa* 45 (1973): 241–62.

[36] See, for example, the summary of Gerald O'Collins, S.J., in "The Mission Christology of General Congregation 34," *Centrum Ignatianum Spritualitatis* (*CIS*): *Review of Ignatian Spirituality* 27, no. 3 (1996): 39-44.

The Grace of Religion

"Introductory Exhortation (*CommInst* 36–38, nos. 1–7)

In an Iberian world hostile to anything Protestant and suspicious of those who claimed to be enlightened by God (known as the *alumbrados* or *illuminati*), a religious congregation had to be named, established, and confirmed by the pope. But on the very doorstep of Melchor Cano, a Dominican who denounced the Jesuits as ministers of the Antichrist, Nadal does not begin by emphasizing the Pope's approval.[37] Rather, he begins with Jesus, the Second Person of the Trinity, showing that Trinitarian thought and the mystery of the Incarnation, the union of the divine and the human, underlie all that he says: "Since the Lord has given us the grace to call us to this religious order *[religión]*, it will be good to notice what is proper *[proprio]* to it (*CommInst* 36, no. 1). Having issued his manifesto, Nadal plunges into the ultimate mystery of God and his search for humanity mirrored in the union of the divine and human in Christ, and the astounding mystery of flesh and spirit in human beings and humanity's search for God. He defines religion as "the virtue that concerns what touches on divine worship" (36, no. 2), which sounds very much like "praise, reverence, and serve God our Lord" (*SpEx* 24). That "the Lord" [Jesus] is the protagonist in this drama, however, suggests that Nadal has only Christianity in mind. "The Lord" also hints that "touches on divine worship" implies that Christians have a part to play in the life and mission of the Son and that through Jesus they participate in that divine dance called *perichoresis,* in which the Father, Son, and Holy Spirit share the divine life that comes from the Father and take delight in each other, and that Christians share also in the mission of the Holy Spirit, spirit expressing itself in the flesh through the Spirit.

"In this sense," he says, "all Christians are called religious and the religion they practice is called the Christian religion" (*CommInst* 36, no. 2). True enough; but then he continues, "since they serve and honor the true God and worship him," words that today would put an end to the interreligious dialog initiated by Vatican II. Recall Nadal's inability to dialog with the rabbis of Avignon.

The word *religion* harbors ambiguities, as does *religio* in Latin and *religión* in Spanish. All three mean not only a system of beliefs or ultimate values, but also "a religious order" and "the religious life." Thus, a member of the Christian religion might "enter religion," that is, embark on the religious life in a religious order.[38] Nadal moves easily from one meaning to another and, a child of his age, comments, "But those who live out both the precepts and the counsels are more appropriately called religious and

---

[37] *PolChron* 1:298, no. 260.

[38] For a fuller treatment, see my *Impelling Spirit,* 242–46.

more perfectly follow the Christian religion" (36, no. 2). That members of religious orders and congregations more perfectly follow the Christian religion is objectionable in the light of the universal call to holiness underscored by Vatican II; it reflects sixteenth-century hierarchical thinking rather than the egalitarian thinking characteristic of the twenty-first century.[39] That they are more appropriately called religious is another matter. God, indeed, calls all to holiness, to seek and find God; but, as Sandra Schneiders has pointed out, no other primary life commitment defines religious except the quest for God.[40] This does not imply that members of religious orders and congregations are more religious than other people. They are religious in a different way.

Nadal's first exhortation is almost a commentary on the passage from Vatican II quoted at the beginning of this chapter. Like the council, Nadal maintains that Jesus also wishes to be served and worshiped in ways distinguishing one religious order from another (36, no. 2). He aroused St. Francis to help the Church and gave him a special grace; he also inflamed Ignatius, communicated a particular grace to him and to his followers through him, thus distinguishing the Society from other religious orders (37, nos. 4 f.). The diversity of graces and stimuli in religious orders are like the diversity of graces in the sacraments: each sacrament contains and gives grace, each justifies us before God, yet each has its own particular grace. Baptism gives us birth, confirmation strengthens us, the Eucharist nourishes us, and so forth. Likewise, Jesus bestows different graces on religious orders to serve God in different ways, adorning the Church with a variety of gifts through one and the same Spirit (37, no. 6).

Religious Institutes

Amid the "wonderful variety of religious communities" that have "come into existence," the graces proper to each institute create different ways of "enabling the Church to be equipped for every good work"— different ways of continuing the divine missions, of continuing the Trinitarian work of the Incarnation through giving oneself wholly to God in Christ, thereby attracting different people in accordance with each one's

---

[39] Some reflections on this "unholy marginalization of the laity" appear in the excellent article "'Perfection in Whatever State of Life': Ignatian Spirituality and Lay Holiness," by Maria Clara Bingemer, *Review of Ignatian Spirituality* 28, no. 86 (1997): 39–56. Note that the new Code of Canon Law distinguishes between "lay life" and "religious" or "consecrated life." Canon 573 speaks of religious as "totally dedicated to God . . . by a new and special title," and c. 607 describes religious life as "a consecration of the whole person," as though baptism is not already a consecration of the whole person to God.

[40] Sandra M. Schneiders, I.H.M., *Finding the Treasure: Locating Catholic Religious Life in a New Ecclesial and Cultural Context*, vol. 1 of *Religious Life in a New Millennium* (New York: Paulist Press, 2000), 36.

own particular grace.[41] God's action in moving Ignatius is peculiar to the Society, but it is for the good of the whole Church. God also moved Basil and Anthony, Augustine and Benedict, Dominic and other founders in ways peculiar to each, also for the good of the whole Church. All these share the call to minister to God's Church and to the whole world, but in different manners, just as the three divine Persons share the same nature, but are distinct in the way they do so.

Religious institutes differ and enrich the Church and each other, just as cultures differ and enrich each other and the whole world by their differences. Every culture is a way of living the human life, and one must always be cautious about pronouncing one culture "more advanced" than another, for each has its own way of expressing and prioritizing human values. So also one religious order differs from another by its "genetic code," the particular way it incarnates the Christian life. They do not differ by something Christian that one has and the other lacks, but by the way they manifest and live the Christian life in its entirety. As Thomas Aquinas once said, the differences do not imply that members of one institute hold something back from God while those of another institute hold back something else.[42] To call the Jesuit Rule a "pathway to God" is not to assert that it is the only way to God.[43]

Each religious order has the grace of what Nadal in his earlier years called the "monastic" life, using the term much the way Sandra Schneiders does in presenting monasticism as the paradigm of the spirituality that drives human beings to seek the fullness of human life. The monastic ideal and the ideals of those whose lives exclude all that interferes with their aim are the visible expressions of that profound desire in human beings to "go beyond"; but monks are not the only ones who thirst "to reach the unreachable stars." In this sense, religious orders and congregations, no matter what their form, are monastic in their inner being and embody the monastic ideal.[44] Even so, "every calling and grace and movement and influence enjoys its own peculiar gift, a divine power that works in each to bring it to the perfection of its own particular form."[45] In later years, after fighting against monastic *practices* in the Society—what Schneiders calls the "monastic lifestyle" and others would prefer to call "monastic way of living"—Nadal regretted placing all religious orders under the monastic

---

[41] See "Exhort. 1554 Hisp." (*CommInst* 37, no. 7); "Exhort. 4 in Alcalá" (1561) (ibid., 335f., no. 94); "Dialogus II (1562–65)" (ibid., 660–661).

[42] *Summa theologiæ* 2ª 2ᵃᵉ, q. 188, a 1, ad 1.

[43] Pope Paul III, *Regimini militantis Ecclesiæ* (1540) and Pope Julius III, *Exposcit debitum* (1550). See *ConsCN* 3–14.

[44] Schneiders, *Finding the Treasure*, 8 f.

[45] See also "Annotationes in Constitutiones" (1556) (*CommInst* 120 f., nos. 30 f.); "Exhort. 4 in Alcalá" (1561) (ibid., 335 f., no. 94); "Dialogus II" (1562–65) (ibid., 660).

umbrella, stating bluntly that the Society is not monastic in nature and should not be judged by monastic norms; rather, it has its own peculiar gifts.[46]

Thus, "the particular manner of Jesuit obedience is a special grace that God our Lord has given to the Society" (38, no. 7), what Schneiders calls "accentuated witness"; but that does not keep obedience from having a special role in other religious institutes as well.[47] We might speak also of the accentuated witness of Carthusian silence or Franciscan poverty, the nurturing love of a mother, the providential care of a father, or the mutual love of husband and wife.[48] All on the face of the earth, whatever their religious background, have their own special graces and their own unique way of revealing the depths of the richness of God. That is why we can all learn about our own personal vocations from those of others, since all are

---

[46] Christian living embraces various levels: (1) a way of living common to all, consisting in sharing profoundly through Christ in the life of Father, Son, and Holy Spirit; (2) a way of living common to all religious, consisting in choosing no other polarity in their life than God, with celibacy at its core (monasticism as the paradigm of spirituality); (3) various ways of living out that celibate commitment: cenobitic monasticism according to various rules, hermit monasticism, canons regular, clerks regular, and so on. Cecilia W. Wilms comments: "One is called and committed to a way of *life;* one expresses the commitment through a *lifestyle* congruent with it. Hence the way of *life* comes first, is basic, essential; the *lifestyle* follows and is secondary and contingent" ("Thoughts in Solitude," *Raven's Bread* 1, no. 2 [1997]: 1). Roberto de Nobili in India and Matteo Ricci in China shared the common way of living of all Jesuits; their lifestyle was very different from that of most. The lifestyle of Jesuits who live and work on reservations with Native Americans differs considerably from that of many other Jesuits living in cities. See "De professione et choro" (*EpistNadal* 4:174). For the continuity between the spirituality of the Society and the monastic spirit, see, Karl Rahner, S.J., "The Ignatian Mysticism of Joy in the World," in *Theological Investigations,* trans. Karl-H. and Boniface Kruger (Helicon Press, Baltimore: 1967), 3:277–93.

[47] Schneiders, *Finding the Treasure,* 16. Like everything else in the Society, obedience has to do with mission, with being sent, far different from monastic obedience where the norm is stability. See Rafael M.ª Sanz de Diego, S.J., "La novedad de Ignacio de Loyola ante un mundo nuevo," in *Ignacio y su tiempo,* 924.

[48] Joseph de Guibert, S.J., has adequately and expertly dealt with the problem of the distinctions among religious institutes: "En quoi diffèrent réellement les diverses écoles catholiques de spiritualité?" *Gregorianum* 19 (1938): 263–79; id., *Leçons de théologie spirituelle* (Toulouse, 1943), 108–22; id., *The Jesuits: Their Spiritual Doctrine and Practice: A Historical Study,* trans. W. J. Young, S.J. (St. Louis: The Institute of Jesuit Sources/Chicago: Loyola University Press, 1964), 1–17. See also Günter Switek, S.J., "Die Eigenart der Gesellschaft Jesu im Vergleich zu den anderen Orden in der Sicht des Ignatius und seiner ersten Gefährten," in *Ignatianisch: Eigenart und Methode der Gesellschaft Jesu,* ed. M. Sievernich, S.J., and G. Switek, S.J. (Freiburg: Herder, 1990), 204–32; Jean Beyer, S.J., "Novità della Compagnia di Gesù nelle strutture degli ordini religiosi," *Vita consacrata* 27 (1991): 733–44; Estanislao Olivares, S.J., "Aportación de la Compañía de Jesús a la vida religiosa en su época," *Manresa* 56 (1984): 229–59, 345–64.

called to be fully and unequivocally who we are.[49] Living our personal call is a gift to all the rest.

Grace of the Jesuit Vocation

CommInst 38–46, nos. 8–19

How did the Society come into existence, and how does it differ from other religious institutes? "This is how it happened," Nadal said:

> God our Lord, through his infinite goodness, impelled Father Ignatius [of Loyola], arousing in him his own special grace, . . . his Divine Majesty providing for his Church and the whole world, helping on two major issues: (1) joining learning to spirituality and (2) directing both to the good of the neighbor. Some people have brains but no heart and others are all heart with no brains; some have both, but very few serve the Lord by directing both to the help of the neighbor. (*CommInst* 38, no. 8)

Nadal himself was a living example of joining learning and spirituality, the embodiment of two ideals the Constitutions hold in tension: depend on the means that unite a person with God (no. 813) and develop human skills to be a ready instrument for ministry in God's hand (no. 814). Flesh is channel for spirit, ineffectual without spirit. To be rooted in the earth and rooted in God is to participate in the self-emptying of the Word made flesh sent to save the human race from sin.

The wedding of learning and spirituality is like the wedding of the human nature with the divine in the Word, embedding the Word in the world, embracing the world, yet exiling the Word in a world that rejected him: "He came to what was his own, and his own people did not accept him" (John. 1:11). In the sixteenth century, uniting learning and spirituality challenged the easy mores of the ecclesiastical and secular world, the lazy thinking that easily leads to heresy. Today, to join learning and spirituality is the unpardonable sin in a postmodern, secular world, a blunder punishable immediately by academic and social exile. To wed learning with spirituality is a special grace of the Society—flesh and spirit continuing the Son's mission, helping people, and sharing the plight of the stranger and homeless refugee. Nadal would one day say that pilgrimage (being on the move for God's sake) is ultimately the best possible home for a Jesuit.[50] Others share that grace of uniting learning and spirituality in ways distinctive and appropriate to each; but all Christians are like Jesus, strangers in their own home, exiles on the move.

---

[49] Many Protestant groups find profit in the Spiritual Exercises today. For a reflection on the value of Ignatian prayer in today's world, see José Arroyo, "La tradición orante ignaciana y su valor actual," *Confer* 23 (1984): 121–33.

[50] "In Examen annotationes" (1557) (*CommInst* 195, no. 175).

At this point, without realizing what he is doing, Nadal begins to outline various ways in which we can come to know the grace of the Society. He speaks of the graces God bestowed upon Ignatius, "giving him especially an intense desire for the greater honor and glory of his Divine Majesty" (38–40, nos. 9–12), the gift of the Exercises "guiding him in this way to give himself wholly to [God's] service and the salvation of souls," especially the considerations on the Call of the King and the Two Standards, which oriented his life toward others and brought about the founding of the Society (40 f., nos. 13 f.); and, finally, sending him the many sufferings and persecutions he and the Society underwent after the manner of the apostles and the primitive Church (41–46, nos. 15–19).

As the years passed, Nadal returned to these themes time and time again, developing them all the while, presenting them as ways of illuminating the special grace of the Society of Jesus. They will form the backbone of this book: (1) the way God worked a transformation in Ignatius (2) through the Spiritual Exercises, especially in the meditations on the Call of the King and the Two Standards, (3) to make him into a man totally committed to the salvation of all those for whom Christ died, which is the end of the Society, (4) all of this according to the pattern of Jesus and the primitive Church. Sometimes he omits the fourth one, sometimes he makes it first, sometimes he adds another that is rather complex and could be called "the Jesuit way of proceeding," our way of doing what others do somewhat differently. The rest of the material in the exhortations of 1554 in Spain seems to fall under that category.[51] Nadal spent much of his energy in establishing good order in the young Society, putting into practice what Ignatius called the Society's "way of proceeding." He also spent time explaining two documents the members of the Society had not yet seen or studied: the *General Examen* and the *Constitutions,* with the latter's ten parts covering everything from admitting new members to dismissing them; their training in the novitiate and during their time of studies, culminating in their taking final vows; the personal

---

[51] Sometimes Nadal limits himself to (1) Ignatius as model, (2) the Call of the King and the Two Standards, and (3) the end of the Society. In *Contemplation in Action* I followed this threefold division. Most of the manuscripts containing his exhortations in Alcalá in 1561, however, add a fourth way: through the Society's way of governing or "way of proceeding," for Nadal saw in the Constitutions a reflection of the Gospels that are a source of life in the Church ("Exhort. 2 in Alcalá" [*EpistNadal* 5:262, no. 33]). A variant reading from a Toledo manuscript, presented in the footnotes on pp. 262 and 264, gives as the first of five ways the imitation of Jesus and his disciples and the primitive life of the Church, for Nadal was convinced a Jesuit could see therein his vocation as in a mirror. Because the Toledo manuscript adds fullness to Nadal's presentation, I have chosen to add the fifth way, but since the Jesuit "way of proceeding" runs through all the ways, I have chosen not to treat it separately.

life of the professed members and the work they do; and the corporate life and good health of the whole Society. The following chapters will detail Nadal's immersion in that task of explaining the Society's Institute, the method he used, and the theology on which he based his explanations.

Before taking up one by one the four ways of discovering the grace of the Society, however, we will gain a broad perspective on Jesuit spirituality by further exploring some of the riches in these early exhortations of Nadal; they will help us determine the grace proper to the Society. To accomplish this task the rest of this chapter will consider some of his reflections on the General Examen, and the next chapter some of his reflections on the Constitutions.

The Least Society

General Examen
"Exhort. 1554 Hisp."

The *General Examen* provides prospective companions information they need about the Society, and seeks information that the Society needs regarding candidates. The *General Examen* began then much as it does now:

> This least congregation *[congregatión]*, which at its original founding was called the Society *[Compañía]* of Jesus by the Apostolic See, was first approved by Pope Paul III of happy memory in 1540 and later was confirmed by the same in 1543 and by Julius III, his successor, in 1550.[52]

Addressing new companions in the second exhortation in Spain in 1554, and having already established divine approval (see chap. 1), Nadal devotes no time to papal approval. He explores instead the first three words of the *General Examen*. "This least Society," he says, using "Compañía" instead of "congregatión."[53] Call it what you will, the emphasis is on *least*.

---

[52] My translation of *Textus B,* found in *Constitutiones* 2:5–7. Nadal's reference a few pages later to the Preamble of the *Constitutions* (nonexistent in *Textus A* [1550]) indicates that he had a more recent text than that of 1550. Remember that Nadal's copy of the text is B^1; B was in flux at the time and took its final form with the death of Ignatius in 1556.

[53] Commenting on the same passage in 1557, Nadal says: "It was important to call it a congregation, as a sort of genus, before calling it a society. Congregation suggests a sense of obedience such as is desired in the Society: that we are a flock led by a superior, like sheep not opening the mouth of our will and judgment" (see Isa. 53:7) ("In examen annotationes" [*EpistNadal* 5:134 f., no. 1]).

The Society as Servant: Second, Third, and Fourth Exhortations

CommInst 48–70, nos. 25–78

> Note that this is what Ignatius is accustomed to call the Society when dealing with matters of great importance and when writing to some prince; and this is the way we should all think of it; namely, that we are the least of all religious and the servants of all, that we should look upon and venerate all as our superiors, and that this ought to be a great consolation to us. It is in harmony with this attitude that, although we are religious and the Society is a religious order, Fr. Ignatius never calls the Society such, but out of humility speaks of a congregation and of a society. (*Comm-Inst* 48, no. 25)

Although the term "least Society" belies the common perception, it lays bare the heart of the Jesuit ideal in the Third Degree of Humility: when the glory of God is equal, to prefer "poverty with Christ poor, rather than wealth, contempt with Christ laden with it rather than honors, . . . to be regarded as a useless fool for Christ, who before me was regarded as such, rather than a wise or prudent person in this world" (*SpEx* 167). The name itself, Society of Jesus, continues the emptying process, *kenosis,* of the Incarnation. "The Son of Man came not to be served but to serve" (Mark 10:45), and so, too, the Society of Jesus. Nadal begins where Simón Rodrigues was strong, with a sense of humility, that is; but he moves away from the personal and exotic humiliations that Simón emphasized, preferring instead a community grace of service: the Society's grace of continuing the mission of Jesus (who identified himself with the Suffering Servant of Second Isaiah), acting therefore as servant of the servant Church and servant of the pope in his role as the Servant of the Servants of God. In doing so he adumbrates decree 2 of General Congregation 34, *Servants of Christ's Mission,* which outlines the struggles of the Society today in every part of the world, with emphasis on the presence of the Risen Lord in our lives. To be servants of all means to be servants especially of the poor. To be servants means to be servants of justice, to welcome cultures other than our own, to collaborate with others, and to listen to and dialog with other traditions. Servanthood differs from servitude. Przywara calls it "messenger-service"—what the service angels (messengers) provide as they care for human beings.[54]

Explaining the name of the new Society, Nadal notes first that "our way of living is described in the bull as a 'militia' because of the terminology Ignatius used in the *Exercises* about Christ's conducting a war against the world, the flesh, and the devil; the Society strives with all its strength

---

[54] Erich Przywara, S.J., "God in All Things," *Sursum Corda* 12 (1972): 154–64, 202–13, esp. 163.

to follow the standard of Christ." He then reports two remarks that he has heard, one from Laínez, the other from Ignatius. He recalled Laínez saying:

> When the Society's confirmation was under discussion, Fr. Ignatius was on his way to Rome with Fathers Favre and Laínez, and while he was at prayer he had a vision of Christ with his cross. As God placed Fr. Ignatius in service at the side [of Christ], he said to him: I SHALL BE WITH YOU [plural], by which he clearly indicated that God chose us to be companions of Jesus.[55] This is a special grace granted by God to the Society. Note that Christ, being raised from the dead, will never die again [Rom. 6:9], but he still suffers the cross continually in his members, so that he said to Paul: Why do you persecute me? [Acts 9:4]. This, then, is what God calls us to, to follow Jesus in this militia, each one taking up his cross and suffering for the sake of Christ. In this we ought to be inspired and comforted, namely, that we follow Christ and are made his companions through the cross. What else did Christ have or want in the world other than labors, persecutions, and the cross for the glory of God the Father and the salvation of us all? We also want it, then, giving up our lives, if need be, for the sake of the brethren. (*CommInst* 51 f., no. 30)

Ignatius, he says, responded to someone who suggested that the Society should have a different name, "The name that it has and uses only God can change" (52, no. 31).

Nadal continues to explain the Society in incarnational terms: "The end of the Society is the very highest, the salvation and perfection of souls for the greater glory of God, imitating Christ not only in prayer but also in work, using whatever can be of help, acting always with intense love" (53, no. 33). Doing so demands poverty or purity of spirit, and the vows strip away whatever impedes the fervor and zeal needed (54, no. 36).

Advancing the theme in the third exhortation, Nadal states that the vows in their diversity, like those of rendering full obedience to the pope and of going where he sends someone, create a crescendo of marvelous symphonic harmony engaging every kind of talent. To the living-out of the vows add spiritual exercises like prayer, meditation, and the like, which are the source *(principium)* of all the Society does, the means *(media)* used, and the term *(finis)* of every action. Finally, the members live out the virtues in a way peculiar to this particular religious order; for example, in the way of obeying, the way of preaching, the way of dealing with the neighbor (57 f., nos. 43–46). Let one sentence summarize how spirit gives life to flesh: "Everything has this purpose, that [the Society's] members may *live spiritually* and *walk according to the spirit,* and strive to lead

---

[55] Different authors report different words, and for some the words belong to the Father, while for others they come from the Son. See the lengthy n. 16 to Nadal's text in *CommInst* 51.

others to do the same, which they do through preaching, confessions, etc."
(57 f., no. 45, emphasis added).

These words summarize what it means to be a "mixed" order, one
concerned not simply with asceticism or with asceticism and the corporal
works of mercy, nor simply with contemplation. To walk "according to the
spirit," that deepest part of the human being where we are most in touch
with God, is to walk according to the Holy Spirit. Austerity provides a
good example. The Society's work demands constant and continuing
interior mortification (59, no. 50). Although the Society imposes no
regular bodily penances on its members, it does not reject penances but
uses them "insofar as they are necessary or useful or appropriate for our
end and our Institute and in a way that feeds the spirit" (60, no. 51).
Studies, too, must be connected with the spirit, else they can do harm. In
an atmosphere where the intellect flourishes, both students and superiors
need to make sure that the affective powers of the students do not wither
and die. Studies are to serve the spirit, not destroy it (64, no. 61). Study
shares in the Holy Spirit's mission.

In the fourth exhortation Nadal gives walking in the Spirit a communal note: "Walking (as we have said) in simplicity and clarity, the
Society wishes for an exact knowledge of all the members so that it might
provide better for each one in the Lord" (67, no. 72). He also remarks that
the Society can be more sure of a candidate who has come through the
internal motion of the Holy Spirit rather than by human persuasion (69,
no. 78). Later, in his "Notes on the Constitutions," he insists that God is at
the heart of the whole process, arousing, moving, inspiring, while the
person called hears, receives the word, follows. All is from God: the call,
the ability to hear, to say yes, and to follow (120, no. 29). To answer the
call is to praise, reverence, and serve God.

In all these passages Nadal describes the way one Christian group
participates in the emptying process that joins them to Jesus and enables
them to continue his mission. Even the need for superiors to know each
member well, a special characteristic of the Society, enables them to send
the right persons on a particular mission. The Father sent the Son into the
world, each knowing the other thoroughly (Matt. 11:27), and the Father
and Son sent the Holy Spirit with total confidence that the Spirit would
teach all that they wished the Spirit to teach (John. 14:26, 15:26).

Suffering Servant

Fifth Exhortation (*CommInst* 79–82, nos. 113–15)

The mission of Jesus leads to suffering and death. Nadal explains
the high expectations the Society has of its candidates. He reflects on the
renunciation of property, the lack of external ceremonies, the demands of
common life, and the meaning of being dead to the world (*CommInst* 70–

73, nos. 79–85). He emphasizes the need to walk in the Spirit, explaining the experiments or trials of the novitiate that teach a novice to pray (73–78, nos. 86–103), and comments on sickness, poverty, and the revealing of one's inner life to the superior (78–81, nos. 104–12). The examination of a candidate comes to a climax by reminding him of the need to follow Christ in suffering, making decisions similar to his. The examiner urges the candidate to reflect carefully on the passage in the *General Examen* that insists "to how great a degree it helps and profits in the spiritual life to abhor in its totality and not in part whatever the world loves and embraces, and to accept and desire with all possible energy whatever Christ our Lord has loved and embraced."[56] Nadal points out that Christ suffers today in the Church, and that Jesuits should fill up what is wanting in Christ's sufferings (Col. 1:24). The cross of Christ is not just physical suffering but ignominy as well, and for this reason Jesuits should reject what the world loves and embrace the opposite with boundless joy.

> Sometimes Ignatius used to say to me, "If I had to give an account to God alone, I would go through the world naked, lathered with honey and feathered, wearing a necklace of claws: a jest and a joke to all, mocked as a fool." He said this because he longed to follow Christ in ignominy, and we should desire the same, believing that there is no honor except to suffer insults for Christ. (81 f., no. 113)

A candidate for the Society should be asked if he has that desire, or at least the desire for that desire; and if he does not, he does not belong in the Society. If he does have the desire, he should be asked a final time if he is ready to suffer insults heaped on him by anyone at all after he has joined the Society, and if not, he should not be accepted (82, no. 114).

What Ignatius has in mind is full participation in the mission of Jesus, in the whole Trinitarian plan for salvation. Does the candidate hear all that the divine persons imply in the mission of the Son to become man? Is he fully in love with Jesus and willing to be like him in every way? Mary's full acceptance of the angel's message offers the model for the candidate's response: "walking in the Spirit" is the norm for everything. The phrase has strong biblical roots and is a favored expression of both Ignatius and Nadal. It will be explored at greater depth in the next chapter.

Conclusion

In 1554 Nadal scarcely or only slightly developed the ways of discovering the grace proper to the Society. He developed these ways more explicitly as the years went by and he became more proficient in the extraordinary

---

[56] *Constitutiones* 2:85; for an English translation, see *ConsCN* 101 (p. 46); see Ruiz-Jurado, "La perspectiva," 242–47; also see n. 16 in *CommInst* 51, no. 30.

work Ignatius entrusted to him. Each theme will provide one or more chapters for this book as we delve more deeply into the graces proper to the Society. Because each theme, however, is embedded in all the other themes, a particular theme may appear for a brief moment to assist in explaining another theme. I have chosen to follow the order of the Toledo manuscript mentioned in an earlier footnote, seeking the grace of the Society by reflecting on (1) the desire to follow Jesus and the apostles stirred up by (2) the experience of the Call of the King and the Two Standards as seen in the Spiritual Exercises, and leading to (3) the end of the Society and its ministries (4) according to the pattern of Ignatius himself.

Nadal's reflections on the *General Examen* and the beginning of the *Constitutions* illumine the grace proper to the Society of Jesus.[57] Toward the end of his life, he edited, corrected, revised much of the work he had done earlier, including the instructions that General Congregation 2 had asked him to prepare for provincials.[58] In his mature thought he states without hesitation:

> Since through the kindness of God we have received our own kind of vocation, grace, institute, and end, everything should be regulated accordingly. And so it proves nothing as far as we are concerned if someone says, This is the way the Dominicans act, or the Franciscans, and therefore we should do the same. For they have received their own grace, their own institute, and so have we our own, through the grace of Jesus Christ.[59]

Many are the ways to walk the path of Jesus. The grace proper to the Society of Jesus is the particular way in which the Society envisions the Christian life. Grace, as a participation in the life of the Trinity, incarnates in some way the life of Jesus, whose personality is so rich that no one person or group, or all men and women together, can image it perfectly. As Jesuit Gerard Manley Hopkins expresses it,

---

[57] Addressing the scholastics in Rome in 1557 after the death of Ignatius, Nadal says, "Let us see how our Society received a particular grace common to all institutes; and then also a very special grace, just as others have their graces" ("Adhortationes in Collegio Romano," 1557 [hereafter *AdhortRom*] in *Font.narr* 2:4, no. 7); see the entire section found ibid., 2:3–7, nos. 2–18. Authors who discuss the particular grace of the Society include Thomas H. Clancy, S.J., "The Proper Grace of the Jesuit Vocation according to Jerome Nadal," *Woodstock Letters* 86 (1957): 107–18 (reprinted in his *Introduction to Jesuit Life* [St. Louis: The Institute of Jesuit Sources, 1976], 271–82); Leonardo R. Silos, S.J., "Cardoner in the Life of Saint Ignatius of Loyola," *Archivum historicum Societatis Iesu (AHSI)* 33 (1964): 3–43, especially pp. 27–37; John H. Wright, S.J., "The Grace of Our Founder and the Grace of Our Vocation," *Studies in the Spirituality of Jesuits* 3 (February 1971): 1–31; Gervais Dumeige, S.J., "The Grace Bestowed on the Founder—For All the Companions," *CIS* 19, no. 1 (1988): 62–71.

[58] Nicolau, *Jerónimo Nadal,* 108 f.

[59] "De ratione instituti," in "Instructiones" (*EpistNadal* 4:514).

> . . . For Christ plays in ten thousand places,
> Lovely in limbs, and lovely in eyes not his
> To the Father through the features of men's faces.[60]

A grace proper to the Society or any other institute reproduces Christ in the lives of its members in a unique though partial manner. Through light and shade it expresses the particular beauty it has caught in the features of Christ's holy face. It also expresses its own limitations.[61] Only other light and shade can capture other beauty in that face. "Light and shade" suggests that the grace proper to one institute is not exclusive to that institute; in each the grace will have a different look. In this way each is a gift to all the others, God's gift, which means that God's gift of Franciscan spirituality is not limited to the way it is lived by the community called the Friars Minor, but can inspire anyone through its basic thrust and attitude toward God and the rest of the world. Just so, many people who have no desire to join the Jesuits find inspiration in Ignatian spirituality and Ignatian prayer, the kind of spirituality and prayer that Jesuits practice.

As Vatican II stated in the quotation at the beginning of this chapter, it is "in keeping with the divine purpose" that "a wonderful variety of religious communities came into existence." They do not all have the same special gifts, but their combined gifts contribute "to enabling the Church . . . to be equipped for every good work . . . and to be prepared for the work of the ministry." From Nadal's remarks we can conclude that a "peculiar" or "proper" gift or grace is one that is suitable to a particular institute because of its particular aims and methods, bearing witness to and accentuating some aspect of the mystery of Jesus.

Just as the way the Jesuit-influenced Rubens envisions the crucifixion differs from Giotto's or El Greco's, so also the Ignatian way of envisioning the Christian experience differs from the Franciscan or Carmelite. Giotto has painted a crucifixion scene, somewhat primitive, austere: the figure on the cross with arms outstretched as though embracing his friends who, overcome by emotion, suffer with him; his head slightly turned from his enemies; angels serving him; the scene is as peaceful and serene as Francis himself. El Greco has painted one in which there is no

---

[60] Poem 57, "As kingfishers catch fire, dragonflies draw flame," in *The Poems of Gerard Manley Hopkins*, ed. W. H. Gardner and N. H. MacKenzie, 4th ed. (London: Oxford University Press, 1967), 90.

[61] "His person is so rich and his personality so inexhaustible that it is impossible to reduce his face to a single expression" (Peter-Hans Kolvenbach, S.J., "Ignatius of Loyola: Experience of Christ," in *The Road from La Storta* [St. Louis: The Institute of Jesuit Sources, 2000], 21–32). For a reflection on the limitations of Jesuit or any other spirituality, see Andrew Hamilton, S.J., "In Sin Was I Conceived," *Review of Ignatian Spirituality* 29, no. 88 (1998): 43–50; Frank J. Houdek, S.J., "The Limitations of Ignatian Prayer," *The Way*, Supplement no. 82 (1995): 26–34.

sign of earth. The cross with its burden is flung against the sky like a mighty spear piercing the heavens, not unlike the writing of John of the Cross. Rubens, on the other hand, has painted one of violent confusion: three crosses, two bodies writhing and one relaxed in death, the centurion on a horse withdrawing his spear, a horse stomping, women sobbing, a strong clash of colors, a banner flying above the cross: "Jesus of Nazareth, King." All this is realistic rather than ideal, an image, if you will, of Jesuit spirituality.[62] Every Christian is initiated into the Christian way by baptism, by the saving action of God, called to be a coheir with Christ, imitating his struggle, sharing in his work and in his triumph. How different groups and persons go about implementing that end determines the distinctions that mark the people of God.

A Jesuit looks beyond himself, but what Christian does not? A Jesuit's life revolves around the Cross of Jesus, but what Christian's life does not? A Jesuit's life is in praise of the Holy Trinity, but what Christian's life is not? What is proper or peculiar is the way of looking beyond, the way life revolves around the Cross, the way one's life is a hymn of praise, a song of love. Looking beyond, embracing the Cross, praising the Trinity—all are done in and through living out the way of life to which each is called. Nadal is just beginning to articulate what that means for a Jesuit: it will have something to do with the greater glory of God, the intensity of the desire to serve, the directing of everything toward the service of others, the intensity of love in embracing the Cross; it will have something to do with accepting, approving, and embracing with love whatever God has created, not fleeing from it. That is what is implied in the paragraph from General Congregation 34 quoted at the beginning of this chapter: "As the Society of Jesus, we are servants of Christ's mission. . . . The Society has also become a body more diverse than ever before, engaged in a variety of ministries at the crossroads of cultural conflict, social and economic struggles, religious revivalism and new opportunities for bringing the Good News to people all over the world."[63] (d. 2, nos. 1 f.).

This chapter has introduced the theme of a special grace proper or appropriate to the Society of Jesus and has looked at some reflections of Nadal on the *General Examen* that illumine this special grace. The next chapter reflects on some of Nadal's comments on the *Constitutions* in his first trip to Spain in 1554, presenting a broad sweep of Jesuit spirituality that reveals more fully in a general way the grace proper to the Society of Jesus.

---

[62] André Wankenne, S.J., "Painters of the Passion," *Lumen Vitae* 9 (1954): 484–98.

[63] *DocsGC34* 15 f. (pp. 25 f.).

Chronicle for Chapter 3

The extraordinary public mortifications took on a new life in the holy season of Lent, at the end of which, on Holy Thursday Fr. Nadal came . . . and explained all the *Constitutions*. . . . With his coming the affairs of the college took a turn for the better, and we learned more about the Society and its Institute to our great joy. . . . One of the more important things he set in order was the study of the arts and theology by persuading everyone how important it is to approach them fervently and seriously, not only because of the fruit the Society will reap for our neighbor, but also for our personal growth and the increase and spiritual prosperity of religion.

—Diego Guzman, S.J.

Nadal's Life and Travels

1554

Visits Toledo

Feb. 6–March 5: Alcalá; rules, exhortations, leaves for Valladolid

March 20: Leaves Valladolid for Plasencia, having understood better de Pedroche's charges against the Spiritual Exercises (chap. 6); at Salamanca, exhortations, considers Cano's charges against the Society (chap. 5)

April 4: Medina del Campo (22 days); new provinces and provincials (chap. 4); Tordesillas; visits Borgia; Valladolid, visits Araoz

May 15: Leaves Valladolid for Burgos; Palencia, Treviño, Oñate; visits Loyola

June (before the seventeenth): At Saragossa, exhortations

July: Cuenca, Valencia, Gandía, Murcia

August or September: Leaves Murcia for Alicante, boards ship to Barcelona

Sept. 20: Arrives at Barcelona but has to return to Salou and go to Barcelona by land

Sept. 29: Leaves for Genoa; storm forces a stop at Marseilles

Before Oct. 4: Arrives in Genoa

Oct. 18: Arrives in Rome

Nov. 1: Elected vicar-general

Chapter Three

WALKING IN THE SPIRIT

Under the impulse of love, which the Holy Spirit pours into their hearts (cf. Rom. 5:5), they live more and more for Christ and for his Body, the Church (cf. Col. 1:24). The more fervently, therefore, they join themselves to Christ by this gift of their whole life, the fuller does the Church's life become and the more vigorous and fruitful its apostolate.

Vatican II, *On the Up-to-Date Renewal of the Religious Life.*

This chapter considers how Jesuits are called to live "under the impulse of love, which the Holy Spirit pours into their hearts" and to "live more and more for Christ and for his Body, the Church," thus joining "themselves to Christ by this gift of their whole life." To show how the Society responds to this call in its own particular way, according to its own spirituality and particular grace, this chapter introduces some reflections Jerónimo Nadal made on the Society's *Constitutions* in the exhortations he gave in Spain in 1554. For its own part, General Congregation 34 in 1995 expressed the Society's call in these words:

The Church, whose mission we share, exists not for itself but for humanity, bearing the proclamation of God's love. . . . Its aim is the realization of the Kingdom of God in the whole of human society, not only in the life to come but also in this life. . . . We exercise our Jesuit mission within the total evangelizing mission of the Church. . . . St. Ignatius was clear that, as the Society was not instituted by human means, so its ministries are preserved and fostered only by the all-powerful hand of Christ. Thus, as we receive our mission from Christ, whatever fruitfulness it bears is entirely dependent on his grace. And it is the Risen Christ who calls and empowers us for his service under the banner of the Cross.[1]

---

[1] *DocsGC34*, nos. 24, 27 (pp. 24, 29).

History

During his student days at Alcalá and again in Salamanca, because Ignatius paid close attention to "the impulse of love" flowing from the Holy Spirit, some suspected him of being one of those "enlightened ones" known as *illuminati* or *alumbrados* in Spain. Like Ignatius, these people paid much attention to the Holy Spirit. However, because they paid little attention to the relationship of the Spirit to the Church, they did not, like Ignatius, "live more and more for Christ and for his Body, the Church." "By their fruits you shall know them," and the life of Ignatius always proclaimed his orthodoxy. He had little use for mysticism not grounded in the everyday life of the Church. He would have applauded the mysticism encapsulated in the words of General Congregation 34 quoted above.

In 1539, before the Pope's oral approbation of the Society of Jesus had been properly solemnized in writing, Pope Paul III appointed Bartolomeo Guidiccioni vicar of Rome and created him a cardinal. Guidiccioni had been the vicar of Parma when Alessandro Farnese was bishop of Parma before becoming Paul III. Since Guidiccioni was strongly opposed to any new religious order—indeed, was convinced that the existing ones should be radically reduced in number—it required the greatest delicacy to persuade him to support the approbation of the Society. At first he would not even look at the proposed bull of approval, nor would he discuss the matter with Ignatius or any member of the Society. After the Society had offered many prayers and Masses, however, he had a change of heart and became an enthusiastic supporter of the Society. Years later Nadal reported that it was even said that the cardinal thought all religious should belong to this one order alone! (*CommInst* 49, no. 28). Undoubtedly the story of the cardinal's final reaction to the proposed solemn approbation of the Society had become exaggerated beyond measure over the course of the fifteen years between the event and Nadal's report. The main point, however, is that Ignatius worked within the framework of the Church to win over an obdurate churchman.

A Pause for Prayer

The "impulse of love, which the Holy Spirit pours out" upon those who are open to receive it, manifests itself at the very beginning of the Spiritual Exercises:

> **First Principle and Foundation: "We ought to desire and to choose only that which is more *[magis]* conducive to the end for which we are created"** (*SpEx* 23).

In this chapter we reflect on the spirit of love and generosity characteristic of the Society, and we ask again for what
we want: the outpouring of the Holy Spirit's impulse of love,
the grace of generosity, making us willing to give to God all
that we have and are, for he has given all to us.

Society of Jesus, Society of Love

Jesuit *Constitutions*

"Exhort. 1554 Hisp." (*CommInst* 35–105)

Addressing Ignatius as "your holy Charity" throughout a lengthy letter
from India, Francis Xavier remarked, "It seems to me that 'Society of
Jesus' means to say 'a Society of love and conformity of minds,' and not
'of severity and servile fear.'"[2] The translator of the letter comments in a
footnote, "Nadal was of this same opinion: 'It is my opinion that the
future of the Society will be much more perfect if we would expel all fear,
and were led by pure charity and a sincere love of virtue.'"[3]

Perhaps that is why Nadal has an astonishingly summary approach
to the *Constitutions,* in sharp contrast to his detailed explanation of the
General Examen we saw above. Delivering his sixth exhortation in Spain in
1554, he briefly addresses the Preamble to the *Constitutions,* and comments on the admission of candidates (Part I) and the dismissal of members (Part II). He summarizes the other eight parts of the *Constitutions,*
which treat daily living in the Society, by speaking on prayer in the
seventh exhortation and obedience and chastity in the eighth. For him, it
would seem, life in the Society can be summed up in words suggested by
Luke 11:28: "Blessed are they who hear the word of God [prayer] and
obey it [obedience]," adding on our own, "in love" (chastity), key words to
bring out some of the overtones in the phrase "walking in the Spirit."

---

[2] From Cochin, January 12, 1549, in *The Letters and Instructions of Francis
Xavier,* trans. and intro. by M. Joseph Costelloe, S.J. (St. Louis: The Institute of Jesuit
Sources, 1992), 217.

[3] Ibid., n. 8. The Nadal quotation is from *Scholia in constitutiones et declarationes
S.P. Ignatii (Prato: Giachetti & Sons, 1993),* 219; for a more modern edition of this
work, see *Scholia in Constitutiones S.I.,* ed. with prolog and notes by Manuel Ruiz
Jurado, S.J., Biblioteca Theologica Granadina, vol. 17 (Granada: Faculty of Theology,
1976), 254. All future references to the *Scholia* will be to the Ruiz Jurado edition; it
will hereafter be abbreviated to *NadSchol.* Note that the Preamble to the *Constitutions*
defines the primary motive governing members of the Society as "the interior law of
charity and love which the Holy Spirit writes and imprints upon hearts" (134$^{v.3}$ [p. 56]).

Omitting Nadal's remarks on admission and dismissal, this chapter considers only the comments on the Preamble in the sixth exhortation, those on prayer in the seventh, and the remarks on obedience and chastity in the eighth exhortation. The *Spirit* is the source of *prayer,* from which flows *love,* which expresses itself in *chastity* and *obedience.*

The Holy Spirit of Love

Preamble to the *Constitutions* (*CommInst* 82–86, nos. 116–23)

The Preamble to the Constitutions did not exist in the earliest version; but it was part of Nadal's text, appears in Text B (1556), and apparently underwent no evolution. Just as Nadal's opening comments on the *General Examen* suggest that the Society of Jesus is the direct result of a choice of the incarnate Word, so also the Preamble suggests that Ignatius views the Society in the same way. In the contemplation on the Incarnation in the Exercises, Ignatius envisions the three divine Persons "over the whole world bent," brooding on the sin and joy, laughter and pain, birthing and dying of men and women of every race and color and language. The Persons are not brooding in judgment, affronted by offenses and insults, angry and seeking vengeance; divine justice is not at stake. They decide to send the Son to be one of us, to make choices to save us from sin. Ignatius is profoundly conscious of the Society of Jesus as an instrument of Jesus.

The first paragraph of the Preamble begins with (1) God's action over the whole Society, (2) sweeps down to the Holy Spirit's action in each member, and (3) ends in our own actions:

> Although God our Creator and Lord is the one who in his Supreme Wisdom and Goodness must preserve, direct, and carry forward in his divine service this least Society of Jesus, just as he deigned to begin it, . . . [*ConsCN, C:* 134 (p. 56)]

For Ignatius and Nadal, God our Creator and Lord is Jesus, so Nadal comments, "God is the source of the Society." Ignatius makes two points: (1) God's infinite wisdom and goodness started the Society; (2) on God's infinite wisdom and goodness the Society depends; in that alone our hope is anchored. The whole reality of the Society can be reduced to that; all we do proceeds from the wisdom and goodness of God as from its primary source (*CommInst* 83, no. 117).

> and although on our own part what helps most toward this end must be, more than any exterior constitution, the interior law of charity and love which the Holy Spirit writes and imprints upon hearts; . . .

Here Nadal introduces the theme of love, the "warm breast" of the Holy Spirit, love which in the years to come he will often call a special grace of the Society. He sees the Society as an instrument extending the Father's loving act of missioning the Son for the salvation of the human race. To be an instrument of love demands a response of love. He emphasizes God's primary role in the Society by repeating what he has already said and adding more:

> God rules and governs the world (and hence the Society) by his wisdom and providence, and he carries this out through his mercy and goodness. Hence, Ignatius adds goodness to the wisdom of God that draws the Society into existence. This law of love is impressed in our hearts. . . . The Society originates in the same love that brought about the Incarnation and the suffering of Jesus. . . . And so we ought to proceed with hearts filled with love and passionate desire. (83 f., nos. 118)

Thus the Society extends the providential love of the Incarnation through its apostolic endeavors. Ignatius continues:

> nevertheless, since the gentle disposition of Divine Providence requires cooperation from his creatures, and since too the vicar of Christ our Lord has ordered this, and since the examples given by the saints and reason itself teach us so in our Lord, we think it necessary that constitutions should be written to aid us to proceed better, in conformity with our Institute, along the path of divine service on which we have entered.[4]

A world of sin is not a world of disaster. Divine providence is at work, divine love is at work, a call goes out to all creation to cooperate in love. In a world-affirming paragraph, Nadal states that we should use all human means to achieve the greater glory of God, offering to God all that might be used incorrectly, using them correctly instead. What others use for vanity, we use for the service of God (*CommInst* 84, no. 119). We offer to God in sacrifice what others misuse in sinning against him. This is spiritual liberty, to use creatures for the glory of God without any inordinate affection (84, no. 120). Today's ecological consciousness suggests that "to relate to creatures" would be better terminology than "to use." On Nadal's mind is the practice of the "enlightened" *[alumbrados]* or "abandoned" *[dejados]* in Spain, who paid no attention to cooperating with grace.

The salvation of the human race has not been left to chance. The supreme wisdom and goodness of God governs the Society of Jesus, which is not a human work depending on the powers of men to preserve it, to govern it, to make it grow and progress. The Society's members need, more than anything else, the action of the Holy Spirit. The Formula of the Institute takes it for granted that the Holy Spirit *impels* each member of the Society.[5] The Latin word, *impellit*, is far stronger than "moves." The Spirit is the driving force behind each one.

---

[4] *Constitutiones* 1:17, no. 3; 28, no. 4; 378, no. 4. Or see *ConsCN* 134 (p. 56).

[5] *ConsCN* 4 (p. 8).

Continuing his comments, Nadal calls to our attention that Ignatius often repeats the words "in our Lord." By these words Ignatius "wishes to express a sense of the spirit in all we do; for we do not act of ourselves, but in Christ, in his grace, by virtue of his power, as though to say: I work—no, not I, but Christ works in me and I in Christ" (84 f., no. 121). "In" suggests abiding intimacy: we are rooted and grounded in Christ. To walk in the Spirit, therefore, means acting in our Lord; to act in our Lord requires walking in love.

Dante Alighieri expressed the whole idea well when he wrote of *l'amore* (love): "L'anima non va con altro piede" (The soul can walk on no other foot).[6] Dante, in fact, anticipates Ignatius and Nadal by spending a whole canto speaking of the primal motions of delight that fill the heart, of the inborn freedom of discernment, and the grace of eager fervor. In Dante's *Commedia* God deals with the simple soul *(l'anima semplicittà)* as it comes trembling out of the hands of a joyful maker, tending toward delight, needing to be schooled.[7]

Nadal wants no harm to come to the eager young members of the Society, desiring rather that they be stirred and stimulated to passionate love. "Wherefore," he writes, "we should strive with all our might to impress deeply into our hearts this *spiritual way of living*" (85 f., no. 123). The words in italics were added in the margin of the manuscript in Nadal's own hand.

Seventh Exhortation: On Prayer ("De oratione")

"Exhort. 1554 Hisp." *(CommInsti* 89–98, nos. 136–63)

Nadal did not coin the phrase "simul in actione contemplativus" (contemplative likewise in action) until 1557, as he was reflecting on the prayer and life of Ignatius; but whenever he speaks or writes on the prayer of the Society, he uses equivalent ideas. He often repeats, not always in the same order, certain presuppositions regarding prayer; that is, the kind of prayer appropriate for the Society and the relationship between work and prayer.[8] He introduces subtleties about body and spirit, the human and the divine, that had escaped the notice of many of the early Jesuits. He is diplomatic and sympathetic in addressing communities jealous of their customs.

One presupposition already present in the exhortations he delivered in Spain in 1554 asserts that the intellect serves the spirit in prayer, but

---

[6] *Purgatorio*, c. 18, 44.

[7] Ibid., c. 16, 84–105. I owe these remarks on Dante to a conversation with and a note from Gretel Buchmann.

[8] I owe these presuppositions to the insight of Hermann Rodriguez Osorio, S.J., in his "La oración en las pláticas espirituales de Jerónimo Nadal en Coimbra (1561)," *Manresa* 70 (1997): 253–73.

thoughts and insights are not the essence of prayer. One who prays acquires a certain light beyond the natural light of the intellect and the light one gains from studying Scripture and ordinary matter; "but it is not contemplation without the union of love, else prayer would be without fruit. The beginning and the end is love: for the greater glory of God, and out of the fullness of love" (91, no. 144).

A second presupposition is that Jesuit prayer turns outward, not inward, and fulfills itself in passionate concern for others:

> The prayer of the Society, then, assists execution. . . . I must take care, therefore, that my prayer moves into praxis with feelings that fit the action, so that preaching, lecturing, etc., are done with relish, else whoever acts under the influence only of the natural light of reason and that special light gained from Scripture is like a tinkling cymbal. What we have been talking about Father Ignatius calls "walking in the Spirit." (92, no. 145)

We shall return to "walking in the Spirit" after seeing the third presupposition, dealing with prayer. This presupposition grounds the previous two mentioned above: the God to whom we pray is the God of history, one who reveals himself to us in the daily events of human life.

Jesuit prayer is not a retreat from the world. Lévesque contrasts the Ignatian approach to that reflected in Augustine's famous remark, "God is more intimate to me than I am to myself." Ignatius does not find God primarily in the most profound depths of his own soul, but in the most profound depths of God's creatures.[9] Ignatius wrote to Borgia using words reminiscent of St. Paul's "He emptied himself" (Phil. 2:7): "Those who go out of themselves enter into their creator and lord, and are vigilantly mindful and attentive, have the consolation of experiencing how our whole eternal good is in all created things" (*EpistIgn* 1:339). "Note," Nadal says on his first trip to Spain, "that the leftovers of reflections and insights [*reliquiæ cogitationum*] remaining after prayer help in work, since they are connected with what one has experienced in prayer" (92, no. 146). Nadal is addressing those who are learning. Work is neither contaminated nor contaminating, but the human spirit is limited. As Ignatius wrote to Borgia, the creator is to be found in all created things, so that impediments come from us, not from God or God's creatures. "Both before and after I am totally an impediment," he wrote (*EpistIgn* 1:340). I can find God in prayer and in work, but I get in the way and must return in prayer to its source, the Holy Spirit, learning gradually to find prayer and God in the work itself.[10] "The spirit becomes worn out by work," Nadal says, "and

---

[9] Fernand Lévesque, "Contemplation et action chez saint Ignace," *Cahiers de spiritualité ignatienne* 3 (1979): 23.

[10] See Herbert Alphonso, S.J., "La vida diaria como oración," in *Ejercicios espirituales y mundo de hoy,* Congreso Internacional de Ejercicios, Loyola, 20–26 septiembre de 1991, ed. Juan Manuel Garcia-Lomas (Bilbao: Mensajero, 1991), 265–78.

so it is necessary to return to prayer frequently and to make, as it were, a circle from prayer to work and from work to prayer" (92, no. 147).[11] Understanding does not suffice for virtue and perfection; one must also taste what one grasps in prayer (93, no. 154). We need to seek "the greater glory of God, not half-heartedly, but passionately, a special grace and capacity granted by our Lord to the Society" (94, no. 156). "We ought to especially take great care, as Ignatius advises, to find God in all things, and in this lies our greatest consolation" (95, no. 157).[12]

We should live, therefore, Nadal continues,

> first of all in spirit and in truth: energetically pursuing the truth; and secondly we should live with courage and gentleness . . . after the manner of divine wisdom, which is the origin of the Society and the source of its growth; . . . [and we should proceed] courageously: with constancy, precision, and fervor; and gently: with discretion, eschewing undue severity.[[13]] To live courageously and in gentleness is to walk in truth and in love. (95, no. 158)

Walking in the Spirit

The phrase "walk in the Spirit" is found in Galatians 5:16. The Latin Vulgate that Ignatius and his companions used has "Spiritu ambulate" (translated in the Douay-Rheims English version as "Walk in the Spirit"). The phrase is also suggested by Galatians 5:25: *Si spiritu vivimus, spiritu et ambulemus* (in the Douay-Rheims, "If we live in the Spirit, let us also walk in the Spirit"). The words appear again in a passage in the *General Examen* that would suit Simón Rodrigues's desire for humility: "Just as the men of the world who follow the world love and seek with such great diligence honors, fame, and esteem for a great name on earth, as the world teaches them, so those who proceed spiritually *[los que van en spíritu/procedunt in spiritu]* and truly follow Christ our Lord love and intensely desire everything opposite" (101[v. 3] [p. 46]).

---

[11] Nadal often returns to this idea: "Annot. in examen," in *CommInst* 143, no. 27; "Plática 11ª en Coimbra," in *Pláticas espirituales del P. Jerónimo Nadal, S.I., en Coimbra (1561),* ed. with notes by Miguel Nicolau, S.I. (Granada, 1845), 127, no. 9; "Exhort. 3ª & 12ª in Alcalá," in *CommInst* 328, no. 85; 456, no. 240.

[12] See also Lévesque, "Contemplation et action," 23–25; Michel de Certeau, S.J., "L'Universalisme ignatien: mystique et mission," *Christus* 13 (1966): 180–182, for remarks on study and prayer.

[13] In the complete text there is an allusion here to "Attingit ergo a fine usque ad finem fortiter, et disponit omnia suaviter" (Wisd. of Sol. 8:1), translated in Douay-Rheims as "She reacheth therefore from end to end mightily, and ordereth all things sweetly." NRSV renders the passage, "She reaches mightily from one end of the earth to the other, and she orders all things well."

"Walk [peripateite] in the Spirit," St. Paul told the Galatians, "and you will not fulfill the lust of the flesh" (Gal. 5:16). *Peripatein* means to walk up and down, as in a cloister; but it also means pacing back and forth in front of a class as the peripatetic teachers did in Athens, thinking, pondering, reflecting even as they taught. The word suggests an awareness of what one is doing, like Hannah Arendt's, "Think what you do," an abiding in the Spirit, a sort of stability in the Spirit.[14] Many today translate *peripateite* as "live," and Paul's remark as "live in the Spirit."

A few verses later Paul says, "If we live [zomen] in the spirit, let us walk [stoichomen] in the Spirit" (Gal. 5:25). *Zoein* means "to be alive" as opposed to being dead. *Stoichein* means "to walk in a line," not Indian file, one behind the other, but side by side as in a battle line, "to walk in step, to be in harmony with." It, too, is associated with teaching. One in harmony with the Spirit teaches by living.

Stoichein mia means to be content with one wife or to walk with one wife. Let those who like the military metaphor advance against the foe side by side with the Holy Spirit; let those who prefer companionship advance side by side, hand in hand with the Holy Spirit, fearing nothing— not because the Spirit is with them, protecting them from their follies, but because they are with the Spirit, who knows where they are going and cannot fail to arrive at the goal. In either case, they are advancing (not just walking back and forth), abiding all the while in the Holy Spirit. Whatever the image, stability is in the Spirit. St. Paul's "If we live in the Spirit [zomen pneumati], let us also walk in the Spirit [pneumati kai stoichomen]," suggests something natural (zoological), already pervaded by Spirit but also open to being transformed by the Spirit. In Ephesians 5:2 the transformation is clear: "Live in love," the translators say, instead of a more literal "walk in love" (Latin: *ambulate in dilectione;* Greek: *peripateite in agape*), which surely means walking in the Spirit, who is love.

Paul exhorts believers to walk *(peripatein)* worthy of God (1 Thes. 2:12), of the Lord (Col. 1:10), of their calling (Eph. 4:1), to walk as children of light (Eph. 5:8). He urges them to walk in step with *(stoichein)* the faith of Abraham (Rom. 4:12). Those who walked in sin do so no longer (Col. 3:7); although believers do, indeed, walk *(peripatein)* in the flesh, they do not walk according to the flesh (2 Cor. 10:2–3).[15] In communicating himself to them, God gives them a new orientation and a new vision: rooted and grounded in Christ, they see the way he sees.

---

[14] Suggested by an unpublished talk by Robert J. Egan, S.J., "To Think What We Are Doing," given at a philosophical symposium at St. Michael's Institute, Spokane, Wash., in November 1996.

[15] *Theological Dictionary of the New Testament,* s.vv. peripateo and stoicheo.

In one eternal moment of happy, wild, and unrepented freedom, the divine Word freely chooses to become flesh, to take as his own a human nature like our own, and in that same delirious eternal moment God makes walking in the Spirit possible by freely choosing to communicate himself to us as well, bestowing his own divine nature upon us in such a way as to leave our human nature intact, and to let our human nature remain ours and not become his.[16] The Spirit points us in a new direction, impelling us freely beyond any purely human goals to the fullness of life in the Father, Son, and Holy Spirit; and the Spirit gives us in faith some glimmer of what that life means for us even in this life on earth. We share that life, not after the manner of the Father who sends the Son, but after the manner of the Son whom the Father sends. Sent like the Son, in and with the Son we participate in his mission of salvation. Moreover, in union with the Father and the Son, we breathe forth the Holy Spirit in his mission of sanctification, and thus participate in the mission of the Holy Spirit as well. From now on we are on a collision course with those who follow the "ways of the world" and cannot understand what we perceive at least "darkly." This life in the Trinity is what it means to be a Christian. Henceforth, if we live in Christ, we live and walk in the Spirit, freely moving where the Spirit moves, freely choosing what the Spirit chooses, freely loving as the Spirit loves.

Walking in the Spirit, then, encompasses more than being in tune with the Spirit; it emphasizes that the Spirit is calling the tune and initiating the music, prompting the walker to fall in step. One filled with the Spirit does not possess a quality deserving of congratulations, but is the object of the Spirit's action, the Spirit who has the quality of filling others; one seized by the Spirit or impelled by the Spirit is the object of the Spirit's seizing and impelling power. If walking in the Spirit entails proclaiming the Good News in the Spirit, loving in the Spirit, praying in the Spirit, and delighting in the Spirit, it reveals even more that the Spirit is proclaiming the Good News in the one who walks in the Spirit, that the Spirit is loving in, praying in, delighting in the one walking in the Spirit. The Spirit makes the moves in the one who through the Spirit freely moves.

Walking in the Spirit evokes "St. Patrick's Breastplate," the Celtic prayer-poem that celebrates the living presence of Christ in every situation:

> Christ with me, Christ before me, Christ behind me, Christ in me, Christ beneath me, Christ above me, Christ on my right, Christ on my left, Christ

---

[16] The last half of this sentence is deliberately modeled on a sentence of Philip Endean about the mystery of the divine and human in Jesus, making the necessary adaptations.

when I lie down, Christ when I sit down, Christ when I arise, Christ in the heart of every man who thinks of me, Christ in the mouth of every one who speaks of me, Christ in every eye that sees me, Christ in every ear that hears me.[17]

Walking in the Spirit celebrates the continuing loving presence of the Spirit in whom one's life is rooted.

Time for Prayer and Quality of Prayer

Nadal comments that the *Constitutions* say little about prayer, for they presuppose that one has made the Spiritual Exercises; then he raises the question why the *Constitutions* provide so little prayer time for those in studies: daily Mass plus an hour of prayer including two examens. He replies that since those who have gone through all the experiments and probations of the novitiate, including a thirty-day retreat to equip themselves to undertake studies profitably, "will already have a taste for prayer, we have to fear that they might neglect study for prayer rather than not give enough time to it, . . . study that is extremely necessary for the end we have in view." Ignatius had to overcome this same problem in his studies in Barcelona (95 f., no. 159).

Nadal's task involves raising consciousness, assisting men to make whole the religious life they tend to compartmentalize. In their lives of prayer and study and work with their neighbor, Jesuit students are to do what monks do in their lives of prayer, study, simple manual labor, and interaction with each other. "The time is enough," Nadal says, and to support his stance makes four assertions (96, no. 160).

1. "Directing studies toward the goal or end of the Society is prayer in its turn, since it is the will of God" (96, no. 160).

Perhaps the briefest expression of the end of the Society is in the *Constitutions:* "the service of God our Lord by helping souls" (204[v.3] [p. 92]). Directing studies to the service of God rather than to one's own glorification is a self-emptying that requires "the raising of the mind and heart to God," the very definition of prayer. Hence, study is an act of worship and service continuing the mission of the Son and the Spirit.

Study in the Society is more than an intellectual probe into the mystery of the universe. Illumined by love and a desire to serve, those who study pierce the Trinitarian presence at the heart of reality. To be saturated in that mystery is to be saturated in prayer.

2. "The presence of God that we ought to have and can have in all things, what else is it than prayer?" (96, no. 160).

---

[17] *The Liturgy of the Hours* (New York: Catholic Book Publishing Co., 1975), 1:1671, app. 4.

When Simón Rodrigues came to Rome for the consultation on the Constitutions in 1551, one of his companions was Antonio Brandão, a priest student, who asked Ignatius, "On what things should we meditate more as more relevant to our vocation?" Ignatius replied:

> Keeping in mind the end of study, because of which the students cannot make long meditations, beyond the [usual daily] exercises . . . they can practice themselves in seeking the presence of our Lord in all things, as in relating to others, in walking, in all they see, taste, hear, understand, and in all they do. For it is true that the Divine Majesty is in all things by his presence, his power, and his essence. This method of meditating, finding our Lord God in all things, is easier than raising ourselves to the more abstract divine truths, making ourselves present to them with effort. This is a good exercise to dispose ourselves for great visits from our Lord even in a short prayer.[18]

Monks always speak of seeking God; to seek God is their perennial task as Christians, to seek a *Presence*, someone who is already there. We do not *put ourselves* in God's presence, as some say; we *are* in God's presence at God's initiative, confronting Father, Son, and Holy Spirit everywhere. If we must seek that Presence and practice ourselves in seeking that Presence, to that extent we are not alive to reality, we are not awake. The Buddha told his followers to wake up; Jesus told his to stay awake, to watch. To wake up, to stay awake, to watch, and to attend to Presence, to respond to Presence, involve being filled with awe and reverence; and that is prayer. But to be aware of Presence takes practice, effort, repetition, correction, determination; but it results in skill, freedom, and spontaneity.

To find God in all things is to "see in ordinary everyday occurrences the power and wisdom of God, even where others perceive only stumbling-blocks and scandal."[19] The wonder that is the Incarnation, however, has made it clear that to find God in all things does not mean to find God rather than the things, or to find God and not see the things, but to find God *in* things, *all* things, seeing God and seeing things in their proper relationship to God.[20] That finding God in all things disposes us for "great visits from our Lord" suggests that we find in creatures God searching for us. It also underlines that we are living in a sacramental universe.

---

[18] Letter written by Polanco on behalf of Ignatius to Father Antonio Brandão, June 1, 1551 (*EpistIgn* 3:510). See also Dario Lopez Tejada, "La paz interior, y el buscar y hallar a Dios en todas las cosas," *Revista de espiritualidad*, 24 (1965): 475–504; Miguel Nicolau, S.J., "La oración de San Ignacio: Fórmulas que la expresan," *Manresa* 28 (1956): 94–96.

[19] Philip Endean, S.J., "The Ignatian Prayer of the Senses," *Heythrop Journal* 31 (1990): 391–418.

[20] See Simon Decloux, S.J., "L'Actualité de la spiritualité ignatienne," *Nouvelle Revue Théologique* (NRT) 112 (1990): 641–59.

"Rather than looking for God in a flight from materiality and the realm of the senses, then, it suggests that matter itself is holy, and that things themselves in the very suchness of their being may become diaphanous with God's presence."[21]

3. "To God obedience is a most pleasing prayer and sacrifice" (96, no. 160).

All creatures are called to obey God; in religious life men and women obey God also in the superior. In Cologne in 1567, Nadal stated sharply the act of faith involved in obedience:

> You do not obey [the superior] as a man; otherwise there is no reason to leave your parents and to obey means nothing. We have it from our vocation that Christ is to be obeyed through an intermediary. For he calls you and sends you into the Society; therefore, he wishes you to be governed by the Society. Therefore, you obey God in this man, and hence you ought to perceive God in this man. Thus you give up nothing in obedience.[22]

Obedience runs on an act of faith, the raising of the mind and heart to God. It is not the slavish execution of another's will; rather, it recognizes the providential and salvific action of the triune God leading all things to their proper end. Przywara remarks that finding God in all things is the ultimate aim of the Exercises, and this aim finds its form and fulfillment in holy obedience.[23]

God to whom we raise our minds and hearts is self-forgetting: Father, Son, and Spirit are other-oriented. Piet de Vries remarks: "[We] can only find God in all things if and when we forget ourselves. . . . we must and can practice this self-denial, because God is unceasingly beckoning us."[24] Penance is self-forgetting, as is obedience: the ultimate penance, the ultimate prayer. This is the end of asceticism, unoccupying the self to make room for the Spirit.

4. "Constant examen and daily meditation, besides reading at table, holy Mass, sermons, spiritual conversations, and other things of this sort, all of them should be considered a continual and ever flowing prayer" (96, no. 160).

---

[21] Robert J. Egan, S.J., "Jesus in the Heart's Imagination," *The Way*, Supplement no. 82 (1995): 64.

[22] "Exhort. 1567 Colon." (*CommInst* 799, no. 50).

[23] Przywara, "God in All Things," 203.

[24] Piet Penning de Vries, S.J., "All or Nothing: Carmelite Spirituality against an Ignatian Background," trans. Mrs. W. Dudok van Heel, *Spiritual Life* 17 (1971): 60.

Far from causing one to neglect prayer, the Jesuit way of life fosters prayer at every moment.

In all his remarks on prayer, Nadal stresses both the role of God and the role of the one praying. God beckons those praying, stirs, invites, purifies, strengthens, and encourages them to many ways of raising the mind and heart to the Father, Son, and Holy Spirit. God supports those praying even as they fail or fall short. The story of prayer throughout the day is a story of slowly and deeply dying to self, and opening to the presence of God like a flower gently blooming. Undergirding each of Nadal's assertions is a demand for self-discipline and maturity: to be intent on doing God's will, to be aware of God's presence at all times, to practice obedience that frees a person to love, to practice prayerful acts throughout the day—all these mean death to the false self and open a person to fullness of life in the Spirit. Add the discipline demanded in studies and ministries themselves and in living in community, and those who study should be mortified indeed.

Decisive Action . . . and Indecisive

On his official visit Nadal takes action. He implements the vision of the Society articulated by Ignatius and delineated in the *Constitutions*. In Alcalá, for instance, the community allowed themselves only six hours of sleep, spent an hour in prayer in the morning and another in the evening, fasted on Fridays and Saturdays, made a fifteen-minute visit to the Blessed Sacrament after dinner and supper. Nadal cancels the hour of prayer in the evening, cuts out the fasting, requires seven hours of sleep, and shortens the visits to the Blessed Sacrament.[25] His action makes a powerful statement.

Yet he waffles, and will pay dearly for it later. In an apparent attempt to be easy on the young Jesuits and, in accordance with an instruction from Ignatius to adapt the rules to the circumstances of persons and places, he makes a decision Ignatius will adamantly reject.[26] Nadal yields in part to the desire of the scholastics for more prayer. "Note," he says, "that now an hour and a half is given to prayer, but later only one hour will be allowed" (96, no. 161). He has cut out the evening hour of prayer, but one hour in the morning still remains, plus two examens, for a total of an hour and a half, even though he knows that the time will eventually be cut to a total of one hour (96 n.41) Nadal is about to learn a lesson from Ignatius he will not forget.

---

[25] Antonio Astrain, S.J., *Historia de la Compañía de Jesús en la Asistencia de España*, 7. vols. (Madrid, 1902–25), 1:397.

[26] Instruction of Ignatius to Nadal, Rome, April 12, 1553 (*EpistIgn* 5:13, no. 2).

Superabundant Prayer

Even so, Nadal finishes the sentence with another powerful statement: "Although, as is clear from what has been said, when someone has so many ways which help prayer and give rise to it, he can have many hours for prayer if he has any facility in it." Without pausing, he adds an extremely telling remark about Jesuit prayer, "For in all these things one can pray. Indeed, when the time of studies is totally directed by the spirit, everything can be considered prayer. . . . In brief: the Society claims to find prayer and God and devotion in everything" (97, no. 161).

The first companion to join Ignatius and the first to be ordained a priest, Pierre Favre, was a quiet man who won friends wherever he went through his complete devotion to the love and service of Jesus, his prayerfulness, his gentleness of spirit, and his quiet listening in the confessional. Said by Ignatius to be the one most skilled in directing the Spiritual Exercises,[27] he provides in his *Memoriale* a good example of a Jesuit version of walking in the Spirit:

> On the day of the Ascension, there came to me a clear understanding of what it means to seek God and Christ outside and above every creature, with a will to know him as he is in himself. . . .
>
> This is a true uplifting of the mind and the spirit, for it is from a knowledge of creatures and the attraction they hold for us that we should ascend to a knowledge and love of their Creator, without in any way dwelling on them alone. . . .
>
> Oh, that the time may soon come when I contemplate and love no creature without God, and rather, contemplate and love God in all things or at least fear him! That would raise me to the knowledge of God in himself and, in the end, all things in him, so that he would be for me all in all for eternity.
>
> To ascend by these degrees, I must strive to find Christ, who is the way, the truth, and the life, first in the center of my heart and below, that is, within me; then above me, by means of my mind; and outside me, by means of my senses. I shall have to beg power from the Father to do this, for he is said to be "above"; wisdom from the Son, who on account of his humanity is said to be "outside" in a certain way; and goodness from the Holy Spirit, who in some way can be said to be "below," that is, within us.[28]

To make Favre's remarks more concrete and further illumine the meaning of "walking in the Spirit" and its all-pervading character, we turn to Nadal's comments on the *Constitutions* and their treatment of chastity and obedience. Although Nadal spoke first of obedience and then of

---

[27] Luis Gonçalves da Câmara, S.J., "Memoriale," in *Font. narr* 1:658, no. 226.

[28] "The *Memoriale* of Pierre Favre," trans. Edmund C. Murphy, S.J., in *The Spiritual Writings of Pierre Favre* (St. Louis: The Institute of Jesuit Sources, 1996), 243–45, nos. 305–7.

chastity, the order he followed is reversed here, for the *Constitutions* treat chastity before obedience.

Chastity (CommInst *103–5, nos. 182–87*)

Text A of the *Constitutions* (1550) does not mention the vow of chastity. Nor does anything suggest that the fathers Ignatius called to discuss the text found this omission remarkable. The minutes of the meeting contain no suggestions regarding Part VI and its explanation of the vows of obedience and poverty. Nonetheless, Ignatius inserted into Text B (received by Nadal in Portugal) an introductory remark concerning the self-knowledge fully formed Jesuits need in order to employ themselves more fruitfully in the ministries of the Society in the service of God and their neighbor. The closing words may have startled Nadal, for it is not clear that "[w]hat pertains to the vow of chastity requires no interpretation, since it is evident how perfectly it should be preserved, by endeavoring to imitate therein the purity of the angels in cleanness of body and mind. Therefore, with this presupposed, we shall now treat of holy obedience."[29]

Nadal dryly comments, "Father Ignatius talks little of chastity, but he says a lot" (103, no. 182). True enough, but one should note that Ignatius makes his trenchant statement on chastity *before* any prescriptions regarding obedience, whereas Nadal's commentary reflects on chastity *after* he has discussed obedience. The difference is significant, for Nadal's order suggests that chastity is a matter of obedience, a duty to be fulfilled, whereas that of Ignatius suggests that obedience is a matter of chastity, that the one who is fully chaste is open to the fullness of obedience. Chastity is a response of love to the call of Christ, a full and complete commitment to the person of Jesus, and everything else in Jesuit life flows from it. Obedience flows from love, is an act of love, rather than love being an act of obedience. Ignatius is almost silent on chastity, not out of a prudish reluctance to speak of it, but because the need for chastity was so clear to him that he thought it would be clear to everyone. Furthermore, after this section on chastity the reader will understand better and affirm more easily Nadal's remarks on obedience.

When Nadal explains the vow of chastity, he focuses on the experience of Ignatius who "when he left his homeland [to go to the Holy Land], fearing for his chastity, took a vow, taking our Lady as his advocate, and he experienced this as a special grace" (103, no. 182).

One can respectfully wonder whether Ignatius and Nadal discussed this experience of Ignatius, for the above passage about leaving home draws on a lengthy letter Laínez wrote to Polanco in 1547. In response to

---

[29] *ConsCN* 547ᵛᵛ, ⁵⁻⁶ (p. 220). For my earlier reflections on this passage, see Joseph F. Conwell, S.J., "Living and Dying in the Society of Jesus or Endeavoring to Imitate Angelic Purity," *Studies in the Spirituality of Jesuits* 12 (May 1980): 1–63.

a request for information regarding the founding of the Society, Laínez stated that when Ignatius left his ancestral home, he was convinced that austerity was the measure of sanctity. Determined to live an austere life and not asking for any advice, "he decided to leave his house, to renounce his homeland completely, his relatives [the very words used of Abraham in Genesis 12:1], and his own body, and to enter upon the pathway of penance." Moreover, "since he had a greater fear of being overcome in matters of chastity than in anything else, on the way he made a vow of chastity to our Lady, to whom he had a special devotion." Laínez wrote that Ignatius had previously been attacked and overcome in matters of the flesh, but that from this time on he had been gifted with chastity in the highest degree.[30] Undoubtedly this narrative represents what Laínez remembered of the story that Ignatius had told him some years previously and also reflects to some extent how Ignatius then remembered the events.

Six years later, in the story of his life that Ignatius began to dictate to Luis Gonçalves da Câmara (a story da Câmara wrote down almost immediately), Ignatius has different recollections of the details of events thirty years earlier. To da Camâra he speaks about his desire to go to Jerusalem and to do all the penance generosity demands, says nothing about a vow of chastity, nothing about fear; but he does say that in the context of his desire to go to Jerusalem and do penance, Mary and the Child appeared to him, and after that he did not yield in the least way to anything against chastity. He even indicates the date on which he tells the story, August 1553 (four months after Nadal had left Rome for Spain).[31] In this telling his chastity seems to result from his experience of the loving and transforming presence of Mary and the Child rather than from a sense of fear or obligation.

Perhaps with the passage of time Ignatius remembered the details differently because certain memories had been healed. Perhaps his experiences between the time that the events took place and the time he told his story to da Câmara transformed his whole understanding and experience of chastity. There is certainly no suggestion that he walked in fear; rather the vision of our Lady at Loyola resulting in chastity (love) confirmed his desire for pilgrimage to Jerusalem, which his experience at Manresa transformed into helping souls: mission.[32]

---

[30] *Font.narr* 1:74–76. For the editor's preface to the letter, see ibid., 54–69; for the complete letter (Spanish original and Latin translation), see ibid., 71–145.

[31] Luis Gonçalves da Câmara, "Acta P. Ignatii," in *Font.narr* 1:374–76, no. 10; for an English translation see *A Pilgrim's Testament: The Spiritual Memoirs of St. Ignatius of Loyola (PilgTest)*, trans. Parmananda R. Divarkar, S.J. (St. Louis: The Institute of Jesuit Sources, 1995), 10, no. 10.

[32] *PilgTest* 10, no. 9 f.; 60 f., no. 45.

Nadal continues his comments. We should not be surprised, he says, that Ignatius proposes the angels for our imitation, since we strive to imitate Christ (which is an even loftier goal) and also to imitate God (103, no. 182). The purity sought is not having any exterior or interior impurity, so bad habits should be countered by their contraries and by mortification (103, no. 183). He notes that angels have no attraction to bodies, nor can they have such an attraction. The quality of not being attracted to bodies is the quality in angels, he says, that we ought to imitate, overcoming the perverse energies of our fallen nature through divine grace (103, no. 184).

This passage is not Nadal at his best. First of all, he presents for imitation a negative quality in the angel, the angel's inability to be attracted to bodies. Is there nothing positive in angelic purity for human chastity to imitate? Second, he expresses a profoundly negative view of the human body. Does the human attraction to bodies really flow from "the perverse energies of our fallen nature"? Would Adam and Eve (to speak biblically) have felt no attraction to each other if there had been no sin?

Commenting in 1558 on the same passage in the *Constitutions,* Nadal begins on a positive note, "There is no perfection of chastity that Ignatius did not encompass in these few words." The word "endeavoring," he says, indicates the religious intensity we should have at all times, and "imitate angelic purity" indicates the scope of the endeavor, a goal we cannot attain in this life, but something we can strive to imitate. We strive to attain through chastity what the angel has by nature. This means for us that our feelings would be affected minimally or not at all and would be unmoved by the attractions of carnal delight. The goal is "to maintain freedom and purity of spirit in the Lord whenever we have to deal with such matters, or whenever thoughts of such things come to us, or feelings or temptations or any carnal movements whatsoever."[33]

Speaking to the Jesuits of Cologne in 1567, Nadal repeats that angels do not experience sensuality, nor can they be moved by passions. "What they have by nature, we gain by grace," he explains (796, no. 45). He then describes various levels of chastity, the highest of which is attained "when there is not the least disturbance even though one reads something lascivious, or hears it, or sees it. This is what we should strive for" (797, no. 46).

If a human person does, indeed, achieve this goal, it is because a person can be so caught up in the reality of God or so absorbed in the immediate human situation and so intent on doing God's will, like an angel, that human passions can be fully engaged elsewhere and cease to be a real source of disturbance. This raises the question: In what does

---

[33] *NadSchol* 146 f.

angelic purity consist? Is it more than *not* feeling attraction and *not* being able to feel attraction to carnal pleasure?

Critique

Nadal might have been more positive in his presentation had he reflected less on *nature* and more on *action* or *function,* less on the angel's nature as *spirit,* a being without a body, and more on the angel's function as *messenger,* which is what the word "angel" means.[34] Through grace we participate in the divine nature, but in our desire "to imitate Christ and God" we imitate their *role* in the salvation of the human race. The triune God of the contemplation on the Incarnation relates to our sinful world with compassion and love and great tenderness, embracing all our hopes and joys, our pains and sorrows, our sins and virtues, and communicates all that to us in and through the Son, calling us to imitate them in their saving action, as the angels do.

How, then, does a human being with a body imitate an angel who participates in that same divine mission?

First of all, the Incarnation loudly proclaims that the body is sacred. Father General Kolvenbach points out that Ignatius calls the soul of Christ "blessed" when it is separated from his body after death, not because it is free from the body, but because it is united to the divinity. Although the Spiritual Exercises are "fully conscious of the vulnerability of the body," the text "contains no word of contempt with respect to the body." The text, Kolvenbach continues,

> breathes forth an air of confidence in regard to the composite human being; it grows out of the conviction that God will make himself known and recognized when we 'put in order' (*SpEx* 21) the duality between body and soul in the line of a constitutive and constructive dialogue—not when we reduce ourselves to pure spirit, or when we make rigid this duality in irreconcilable opposition. . . . [Ignatius is] quite conscious . . . that the human person is involved in space and time through the instrumentality of the body, and that in this the body constitutes the condition for all openness and relationship to the world, to others, and even to the wholly-OTHER that is God.[35]

Since they have no bodies, angels can neither be chaste nor unchaste, but we can *imitate* their *openness and relationships,* the *purity* of the angels as *messengers,* even though we can never achieve it fully. The angel is transparent or translucent to God as God is, to others as they are, to the world as it is, with all relationships in their proper order. There is no self-seeking

---

[34] See the remarks of Przywara in "God in All Things," 163 f., 202 f.

[35] Peter-Hans Kolvenbach, S. J., "'Christ . . . Descended into Hell,'" in *The Road from La Storta* (The Institute of Jesuit Sources, St. Louis, 2000), 77.

in an angel, no deceit, no way of relating dishonestly. A fallen angel, an "impure" spirit, is isolated, filled with deception, totally closed to any relationship with the world, with others, and with God except to hold them all at arm's length, as it were—and God would not dream of using one as a messenger!

Common to the stories that Ignatius told about himself to Laínez and da Câmara are chastity, penance, total renunciation, and *journey*. They form a matrix of his initial opening to both God and the world, an opening that would gradually become total in its commitment to both God and the world. Likewise, in the *Formula of the Institute* the only mention of chastity is in connection with belonging to a community ready to be *sent* anywhere in the world to bring God's word. The revised *Formula* approved by Julius III in 1550, with which Nadal was perhaps more familiar, joins poverty and obedience to chastity, obscuring the special connection between chastity and being sent anywhere in the world, but at the same time directly connecting poverty and obedience as well with being *sent*.

Chastity in the Society has an apostolic purpose, as does obedience and poverty as well. Chastity in the Society endeavors to imitate the purity (*puridad*) of the heavenly messenger in cleanness (*limpieza*) of body and mind. To clarify with a pun, the meaning of *limpieza* was limpidly clear to the early Jesuits. In the Spain of Ferdinand and Isabella, who tried to drive the Jews and the Muslims out of the country, and long after their time, many Christians cried out for *limpieza de sangre* (blood purity: not a single drop of Jewish or Moorish blood in their veins!). Ignatius would have been proud to have the blood of Jesus' relatives flowing in his veins, and he and Nadal fought every demand of the upper classes to exclude from the Society anyone with Jewish or Moorish blood.[36] Limpidity implies clearness or transparency. It suggests the crystal that is of earth, but has great clarity. Limpidity can be used of material or immaterial things: not a drop of blood! not a speck of unchastity! In the Formula chastity precedes *mission*. In the Constitutions chastity precedes obedience, being *sent*. In the Constitutions Ignatius is not concerned about the purity of a spirit that has no body. He is concerned with *imitating* in the *mind* and in the *body* the purity of one *sent* by God, the purity of a messenger of God's word.

---

[36] According to a 1573 report of Pedro de Ribadeneira, S.J. (*Font.nar* 2:476). Bangert, *Jerome Nadal,* 103–9; James W. Reites, S.J., "St. Ignatius of Loyola and the Jews," *Studies in the Spirituality of Jesuits* 13 (September 1981); Francisco de Borja Medina, S.J., "Ignacio de Loyola y la 'limpieza de sangre,'" in *Ignacio y su tiempo,* 579–613; José Luis Orella Unzué, "La Provincia de Guipúzcoa y el tema de los judíos en tiempos del joven Iñigo de Loiola (1492–1528)," *Ignacio y su tiempo,* 847–68; Pedro de Ribadeneira, S.J., "De prognatis genere hebræorum Societatis aditu non excludendis," in *Patris Petri de Ribadeneira Societatis Iesu sacerdotis Confessiones, epistolæ, aliaque scripta inedita,* 2 vols., vols. 58, 60 of MHSI (Madrid, 1920–23), 2:374–84.

The difference is important. A spirit has no admixture of earth. On the other hand, according to Thomistic doctrine an angel is one sent to earth, a messenger bringing God's word to earth. As spirit, the angel's choice is immediate and definite, once and for all. A human being, however, is of the earth, bound to time; a human choice, even one made once and for all, has to be renewed a thousand times a day. The purity of the angel is its total openness to God, its total focus on God's will, on transmitting God's message. We are of the earth: we walk in the flesh, indeed; but in and through the Spirit we choose not to walk according to the flesh. Chastity in the Society is about total transparency in the ministry of God's word, the crystal-like transparency of a mind and body solely centered on delivering God's message.[37] Walking in the Spirit, we preach God's word; indeed, we preach God's word simply by walking in the Spirit.

The foundation and source of chastity, its whole meaning, is love. Unchastity is either disordered love or disordered passion that pretends to be love. Ignatius moved from a chastity that fears and shrinks from the world to a chastity that loves the world and goes out to it the way the Son entered fully into it. Regrettably, Nadal did not seem to grasp the significance of this change in Ignatius. Had he done so, he would have had a rich theme to work through all his exhortations and might have saved the Society and Francis Borgia much later grief.

Nadal certainly grasped the need to go out to the world passionately and lovingly, with all relationships properly ordered, but he was profoundly aware of human disorder. His occasional bouts with irritability may indicate a lack of openness toward others, a disorder of affections, a refusal to accept others as they are. Do the most fundamental failures against chastity manifest themselves, not in sins of the flesh, but in all those ways in which human beings block others out of their lives through lack of love? To love others means to be open to be sent to minister to them.

True *limpieza,* that cleanness of body and mind that imitates the angels, is the purity of walking in the Spirit, of being ready to be sent by the Spirit anywhere, to anyone, and that is why in the Constitutions Ignatius made his enigmatic statement on chastity *before* speaking about obedience. That is why in the first version of the *Formula* he thought it

---

[37] My office is located near the entrance to the building. Not infrequently the United Parcel Service (UPS) driver knocks on my door to deliver a package for someone in the community. He does not dally in talk about the weather or the latest ball game, or in search of a cup of coffee. He conveys, rather, a sense of urgency, a desire to deliver the package and be gone. He is a messenger, period; but I miss the compassion, love, and greater tenderness of an angel.

sufficient to mention only the solemn vow of chastity before describing the Jesuit way of life. Chastity says it all!

Obedience (CommInst 98–103, nos. 164–81)

Obedience is another name for walking in the Spirit, lovingly cooperating in God's work of salvation. Religious obey God in a special way by obeying superiors according to the demands of each institute. The Society's obedience is about being open and loving enough to be sent to minister to others. Ignatius might just as easily have recommended imitating angelic obedience.

In the first exhortation in Spain, Nadal cited obedience as an example of the special graces granted to the Society, an apt illustration after the Portuguese Jesuits' experiences under Simón Rodrigues. In the eighth exhortation he repeats that, among the gifts the Lord has granted to the Society, a particular manner of obedience is to be found (98, no. 164). Jesuit obedience is not satisfied with an exact or even a willing execution of an order; it demands intellectual assent to an order, agreement with it. Remember that in the contemplation on the Incarnation the three divine Persons discuss the plight of the human race, and they *agree* with the wisdom and goodness of the decision that the second Person should become man, and so on. This panorama is Nadal's model for discernment and obediential wisdom. Nadal adds that obedience is not a matter of syllogisms or reasoning: that the superior wills something and orders it is reason enough for one to accept it as the will of God (99, no. 165). It is not enough for the intellect to be held captive; perfect obedience requires that the intellect assent fully to the superior's command. Nor can one plead impossibility, for the intellect can be persuaded, as is clear in matters of faith (99, no. 166).

The will is blind, but blind obedience is not irresponsibility; it is blind only to the obstacles to fulfilling a command, and looks at and considers whatever can help in carrying it out. Just as the illumination given to saints shrouds low and trivial things in darkness and floods the lofty with light, so does the light that comes from obedience (99, no. 166 f.). Thus Nadal dismisses the kind of blind obedience that flails about in the dark or neglects to examine the moral aspects of a command.

Obedience challenges one to creativity, to being godlike, to attention and reverence and love like that of the Spirit of God hovering over the waters at creation, to quiet yet excited and loving awareness of the possibilities in creating out of chaos. In faith darkness is luminous. To obey God is to walk a path so illumined as to shade out low and trivial things. To obey God is to pray profoundly. So also is to obey God in the superior. To obey is to *walk in the Spirit* of love.

Centuries earlier, the prophet Micah provided an apt summary of Nadal's message: "Three things I ask of you, to do justice, to love tenderly, and to be ready to walk with God" (6:8).

- to do justice: to reverence God in every act, and in every act to reverence all God has made (prayer and obedience united in the First Principle and Foundation)

- to love tenderly: to obey the command to love God with all your heart and all your soul and all your strength, and your neighbor as yourself

- to be ready to walk with God: to be willing, like Abraham, to walk into the unknown, confident of God's faithful and guiding presence—to walk in the Spirit

To do justice is to love God, and to love God is to obey God, and to obey God is to walk in the Spirit. In 1995 General Congregation 34 not only reaffirms the concern of earlier Jesuit congregations for the end of violence and discrimination, for countering poverty and hunger, for addressing the exploitation of women; but it underlines as well our increasing consciousness of other dimensions in the struggle for justice in our own times: abuses of human rights on the international level, the interdependence of all peoples in one common heritage, the culture of death that dominates our times, concern for the environment, the marginalization of vast numbers of people, the oppression of indigenous peoples, the exclusion of many from the benefits of society, the exploitation and oppression of refugees in all parts of the world.[38]

Conclusion

Both living as servant and walking in the Spirit take many forms, another way of saying that there are many ways of living the Christian life. Every Christian way of life, however, follows the pattern of the life, death, and resurrection of Jesus, and requires participation in his mission and that of the Holy Spirit. If mission defines the religious vows for a Jesuit and illumines the Jesuit way of life, then mission should illumine every Christian way of life even though a particular way may find its major charism in some other manner of imitating the pattern laid out by Jesus. In like manner, the chaste love of a married couple for each other and their children illumines the kind of love that should exist in a community of religious or in the heart of a hermit. The charism of one way of life exists somehow in the charisms of the rest. Every charism in the Church comes from "the impulse of love which the Holy Spirit pours into their hearts," as

---

[38] D. 3, "Our Mission and Justice," in *DocsGC34* 39–48, nos. 50–74; d. 14, "Jesuits and the Situation of Women in Church and Civil Society," ibid., 171–78, nos. 361–84.

Vatican II stated in the passage quoted at the beginning of this chapter, and under that impulse we all "live more and more for Christ and for his Body, the Church."

Different states of life follow different formats, so that those who have entered upon a particular way of life are likely to confront somewhat similar sets of circumstances in which to follow the pattern set by Jesus, while those in another state of life confront other conditions and circumstances. Married people confront circumstances not confronted by religious and vice versa. The daily routines of Jesuits, Carmelites, Carthusians, and married or single laypeople are far from similar, but they all follow the pattern of Jesus. In the end, however, within those differing formats with their differing perspectives and charisms, what makes each life a different and partial expression of the fullness of Jesus is the concrete way in which we confront the actual circumstances of our daily lives. *The more fervently, therefore,* we join ourselves *to Christ by this gift of* our *whole life, the fuller does the Church's life become and the more vigorous and fruitful its apostolate.* Mission may define the vows of Jesuits, and divine praise define them for someone else, and Christian restraint and joy define the relation of married people to the good things of this world; yet each of us, within his or her state of life, has to make God the definitive norm. Return for a moment to the passage from General Congregation 34 near the beginning of this chapter. Similar passages could be written of every Christian way of living:

> The Church, whose mission we share, exists not for itself but for humanity, bearing the proclamation of God's love. . . . Its aim is the realization of the Kingdom of God in the whole of human society, not only in the life to come but also in this life. . . . We exercise our Jesuit mission within the total evangelizing mission of the Church. . . . [*DocsGC34* 24 (p. 27)]
>
> St. Ignatius was clear that, as the Society was not instituted by human means, so its ministries are preserved and fostered only by the all-powerful hand of Christ. Thus, as we receive our mission from Christ, whatever fruitfulness it bears is entirely dependent on his grace. And it is the Risen Christ who calls and empowers us for his service under the banner of the Cross. (27 [p. 29])

This chapter reflected on some broad aspects of Jesuit spirituality. The next chapter looks at the desire of Ignatius to walk in the footsteps of Jesus and explains how this desire took concrete form in the Society of Jesus. It should help reveal more precisely the Society's proper grace.

Chronicle for Chapter 4

Father, may God bless Master Stephen [Baroëllo] for knowing me well. I truly recognize that it is so: I am arrogant, distant, and severe, and also what he does not mention, hasty, indiscreet, and negligent.

—Nadal to Ignatius

Nadal's Life and Travels (1555–1556)

1555

Jan. 7: Rome; learns of Xavier's death

Jan. 12: Nadal and Laínez named theologians to papal legate at Augsburg

Feb. 18: Nadal and Laínez named commissaries general for Italy, Austria, etc.

Feb. 19: Nadal leaves for Augsburg by way of Florence, Bologna, Trent

March 24: Arrives in Augsburg

April 19–23: Dillingen; goes to Regensburg

May 1–June 20: Vienna

July 4–19: Venice and Padua, exhortations

July 20: Bassano to visit Simón Rodrigues (2 days)

End of July to mid-Sept.: Visits colleges in Argenta, Ferrara, Modena, Bologna; visits Rodrigues a second time

After Sept. 12: Visits colleges in Genoa, Florence

Oct. 5 or 6: Arrives in Rome

Oct. 21: Sent to visit Spain again

Oct. 23: Leaves Rome for Genoa via Florence

Dec. 13: After long wait in Genoa, embarks for Alicante

1556

Jan. 1: Arrives at Alicante, goes to Elche, Murcia

Before Feb. 1: Valencia (10 days), Cuenca, Alcalá, Plasencia, where he meets Borgia

Feb. 1–17: Valladolid, Plasencia, Oropesa; leaves for Escalona

Feb. 26: Still in Escalona, begins writing on Constitutions, later returns to Plasencia

March-April: Valladolid, where Cano is preaching against the Society; to Simancas

June 11– July 6: Valladolid

July 31: Ignatius dies; Nadal in Simancas

Chapter Four

IN IMITATION OF JESUS
AND THE PRIMITIVE CHURCH

> The up-to-date renewal of the religious life comprises both a constant return to the sources of the whole of the Christian life and to the primitive inspiration of the institutes, and their adaption to the changed conditions of our time.
>
> —Vatican II, *On the Up-to-Date Renewal of the Religious Life*

For a Christian, to share in the life of the Trinity through the Son means to incarnate in a personal way the life, passion, death, and resurrection of Jesus, and to do the same in a communal way in the Church. The Acts of the Apostles and other New Testament writings spell out the *communal* pattern for our lives. The apostolic age stands as a model not only of how to live as followers of Jesus but of how God acts in his people throughout history.

Today the apostolic life has come to mean a life devoted primarily to working with people as opposed to a life devoted primarily to prayer. This contemporary view of the "apostolic life" is not only restrictive and confining but is strikingly out of touch with its own roots. Throughout the Christian ages the apostolic life has meant the life of the apostles, life as lived in the primitive Church, a life that is both summarized and very likely idealized, for example, in the Acts of the Apostles:

> They devoted themselves to the apostles' teaching and fellowship, to the breaking of bread and the prayers. . . . All who believed were together and had all things in common; they would sell their possessions and goods and distribute the proceeds to all, as any had need. Day by day, as they spent much time together in the temple, they broke bread at home and ate their food with glad and generous hearts, praising God and having the goodwill of all the people. (2:42, 44–47)
>
> Now the whole group of those who believed were of one heart and soul. (4:32)

The name of the Society of Jesus suggests and demands "a constant return to the sources of the whole of the Christian life." In its efforts for the renewal of the Society at the end of the second millennium, General Congregation 34 reasserted the Society's special vision of Christ in order to underline the Society's way of re-creating in our own day the life of the early Church:

> The way in which Jesuits exercise their ministerial priesthood takes its character from our apostolic mission to labor with Christ in proclaiming the Kingdom. Our first companions envisaged a universal, itinerant ministry of evangelization, teaching, works of charity, and poverty of life: an evangelical *imitatio apostolorum,* a radical pattern of evangelical discipleship, was to be the wellspring for what they did as priests.[1]

History

From the beginning of Christianity, founders of religious orders have justified each new vision of the religious life by claiming that it was apostolic, meaning that it was in continuity with the apostles and the primitive Church. The founders differ in their perspective on Jesus and the way they envision the primitive Church. Each religious order has attempted to incarnate in its own time the spontaneity and vigor of the Church of apostolic times: the prayer, the union, the teaching, the concern for one another and for the poor in the sharing of goods. Just as "apostolic times" means the time of the apostles, so also Benedict used "apostolic" to mean "of the apostles"; for example, the "recommendation of the Apostles" and "saying of the Apostle."[2] Those seeking to renew the monastic life in the eleventh century wanted to imitate "the life of the apostolic community in Jerusalem, in poverty, simplicity, and mutual charity." The Franciscans endeavored "to restore in their own lives the religious practice, the poverty, and humility of the primitive Church, . . . imitating quite explicitly the apostolic life." An anonymous medieval author eulogizing the Order of Preachers praises "the apostolic life, which is to leave all things for the sake of Christ, and in poverty to serve him and preach him." In stressing unity the Augustinian tradition was trying to return to "the apostolic life." Each embraced the full life of the primitive Church, but each chose to emphasize a particular aspect of apostolic life.[3] None set out

---

[1] *DocsGC34,* d. 2, "The Jesuit Priest: Ministerial Priesthood and Jesuit Identity," 25, no. 16.

[2] *The Rule of St. Benedict,* ed. Timothy Fry, O.S.B. et al. (Collegeville, Minn.: The Liturgical Press), chap. 2[v.23]; chap. 31[v.8].

[3] Louis J. Lekai, S.O.Cist., "Motives and Ideals of the Eleventh-Century Monastic Renewal," in *The Cistercian Spirit: A Symposium,* by M. Basil Pennington, O.C.S.O. (Shannon: Irish University Press, 1970), 39. Cistercians are divided into the Sacred Order of Cistercians, who do some teaching and pastoral work, and the Order of Cistercians of the Strict Observance. See Jacques de Vitry, *Historia orientalis,* quoted in Cajetan Esser, O.F.M., *Origins of the Franciscan Order,* trans. Aedan Daly, O.F.M., and

to imitate the limitations and faults of the apostles, but all of them managed to do that as well!

A Pause for Prayer

To be a Christian is totally a gift; one can only accept all from God and return all to God. In the fifth annotation at the beginning of the *Spiritual Exercises,* Ignatius advises the one making the Exercises how to enter into them:

> **The Fifth. The persons who make the Exercises will benefit greatly by entering upon them with great spirit and generosity toward their Creator and Lord, and by offering all their desires and freedom to him so that his Divine Majesty can make use of their persons and of all they possess in whatever way is in accord with his most holy will** (*SpEx* 5 [p. 22]).

We ask for the grace of gratitude and openness, so that in us and through us God may re-create in our own times and circumstances the spirit of the primitive Church as a witness to the divine life that God wishes to bestow upon all.

New Assignments for Nadal

When Nadal reached Rome after his visit to Portugal and Spain in 1553–54, Ignatius's health was so poor that he was confined to bed most of the time.[4] His consultors persuaded him that he needed someone to act in his name with full authority and thus relieve him of much of the work of governing the Society. Ignatius ordered all the priests in Rome to offer

---

Dr. Irina Lynch (Chicago: Franciscan Herald Press, 1970), 40; see *The Rule of St. Augustine,* trans. Raymond Canning, O.S.A. (Garden City: Doubleday, Image Books, 1986), 7; "'Tractatus de approbatione Ordinis Fratrum Prædicatorum,'" ed. Th. Käppeli, O.P., *Archivum Fratrum Prædicatorum* 6 (1936): 145. For the different ways of viewing the apostolic life, see Simon Tugwell, O.P., "The Apostolic Life," appen. 2 of *The Way of the Preacher* (Springfield: Templegate, 1979), 111–16.

[4] For years Ignatius suffered stomach pains, which were attributed to his severe fasts during the period at Manresa. The autopsy after his death, however, revealed that he suffered from gallstones, and that these had passed from the gall bladder into the portal vein, causing pain to radiate into the stomach. A twentieth-century physician observed that the pain must have been excruciating. See Cándido de Dalmases, S.J., *Ignatius of Loyola: Founder of the Jesuits: His Life and Work* (St. Louis: The Institute of Jesuit Sources, 1985), 288 f.

three Masses and to pray over the proper person for this office. Polanco wrote that thirty-one or thirty-two of the thirty-four priests present chose Nadal (*EpistIgn* 8:43).

Nadal notes that before the election Ignatius inquired about the charge that Nadal had been "too hasty, abrupt, and impetuous" in his manner of governing in Messina. Cornelius Wischaven, who had been in the community there, rather harshly supported the charge. Nadal noted in his diary that he freely admitted it and begged pardon for his "deplorable weakness" (*EpistNadal* 2:33). Apparently the electors were more impressed by his humility than by his irascibility. Two weeks later Polanco wrote that Nadal had begun well, "greatly relieving our Father from the unbearable burden of business that he carries" (*EpistIgn* 8:43).

Later Nadal described to Ignatius the conditions in Spain: some complained of too little time for prayer; some insisted that the Society could not continue without more prayer time; when questioned by others, some found it embarrassing to admit that they devoted but one hour to prayer during the whole day. Nadal inclined in their favor, and suggested making some concession, to this province at least.[5]

Despite his illness, Ignatius so vigorously rebuked Nadal that Gonçalves da Câmara, who was present, was amazed not only at the strong reprimand but also at Nadal's patience in enduring it. Ignatius said that never would he abandon the conviction that an hour of prayer was enough for students, presupposing mortification and abnegation, virtues that make for more prayer in fifteen minutes than an unmortified man will achieve in two hours. He ended by saying, "For a truly mortified man, a quarter of an hour suffices to unite him with God in prayer."[6] Clearly Ignatius had in

---

[5] Da Câmara, "Memoriale," *Font.narr* 1:644, no. 196. Da Câmara wrote the "Memoriale" in Spanish in the course of several months in 1555. The events recorded in Spanish did not necessarily happen the same day the author wrote them down. In 1573 he inserted commentaries in Portuguese throughout the work. See "Memoriale," 531 f., no. 9; 534, no. 12; letter to Father General Everard Mercurian, April 14, 1574 (ibid., 532 f. n. 11). The passages referred to here are in Portuguese, written long after the event.

[6] Da Câmara, "Memoriale," 644, no. 196; 676 f., no. 256; See Pedro Leturia, S.J., "La hora matutina de meditación en la Compañía naciente," *AHSI* 3:62 f. Note that Nadal is urging more prayer for the scholastics only and is not urging an increase of time for all (*CommInst* 96 n. 41). In the second of these passages, da Câmara adds that Ignatius had recently said to him, "Of a hundred men given to long prayers, the majority of them ordinarily come to grave consequences"; but in the first passage da Câmara quoted Ignatius as saying that ninety out of one hundred were deluded, and he thought maybe Ignatius had said the number was ninety-nine. Da Câmara maintained that Ignatius esteemed the spirit of mortification more than prayer. When da Câmara one day referred to a man as very prayerful, Ignatius retorted that he was very mortified (*EpistNadal* 1:644, no. 195). Ignatius saw that apostolic action on behalf of others out of love demanded much self-abnegation and mortification. See Stierli, "Ignatian Prayer,"

mind that the discipline of studies and the affective maturity required to live in community demand that the scholastics must daily be living out the norm presented in the *Exercises:* "[T]he more one divests oneself of self-love, self-will, and self-interests, the more progress one will make" (no. 189$^{v.10}$). His response suggests the depths to which one must forget oneself in order to practice his world-affirming mysticism and find God in everything.[7]

Da Câmara makes the illuminating comment that Ignatius very easily gave penances and rebukes in small matters and often said that in giving penances it is good to be liberal. He reported that Ignatius often raised the spirits of his subjects by praising them for what they had done and treating them with tenderness, unless it was Nadal or Polanco, whom he treated harshly.[8] This was how Ignatius dealt with those he knew were of solid virtue.[9]

After only four months at home, the new vicar-general was on the road again in the new year. He noted in his diary that the Society had been asked to send two men to the Catholic-Lutheran meeting at Augsburg as theologians to the papal legate, Cardinal Morone. Ignatius chose Laínez and Nadal (*EpistNadal* 2:33). On February 18 Ignatius named Nadal commissary general, with full power of the general while visiting Italy, Austria, and other regions to promulgate the *Constitutions*. Laínez also possessed the full power of the general. When separated, each had full power; when together, they had to agree on any decision regarding the Society.[10] Nadal left Rome on February 19, 1555.[11] His diary notes that

---

137, 147 f., 162 f. St. Benedict also advocated short prayer unless lengthened by divine grace (*Rule of St. Benedict,* chap. 20$^{v.4}$).

[7] The term "affective maturity" is from "Jesuit Corporate Identity: Promoting Unity and Cohesion in the Society of Jesus," by Franz Meures, S.J., *Review of Ignatian Spirituality* 29, no. 3 (1998): 23–40. De Vries compares the *nada* of John of the Cross to the *todo* of Ignatius, negative asceticism to positive mysticism, to bring out the qualities of each: John's *nada* gauges the depths of Ignatius's self-denial, and the "in all things" of Ignatius "enables us to feel the intensity of the intimate encounter with God that kept alive Saint John's predilection for the cross" ("All or Nothing," 60). John of the Cross, of course, born in 1542, was at this point in our story only a schoolboy.

[8] *Font.narr* 1:587, no. 102.

[9] Jiménez, "Commentarium" (*EpistNadal* 1:35). Jiménez was not an eyewitness of Ignatius's mode of governing, but learned many things about Ignatius from Nadal and others. He entered the Society in Rome in 1558 and was Nadal's socius during his visitation of Spain and elsewhere in 1560–61.

[10] *EpistIgn* 8:436 f., along with an explanatory document, 438–41; see also Ignatius's letter in *EpistNadal* 1:279–82, as well as a lengthy explanatory document in footnotes.

[11] Da Câmara, "Memoriale" (*Font.narr* 1:621, no. 152). Bangert gives February 16 as the date (*Jerome Nadal,* 140), but his computation seems to be incorrect. See the

Laínez joined him in Florence. Nadal admits, "I hardly ever got along with him, and on the way I attacked *[impegi]* him during some argument. I acted harshly again in Augsburg. It was clearly weakness on my part" (2:34). Much reflection suggests that this is an example of how Ignatius tested his best men. Could they walk in the Spirit together?

Nadal's Mission to Spain (1555–1556)

In 1553 Ignatius sent Nadal to Spain with powers that astounded him. In 1555 Ignatius sent him to Spain again on a mission with so little power that he found the mission impossible.

Towards the end of his first visit, Nadal had carried out instructions from Ignatius to divide Portugal and Spain into four provinces.[12] Diego Miró was to be provincial of Portugal; Antonio Araoz, instead of being provincial of the whole of Spain, would be in charge only of Old Castile; Francisco Estrada would become provincial of Aragón; and Miguel de Torres, provincial of Betica (Andalucía). Over all four was to be Francis Borgia as commissary general, with all the powers of the general. Araoz was not pleased at the division. Estrada protested the assignment, and Nadal softened it by giving him an assistant. Borgia admitted Bartolomé de Bustamante to the profession of four vows (with the approval of Ignatius) without saying anything to Nadal. He feared the latter might interfere because Bustamante had made his first vows only a few months earlier.[13] This was not a good way to establish a healthy relationship with one holding the power of the general.

On October 21, 1555, no more than eighteen days after Nadal had returned to Rome from his tour of Germany, Austria, and Italy, Ignatius commissioned him to go a second time to Spain on a mission for the Roman College (*EpistIgn* 10:16–18). On that day Ignatius wrote a letter to Borgia, another to Araoz, and one to Nadal explaining that mission.

In the first letter, Ignatius told Borgia that Nadal was coming to help him in various ways, that Nadal's power as vicar-general with full power of the general was suspended during the visit, but that nevertheless Nadal had authority in certain matters in instructions he could show him (10:14 f.). He told Araoz that Nadal's mission was a particular one, not general, that Nadal had authority over everyone, including rectors and provincials, that he could send them anywhere inside or outside Spain

---

letter of Ignatius to Laínez in *EpistIgn* 8:425, in which Nadal leaves Rome on Tuesday. Later da Câmara refers to "last Saturday" and the footnote indicates February 23 (*Font.narr* 1:652), making the preceding Tuesday February 19. See Ruiz Jurado, "Cronología," *AHSI* 48:258.

[12] Letter of Ignatius to Nadal, January 1, 1554 (*EpistIgn* 6:122 f.).

[13] *NadalEphem* (*EpistNadal* 2:25 f.).

(10:15 f.). He told Nadal that he should help Borgia in any way he could, adding that, although his powers as vicar-general were suspended during his visit, no one in Spain was his superior nor was anyone subject to him. Regarding the Constitutions and rules, he should deal with rectors and provincials, and do whatever he deemed necessary with Borgia's approval (10:16–18).

The abundant lack of consistency in the three letters created confusion, as Nadal soon discovered. Had Ignatius simply nodded, like Homer, or was this inconsistency deliberate on his part, another example of how he tried those he trusted most? Is he training them, especially Nadal, in the primitive inspiration of the Institute, teaching each of them how to deal with the less-than-perfect human beings in the Society? Nadal wrote in his diary about the events in Rome prior to receiving the mission to go to Spain:

> Here [in Rome] I did nothing ex officio, but I understood that Ignatius was displeased that I had not dealt with Fr. Laínez the way he had hoped I would. Before I went to see Fr. Ignatius, I ran into Frs. Laínez and Salmerón, who told me that I was going to be sent to Spain immediately, and it displeased Fr. Ignatius that I heard of the mission from them first.[14]

Ignatius had been displeased with Nadal over his stance on more prayer for the Jesuits in Spain; he was now displeased that Nadal had not been able to rise above personal animosities in dealing with Laínez when Ignatius deliberately paired them as joint holders of his power as general and sent them to Germany; and he was further piqued that Nadal had learned of his mission to Spain from Laínez and Salmerón rather than from himself. Ignatius might very well have judged that his favorite needed more testing. What better way could he test both his ability to govern and his virtue than by arranging for him to deal with Borgia, a seasoned administrator and a holy man, swift at making decisions, but lacking the usual novitiate experiences and somewhat deaf to what his superior told him?

After encountering delays from storms at sea and danger from pirates, Nadal arrived in Spain on January 1, 1556. Bustamante was now provincial of Betica, and Torres had replaced Miró in Portugal. Perhaps storms and pirates were God's way of preparing Nadal for the tempestuous times ahead.

Nadal noted in his diary that Borgia and Araoz were not getting along, with the result that Araoz was governing less and Borgia was governing more. Much that Nadal had accomplished in Spain in 1554 he found was being undone. Nor did Borgia appreciate Nadal's observations that he was violating the Constitutions in various matters. Neither Borgia

---

[14] Ibid., 38.

nor Araoz had grasped or accepted the pleas of Ignatius for moderation and disagreed with the provisions regarding the amount of time to be given to prayer. When Nadal told Borgia that Ignatius had commissioned him to admonish Francis about his excessive penances, Borgia testily replied that the two of them would drive him to the Carthusians. How hard it was to transform external ascetical practices into the internal discipline needed for daily meeting one's neighbors' spiritual and corporal needs!

Borgia obviously interpreted the instructions from Ignatius to mean that while in Spain Nadal was Borgia's subject. On one occasion he suddenly ordered Nadal to explain the Society's Institute in Latin to a group of monks he had invited to dinner. Without preparation Nadal did so easily enough, but he experienced that Borgia "had imperiously *[ex imperio]* constrained me to do it without any warning." In the Jesuit vocabulary on obedience, several words might be translated "command" but *imperium* is not one of them. *Imperium* suggests a sovereign lord, which Borgia was not in relation to anyone in the Society, and especially not to Nadal. They should have clarified their mutual relationship, but neither chose to do so. Nadal must have struggled with his own humble image of himself and his desire to carry out the mission Ignatius had given him. But Borgia's personality was formidable and confronting the former duke no easy task. When Nadal recognized that his help was considered interference, he began to withdraw and ceased his admonitions. He had not yet grown enough to live in the pain. At some point he began to write on the *Constitutions*. Out of his flight from pain God drew much good.

Estrada, too, added to Nadal's burden. He kept complaining about the assistant Nadal had given him, but the irascible visitor finally replied so sharply that Estrada quit bothering him.[15]

Ignatius seems to have failed in consistency or else was overzealous in testing his vicar-general; Araoz failed in humility; Estrada became a whiner; Borgia was indocile and overeager, Nadal not assertive enough. A distant commentator can be too critical, demanding perfection of everyone. Through it all God was creatively and quietly at work drawing good out of chaos.

Return to Rome

News from Ribadeneira to Borgia that Ignatius had died on July 31, 1556, interrupted Nadal's writing. Was Nadal still vicar-general after the death of Ignatius? He deemed that he was, and Borgia and the provincials agreed. A few days later news from Polanco conveyed surprising news: Laínez had been elected vicar-general and a general congregation had

---

[15] This account of Nadal's experiences is drawn from *NadalEphem* 41–43.

been summoned for 1557 (later changed to 1558). Nadal was not disturbed by the news. Should he return to Rome? He thought he should; but Borgia, Araoz, Estrada, and Bustamante did not concur. He did not like their position, thought there was something suspicious about it, sensed that they were not being forthright, and later thought they might be looking toward an election that would not take place in Rome. No longer meek and unassertive, he spoke his mind clearly, manifested his displeasure at their position, indicated that he was offended by their action, and declared that he would leave at once, a promise he prepared to carry out that very day. Borgia and the others were incensed at his candor and kept arguing with him; but Nadal was in no mood to be mild-mannered, so he told Borgia that he respected him not for who he had been but for who he was.[16] His response to the former duke was a strong rebuke, but it was also a response of love. Perhaps that was what Ignatius had had in mind. At any rate, Nadal was not about to embrace anything that smacked of the secular or political. He preferred to "leave the letter unfinished" (*ConsCN, C:* 547) and go where God was calling him. Once again Nadal was teaching by doing.

As Nadal threw his few possessions together, one fear dominated his mind: Would he in the end have to travel on a broken-down old nag? He was so upset that when he accepted a friend's offer of a splendid mount, he showed but meager appreciation. On the way his companion's horse took a dangerous fall, but the companion was miraculously uninjured. Nadal, too, faced many a danger from the rocky ground in crossing the mountains. He did not reach Rome until December 10.[17]

There he faced the confusion Polanco had unwittingly created by convening a gathering of the local professed fathers to elect a vicar-general. The proper convener should have been the rector of the house where Ignatius died, Cristóbal de Madrid. Those convened elected Laínez vicar-general, but since the electors had been improperly convened, who was the legitimate vicar-general: Nadal or Laínez? In an already tense atmosphere enhanced by the outbreak of war between Spain and the Holy See, Nadal supported Laínez.[18] Nadal also faced down Bobadilla in a bitter fight over the role the remaining founding fathers would play in the coming congregation to elect a new Father General, a fight that in the end Nadal called a tragedy.[19] If he would not be assertive for himself, he would be assertive for the sake of the Society.

---

[16] Ibid., 48 f.

[17] Ibid., 49.

[18] Bangert, *Jerome Nadal,* 170.

[19] *NadalEphem* tells the whole story of the congregation (50–64); or see Bangert, *Jerome Nadal,* 173–92. See also Manuel Ruiz Jurado, S.J., "La figura de Jerónimo Nadal en la primera crisis grave de la Compañía (1556–1557)," *Manresa* 52 (1980): 135–54.

Perhaps this is what Ignatius had in mind when he placed Nadal in a vulnerable position first of all vis-à-vis Laínez in Italy, Germany, and Austria, and secondly vis-à-vis Borgia and Araoz and the whole of the Society in Spain. Nadal had to live in an imperfect Society and make the best of it. Gradually he matured through these experiences of imperfection. In later years both Diego Laínez and Francis Borgia as generals of the Society recognized his competence and skill and love of the Society. Like Ignatius, they too made him official visitor of all the provinces of Europe.[20] Nor did the story end with them. When this great traveler was in his sixties, the fourth general, Everard Mercurian, also sent him to patch up difficulties in Germany. Frequently he urged the peacemaker to finish as soon as possible the book of meditations he was writing.[21]

Reflection

To omit this section is very tempting. Everyone prefers superiors who do not make mistakes, friends who do not annoy, acquaintances who do not disappoint, co-workers who do not disagree. Everyone prefers the kind of world that does not exist. Yet, how could such a world exist? God has gifted everyone with flawed superiors, flawed friends, flawed acquaintances, flawed co-workers—flawed: everybody is flawed. Ah! There's the rub. That flawed world is far better than the dream world anyone has created. God creates out of chaos, and in a world marred by sin and blemished by limitations of every kind, God is calling everyone to creativity.

Michelangelo created David out of a piece of marble "already roughhewn . . . and badly hewn" by another sculptor.[22] Our call is likewise a challenging one: to use our imaginations to create out of the material at hand. Our prayer is emptiness, openness to receive and to let God create within us whatever he envisions. We are called to accept willingly, to accept joyfully, what we have been given, not what we wish we had been given. We are called to be and live who we actually are, not the person we would like to be. The theme of this section—flawed human beings accomplishing God's work—runs through our lives. Without it we cannot respond in any way to the invitations contained in the rest of the book, nor in the rest of our lives.

---

[20] *Lainii monumenta: Epistolæ et acta Patris Jacobi Lainii secundi præpositi generalis Societatis Iesu, 8 vols.,* vols. 44, 45, 47, 50, 51, 53, and 55 of MHSI (*EpistLain;* Madrid, 1912–17), 1:ix-x; letter of Laínez to Antonio de Córdoba (ibid., 5:303); letter of Nadal to the Jesuits in Rome (ibid., 4:771).

[21] For example, see *EpistNadal* 3:698, 705, 708, 711, 721.

[22] Herbert von Einem, *Michelangelo,* trans. Ronald Taylor (London: Methuen, 1973): 27, with documentation in n. 8; Ascarico Condivi (ca. 1520), *The Life of Michelangelo,* trans. Alice Sedgwick Wohl, ed. Hellmut Wohl, 2nd ed. (University Park: Pennsylvania State University Press, 1976), 27 f.

Everyone likes Peter the apostle, flawed, terribly flawed and vulnerable. To him and to the rest of the flawed band of apostles Jesus said, "As the Father has sent me, so also I send you; receive the Holy Spirit." The Son and the Spirit carry on their missions through and with and in imperfect human beings; there are no others. That is why I have included this section in a chapter that undertakes to see Ignatius and his companions—flawed, every one of them—setting out to imitate Jesus and the apostles in the primitive Church.

In the Likeness of Jesus, the Apostles, and the Primitive Church

When convalescing at Loyola after being hit in the leg by a cannonball while defending the city of Pamplona against the French, Ignatius experienced a call to do penance and to go on pilgrimage to the Holy Land. He wanted to follow in the very footsteps of Jesus. What would he do there? All he thought of was fasts and disciplines. Something startling happened to him on the way to Jerusalem that would change his whole approach to pilgrimage. The present chapter will look at this profound transformation in the decision Ignatius had made on how he would spend the rest of his life.

Preaching and Persecutions

"Exhort. 1554 Hisp." (*CommInst* 40–46, no. 13–19)

Through his experiences at Manresa, especially through considerations of the Call of the King and the Two Standards, God drew Ignatius to a new vision of how to serve him, and that vision became the end of the Society of Jesus (*CommInst* 40, no. 13). The next chapter will look at those two transforming meditation experiences, and the following chapter will consider in more detail the end of the Society. This present chapter simply looks at the change that took place in Ignatius's proposal to spend himself in a life of doing penance: a determination to place moderate external austerities at the service of the internal discipline needed for a life in service of others.

While at Manresa Ignatius abandoned his proposal to live a life of penance, determining instead to work for others where Jesus had worked. When he was not allowed to work in the Holy Land, he concluded that he needed first to study. He began to pursue this plan in Spain first of all and then in Paris, gathering all the while some companions in the latter city. After preaching in various places and performing other good works, they drew up the way of living outlined in the bull of confirmation (40 f., no. 14). Nadal saw a similarity between the founding of the Church and the founding of the Society. God our Lord founded the Church through the many labors of his Son and those of his Body, the Church, and in this way the Church grew. In the same way, through his infinite mercy he bestowed the grace to be like his Son in some way and to found the Society the way the Church was founded; namely, through the persecutions that Ignatius suffered in Alcalá, Salamanca, Paris, and other places not only through the hands of others but through the profound poverty he endured in Paris. He was gravely ill, and he suffered much by having to abandon his taste for prayer for the sake of needed study; but he knew this was God's will (41f., no. 15).

The Society, too, endured persecutions. In Rome, before the Society was confirmed, the companions preached against the teachings of a priest whose doctrine was suspect and three of whose friends (two dead by that time and one imprisoned by the Inquisition) accused the companions of having been run out of Spain, Paris, and Venice before taking refuge in Rome. The companions had no help except God, who sent persons from those places to testify that the charges were false. Ignatius went to the Pope and obtained a public sentence on behalf of the Society (424–44, no. 16). After its confirmation the Society was again attacked in Rome (44, no. 17); finally, the persecution of the Society in Portugal succeeded only in promoting its growth (45, no. 18).

Another similarity to the apostles and disciples of the Lord is that, just as they lived without a written Gospel, so the early Society managed without written constitutions. Moreover, they were sent out to preach, just as the apostles were. Ignatius had to say to his followers what Peter said to the early Church: "You know our way of living; now go and live it." Just as the growing Church in the course of time needed to write down its way of life, so also as the Society grew it became more and more urgent for Ignatius to write constitutions for the Society (45 f., no. 19). Nadal sketches them briefly (46 f., nos. 20–24). Thus ends the first exhortation.

Following Jesus on the Road

Notes on the *Constitutions,* 1556 (*CommInst* 123–27, nos. 40–50)

The *Constitutions* begins by treating candidates to the Society, then novices; next it moves through scholastics and brothers to those with final vows, living the full life of the Society. Incorporation into the Society, therefore, is a gradual process: step by step one enters into the body of the Society, finally sharing in the responsibility for the life, growth, and preservation of that body. As the young Jesuit grows in spirit and aspires to spiritual heights, he also gradually moves more fully into his own physical body, embodying in concrete ways his spiritual aspirations. The temptation for beginners is to be too spiritual. Their desire is to rise above the world, to ignore the body (let their hair and nails grow long), to starve the body, to torment the body, or to withdraw from the world as though it were not there, as though the Incarnation were a denial of the body rather than an embrace of all its limitations. To go up is to go down, and to grow spiritually is to enter more fully into the world God created to unite us to the divine and fill us with divine life.[23]

In the 1556 "Notes on the *Constitutions*," Nadal reflects more deeply on how the Society imitates the life of the primitive Church. Although on occasion he draws a parallel that might seem to be merely external, even then he is picking out instances of how the Society differs from other religious orders. Just as Jesus and the apostles lived on the road, moving from place to place, so Nadal will increasingly underline the pilgrim nature of the Society, living on the road, in exile. In summary fashion the *Formula of the Institute* outlines Jesuit life as being *sent* to serve Christ and his Church under the Roman Pontiff. A Jesuit is to be filled with love and totally available through chastity, traveling lightly or wholly unburdened through poverty, and eagerly ready for anything through obedience. The *Constitutions* fill out the details: Part VI expands on prayer, mortification, and the vows; Part VII describes the mission; Part VIII speaks of the union of minds and hearts.[24] All those parts of the *Constitutions* could be considered a reflection on the words of Jesus criticizing the way of the world: "It will not be so among you; but whoever wishes to be great among you must be your servant" (Matt. 20:26). In this way the Society continues the mission of Jesus and the Apostles.

After carefully outlining the activity of God in the Church throughout the centuries, Nadal boldly but humbly asserts that God, one and triune, has bestowed the grace of the Church on this least congregation and has made it in his mercy a compact version *(abbreviatum quoddam verbum)* of the monastic life; for its Institute not only embraces what is found in other religious orders but includes as well aspects of the life of bishops and parish priests: the ministry of the Word of God and the sacraments, excluding, however, anything contrary to humility or poverty or involving dignities, honors, jurisdiction, or benefices that would impede Jesuits' ability to assist others on the way (123f., nos. 40–44). Nadal offers this clarification regarding the Society:

> With religious orders it shares the vows and embraces a twofold life, active and contemplative, and in each it strives to employ a well-rounded *[perfecta]* and more holistic *[superior]* action for the salvation and perfection of others, so that the active life is efficacious, and the contemplative life is efficacious, and so also is that more holistic life efficacious, with the effect

---

[23] See the constant theme in Bertrand, *Corps pour l'Esprit.*

[24] Peter-Hans Kolvenbach, S.J., outlines the similarity between the way of the apostles and the way of the Society in his "Certain Pathway to God *(Via quædam ad Deum),* in *The Road from La Storta* (St. Louis: The Institute of Jesuit Sources, 2000), 213–15. He refers to recent general congregations to describe a Jesuit as a man on mission (p. 215 and *passim*).

that through the Society's ministry some people become active and others contemplative, and still others embrace that kind of holistic action proper to bishops and those priests who have received from bishops the care of souls. (124, no. 42)

To avoid charges of elitism against the Society or other religious orders engaged in the ministry of the word, we here translate *superior* as "more holistic": ministerial actions that affect the whole persons for whom they are done, more than doing penance, practicing virtue, and engaging in corporal works of mercy.[25] In holistic actions one feeds the hungry because they are hungry and in order to enable them to hear the word of God; and one preaches the Word of God so that the hearers might not only change their lives but become preachers of the Word in some way themselves.

Jesus did more than meet people's needs: sometimes he asked them to follow him, sometimes to remain silent, sometimes to proclaim what God had done for them. In like manner, bishops do more than meet the needs of people; they try to involve as many as they can in helping others in prayer or work or ministry of Word and sacrament. Try to realize the difficulty Nadal faced in explaining the Jesuit way of life even to his own Jesuit brethren. In similar fashion Humbert of Romans in the thirteenth century made little impact at first in explaining that preaching is the foundation of the whole way of life of the Dominicans, so daring was it for priests to undertake a life of preaching, which was usually understood to be the office of bishops.[26]

Following the threefold moments in the call of the apostles as Ignatius presented them in the *Spiritual Exercises,* no. 275, Nadal says that the apostles were first called to come to know Christ, and through Christ's grace the members of the Society come to know the Institute during first probation. The apostles were then called to follow Christ, to learn from him, to prepare themselves for ministry; second probation and studies prepare Jesuits in the same way (125, no. 47). Here Nadal might have put greater emphasis on how much the Spiritual Exercises enable Jesuits to come to know Christ and love him, following him from the Incarnation to the Ascension, not only in the thirty-day retreat but through daily saturation in the mysteries of the life of Christ.

---

[25] In *Contemplation in Action* I translated *superior* as "higher." The words "higher" or "better" seem to me now to be too vague, and also seem to suggest difference in quality rather than difference in nature. Nadal, in fact, puts active people side by side with contemplatives in a partnership in Christ, "so that the actives . . . are helped by the contemplatives . . . through their prayer joining contemplation with action in Christ" ("In exam. annot." [*CommInst* 158, no. 66]).

[26] See *Early Dominicans: Selected Writings,* ed. Simon Tugwell, O.P., The Classics of Western Spirituality series (New York: Paulist Press, 1982), 181; id., *Way of the Preacher,* 23ff.

Then the apostles were sent to preach the Gospel and administer the sacraments to every creature; that is, to bring the Word of God and the care of souls to all. The members of the Society, too, preach the Word and care for souls, although not by reason of either jurisdiction or office (125 f., no. 48). Here Nadal might have emphasized the activities of the apostles in Scripture and the labors in the vineyard of the Lord described in Part VII of the *Constitutions:* being sent by Jesus, the Holy Spirit, or the vicar of Christ, staying or moving on depending upon the fruit of the work being harvested or the call of the superior to seek the greater glory of God.

Just as the apostles freed themselves from other cares that interfered with prayer and the ministry of the Word, so also the Society has coadjutors to free the professed for ministry. The apostles were sent everywhere (no doubt, Nadal naively says, by Peter); and his successor, the Roman Pontiff, sends members of the Society throughout the world. The apostles were pilgrims on the road with no place to stay together, but were always trying to help others; this as well "is the principal end of the Society, not merely to live in a community of brothers but to be on pilgrimage and to fish for men and women, and most of all where we see no other fisherman" (126, no. 49).

At the end of the twentieth century and on the eve of the third millennium, General Congregation 34 stated that, because we are "an international apostolic body," certain world situations "cry out for our urgent attention." Without mentioning the above passage from Nadal, but in a similar allusion to the apostles, the congregation listed some of those urgent situations today where, in Nadal's words, "we see no other fisherman" or find the fishermen desperately in need of help to care for the marginalized, unemployed, abandoned, refugees, and displaced.[27]

Nadal went on to state that the apostles proclaimed the counsels, and the Society has vows. The apostles wore no habit, chanted no psalms, and members of the Society have neither habit nor choir (126 f., no. 50). Lack of choir and habit distinguished Jesuits from others in the sixteenth century, not as an idiosyncrasy, but as sign of their new "on the road" spirituality. Nadal quoted Gregory the Great as saying that those who have the care of souls should not have to chant the office in choir. Called from the contemplative life of a monk to become pope, Gregory had to develop a new form of spirituality to enter fully into the busy life of the visible head of the Church.[28]

In 1557 Nadal again boldly compared the spirituality of the Society to that of bishops, even as he disavowed any share in the powers of the episcopal office. The end is the same but the way of proceeding is different:

---

[27] "Our Mission and Justice," in *DocsGC34* 60–65, nos. 11–16.

[28] See in the breviary his own homily on Ezekiel in the office of readings for his memorial on September 3.

> The institute of our Society imitates the life of the apostles and of the bishops who succeed them, but in a state of humility, even external, and in poverty. This is the amazing grace of Christ Jesus. For we have the same end, [although] . . . [w]e have no office, no income, no jurisdiction; we do not ordain or confirm. (204 f., no. 203)

Although centuries earlier Thomas Aquinas had compared the life of what some call "mixed" orders to that of bishops, in that such religious live a combination of the active life and the contemplative life, the comparison with bishops would shock any Jesuit audience into listening more carefully.[29] Like Humbert of Romans, Nadal is talking about a spirituality, a way of living, a way of engaging the world. Jesuits engage the world the way bishops engage the world by entering into it, as Gregory the Great found out, not the way monks engage the world by withdrawing from it. He emphasizes the spiritual tasks of ministering the Word, of caring for people, tasks to which the Jesuit is called by reason of his Church-approved Institute, not by way of exception, as a monk might be called. For Jesuits he deliberately rejects other aspects of episcopal life: office, income, jurisdiction, or the power to confirm and ordain.

Imitation of Apostles

Observations on Prayer, ca. 1559 (MHSI vol. 50a, 191 f., no. 626)

Nadal's reflection continued, and about 1559 he jotted down some notes for himself in what came to be called his *Observations on Prayer,* notes that express more fully what he means by saying that Jesuits imitate the apostles and the bishops who are their successors. Following the remarks of Ignatius in the *Spiritual Exercises,* no. 275[v.3], he has the apostles leaving everything at first but not perfectly, in the same way that Jesuit novices and scholastics can still retain ownership (though not use) of property. He sees parallels with the six experiments of the novitiate. The apostles were taught how to pray, and they took time for prayer, as Jesuits do in the thirty-day retreat. They healed the sick, and Jesuits have an experiment in a hospital. They went out on pilgrimage, and so do Jesuits. They bought food and prepared it for the people, and Jesuits have the kitchen experiment and other manual tasks around the house. They taught others to the best of their ability, just as Jesuits teach Christian doctrine to the uninitiated. They were taught the Good News by Christ, which is the daily lot of Jesuit scholastics and student brothers. As formed ministers, they were sent into the whole world to proclaim the Gospel, as are Jesuit priests with final vows. The professed are like the apostles, the spiritual coadjutors like the disciples, and the temporal coadjutors like the

---

[29] *Summa Theologiæ,* 2ᵃ 2ᵃᵉ q. 188, a. 6.

deacons (191, no. 26).[30] For Nadal's purposes the apostles were closer to Jesus and were devoted to prayer and the ministry of the Word; the disciples were more loosely connected with Jesus than were the apostles; the deacons took care of waiting on table and supplying other needs of the community. The reality was more subtle, as we see in the cases of Stephen, a deacon who performed wonders and gave testimony to Jesus, and of Philip, a deacon who proclaimed the Word and baptized.

The Call

Fifth Exhortation in Coimbra, 1561 (*Pláticas espirituales*, 79–81, nos. 6–9.)

By 1561 in Coimbra Nadal was sure of his ground. In a few paragraphs he summarized all that has been said above, inserting this material into his exhortation concerning the Spiritual Exercises and the Call of Christ. In this context he reflects on the call of the apostles, connecting it with the call of the evangelists, the disciples, and the saints and servants of God throughout the ages, even the least Society of Jesus (*Pláticas*, 79, no. 6). Unlike the apostles, Jesuits are called to obedience, not to dignities; they are to be "poor common servants without honors" (79 f., no. 7). Coming to know Jesus, participating in the healings, moving from town to town, preaching, feeding the crowds—all find an echo in the mysteries of the life of Jesus contemplated during the Second Week of the Exercises and in Jesuit work in hospitals, on pilgrimage, preaching, teaching, and serving others in a variety of ways (80, no. 8). In the consideration on the Call of the King, Nadal sees direct continuity between the Society of Jesus, the Christian ages, and the primitive Church (in which, according to Acts, the Holy Spirit is the immediate ambience of its decision making; 80 f., no. 9).

The meditation on the Call of the King takes its imaginative form from Crusading events contemporary to Ignatius; the content is pure Gospel, an invitation to the countercultural refugee life of the primitive Church. Part VII, too, of the *Constitutions* treats of those Jesuits who are "dispersed into the vineyard of Christ our Lord," explaining in broad outline how to serve the needs of people after the pattern of the primitive Church. General Congregations 32, 33, and 34 spell out in explicit detail how to lead that life in the contemporary scene.

Spirit, Heart, Praxis of Refugees

First Exhortation at Alcalá, 1561 (*CommInst* 224–31, nos. 5–11)

Sent by Laínez to the Iberian Peninsula once more, Nadal began his exhortations in Coimbra and Alcalá in 1561 by indicating that Father

---

[30] For the meaning of the terms professed, spiritual coadjutors, and temporal coadjutors, see chap. 1 above.

General Laínez had wanted to come to Portugal and Spain to explain the decrees of the First General Congregation, but the Pope had needed him in Rome. Instead Father General had sent Nadal himself in spite of his deficiencies: no one else could be spared; he was the one who would be missed the least (*CommInst* 224, no. 5). Nadal's humility is real.

Just as Ignatius began the *Spiritual Exercises* with the presupposition that one should listen with an open heart to what another has to say (no. 22 [p. 31]), so Nadal set down the presupposition that everything he said and everything his audience heard should be given and received *spiritu, corde, practice*.[31] These three Latin words summarize all that Nadal wanted to say in his exhortations in 1561. He explained them in the first exhortation at each institution.[32] They are placed here since they convey the interior spirit of the Society and the primitive Church: *spiritu*, finding its source in God; *corde*, with true charity and love; *practice*, in praxis—not in word alone but in deed, in the practical carrying out of the end through obedience to God in the Church.

By *spiritu* Nadal means the same as St. Paul when writing to the Galatians: "Live by the Spirit *[Spiritu ambulate]*, I say, and do not gratify the desires of the flesh" (Gal. 5:16), and he means the same as Ignatius writing in the *General Examen*: "Those who proceed spiritually *[spiritu]* and truly follow Christ our Lord love and intensely desire . . . to clothe themselves with the same garb and uniform of their Lord . . . to suffer injuries, false accusations, and affronts."[33] To live *spiritu* means that the Spirit has taken charge of one's life; it means that one should conform oneself in all things to Christ, make choices in accordance with the graces of the vocation God has given in Christ. To live *spiritu* is to find one's source in God alone, to refer everything to the infinite goodness and wisdom of God, who rules the whole Society, to found one's ministries and actions on no creature, to depend on no creature; it means to receive strength from no creature but only from God, one and three, through Christ, to refer nothing to creatures but only to the triune God. To live *spiritu* means, indeed, to depend on the prayers of the saints and every created help, but in such a way that all their power comes from God. To

---

[31] For reflections on *spiritu, corde, practice,* see Raymond Hostie, S.J., "The Cycle of Activity and Prayer according to Father Jerome Nadal," in *Finding God in All Things: Essays in Ignatian Spirituality,* trans. William J. Young, S.J. (Chicago: Henry Regnery Co., 1958; originally in *Origins* 6 [April 1955]), 154–58.

[32] The exhortations are in Spanish, but one manuscript from 1576 contains a Latin version of the first three exhortations in Alcalá corrected and expanded in Nadal's hand, as the editor indicates in *CommInst* 213 f. My remarks are based on both the Spanish and the Latin versions of the first exhortation (ibid., 226–31), and on Nadal's treatment of the same subject in "Plática 1ª en Coimbra (Nicolau, *Pláticas espirituales,* 43–45).

[33] *ConsCN* 101^w.3–4 (p. 44).

live *spiritu* is "to be willing to walk with God" wherever he goes, as we read in Micah 6:8. Nadal is describing the radical openness to the Holy Spirit found in the primitive Church. Everything is prayer.

There is nothing speculative about living *corde*, with one's heart. Love should inspire every action. We should *hate* sin and *long for* virtue. Love links to understanding: we should hear the voice of God with gusto, with devotion, with tenderness, loving him and directing our affection to him in all that we do. To live *corde* is "to love tenderly;" to live *corde* means that all our actions genuinely and affectively proceed from the love of God, our true heart. On fire with God's love and united with him, we bring love and union to all that we do: preaching, hearing confessions, studying, cooking, teaching, directing retreats, being chaplains in hospitals and prisons—whatever we do. Every kind of work, high or low, becomes our joy and consolation. To live in this manner is to live *corde*. Everything is prayer.

To live *practice,* in praxis, is to "walk the talk," to be obedient to one's call. Obedience is *practical,* acting out what we believe. To live *practice* is "to do justice." Prayer leads to act. Faith without *praxis,* without action, is not enough. Since God has called us to the service of others, we have to be practical about it, even contradicting heresy by our actions, walking always in the service of God. To act out the faith is to obey God. To act out the faith is to live in union with God, and it extends prayer into all the actions of the day. Everything is prayer.

Indeed, as Leonardo Silos points out, to live *spiritu, corde, practice* is to be caught up in the cycle from prayer to action and from action to prayer, in that reality of being contemplative at all times, even in the midst of action *(in actione contemplativus).*[34]

In the sixth exhortation at Alcalá, Nadal returns to the Latin word *practice,* urging the Jesuits to live practically *(practice),* not in an abstract or theoretical way, but from a heart full of love and the desire to serve God more fully.

> Who is the source of everything? God is. God's goodness and infinite power have done everything for me, and I am worth nothing. . . . Called and drawn to the Society by God's mercy . . . what return shall I make? . . . I shall serve God. . . . I shall seek God's greater glory. I shall seek to suffer for the one who has done all this for me. I have to distinguish myself in doing all that I can in the divine service. (358 f., no. 122)

The triune God calls a person to this way of life, and the proper response is to ask our Lord to plant the grace of that call deep in the

---

[34] Leonardo R. Silos, S.J. "Cardoner in the Life of Saint Ignatius of Loyola," *AHSI* 33 (1964): 29.

empty soil of one's heart, asking each day for our emptiness to be filled with a lively love of the work that comes through obedience, and with an openness for every ministry. Everything about the Society is practical (from the heart), aimed at helping the neighbor. The Society is a continual work of love and an exercise in love (360 f., no. 126). Nadal is telling his Jesuit audience that obedience (attentive listening) is something that God works within an empty and open heart, so that reverence for God and for God's work wells up from within and draws the heart to total commitment to God and to his work.

For Nadal, to live *spiritu* does not imply immediate revelation, although we know that Ignatius, along with his companions, was divinely inspired, as both bulls of confirmation indicate: "inspired, as is piously believed, by the Holy Spirit" (*Regimini,* 1540) and "inspired by the Holy Spirit" (*Exposcit,* 1550). Because Nadal entered the Society in 1545, he apparently had no occasion to know and be familiar with the original form of a proposed papal letter composed by the companions themselves that formed the basis for the later bulls.[35] In it they narrate briefly, in the Pope's name, their choices leading up to their request for approbation as the Society of Jesus. Their choice to be poor, their choice to be priests, their choice to come together, their choice to serve Christ alone and his vicar on earth "with the Holy Spirit, as we believe, impelling you"[36]—all these choices are evocative of the life of the primitive Church and its openness to the movement and inspiration of the Spirit, its listening stance before the Holy Spirit.

The *Formula of the Institute* itself makes two more references to the Spirit, the first urging each one to be aware of "the grace given him by the Holy Spirit" and to stay within its bounds, and the second urging any who join them to take great care to make sure that "the Spirit who impels them" has promised them the grace they need to live out the difficult vocation of being a member of the Society of Jesus.[37] Using terms worthy of the primitive Church, Nadal once described Ignatius as a man who "with great modesty followed the Spirit and did not go ahead of the Spirit.

---

[35] For an extensive treatment of the original draft, see Conwell, *Impelling Spirit,* 585.

[36] *Constitutiones* 1:15, no. 1, lines 9 f.

[37] The full document is entitled "Prima Societatis Jesu instituti summa" (*Constitutiones,* 1:14–21), the pertinent passages being 16 f., nos. 2 f. Both of these passages made their way into *Regimini* and *Exposcit.* Indeed, *Exposcit* adds two more, one in the letter, one in the *Formula.* The letter lists all the works in which the companions had engaged themselves, "each according to the grace given him by the Holy Spirit" (*Constitutiones,* 1:374, no. 2). In the *Formula* one of the reasons added for the vow of obedience to the Roman Pontiff is "for the more certain direction of the Holy Spirit" (ibid., 1:377, no. 4).

Thus he was led gently where he did not know he was going."[38] In the *Formula,* the companions expressed their willingness to surrender to the experience of the "Holy Spirit impelling" them as they took the path toward seeking papal confirmation of their way of life.[39] The *Constitutions* that Nadal promulgated and tried to explain articulate the daily Jesuit way of proceeding and describe a day-to-day experience of walking in the Spirit. Of all who follow them in this vocation the companions expect the same openness to the Spirit, the same ability and readiness to listen, the same eagerness to give all they have to the Spirit's call. *Walking in the Spirit* attempts to underline Nadal's insights and make them accessible to all those drawn to the spirituality that Ignatius and his companions lived and practiced.

Spiritu, corde, practice leaves no doubt of the prominent role of the Holy Spirit in a Jesuit's life, or of his need for a listening attitude before the Holy Spirit in whose ambience he lives. An image comes to mind of a village along an ocean beach: the air may be warm and still, but the inhabitants know that before the day is over a cooling breeze will come to stir the trees and flowers and perhaps even become a mighty wind to fill sails and lift kites. They live in the sure embrace of air that is benevolent and never destructive.

Similarities and Differences

Second Exhortation in Alcalá, 1561 (*CommInst* 256–87, nos. 26–33

When speaking to the Jesuits in Coimbra and Alcalá in 1561, Nadal again places the grace of the Society of Jesus within the context of world and Christian spirituality. Emphasizing the service of God, doing his will, obedience (*CommInst* 256, no. 26), Nadal begins with the saints of the Old Testament (257 f., no. 27] and then introduces the Word made flesh (258, no. 28). "God wants to be served well, better, perfectly," and so he calls different people to serve him in different ways and different religious orders to serve in different ways according to different graces (258–60, nos. 29 f.).

"The grace of religion itself," Nadal insists, "is itself a gift of God. Who can glorify self? All is gift. . . . We did not make ourselves religious; God did it. Grace is not from Ignatius. What could he do? God moved him and moves us as well. . . . This is not the work of a human being no matter how powerful" (260, no. 31).

---

[38] "Dialogus II" (1562–65; *CommInst* 625, no. 17, lines 46–50).

[39] *Constitutiones* 1:25, no. 2, line 22.

In Alcalá Nadal expanded some of his ideas.[40] First of all, he notes as before that all religious orders are established in imitation of Christ and of the primitive Church. He opines, therefore, that certain characteristics of the Society indicate a similarity to that first state of the Church. He draws a parallel between Jesus' withdrawal into the desert for forty days of penance and fasting and the time Ignatius spent in penance and fasting at Montserrat and Manresa. The difference, of course, is that the penance of Ignatius was that of a sinful man.

Both Jesus and Ignatius found companions. The difference is huge: "Our Lord gathered a company of twelve men; our Lord also willed to give his servant [Ignatius] a company of ten." Jesus is head of both groups. Nadal is so aware of the continuity of the two choices that he tries to stretch the ten to twelve by adding Bachelor [Hozes] who died in Padua before the Society was founded, and Cáceres, who signed the original Formula but left the group—or in Nadal's harsh parallel, "stayed in Paris to finish his studies and apostatized like another Judas."

Nadal modestly sees the apostles, disciples, and deacons as more advanced on the road to perfection than their Jesuit counterparts, the professed, spiritual coadjutors, and temporal coadjutors, who ought to strive with God's grace to be like their ancient predecessors.[41] Nadal so reverenced the apostles and disciples that he turned a blind eye to their obvious defects.

He goes to the heart of the Christian experience, however, when he talks about the trials and persecutions endured by our Lord, his apostles and his disciples, and about the struggles of the primitive Church to establish itself in the midst of persecutions; then he compares them to the trials and persecutions endured by Ignatius and the Society's members. Nadal does "not know whether another religious order has ever endured more persecutions and difficulties, long-lasting and still ongoing, than this one, which seems to have someone almost everywhere who persecutes it, at least in words."

The intent of Christ and the apostles and the intent of the Society is identical: with self-sacrificing zeal "to save souls, to convert non-believers and to draw believers to greater perfection." The Society shares with the apostles and disciples the experience of dispersion and of being sent; and just as the primitive Church converted many unbelievers right from the start, so also did the Society, for example, in India. The primitive Church had "one heart and one mind," and so does the Society, even though its members come from different countries. Some of these parallels rely heavily on externals, perhaps even on mere coincidence, but the overall

---

[40] *CommInst* 262, no. 33; see Q's variant reading for lines 78–81 toward the bottom of pp. 262 and 264. See editor's remarks, ibid., 208, A, no. 1.

[41] See n. 30 above.

picture is impressive; and it is important to be aware that the young Society, like every new religious order, saw itself as blessed with the grace to live in its own time the life of the primitive Church.

General Congregation 34 echoes its awareness of a similar grace today by entitling its second decree "Servants of Christ's Mission." Referring to the 1550 text of the *Formula,* which says that Jesuits are also to be engaged in reconciling the estranged, passionately assisting those in prisons and hospitals, and performing other works of charity, the congregation states, "We have recovered, for our contemporary mission, the centrality of working in solidarity with the poor in accord with our Ignatian charism." The congregation quotes "as a prophetic text for our time" what Ignatius directed Polanco to write to the community at Padua in 1547, where a benefactor was slow to release funds to the Society, with the result that the scholastics studying there were underfed and sick with fever:

> So great are the poor in the sight of God that it was especially for them that Jesus Christ was sent into the world: "By reason of the misery of the needy and the groans of the poor, now will I arise, says the Lord" [Ps. 11:6]. And elsewhere, "He has anointed me to preach the Gospel to the poor" [Luke 4:18], a word which our Lord recalls when he tells them to give an answer to St. John: "The poor have the Gospel preached to them" [Matt. 11:5]. Our Lord so preferred the poor to the rich that he chose the entire college of his apostles from among the poor, to live and associate with them, to make them princes of his Church and set them up as judges of the twelve tribes of Israel—that is, of all the faithful—and the poor will be his counselors. To such a degree has he exalted the state of poverty! Friendship with the poor makes us friends of the eternal King.[42]

Call: Love! Live!
Fifth Exhortation in Alcalá, 1561 (*CommInst* 345–56, nos. 107–13)

The Gospels and Acts are full of stories of calls: calls of the apostles, calls of individuals like the lame man or the Ethiopian eunuch, calls of crowds and communities like the thousands on Pentecost, or the family of Paul and Silas's jailer. These calls continue today. "A great help in coming to know the Society," Nadal said in Alcalá, "is for each one to consider what he went through to arrive at his own vocation, how God snatched him out of the world" (*CommInst* 345, no. 107). The call each Jesuit

---

[42] *DocsGC34* 31 f., no. 33. Polanco's letter, dated August 7, 1547, appears in *EpistIgn* 1:573 f. For an English translation of this letter, see *Letters of St. Ignatius of Loyola,* trans. W. J. Young (Chicago: Loyola University Press, 1959), 147 f.; also see Young's footnote on p. 146, quoting a letter from Ribadeneira about the food. The original text of Ribadeneira's letter is found in *Epist.mixt* 5:649 f.

receives is the call the Society receives. What better way of knowing the Society than to reflect on one's own call (and that of one's companions)? It is a story of unmerited grace and mercy, of being awakened and stirred, of being led by divine providence and gifted with the ability to say yes (whereas the young man in the Gospel said no): a mind enlightened, a will made ready, a heart gifted with consolation to follow Jesus in poverty, chastity, and obedience. The story has a good beginning; all must continue to respond in the same manner (345–47, no. 107 f.).

The Gospels insist on our loving one another, and St. Paul not only eulogizes love but demands it. Acts is a story of love, of being one in mind and heart, of the love of God for his people, and the love of his people for one another. Another way of knowing the Society, says Nadal, is through love. "Nothing helps so much to the knowledge of something as to love it. . . . What I love I work hard to obtain. . . . If you want to know God intimately, love him, let your heart rest in him. . . . 'To the one who loves me,' said the Lord, 'I shall manifest myself to him'" (John 14:21; 347, no. 109). God gives to a lover a knowledge of the Society (348, no. 110). Love of the Society means every part of it in every part of the world and everyone in it (348, no. 111). Love the call that God has given you, Nadal is saying to his audience; love that call and you will come to know it better and appreciate it more.

In the Sermon on the Mount Jesus calls for practicing virtue, and each Gospel and epistle spells out for the community it addresses the meaning of Christian virtue in the context of their lives. Acts is a story of sharing inner goodness as well as exterior goods. Another way of coming to know the Institute of the Society, Nadal insists, is through the exercise and practice of virtue, especially simplicity, straightforwardness, and genuine humility. Look at the compendium of all the virtues: obedience. All ministries of the Society are not for all, nor do all the members engage in all of them; but the Institute of the Society is exhausted in one word: obedience (349, no. 112). "Obedience will give us a religious knowledge of the Society" (350, no. 113). In view of the order in which he approaches the topics, first love and then obedience, Nadal indicates that obedience is always primarily an act of love. Like the director described in *Spiritual Exercises,* no. 15, the superior attends carefully to the love relationship between Creator and creature, Lover and beloved.

Concluding Reflection

Peter addresses the Church as "exiles of the Dispersion" and "aliens and exiles" (1 Pet. 1:1, 2:11). Adam, of course, was the first exile, a refugee from his home through his own faulty choice, and Cain the second, "a fugitive and a wanderer on the earth" (Gen. 3:23, 4:12). The first voluntary refugee is Abram, called by God to leave his country and his kindred and his father's house to go to a land God would show him (Gen. 12:1). Christ, however is the ultimate refugee, both voluntary and involuntary. By the Incarnation he empties himself and takes the form of a servant; he "vacates" his status as God, makes no human claim on divine prerogatives. As man, even before he is born, he leaves Nazareth for Bethlehem; scarcely born, he goes into exile in Egypt; returning from exile, he accompanies his family to Nazareth because Judea is not safe. As an adult, he leaves Nazareth and his mother and goes to the Jordan, thenceforth to wander through Judea and Samaria and Galilee and the surrounding territories; when he attempts to teach, he is even banished from his home town of Nazareth. He is the ultimate pilgrim making his way to the shrine that is his Father. He is the pattern for the life of the Church, of the Society, of all Christians, indeed, for the life of every man, woman, or child. None escapes that pattern: all can embrace it. To be a Christian, a companion and follower of Christ, is to let the life of Christ happen within each Christian, to let the pattern of his life take shape in each Christian's life. That is why, in the words of Vatican II quoted at the beginning of this chapter, "[T]he up-to-date renewal of the religious life," indeed of the Christian life, "comprises . . . a constant return to the sources of the whole of the Christian life," and for religious, "to the primitive inspiration of the institutes, and their adaption to the changed conditions of our time."[43]

The prayer of Jesus reveals that reverential and obediential openness to the Spirit that demands readiness to make choices regardless of the cost. His prayer patterns the prayer of the primitive Church; his way of praying is the way Christians are called upon to pray today. Walking in the Spirit means, first of all, the emptiness that lets the Father and the Son breathe the Holy Spirit into the human heart; and second, it means both breathing out and breathing in the Spirit of God: breathing out upon the world the Holy Spirit who fills the heart, breathing in from the world thus inspirited the same Holy Spirit who is the breath of life for all. Only lungs filled with breath can breathe out; only empty lungs can breathe in, lungs open to receive.

Jesus prayed like that. He stood in the waters of baptism and marveled at the coming of the Holy Spirit upon him, at the voice that came from the heavens acknowledging him as God's beloved (Mark 1:11). What a powerful prayer experience when the Spirit drove him into the desert, where he tangled with evil and dwelt among wild beasts and associated with angels (Mark 1:12 f.). After a day of hard work, he retired into a place of solitude and prayed, and the Spirit instructed him to move on in spite of his success (Mark 1:35–38). When he seemed to be accomplishing the most, he would go off into secluded spots and pray (Luke 5:16). He prayed all through the night before he chose his apostles (Luke

---

[43] "Up-to-Date Renewal of the Religious Life," in *DocsVatII*, no. 2 (p. 612).

6:12 f.). He looked up to heaven and sighed before curing the deaf man who was unable to speak clearly (Mark 7:35); and after he fed the five thousand, he went off by himself on the mountain to pray (Mark 6:46), for the people wanted to force him to be king (John 6:15). He prayed in gratitude to God for revealing himself to the lowly (Matt. 11:25), and he prayed for little children (Matt. 19:13). He prayed when transfigured on the way to Jerusalem (Luke 9:28), and he prayed when he was troubled (John 12:27). He prayed during his last meal with his apostles (John 17), in the garden when he felt agitated and alone (Mark 14:33–39), and on the cross when he felt abandoned even by his Father (Mark 15:34). He prayed when blessing bread at Emmaus (Luke 24:30), when he breathed the Holy Spirit on his apostles (John 20:22), and when he told them goodbye (Luke 24:51). For the most part, his prayer was for the sake of others rather than about himself. His prayer set the pattern for the primitive Church; his way of praying is the way we are called to pray today.

The prayer of the Society accords with the grace of the Society; for, in the words of General Congregation 34 quoted at the beginning of this chapter,

> The way in which Jesuits exercise their ministerial priesthood takes its character from our apostolic mission to labor with Christ in proclaiming the Kingdom. Our first companions envisaged a universal, itinerant ministry of evangelization, teaching, works of charity, and poverty of life: an evangelical *imitatio apostolorum*, a radical pattern of evangelical discipleship, was to be the wellspring for what they did as priests.[44]

The life of Jesus as portrayed in the Gospels, the life of the apostles and disciples and deacons as seen in the Acts of the Apostles, and the entire life of the primitive Church as outlined in Paul is life impelled by and lived in the Spirit.[45] The Holy Spirit descends upon Jesus, fills Jesus; Jesus is anointed by the Spirit, led by the Spirit, driven by the Spirit, rejoices in the Spirit. At the center of the Church on Pentecost is Mary, the disciple overshadowed by the Spirit, who "treasured all these things in her heart," who had feared that her Son had been overcome by a false spirit (see Mark), who, together with the Beloved Disciple, received the outpouring of the Spirit from the cross, and now models and shares that obediential wisdom born of suffering with all the disciples yearning for the fullness of the Spirit. Scripture explicitly links many men and women with the Holy Spirit. The Spirit also comes upon Simeon, the Samaritans, the Gentiles, the disciples, the Ephesians. The Holy Spirit fills John the Baptist,

---

[44] *DocsGC34* no. 173 (p. 90).

[45] See James D. G. Dunn, *The Christ and the Spirit* (Grand Rapids: Eerdmans, 1998), vol. 2 of *Pneumatology*, 3–21; id., *Jesus and the Spirit: A Study of the Religious and Charismatic Experience of Jesus and the First Christians as Reflected in the New Testament* (Grand Rapids: Eerdmans, 1975), 199–209.

Elizabeth, Zachary, Peter, Stephen, Paul, and Barnabas, not to mention all the men and women assembled on various occasions and the deacons who are to be filled with the Spirit. The Holy Spirit reveals or speaks to Simeon, Philip the deacon, Peter, Agabus, the church at Antioch. Others are guided by the Spirit (Simeon), sent by the Spirit or forbidden by the Spirit (Paul and Barnabas), speak with the Spirit (Stephen), or resolve in the Spirit (Paul in Acts, *passim*) The list would be nearly endless if we included all those "helpers in Christ Jesus" like Priscilla and Aquila, whose names grace the pages of the New Testament. As Peter wrote in his second letter, "No prophecy ever came by human will, but men and women moved by the Holy Spirit spoke from God" (2:21). The Holy Spirit is a very personal presence at the heart of the life of the Church. Like the apostles, we too are invited to "walk in the Spirit."

Even while these passages of Scripture say little about the style or characteristics of the prayer of Jesus or of the apostles or disciples or deacons, they say much about that prayer by suggesting an openness in Jesus and his followers to the movement and inspiration of the Holy Spirit, an attitude of listening to the Spirit, a commitment to obedience to the Spirit. During prayer and outside of prayer, they live in an attitude of readiness for the intervention of the Spirit so that their whole life is prayer. If, then, the grace of the Society is to live in the present a transformed version of the life of the primitive Church, the whole life of the Society, including its prayer, should be life and prayer in the Spirit, always and everywhere that ancient refugee prayer of the Church: Maranatha! "Come, Lord Jesus!" (Rev. 22:20).

This chapter has reflected on how the dream of Ignatius to follow Jesus in the Holy Land was transformed into the Society of Jesus. The next chapter will reflect on what happened to Ignatius on the way to Jerusalem that transformed his intention to do penance there into the determination to continue the preaching and healing ministry of Jesus and the apostles; namely, his experience of prayer at Manresa, especially as expressed in the considerations of the Call of the King and the Two Standards in the Spiritual Exercises.

Chronicle for Chapter 5

[Jerónimo Nadal] can with all justice be called the first theoretician of Jesuit spirituality.

Ignacio Iparraguirre, S.I., *Historia de los ejercicios de San Ignacio*

That aspect of [Jerónimo Nadal] that stands out over all others is that he rightly appears as THE THEOLOGIAN OF IGNATIAN SPIRITUALITY.

Miguel Nicolau, S.J.

Nadal's Life and Travels (1556–1559)

1556

Summer: In Medina and Simanca

September: In Valladolid; hears of death of Ignatius

Sept. 21: Leaves Valladolid for Burgos; stays in Torquemada with a fever

Sept. 30: Leaves Burgos for Rome

Sails to Nice, Genoa; visits colleges in Florence, Siena, Perugia, Amelia

Dec. 2: Arrives in Rome

1557

January: Exhortations at Roman College; named superintendent of Roman College and consultor to Laínez

Conflict with Bobadilla over Constitutions

1558

July 2: Laínez elected general; 4 of 20 votes for Nadal

Sept. 8: Congregation informed that Pope Paul IV wished general's office to be for 3 years and Jesuits to chant the office; Nadal named one of 4 assistants to general; also superintendent of Roman College

1559

August 18: Death of Paul IV

Before Christmas: Experts determine Paul IV's wishes regarding term of office and choir are no longer in force after his death because they were not in writing

Chapter Five

PRAYER INSPIRED BY THE KINGDOM
AND TWO STANDARDS

The up-to-date renewal of the religious life comprises both a constant return to the sources of the whole of the Christian life and to the primitive inspiration of the institutes, and their adaption to the changed conditions of our time.

Vatican II, "On the Up-to-date Renewal of the Religious Life"

The grace proper to the Society and the prayer that is appropriate to that grace flow from "the primitive inspiration of the institute." Nadal finds that inspiration in the Spiritual Exercises, especially in the considerations on the Call of the King and the Two Standards.

From the earliest days Christian leaders chose to express some of the most profound spiritual truths in terminology usually associated with the military. St. Paul used military terms in his epistles to express the conflict between good and evil. Today "sacrament" means a sign and source of Christian grace and life, but in the days of the Caesars *sacramentum* meant an oath, particularly a soldier's oath of allegiance. The Latin term *militare Deo* (to fight for God), at least as far back as St. Benedict in the sixth century, came to mean "to serve God." Perhaps the constant effort to sanctify war has produced the reverse effect: today a person in the armed forces is said to be in the *service*, and is called a *serviceman* or *servicewoman*. The spirit of the times tends to dictate meaning.[1] The

---

[1] For the spirit of the age of Ignatius, see Juan Manuel Cacho Blecua, "Del gentilhombre mundano al caballero 'a lo divino': Los ideales caballerescos de Ignacio de Loyola," in Plazaola, *Ignacio y su tiempo,* 129–59; Luis Suárez Fernández, "El marco histórico de Íñigo López de Loyola y su educación cortesana," in *Ignacio de Loyola en la gran crisis del siglo XVI* (Bilbao: Mensajero, 1991), 103–10; Miguel Angel Ladero Quesada, "Ecos de una educación caballeresca," in *Ignacio de Loyola en la gran crisis del siglo XVI,* 143–50; Julián Marías, "Las generaciones en la época de San Ignacio de Loyola: El mundo de 1491," in *Ignacio de Loyola en la gran crisis del siglo XVI,* 151–58. For a general background on chivalry, see Richard Barber, *The Knight and Chivalry,* rev. ed. (Woodbridge: Boydell, 1995).

Church *Militant* is either a Church fighting against evil (the Church in which the older generation grew up) or a Church at the *service* of the world (the Church since Vatican II). We need to go beyond the image to the reality the image expresses. General Congregation 34 spoke of the conflict between good and evil in terms of *service:*

> Ignatius presents a Christ who is on the move, traveling through villages and visiting synagogues to preach the Kingdom, going where people dwell and work. This contemplative identification of Jesus on mission is linked to the Election of the Exercises. In their own communal apostolic discernment, which led to the founding of the Society, Ignatius and his companions saw this as their unique call, their charism: to choose to be with Christ as servants of his mission, to be with people where they dwell and work and struggle, to bring the Gospel into their lives and labors.[2]

The preceding chapter reflected on the desire of Ignatius to make a penitential pilgrimage to Jerusalem, which God transformed into a desire to preach and care for the poor and sick. This chapter considers how Ignatius expressed his Manresan experience in the *Spiritual Exercises.*

History

In 1526 Ignatius was examined in Alcalá by two officials of the Inquisition, who passed no sentence. The vicar-general of the archdiocese examined him without passing judgment on his teaching. In 1527 the vicar-general examined him again; subsequently, he was confined in the episcopal jail for forty-two days. Even though he was found innocent, he was forbidden to teach until he had studied more. That same year four judges in Salamanca examined him, kept him in prison for twenty-two days, and finally pronounced him free of any error. They permitted him to teach, but imposed certain restrictions upon him. In 1529 the inquisitor in Paris received complaints about Ignatius, investigated them, but did not summon him. In 1535 a new inquisitor in Paris received accusations against him, but also did not summon him; when Ignatius voluntarily presented himself before him, the inquisitor requested a copy of the *Exercises.* After reading it, he praised the book. While Ignatius was in Venice in 1536–37, reports were bruited abroad that he had been burned in effigy in Spain and Paris. A trial proved him innocent. In Rome in 1538 some Spaniards falsely accused him, but the governor of Rome cleared his and his companions' names, whereupon his accusers either fled or were jailed.

---

[2] "United with Christ on Mission," in *DocsGC34* 20, no. 7.

A Pause for Prayer

In the consideration in the Spiritual Exercises on the Call of the King, Ignatius reminds us that we are all called to share the labor, the pain, the glory of Christ:

> **"The Call of the King: 'Whoever wishes to come with me must labor with me, so that through following me in the pain he or she may follow me also in the glory'"** (*SpEx* 95^{v.5}).

> We ask for what we want, which here is for the grace to be open to the transforming power of the Holy Spirit actively working in each of us and in the Church, to be ready to reflect in our own lives the life of Jesus himself and those aspects of the primitive Church that the Lord Jesus calls us to imitate, offering a model for the rest of the Church and the whole world.

Accusations by a Spanish Theologian, Melchor Cano

By 1548 the word was out: "The Society of Jesus is the mother of the Antichrist." In 1547, at the request of Cardinal Mendoza, Ignatius established a college for scholastics at Salamanca with Miguel de Torres as rector.[3] The next April, Torres wrote to Araoz, the provincial, that "that good man who earlier set out to attack us" was using Lent to deliver sermons seemingly aimed at the Society. The "good man" was a Dominican theologian of high repute, who found in the Jesuits' manner of living the exact antithesis of genuine religious life: they omitted or minimized external practices basic to the monastic life. Torres talked to the leaders of the city, who, fortunately, were not impressed by the attacks; he talked to the Dominican himself, who, unfortunately, did not desist from further attacks. Another Dominican, in fact, joined him in the fray (*Epist.mixt* 1:491–92).

Ignatius sent to Salamanca the papal bulls approving the Society and wrote that Pope Paul III had approved the Spiritual Exercises in July.[4]

---

[3] Letters of August or September 1547 to Francis Villanova and Miguel Torres (*EpistIgn* 1:580–82).

[4] Ibid., 2:190. Paul III approved the *Exercises* orally on January 2, 1547, formally on July 31, 1548, both at the instance of Francis Borgia. See *Sancti Ignatii de Loyola Exercitia Spiritualia,* ed. Josephus Calveras, S.I., and Cándido de Dalmases, S.I., MHSI

He cautioned Torres not to make a big fuss about the hostility they encountered (*EpistIgn* 2:192). Writing to Torres he named for the first time the source of the "contradictions," Friar Melchor Cano, O.P., a renowned theologian. "He is very zealous," wrote Ignatius, "but not well informed" (2:213). As a matter of fact, Ignatius and his secretary and research assistant, Juan Polanco, had drawn freely on the Dominican Constitutions in crafting those of the Society. Perhaps the omission of norms Cano considered essential made the result seem to him a monstrous caricature of religious life.

After spending over two weeks assessing the situation, a Jesuit from Alcalá, Juan Álvarez, reported to Ignatius Cano's contention that the Society was rebelling and dissenting from the Church. He preached before the whole university, scandalizing everyone by his vituperations. People turned and stared at Jesuits, although some were obviously in sympathy with them. When Cano criticized those who did not wear a habit, avoided penances, and recited the breviary rather than chanting the office in common (all external ascetical activities), even the children understood that he meant the Society. Praying in church, a Jesuit heard people say, "There's one of those of whom Friar Cano said, 'Beware.'" Cano was so revered that everyone was afraid to speak to Jesuits.

Álvarez spoke to Cano, who denied attacking the Society, asserting that he was saying only what was in Scripture. Álvarez thought this made little difference, for all Cano's hearers understood that he was speaking of the Society. Even though he knew the effect his denunciations were having, he kept up the attack. Álvarez was horrified at the outrageous remarks Cano made to him privately: Cano rejected the Pope's approval of the Society, stating that the *alumbrados* had started out well and then had fallen. He feared that the Society was the mother of the Antichrist, charging that Jesuits go about too freely. They dress, eat, and sleep like laymen; they were going to remove from their necks the holy yoke of religion advocated by the saints of old. Cano saw many signs that the Antichrist was coming, and those pseudoprophets who were to come did neither more nor less than the members of the Society do. He advised all those who want to serve God to join approved religious orders or the well-traveled "cart-road" of the clergy, and avoid the latest novelties (*EpistIgn* 12:487–90).

Meantime, the Master General of the Dominicans, Francis Romeo, wrote a letter to all his subjects commending the Society, not only forbidding them under holy obedience to attack it but urging them to protect and defend it.[5] Ignatius obtained a brief from Paul III naming episcopal

---

100 (Rome: Historical Institute of the Society of Jesus, 1969), 71–78.

[5] The letter, dated December 10, 1548, is given in its entirety in *Vita Ignatii*

judges to proceed against the Society's detractors in Salamanca. He wrote to John of Avila (later to be canonized), apostolic preacher of Andalusia, asking for help. Cano moved many to become disaffected toward the Society, but John of Avila moved many more to favor it and even join its ranks.[6]

The people of Salamanca gradually saw the Jesuits as a living contradiction to Cano's charges, and the controversy died of its own accord. The judicial action envisioned in the papal brief was unnecessary. Fray Juan de La Peña, a Dominican highly esteemed in Salamanca, published a defense of the Society. Not everything new is a novelty, La Peña declared. Innovations have renewed the Church in every age. No heretic has ever subjected himself to the Roman Pontiff, but these Jesuits have vowed to obey him. Not to have a special habit is no insult to other religious orders, the Dominican defender continues, nor is it without precedent in the history of the Church: we are not aware that the order founded by St. Augustine had a habit distinctive from the clothing of the secular clergy; and in the early days of their order, the Dominicans dressed the same as the canons regular. Neither is it unheard of not to admit those who have previously been admitted to another order, for the military orders did the same. Choir is important to religious life, but not so important that an order cannot exist without it, as the Dominicans did for a number of years and were none the worse for it. If preachers and teachers and others can be excused from choir, why cannot a whole order engaged in preaching and teaching and other works of mercy?[7]

Nadal's insistence on the Society's similarity to the early Church responds directly to Melchor Cano's contention that the Jesuits are precursors of Antichrist. In spite of Dominican protests, Cano was still active when Nadal visited Spain in 1554 and again in 1555.[8]

Loyolæ, by Pedro de Ribadeneira, S.J., in *Font.narr* 4:462–65, nos. 73 f.; see also 308 f., nos. 73 f. See *EpistIgn* 2:215, esp. n. 6; *PolChron* 1:267 f., no. 229.

[6] Astrain, *Historia* 1:331–33. The letter to John of Avila and another to Torres mention the papal brief (*EpistIgn* 2:316–20; 330–32).

[7] Astrain, *Historia* 1:333–38, including a lengthy summary of La Peña's apologia preserved by Pedro Ribadeneira in his "Hist. de la Asist. de España" (manuscript preserved in the Archivum Romanum Societatis Iesu, Hisp. 94), bk. 1, chap. 12.

[8] Terence O'Reilly discusses the issues in "Melchor Cano and the Spirituality of St. Ignatius Loyola," in Plazaola, *Ignacio y su tiempo*, 369–80. Although Ignatius was not one of the *alumbrados*, he shared with them the desire to join contemplation and action, confidence in sensible experiences of God's love, and faith in finding divine guidance in life's ordinary decisions.

Chivalric Background of the Kingdom and Two Standards

In a novel about King Harold of England, the narrator is his bodyguard, bound to him in love, gratitude, and admiration since childhood. It was his duty to throw himself between the sword and the King when the two-handed sword thrust came, but he tried instead to parry it with his sword and arm, losing his hand while Harold lost his head. For the rest of his life he was filled with shame.[9] Just so, at Manresa Ignatius experienced his sinfulness to such an extent that he wanted to throw himself down a hole and kill himself; but at the same time aware of the merciful forgiveness of Christ, he was filled with the deepest sorrow and also with profound shame in the presence of his Lord, who gave his own life out of love for him. "What have I done for Christ? What am I doing for Christ? What ought I to do for Christ?" (*SpEx* 53[v.2]). As he hears the call of his God and Savior to follow him, he responds with a total commitment in a bond of love that asks no questions and never hesitates to make decisions that cut him free and render him available for whatever service love demands. The considerations in the Spiritual Exercises on the Call of the King and the Two Standards are about a personal relationship of love with the risen Christ and about willingness to express that love by removing all obstacles to its full flowering in unquestioning love for him and all those for whom he died. God had moved him far beyond the desire to go on pilgrimage to the Holy Land and to do penance there.

The crusading spirit that pitted Christendom against Islam lived on long after the Crusades ended in the defeat of the Christian forces as the thirteenth century came to a close. The conquest of the New World was not only political and economic; it was also a "conquest" for Christ. At the same time that Columbus "discovered" America, his patrons, Ferdinand and Isabella, were driving the Muslims out of Granada and out of Spain (along with "unbelieving" Jews). One of the brothers of Ignatius gave his life in the conquest of the Americas, and another brother (or relative) died in the war against the Turks in Hungary.[10] Hostility between Christian Europe and the Turks erupted into open war off and on throughout the sixteenth century.

In spite of an atmosphere often unfriendly to the Jews, especially in Spain, as general of the Society of Jesus Ignatius was partial toward Jews, obtained a papal brief on their behalf, and rejected the Spanish obsession

---

[9] Julian Rathbone, *The Last English King* (London: Little, Brown and Co., 1997).

[10] Hans Wolter, S.J., "Elements of Crusade Spirituality in St. Ignatius," in *Ignatius of Loyola: His Personality and Spiritual Heritage, 1556–1956* (St. Louis: The Institute of Jesuit Sources, 1977), 37 and n. 38.

with "purity of blood."[11] Note well, however, that both Ignatius and Pope Paul III looked on both Jews and Muslims as potential converts.[12]

At the beginning of the jubilee year 2000, Pope John Paul II made a pilgrimage to the Holy Land, not seeking converts, but striving for reconciliation with Jews and Muslims, a sense of solidarity and unity in the great religions of historic monotheism. In the jubilee year 1550, however, Ignatius presented to Emperor Charles V and his viceroy in Sicily, Juan de Vega, a plan for the Christian fleet in its campaign against Dragut, the leader of the Islamic forces.[13] At the request of Juan de Vega, he obtained from Julius III all the blessings of the jubilee year (normally granted to those who made a pilgrimage to Rome) "for those who fight in the war with the infidels for the glory of Christ and the exaltation of the holy faith"; the more fiercely they fought, the greater would be the blessing, Ignatius assured them.[14] The prevailing attitude of the sixteenth century did not see the relation between the Turks and Europe as a conflict of one people against another, all of them children of God, all of them constituting God's holy people; but rather, people viewed it as a religious war of good versus evil: God on the side of the Christians fighting against the spirit of darkness, and Allah on the side of the Muslims fighting a "holy war."

To return to the new millennium, the United States is engaged in a "war against terrorism," fighting those who for the most part happen to be Muslims, as Europe did in the days of the Crusades, and a terrorist leader who finds terrorism an apt instrument for fighting against what he regards as the injustices of the United States. Both sides rattle swords, invoke God or Allah, and stir their followers to heroic deeds in the name of justice. Some persons look in horror at both the sixteenth and the twenty-first centuries, as they witness the enthusiasm that sweeps over human beings who are convinced they are fighting for a just cause.

The Experience of Ignatius

Born into a world at the twilight of the age of chivalry and still enthralled by the great and honorable deeds of the fictional knight, Amadis of Gaul, when the Crusades were not quite ended and the "unbe-

---

[11] Dalmases, *Ignatius of Loyola*, 180. Reites, "Ignatius and the Jews"; Borja Medina, "Ignacio de Loyola y la 'limpieza de sangre,' in Plazaola, *Ignacio de Loyola y su tiempo*, 579–615.

[12] Philip Caraman, S.J., *Ignatius Loyola: A Biography of the Founder of the Jesuits* (San Francisco: Harper and Row, 1990), 133.

[13] Wolter, S.J., "Elements of Crusade Spirituality"; see also Norman P. Tanner, "Medieval Crusade Decrees and Ignatius's Meditation on the Kingdom," *Heythrop Journal* 31 (1990): 505–15.

[14] *EpistIgn* 3:111–14.

lieving" Turks were still an abiding threat to Europe, Ignatius chose to express his ideal of Christ in the language of Crusaders and conquistadors.[15] The considerations on the Call of the King and the Two Standards are shaped by the crusading spirit of the times.[16]

Ignatius imagined a temporal king "chosen by God our Lord himself"; this king's "will is to conquer the whole land of the infidels," an action thoroughly repugnant to anyone accustomed to interreligious dialog since Vatican II.[17] At the same time the chivalric terminology invokes an image of the rich and deep relationship between a lord and his vassal. Ignatius imagines Jesus as the eternal King who shares everything with his vassals, the pain as well as the glory. On the vertical level, the lord and vassal were loyal to one another: the vassal serving his lord unhesitatingly even unto death, and the lord protecting and providing for his vassal both in good times and in bad. The horizontal level presents the image of vassals bound in loyalty to one another in the service of their lord, utilizing their skills to the utmost for the good of the group and compensating for one another's weaknesses.

The Experience of Nadal

In mid-June of 1551 Nadal wrote to Ignatius that the city of Messina, where he had been sent to establish a school, was fortifying itself against the coming of the Turkish fleet. The Christian spirit of the viceroy, Juan de Vega, was manifest in his appeal for prayers and good works to move the divine mercy to strengthen Christians against the enemy of the Catholic faith.[18] When the Turks threatened the Mediterranean, Nadal threw himself vigorously into a military chaplaincy for six months at Messina, presuming that Ignatius would approve. He joined the Christian fleet and sailed out of Messina on the flagship *Praetoria* at the end of June. A few days later he was clinging to a rock in the sea after being shipwrecked off the island of Lampedusa, east of Cape Bono and south of

---

[15] On Ignatius and chivalry, see Tanner, "Medieval Crusades," 505–15; Manuel Cacho Blecua, "Del gentilhombre mundano," in Plazaola, *Ignacio y su tiempo*, 129–59; Suárez Fernández, "Marco histórico," in Suárez Fernández, *Ignacio en la gran crisis*, 103–110; Ladero Quesada, "Ecos de una educación caballeresca," *Ignacio en la gran crisis*, 143–50.

[16] Georg Eickoff suggests some literary dependence, through Guillaume de Digulleville's *Pèlerinage de la vie humaine* (whose English translation influenced John Bunyan's *Pilgrim's Progress*) on the *Parabolæ* formerly attributed to St. Bernard. See Georg Eickhoff, "Claraval, Digulleville, Loyola: La alegoría caballeresca de *El peregrino de la vida humana* en los noviciados monástico y jesuítico," in Plazaola, *Ignacio y su tiempo*, 869–81.

[17] See Vatican II's declaration on the relation of the Church to non-Christian religions, "Nostra ætate" (October 28, 1965), in *DocsVatII*, pp. 738–47.

[18] *EpistNadal* 1:108, nos. 6 f.

Malta. Isidoro Bellini, a scholastic he had brought along as a companion to preach to the troops, had his arm severed, was rescued, but went down later when the ship broke in two. Nadal managed to catch a rope thrown from another ship and was dragged aboard. The ship took him west of Cape Bono to Aphrodisium (present-day Annabah in the northeastern corner of Algeria), where he spent months preaching to the local populace and also to the soldiers, hearing confessions and preparing for a war that did not come.[19] His military figures, therefore, are drawn more from camp life than from actual battle, an advantage in talking to scholastics preparing for the priesthood or to priests preparing for missions. In 1557 he draws on both meditations in order to describe the Society of Jesus.

> The nature of our vocation is to be a militia under the banner of Christ, as can be seen by all the Exercises, but especially in the meditation on the Kingdom and the Two Standards. In the meditation on the temporal king, we are called by Jesus Christ, the supreme king and leader of angels and men, to comradeship in the war that he is carrying on against the world, the flesh, and foul and hideous demons, until the day when he delivers the kingdom to God, his Father, and brings to naught all principality, power, and virtue. We enlist in that sacred service and inscribe our names with the finger of God. From the meditation of the Two Standards we see that we are to flock to the banner of Christ, to join together with Christ, our emperor, to advance with him into battle, to stand firm in the fight, and from our positions to carry on the combat through him. In this way was Fr. Ignatius first called; in this way Christ calls us through these meditations to the Companionship of his service *[Societatem suæ militiæ];* and thus we read in the *Formula* of our Institute that his vicar on earth, the Roman Pontiff, has given us his name under the standard of the Cross.[20]

The meaning is exceedingly rich; the imagery less so today and open to challenge. The violence of war does not stir every profoundly patriotic heart in a positive manner.

Nadal's penchant for the language of violence in reflecting on the Kingdom and Two Standards, activated in his crusading foray against the Turks while in Messina, no doubt grew and increased during his experiences in Germany in 1555. On his mission to Augsburg, his first encounter with Lutheranism shocked and appalled him. His heart bled for the people as he saw "the extreme misery of this nation, and the open and beastly dominion of the evil one."[21] Germany became for him a major apostolic concern. The Lutheran challenge replaced the Muslim challenge. The early

---

[19] Bangert, *Jerome Nadal,* 75 ff.; some of the story can be pieced together from a series of Nadal's letters from Aphrodisium (ancient Hippo, current Bône or Annabah). See *EpistNadal* 1:109–19.

[20] "In exam. annot.," *CommInst* 136, no. 5.

[21] Letter to Ignatius from Augsburg, March 30, 1555, *EpistNadal* 1:290.

Jesuits approached Germany as they would a battleground.[22] Listening was difficult.

The Imagery and the Content

Today the military metaphor gives one reason to pause. Compare the original from the hand of Ignatius with Nadal's gloss on the same: Nadal's is far more physical, far more combative, far more violent in its imagery. Both Ignatius and Nadal are steeped in the culture of a Christendom radically at odds with the culture of Islam: the "infidel" Turk is beating on the door of Europe, and for Christians to overcome Islam means that they must kill Muslims. The romance of war crumbles and dissolves when it crashes against war's harsh reality. Military images are not as attractive in this nuclear age as they were once upon a time. Nor in a secular and democratic age can one easily imagine a leader chosen by God to achieve a secular goal who would on that account excite unbounded enthusiasm. The image is not the message. Despite the strong imagery, Nadal takes us far beyond the military form of the imagery to the real heart of the matter, the urge to respond concretely to the call of Christ in giving oneself totally to his service out of love.

Translating the main ideas of the Kingdom and Two Standards into contemporary language, General Congregation 34 transforms the wartime terminology of military service and conflict into the peaceable practice of serving one another and engaging in dialog; it summons the Society to experience union with Christ on mission (d. 1), to be servants of Christ's mission (d. 2), to strive to fulfill Christ's mission of justice (d. 3), to seek to let every culture express Christ's mission in its own way (d. 4), and to enable Christ's mission to engage every religion in interreligious dialog to the mutual benefit of all (d. 5).

In changing the imagery in this way, General Congregation 34 takes its cue from Ignatius himself. In the Constitutions, the Kingdom and Two Standards lose none of their brilliance when they shed their military aspects, transformed by Ignatius into the equally brilliant images of the "members of the body of the Society" in Part VI of the *Constitutions* and the "vineyard of the Lord" in Part VII. Keep in mind, then, that the Kingdom and Two Standards are only one way to present a challenge to the value systems of contemporary society. Learning from that way, one can devise other ways more suitable for today's societies, ranging from rigid dictatorships to loose democracies, from First World powers to poverty-stricken Third World countries.

Because of this we distinguish carefully between the form of the considerations and the content or meaning of each. In the hands of Nadal,

---

[22] See Bangert, *Jerome Nadal,* 140–54.

the form is even more martial than in the hands of Ignatius. As seen above, Nadal could be pugnacious, as evidenced by his anger toward the rabbis of Avignon who wanted to make him their chief rabbi, his much criticized methods of governing in Messina, his arguments with Laínez, his conflicts with Borgia, his battles with Bobadilla.

The Grace of the Society

At Montserrat, while on his way to Jerusalem, Ignatius, like a medieval knight, with pilgrim staff in hand made a vigil of arms before the altar of our Lady, having placed there his sword and dagger and clothed himself in his pilgrim burlap. During the months at Manresa that symbolic action took the shape of long hours of prayer and excessive penances; but God transformed the imagery at work in him so that he forgot himself, abandoned excessive penances, made himself available to others: he begged alms for others as well as for himself, taught catechism in the streets, and showed special concern for the sick and the poor in the hospital where he was staying. The pilgrimage to Jerusalem began to take on the shape of a knight-errant's journey in search of mighty exploits to perform. In his exhortations in Spain in 1554, Nadal said:

> Here our Lord communicated the Exercises to him, guiding him in this way so that he might employ himself completely in his service and the salvation of souls. He showed him this especially in two exercises, namely, that of the King and that of the Standards, giving him the while great devotion. Here he understood his purpose in life and to what he should devote himself entirely and what should be the aim of all he did. This purpose and aim is what the Society has today.[23]

All that was worldly in Ignatius God had converted into a driving energy in the service of Jesus, countercultural to the extreme; but Nadal still longed to walk where Jesus had walked.

The Kingdom of Christ

The meditation on the Kingdom, or the consideration on the Call of the King, shows the imaginative form into which Ignatius cast his Trinitarian view of the universe. The Kingdom meditation comes after the exercitants have experienced their own sinful selves as embraced by the love of God and redeemed by the passion and death of Christ, the Beloved Son in whom the Father is well pleased. The redeemed sinner, now forgiven, is invited in this transitional time to meditate on the Kingdom—an incitement to a certain boldness for Christ—to confront and reflect on the

---

[23] "Exhort. 1554 Hisp.," *CommInst* 40, no. 13; also in *Font.narr* 1:307, with slightly different orthography.

answer to the question of the First Week, "What am I going to do for Christ?" Faced by the call of Christ, can one do less than all that one can do? It is in this context that General Congregation 32 declares in its decree 2 that to be a Jesuit today is "to know that one is a sinner, yet called to be a companion of Jesus as Ignatius was," placed with Christ carrying his Cross, who takes us as pilgrims into his company.

In the Kingdom meditation, Christ, leader of the good, desiring to win the hearts of all and guide all things back to the Father, calls upon all to assist him in that cause. The core of the Kingdom meditation is a full response to the call of Jesus. "Those who have judgment and reason will offer themselves wholeheartedly" (*SpEx* 96 [p. 54]). But the key lies in these words: "Those who desire to show greater devotion and to distinguish themselves in total service" to Christ, captured by loyalty to a magnanimous Leader and to all those in his service, bursting with enthusiasm, "will work against their human sensitivities and against their carnal and worldly love, and they will make offerings of greater worth and moment" (*SpEx* 97); that is, they will go against whatever in their own lives is an obstacle to the service of Christ. Being willing to find out what those things are and to do the internal asceticism needed to root them out—part of the pain that leads to glory—is what the response to the call of Christ is all about. Throughout the Second Week of the Exercises, beginning with the Trinitarian contemplation on the Incarnation, the exercitant is invited more and more to take on the livery or uniform of Christ and to be like him.

Fifth Exhortation in Coimbra (1561)

(Pláticas en Coimbra, 78 f., no. 2–5)

Sometimes Nadal softens the military image, sometimes he sharpens it. When speaking to the community at Coimbra in 1561, he refers to the temporal king as gathering "soldiers to lay waste and destroy all of God's enemies";[24] but he does not state, explicitly at least, that those who do not accept the Christian faith are the enemies of God. As for Christ, he says, "holding a mandate from the Father, he desires to make war on our enemies, the world, the flesh, and the devil" (*Pláticas,* no. 3), The enemies are not other human beings but forces that can do spiritual harm, and the weapons of this war are far different from those used on the ordinary battlefield. More in conformity with the language of St. Paul, he says:

> This is a spiritual war, and it is going on today; . . . a wickedly cruel thing because of the death of souls, a thing that all the temporal wars in the world could not bring about: spiritual death, eternal suffering, but also eternal life for souls, which is what God wants, whereas the demons want

---

[24] Nadal, *Pláticas espirituales,* no. 2.

eternal death. In this battle Christ conquered by his death, by means of his Cross, through humility (as opposed to the pride of the evil one) and, being both God and man, by his divine power. All that remains is to secure the victory, making us his companions, and so he calls us to this over and over again. (nos. 3–5)

This worldview certainly contains many of the apocalyptic features of the worldview of Jesus. Albert Nolan comments, "As Jesus understood it, Satan ruled the world. It was a perverse and sinful generation (Mark 8:38), . . . a world in which evil reigned supreme."[25] It may be a spiritual war, but evil has so embedded itself in human institutions that power (economic, political, and so forth) is normally used to dominate rather than to serve and set free (Mark 10:42–45).[26] Perhaps the language of non-violent resistance would be more acceptable today than "battle," "conquer," and "victory," and stir more people to want to join Jesus, who laid down his life out of love.

Third Exhortation in Alcalá (1561)

(*CommInst* 290–329, no. 56–85)

In this presentation the terminology of the parable of the temporal king is more objectionable than the one concerning Jesus himself. To the community at Alcalá in 1561 Nadal speaks of a Catholic Christian (monarch) "who is determined to subject the world to obedience to God and to his holy Church." The spontaneous image is not of Pope John Paul II begging pardon for the sins of the Church and seeking reconciliation with both Muslims and Jews in his jubilee-year pilgrimage to the Holy Land. Rather, visions of arrogant and violent conquistadors with swords and crosses come to mind, of inquisitors quietly handing over recalcitrants to death—anything but the image of the gentle and loving Christ, who lays down his life for even the worst of sinners.

Nadal explains that the imaginative and sensible (the parable of the temporal king) is at the service of the spiritual. Much exists that we cannot see. Something is going on in the Church that is like the enterprise of the temporal king. Christ came to change hearts, to bring the world to his eternal Father. Nadal even modifies the words of Ignatius, who pictures Christ as saying, "My will is to conquer the whole world and all my enemies" (*SpEx* 95 [p. 54]), by clarifying that the enemies of Christ are not unbelievers; rather, Christ's will is "to conquer the world, the devil, and sin," the enemies of the human race. In this enterprise we are God's co-workers (1 Cor. 3:9); this is the grace of being called to any state of life in the Church (*CommInst* 290–95, nos. 56 f.).

---

[25] Albert Nolan, O.P., *Jesus before Christianity* (New York: Orbis, 1992), 60.

[26] See Ched Myers, *Binding the Strong Man: A Political Reading of Mark's Story of Jesus* (Maryknoll, N.Y.: Orbis, 1988), 437–38, and Afterword C, 452–57.

What is more particular and proper to the Society? For the same end for which God established his Church and for the same great enterprise, God has called the Society into being and has enabled it to achieve this end through the means given it for fulfilling its ministries. This is what is meant by the grace of the Institute, the grace proper to the Society (292–95, nos. 57 f.). Then Nadal goes on to say once more that life is a constant battle: we are in the field, encamped against the enemy; we fight, and we fight armed with the favor and grace of God (294–97, no. 59). The clash of combat, however, is not what stirs Nadal as much as the spirit and example of Jesus, who teaches the way to go and the means to use and helps each one along the way (no. 59). "Our Captain carries his cross today in his Mystical Body, the Church, suffers in it and is persecuted in it. See what the Apostle says: 'I fill up what is wanting in the sufferings of Christ for his body, which is the Church'" (Col. 1:24; no. 59). Having supplied the context of the Church's enterprise, Nadal now zeroes in on "what is more particular and proper" to the Society, the call to be outstanding in response to Christ's call.

> Take notice of one thing in this part concerning the means that the Society embraces, which I often think about and which gives me great consolation. Our Father of holy memory was a man of strong mettle, a passionate man; aided by divine grace, he always threw himself into great enterprises; all his works were filled with ardor. And if you look at the Society, her Institute and works, everything is marked by the fire of love, the ardor of love, a never being idle, always energetic, always eager to go to work. (no. 60)

This ardor marks the Society of Jesus: the whole Company is called to be outstanding, passionate, always seeking and choosing the *magis* (more) of the First Principle and Foundation of the Exercises, the *greater* glory of God, the more universal good, the better in service, the more profound in humility, always in the service of Christ carrying his cross in his Mystical Body, the Church. With firm, bold strokes Nadal presses the image far more than does Ignatius.

> Do you not see that we are at war, that we are encamped? A servant of God cannot be indolent and unprepared, with his hands clasped doing nothing. In a war there is always something to be done, there is no place for idleness; there is always a skirmish or an alarm. Or, when it is not the time for fighting, it is time to be getting the weapons ready for battle. This is what goes on in the Society; it is always time either to deal with our neighbor or to fight against evil or against the world, against the evil one. And when it is not time for that, it is time to pray, to study, to perform the other exercises that you see in the Society, all of which are a preparing for war. Even eating and sleeping, things necessary for the body, help towards this end and have to be dedicated to it. (296–99, no. 60)

Nadal's experience in the camp at Aphrodisium (Annabah) in Africa after his shipwreck pursuing the Turks breaks out in every line. The military imagery may be stirring to some, repugnant to others. The reality hidden in the imagery is neither violent nor bloody. The campaign against the evil one begins in the hearts of those who wish to be outstanding. Those who desire to distinguish themselves in the service of Christ "will work against *[agere contra]* their human sensitivities and against their carnal and worldly love" (*SpEx* 97ᵛ·² [p. 54]). The same holds for advancing in prayer:

> To become capable of the perfection and gifts of prayer, we need first to purify our hearts and our consciences of all serious faults and should also truly guard ourselves very carefully from all venial sins and every kind of imperfection. We should strive in the Lord to root out all evil habits and inclinations remaining from past sins, and we should progress from good to better in all the virtues and the particular observances in our way of living.[27]

Agere contra (to go against) does not suggest arbitrary and unbridled exterior mortification, but deliberate choices well calculated to free one for ministry. To go against themselves implies every effort to rid themselves of disordered attachments or tendencies that would blind them as they attempt to discern the Lord's movements within themselves or make them deaf to his call.[28]

In the prayer of the Kingdom, those who act against their own sensuality and self love "will make offerings of greater worth and moment" (*SpEx* 97ᶠ·² [p. 54]). Their prayer will be a constant listening to the Holy Spirit in order to seek the mind and heart of Christ, through him surrendering themselves to the Father rather than to selfish interests or worldly ideals. They will strive to root out of themselves whatever may block the coming of his Kingdom.

Just as in the Constitutions Ignatius moved from Crusader imagery to the more peaceful metaphor of laboring in the vineyard of the Lord, so Nadal mellowed in his talks on ministry as he grew older. In Dialog 2 (1562–65) he describes professed houses as "army camps" from which attacks are made, not against "heretics" and "infidels," but against "the enemy of the human race, demons and vices."[29] In the second exhortation in Cologne (1567), he describes the Kingdom and Two Standards, but Christ has fought the "war against the devil" and won it, and the Church is performing a mop-up operation in this "war against all those things that are opposed to God." He concludes by summing up the Jesuit vocation in

---

[27] "Orationis ratio in Societate," *EpistNadal* 4:680.

[28] "Exhort. 4ᵃ en Alcalá," *CommInst* 340, no. 100.

[29] *CommInst* 773, no. 187.

a very peaceful reflection on the Lord's Prayer.[30] In what is entitled simply "The Sixth Exhortation" (1573–76), he makes no mention of the Kingdom and Two Standards in describing the Spiritual Exercises: the First Week is concerned with contrition for sin, the Second, Third, and Fourth Weeks with the life, death, and resurrection of Christ, in addition to the Contemplation to Obtain Love and some methods of prayer, notes, and observations.[31] In the American-frontier stories of the 1920s, young Indian braves hungered for the warpath, but wise, old chiefs counseled the way of peace. The elderly may be impatient and contentious on occasion, but they have a vast awareness of human imperfection, an awareness that is a share in the pain that leads to glory.

The Two Standards

In the Third Exhortation in Alcalá Nadal continues:

> The second meditation . . . indicates how the Institute is to be lived out; the first, the vocation and call and the end to which he calls us. The second points out more specifically the execution of this call and Institute and vocation.[32]

The consideration on the Kingdom is a call to follow Christ in "emptying himself" and sharing in his mission. The consideration on the Two Standards is a challenge to concretize the choice of means in Christ's service. It appropriates what it means to be totally at the service of Christ and plumbs the full meaning of the generous offerings that those who would be outstanding in the service of Christ make in the Kingdom meditation. Its prayer expresses a profound desire to be like Christ himself in the actual way in which he ushered in the kingdom of God, possessing nothing and rejected by many. The meditation on the Two Standards also introduces the adversary and presents his battle strategy: snares and chains; riches, honors, with pride as the goal; the fashioning of the false self. He sends out his minions. The enemy (the world, the flesh, the devil) is everywhere. The meditation also presents Christ's plan, the exact opposite: interior as well as exterior poverty and opprobrium, leading to humility—the fashioning of the true self. If the enemy is everywhere, so also is Christ. Nadal writes,

> Behold, on the other hand, Christ, Captain of the Church, Leader of the good, eternal light, complete beatitude, infinite perfection in his divinity. Behold him in heaven and in the Blessed Sacrament, where he is really

---

[30] Ibid., 789 f., nos. 25–28.

[31] Ibid., 843, no. 39.

[32] *CommInst* 298 f., no. 61; also see the alternate readings for lines 38 f.

present. Behold him on every side, for he fills all with his divinity. (298–301, no. 63)

Christ also sends out his followers. The military image continues.

He wants us to go forth to the assault, to the skirmish, to enter into battle with the enemy, showing great courage and valor with the grace and assistance of our Captain. And look how necessary it is for us to go to him each day, to find out from him the way to fight, and for him to send us into the battle himself. (ibid.)

The core of the Two Standards is loyalty to Christ as Lord and the consistent choice of his norms over one's own. Riches and honors are examples of obstacles to falling in love, but all must discover within themselves their own obstacles, their own traps, snares, and willful delusions.[33] Once again, there is need to go beyond the image to the meaning. To be a companion of Jesus today, General Congregation 32 says, is "to engage, under the standard of the Cross, in the crucial struggle of our time: the struggle for faith and that struggle for justice which it includes."[34] Both the Kingdom and the Two Standards challenge the exercitant to accept God's grace that frees a human person from the prevailing value system. The medieval goals of riches and honor resulting in pride were, indeed, the values of the upper-class contemporaries of Ignatius, the men to whom he gave the Exercises. Riches and honor and power are appealing today, at least for some. Perhaps they attract upper-middle-class men, but not necessarily the poor, or women, or the marginalized of the new millennium. The poor do not long for yachts, but for a square meal and a square deal. They yearn to be rid of a crippling economic system that makes them poorer while benefiting the already rich. Christ may be calling them to challenge the power of wealth. Many women are looking for meaningful relationships. Christ may be calling them to be more assertive, whatever their husbands may think about that! Ignatius mentions temptations and ideals of the world with which he was familiar—those shared by the nobles and upper classes, rather than by serfs, slaves, and peasants.

Today the Exercises are available to rich and poor alike, to Protestants as well as Catholics, to those of non-Christian religions, to men and

---

[33] See three works by Robert J. Egan, S.J.: "God in All Things: Ignatian Spirituality in the Situation of Postmodern Culture," an unpublished 305–page paper presented as part of the doctoral program in the Graduate Theological Union at Berkeley in 1990; *Ignatian Spirituality: Finding God in Everything,* and *Ignatian Spirituality and Social Justice* (Toronto: Regis College, 1991); "Toward a Postmodern American Catholicism: Ignatian Spirituality and the Mission of a Jesuit University Today," lecture in the Distinguished Jesuit Lecture series at the University of San Francisco, 1999.

[34] *Documents of the 31st and 32nd General Congregations of the Society of Jesus* (St. Louis: The Institute of Jesuit Sources, 1977), 401, no. 2.

women of every class and occupation, to minorities and other marginalized people of our contemporary society.[35] For some the way to humility may be self-affirmation, a refusal to be treated as a thing or a product, a refusal to accept or tolerate the norms and values a faulty social and economic system has thrust upon them, a demand for what is rightfully theirs, something that a power-hungry society has stolen from them. For others the sin of "hiding," the refusal to speak out, is as harmful as the sin of pride.[36] In any case, whether for rich or poor, for men or women, the call is not to conformity to the world, but to Christ both in his condemnation of the world and in his love of the world he has come to save.

Growing up steeped in the ideals of chivalry portrayed in works like *Amadis of Gaul,* and desirous of accomplishing great deeds in the service of God and on behalf of the oppressed and unfortunate, especially of ladies in distress, Ignatius, a passionate man, yearns for great deeds to perform. After his conversion, however, while retaining the ideal of heroic deeds, he totally rejects the motive that inspired the knights of old to unbelievable acts of courage: the driving desire for honor. Vivid metaphor though the martial language of the Two Standards is, more startling is the extremely "unmartial" way Ignatius proposes to conduct the campaign. The hero Amadis would be completely befuddled by the unmilitary choice of weapons. Whoever heard of a military establishment that chose poverty as its first line of defense or attack? What militia instills into its soldiers a desire for humiliation, for being despised, for being insulted? What officer corps advocates humility as its highest ideal? This war entails no body count, no broken bones, no bloody limbs; for the enemy in this war is not Islam or Muslims or other human beings, but "the enemy of human nature," Satan himself. The plan of action is the opposite of warlike. Asking for genuine poverty, pleading for humiliation, this kind of prayer produces a person who is at once passionate and gentle, zealous and vulnerable, eager and caring, a doer who is a listener, one who does justice prayerfully and quietly. The metaphor hides a far deeper reality; in the end the martial spirit quietly changes into zealous love.

Companionship with Christ in prayer opens the way to overcoming evil with good. The burst of enthusiasm prompting the offering of the Kingdom becomes the maturely deliberate prayer of one who has sounded the depths in Christ's life and realizes all his offering implies. The prayer of the Two Standards is that God accept the offering totally; La Storta is

---

[35] See the excellent list of publications in Katherine Dyckman, S.N.J.M., Mary Garvin, S.N.J.M., Elizabeth Liebert, S.N.J.M., *The Spiritual Exercises Reclaimed: Uncovering Liberating Possibilities for Women* (New York: Paulist Press, 2001), 22 n.5; see also Michael Kennedy, S.J., *Eyes on Jesus: a Guide for Contemplation* (New York: Crossroad, 1999).

[36] Patrick J. Howell, S.J., *As Sure as the Dawn: A Spiritguide through Times of Darkness* (Kansas City: Sheed & Ward, 1996), 110–14.

God's assurance that he has done so, that Ignatius and the Society will be with Jesus and receive the full weight of his poverty and insults. Hard things, difficult tasks, have become the ideal of the Jesuit, not because they are hard, but because they are at hand, and because where they are, there is Christ. To be at Christ's side is far from a glorious march behind a conquering Leader who wins merely by appearing on the scene; the combat is glorious, but carried on behind a Leader who conquers through meekness. Satan with all his works and pomps is already vanquished, but hate endures to be defeated again each day through discerning love in companionship with Jesus.

We return again to finding God in all things, now under the formality of finding Christ, Captain of the good, or finding the enemy. For one steeped in the reality of the Incarnation, to discover Satan in the events of life, or to discover Christ there, is to discover a Trinitarian world. To learn how to pray, we have only to find ourselves placed by the Father at the side of Christ bearing his cross. There we see all things in the Trinitarian context that is really theirs; there we are engulfed in the reality that permeates every event of human history; there we discover that the Blood of Christ has stained scarlet every creature on the face of the earth and made it new. In companionship with him and in his service, our prayer is at once a rallying cry and a plea for aid in the struggle, a rallying cry for others to join in his service, a plea to Christ for the strength and courage to walk at his side, a Trinitarian prayer that embraces the universe in the desire to reconcile the world with Christ and with him win back the whole human race to lead them to the Father. The accommodating tone of the decrees of General Congregation 34, which was searching for the common bonds among differing religions and cultures, fits both the Call of the King and the Two Standards: the enemy is not other people or their religion or culture, but evil itself.

Nadal assures his listeners that they can easily find material for prayer each day in what they discovered to be helpful in the Exercises, secure that our Lord will give it to them in his goodness and according to their own receptiveness, aided by his grace. Then he adds:

> For the state of prayer is a state of the spiritual life in Jesus Christ. As he is eternal light and infinite goodness, so he should be known and loved above all else, and in him should be known and loved all the rest. Thus our whole living and understanding should be above and withdrawn from these lower things, so that we do not live or work according to a human spirit, but according to a celestial and divine spirit; and in all things let us see and recognize the divine power and goodness, and let us love and serve it and not be curious or rash regarding ecstasies and visions or launching ourselves impetuously into more than grace itself leads us to.[37]

---

[37] "Orationis ratio in Societate," *EpistNadal* 4:676.

Conclusion

However faulty the images, the Call of the King and the Two Standards present the Risen Lord in a stirring call not only to join him in standing against all that is negative and destructive in the world but also to stand at his side in promoting all that fills the world with life and love. Both are rife with the optimism and love for life of the one who has conquered sin and death. They do not hesitate to link in one image the Crucified Lord and the Risen Lord, Jesus on the cross and Jesus head of the Mystical Body suffering in his members: the battle has been joined, but the battle has already been won even though it continues today. A key moment in General Congregation 34 came when the themes of the Crucified and Risen Lord were conjoined, for example, in decree 2, *Servants of Christ's Mission:* "The Jesuit mission, as a service of the Crucified and Risen Lord, is always an entry into the saving work of the Cross in a world still marked by brutality and evil" (*DocsGC34* 28, no. 26).

In the quotation at the beginning of the chapter, Vatican II stressed "a constant return to the sources of the whole of Christian life and to the primitive inspiration of the institutes, and their adaption to the changed conditions of our times."[38] The very titles of the first five decrees of General Congregation 34 put Christ and his mission at the very center of Jesuit life and suggest both the Kingdom and Two Standards, stated in fresh and creative terms suitable for today:

1. United with Christ in Mission
2. Servants of Christ's Mission
3. Our Mission and Justice
4. Our Mission and Culture
5. Our Mission and Interreligious Dialog

In decree 1 the congregation considered the Society's limitations and weaknesses as well as the life and example of Ignatius. Jesuits do not go on mission as conquistadors, but as "pilgrims on Christ's mission," moving from pilgrim to laborer in the vineyard of the Lord as Ignatius did; and even after the chastening experiences of the last thirty-five years, like the early companions they are "friends in the Lord" who need to listen to the whole Church, especially the pope, and the voices of women, the poor, other religions and cultures, indeed, all the marginalized. Decree 2 continues the theme of the Kingdom, and the next three decrees spell out in contemporary terms the relevance of the Two Standards as a challenge to some of the Society's traditional but outdated ways of viewing Christ's mission. The passage from General Congregation 34 quoted at the begin-

---

[38] *DocsVatII* d. 47, no. 2 (p. 612).

ning of this chapter reminds Jesuits that, just as Jesus worked in the real world of his day, so they must work in the real world of their own day:

> Ignatius presents a Christ who is on the move, traveling through villages and visiting synagogues to preach the Kingdom, going where people dwell and work. This contemplative identification of Jesus on mission is linked to the Election of the Exercises. In their own communal apostolic discernment, which led to the founding of the Society, Ignatius and his companions saw this as their unique call, their charism: to choose to be with Christ as servants of his mission, to be with people where they dwell and work and struggle, to bring the Gospel into their lives and labors. (*DocsGC34* 20, no. 7)

The challenges continue in later decrees dealing with serving the Church, cooperating with the laity, coping with the situation of women in the Church and civil society, of parishes and educational apostolates. It explores the new culture of communication, and in its last decree, *Our Way of Proceeding,* it sounds a call for a deep personal love of Christ, summoning us to be contemplative in action, to be friends in the Lord, in solidarity with those in need, in partnership with others, to be learned men always available for new missions, ever seeking the *magis,* the better thing, the greater glory of God.

This chapter on the Kingdom and Two Standards, in which the central thought is the extent of the conflict between Christ and Satan, reveals that in these two considerations Ignatius conceived an idea of the apostolate that produced the Society, imparting to it its own proper spirit. The prayer proper to that Society is apostolic in nature, a prayer one makes in companionship with Jesus in an atmosphere of mortal conflict that would reconcile the world to itself and to the creator of all: "If anyone is in Christ, there is a new creation: everything old has passed away; see, everything has become new!" (2 Cor. 5:17).

The next chapter envisions the grace of the Society in terms of its end. It is not an active order or a contemplative order, but it embraces both lives, the active and the contemplative, and also that higher active life that enables some to become active, some to become contemplative, and some to assist others to engage themselves in this same higher active life.

Chronicle for Chapter 6

We commend to Your Majesty our beloved son, Jerónimo Nadal
. . . sent there by his Father General [Diego Laínez] to fulfill the
office of commissary and visitor for all the houses and colleges of
the Society, . . . chosen for his outstanding probity, religious commitment, and knowledge.

—Pope Pius IV to King Philip II of Spain

Nadal's Life and Travels (1560–1561)

1560

Nov. 6: Laínez names Nadal commissary general with full power to visit
Spain, France, Germany, and Italy

Nov. 18: Leaves Rome with Jiménez as
secretary

Genoa; waiting for ship, writing

Dec. 18: Leaves Genoa

Dec. 20: Arrives at Nice

Dec. 22: Leaves Nice

Dec. 24: Arrives at tower of Ambuca
near Marseilles

Dec. 27: Departs; storm scatters and
endangers ships; lands between
Cadaqués and Rosas

Dec. 29: Goes on foot to Rosas, then
on to Gerona

1561

Jan. 1: Barcelona; leaves on Jan. 4

Saragossa, Alcalá; talks to Araoz

Feb. 12: Cuenca; returns to Alcalá

Before March 3–20: Toledo, talks to
inquisitor and King's minister

Late March: Avila, Medina del Campo,
and Salamanca

April 6: Porto for several days; visits
Braga, Monterrey; goes to Coimbra
via San Fins, visiting Braga and
Porto again

April 23: Coimbra (almost 2 months);
exhortations

July 14: Leaves for Évora

July 17: Arrives at Évora; sick

July 31–Sept. 10: Lisbon

Sept 12–Oct. 2: Évora; exhortations

Oct. 2–13: Albuquerque, Plasencia,
Alcalá

Oct. 13–Nov. 14: Alcalá; exhortations

Nov. 14: Leaves for Ocaña (2 days)

Nov. 17: Leaves for Toledo (3 days)

Nov. 21–23: Returns to Ocaña

Nov. 23: Leaves for Villarejo (2 days);
goes to Belmonte (day and a half)

Nov. 28: Leaves for Cuenca

Nov. 29–Dec. 5: Cuenca; new college

Dec. 5: Leaves Cuenca for Guadala-
jara, Jesús del Monte, Alcalá

Dec. 9–Jan. 2: Alcalá

Chapter Six

PRAYER BASED ON THE END OF THE SOCIETY

> Since the final norm of the religious life is the following of Christ as it is put before us in the Gospel, this must be taken by all institutes as the supreme rule.
>
> —Vatican II, *On the Up-to-Date Renewal of the Religious Life*

End or purpose is not to be confused with the means available at one point in history. Spiritual renewal modeled on "the following of Christ" does not imply a return to old ways of serving God, but a return to listening to God calling us to move out from the safe and secure into the unknown, the unexpected, the new that is creatively in continuity with the old. This new reality concerns ends and not means, the purpose of life and not the means that were once effective; for "the final norm" is Christ himself. Thus it was the call to the Society from the beginning to participate in the missions of the Son and the Spirit that moved the fathers of General Congregation 34 to send this message to the whole Society:

> When understood in the light of the faith which seeks justice, the criterion of "greater need" points toward places or situations of serious injustice; the criterion of "more fruitful," towards ministry which can be more effective in creating communities of solidarity; the criterion of "more universal," towards action which contributes to structural change to create a society more based on shared responsibility.[1]

History

A religious person is often thought to be someone who seeks personal perfection and union with God. In Christian terms, however, a religious person is one who tries to live the Gospel. Because the Gospel clearly describes perfection as loving God and loving one's neighbor, seeking perfection is not a self-centered activity, but necessarily bears upon the neighbor as well. A religious person, then, seeks communion with God and

---

[1] "Our Mission and Justice," in *DocsGC34* 71 (p. 47), citing *ConsCN, C:* 622[w. 2, 8] (pp. 284 f.).

with others through Christ in the Spirit. Jesus went into the desert to pray and to prepare himself for ministry. The early Christian virgins gave good example to their neighbors by living the Gospel in the midst of the corruption and dissipation of pagan cities. Anthony, the father of monasticism, exerted an impact upon others by abandoning even the good things of the world and going into the desert to find God and to confront the evil spirit. He edified from afar and attracted many others to a similar way of life.

The more radical ways of following Christ tended to become institutionalized, but their main purpose always remained living the Gospel. The first Christian monks were laymen. They did not think of themselves as different from other Christians. They simply wanted to live the Gospel as fully as they could. In the early centuries of institutionalized religious life, contact with human beings was secondary to a life of prayer and penance.

Monastic documents expressed in strikingly different ways the desire to live the Gospel in a radical manner.[2] The *Rule of Benedict* spoke of "doing battle for the true King, Christ the Lord" (Prologue 1). The Carthusians, who cut themselves off completely from the world surrounding them, spoke in their *Customs* of "serving God" (Prologue 2), and the *Older Life of Bruno* said that they wished "to follow the naked Christ naked." The Cistercians wished "to observe the Rule of blessed Benedict in every particular" in utter simplicity and poverty (*Carta Caritatis Posterior,* no. 3). The Carmelites' *Rule of St. Albert* urged them to "live a life of allegiance to Jesus Christ" (2). The Canons Regular read in the Rule of Augustine that they were to "live together in harmony . . . on the way to God" (1.2). Priests attached to the bishop took care of the usual sacramental needs of ordinary people, assisted in emergencies by the few monks who were ordained. Monastic houses for both men and women were noted for their hospitality, especially to the poor, pilgrims, and strangers.

The advent of the mendicant orders in the thirteenth century changed the face of the Church. By then preaching had fallen on bad times. Religious orders assumed part of the task carried out until then by bishops and pastors. Preaching repentance and proclaiming the Good

---

[2] Here are the sources of the quotations that follow from various religious founders and commentators: Fry, *Rule of St. Benedict,* 157; *Vita antiquior Brunonis,* in *Patrologiæ cursus completus, series Latina* (Paris: Barnier), 152, col. 485; Guiges I, *Coutumes de Chartreuse* (Bd de Latour-Maubourg: du Cerf, 1984), 156 f.; Bede K. Lackner, O.Cist., trans., "Early Cistercian Documents in Translation," in *The Cistercians: Ideals and Reality,* by Louis J. Lekai, O.Cist. (Kent State University Press, 1977), 462; *The Rule of St. Albert,* ed. Hugh Clarke, O.Carm., and Bede Edwards, O.D.C. (Aylesford and Kensington, 1973), 79; *The Rule of Saint Augustine,* introduction and commentary by Tarsicius J. Van Bavel, O.S.A., trans. Raymond Canning, O.S.A. (Garden City, N.Y.: Doubleday, 1986), 11; *Francis and Clare: The Complete Works,* trans. and intro. Regis J. Armstrong, O.F.M. Cap., and Ignatius C. Brady, O.F.M. (N.Y.: Paulist Press, 1982), 137; Tugwell, *Early Dominicans,* 457.

News of the Kingdom of God demanded time and energy, but the mendicant orders still retained many monastic practices, like choir, common penances, and wearing a distinctive habit. The *Later Rule* of the Franciscans maintained that "to observe the Gospel of our Lord Jesus Christ [is] the rule and life of the Friars Minor" (1.1). The Prologue of the Dominican *Constitutions* expressed itself in a way that obviously influenced Ignatius: "Our Order is known to have been founded initially precisely for the sake of preaching and the salvation of souls, and all our concern should be primarily and passionately directed to this all-important goal, that we should be able to be useful to the souls of our neighbors." The superior could dispense the members of his community "particularly in things which seem likely to obstruct study or preaching or the good of souls."

The Society of Jesus thus created a shocking disruption of the pattern of centuries because it entirely excluded from its Institute monastic practices that could impede work for the neighbor, rather than merely dispensing from them when necessary.[3] The Society's end was the salvation of souls, both their own and their neighbors', and the members of the Society were to achieve their own salvation by working for that of their neighbors.

A Pause for Prayer

Note on the Three Classes of Persons: "When we feel an inclination or repugnance against actual poverty, or when we are not indifferent to poverty or riches, a great help toward overcoming this disordered attachment is to beg the Lord in the colloquies to choose oneself to serve him in actual poverty (even though it is contrary to our lower nature); and further that one desires it, begs for it, and pleads for it, provided only that it would be for the service and praise of the Divine Majesty" (*SpEx* 157 [p. 69]).

The prayer at the beginning of the consideration of the Call of the King is that we might not be deaf to the call of Jesus, but eager and ready to respond ardently in his service;

---

[3] Nadal relates a little story about Ignatius: "When Fr. Ignatius was asked by a certain father of the Society what had moved him to reject choir, he replied, 'I thought that if we did not have choir, everybody would know that we were taking it easy when they did not see us out helping souls, and this would spur us on to want to help them.' He said this quite ingenuously just as I have told it. But at other times when he was asked about the Institute, he used to refer to that wonderful illumination God granted him at Manresa, which I have talked about elsewhere; as though he had received everything from our Lord right there in a sort of master-designing spirit of wisdom" (*NadSchol* 163.

the prayer of the Two Standards is that we might avoid the deceits of the evil one and know and embrace the path of Jesus. Now we pray that we may seek only what Jesus seeks, what is more for the glory of God and the salvation of the world.

Pedroche's "Censura"

PolChron 3:503–24

In Salamanca Cano sent his copy of the *Spiritual Exercises* to the arch-bishop of Toledo, Juan Silíceo, indicating passages he considered worthy of condemnation.[4] Notwithstanding the Pope's approval of the Exercises and the Dominican Master General's prohibition against attacking the Society of Jesus, Thomas de Pedroche, O.P., a lecturer in theology at the College of St. Peter Martyr in Toledo, added a few notes of his own and in 1553 launched an attack against the *Spiritual Exercises* that included criticism of Ignatius and of the Society of Jesus. The attack took the form of a censure of the book of the *Exercises*.[5] Pedroche quotes the text correctly, but often misinterprets it or judges it harshly.

Pedroche begins his "Censura" with an old bromide already put to rest by the governor of Rome in 1538: he denounced Ignatius as having been "charged with heresy before the Inquisition. One of the abandoned *[dejados]* or enlightened ones *[alumbrados]*, . . . he fled to Rome to escape the Inquisition and the Inquisitors."[6] He scoffs at Ignatius on the grounds that he "was so poorly educated that he did not know how, nor did he have sufficient skill, to write these exercises and instructions in Latin, but instead wrote in the vernacular, in Spanish" (*PolChron* 504 f.).

Pedroche twists Polanco's description of Ignatius in this 1548 edition as "taught not so much by books as by the unction of the Holy Spirit, by inner experience, and by the practice of dealing with souls"

---

[4] *PolChron* 3:336, no. 1.

[5] "Censura exercitiorum S. Ignatii confecta et archiepiscopo toletano oblata anno 1553," published in the appendix of *PolChron* (3:503–24).

[6] Ibid., 504 f. For background on Ignatius and the *alumbrados*, see Alistair Hamilton, *Heresy and Mysticism in Sixteenth-Century Spain: The Alumbrados* (Toronto: University of Toronto Press, 1992); Bernardino Llorca, S.J., *La inquisición española y los Alumbrados (1509–1667)*, Biblioteca Salmanticensis Estudios, no. 32 (Salamanca: Universidad Pontificia, 1980), 86–92; John E. Longhurst, S.J., "Saint Ignatius at Alcalá, 1526–1527," AHSI 26 (1957): 252–56; Luis Fernández, "Iñigo de Loyola y los alumbrados," *Hispania sacra* 35 (1983): 585–680.

(504). He jeers that "[w]hat he knows—and no small amount comes from the abandoned [dexados] and enlightened [alumbrados] ones who, having abandoned and set aside revelation found in books, submit and surrender to what the spirit says to them within their own heart, and they hold as infallible that the spirit of God always speaks to them" (505). Pedroche ridicules, not the Holy Spirit's role, but Ignatius's reliance on that role in the Spiritual Exercises.

He takes even greater umbrage at the Society's name, even though it had been specifically approved by the Pope: "This title, or name, is arrogant, schismatic, and in no small way injurious to the whole Christian people. . . . If they, and they alone, are named and belong to the Society of Jesus, it follows that all the rest belong to and are named the Society of the devil" (506).

Pedroche is suspicious of any talk of the inner working of God in the soul—any consciousness of the presence of the Spirit within—as smacking of the alumbrados, those "enlightened" men and women of the times who were sensitive to what they deemed the action of the Holy Spirit in their lives, but paid little heed to the Church. More or less missing Ignatius's whole point that the service of God is primary, Pedroche finds indifference to all created things contrary to natural law—in particular, not preferring health to sickness and honor to contempt (510–15). That God is working for us in creatures he finds vain and fanciful (518). He rejects what Ignatius writes about identifying consolation through the interior movement that inflames the soul with love of God (520).

Certainly for Pedroche the spirituality of Ignatius and the Society of Jesus is questionable at best and Ignatian and Jesuit prayer are tainted from the start. Between 1554 and 1556 Nadal will write a line-by-line refutation of Pedroche's "Censure."[7]

The End of the Society of Jesus

Ignatius did his best to convince his followers that action on behalf of the neighbor was holy and united them to God. Works withdrawing one from explicit attention to God, if undertaken out of love of God, not only were equivalent to the union and recollection of contemplation, but could be even more acceptable. To Father Emmanuel Godinho, rector in Coimbra, he wrote:

> My very dear brother in the Lord, . . . Regarding the charge of temporal affairs, although to some extent they may appear to be, and even are, distracting, I have no doubt that your right intention and the direction of all you do to the divine glory make your work spiritual and very pleasing

---

[7] See *PolChron* 3:503–24 and *EpistNadal* 4:820–73; some excerpts are in *Font.narr* 1:314–22.

to his infinite goodness. For distractions undertaken for his greater service and in conformity to his divine will interpreted by obedience not only can equal the union and recollection of deep contemplation, but may even be more acceptable as proceeding from a stronger and more fervent charity.[8]

Olivier Mannaerts, rector of the Roman College in 1553–54, reported that Ignatius instructed one man how to be united to God even in the midst of so-called distracting labors:

When one of Ours, whose name slips my mind, complained to him [Ignatius] that he was hindered from interior union with God by externs who frequently were calling him to the door, and that he was much distracted thereby, Ignatius replied: "When people come to see you for spiritual help or consolation, receive them with great charity; but after you have been called, or while on the way, say some ejaculatory prayer, asking God that he may deign to help that soul through your instrumentality, and then give yourself completely to helping the visitor, and thus you will not be distracted uselessly, but will make great advancement. And if you do not feel yourself as united with God as before when you were alone, do not be disturbed on that account, for no distraction will do you harm that has been embraced for the glory of God. But if [the visitors] come just to pass the time of day or talk about useless things, prudently introduce into the conversation thoughts on death, on the enormity of sin, on offending God, on the judgment, hell, examination of conscience and confession, etc., and whenever they come back, talk about these subjects. If they want to be helped, they will come back to get some profit from you; if they do not want to be helped, they will leave you in peace and will not return any more to trouble you."[9]

If some religious were disturbed that the Society set aside monastic practices traditionally regarded as essential to religious life, so did some Jesuits. They clung to them fiercely, fought for them desperately. Twenty years after the founding of the Society, Father General Laínez received many letters protesting that Bustamante, provincial of Betica (Andalusía), was introducing practices from other orders that were alien to the Society. He told the rigorous provincial to cut back on common penances and to reduce the two hours of prayer each day by half. He explained to Busta-

---

[8] *EpistIgn* 4:127. The letter, dated January 31, 1552, goes on to advise that if, nevertheless, looking only to the greater glory of God, Godinho still judges that temporal affiars are distracting, he should refer the matter to his superiors.

[9] "Responsio P. Manarei ad quædam Lancicii postulata," *Scripta de Sancto Ignatio de Loyola*, MHSI no. 20 (Madrid: 1904) 1:515 f. Mannaerts or Manareus (1523–1614), known as the father of the Belgian Province, studied in Louvain, was ordained in 1546, entered the Society in 1550, was named rector of the new college in Loreto in 1554; subsequently he served as provincial of France, assistant for Germany, visitor of the northern provinces, and provincial of Belgium (*Font.narr* 1:602, no. 42). Nadal describes the same Ignatian technique of getting rid of troublesome visitors in his "De ministerio verbi Dei" (*EpistNadal* 4:663 f.).

mante that requiring prayer in common had been rejected by the First General Congregation, which had judged that members of the Society needed to be men who found it fruitful to pray by themselves. Laínez also gently responded to a suggestion from Bustamante that the time might come when prisons could be of some help to recalcitrant subjects, in accordance with the practice in some monasteries, asserting that up to the present the Society had found no need of them.[10]

The considerations on the Call of the King and the Two Standards reveal the personal love for the Risen Lord that animates the Society of Jesus, that drives its members to work tirelessly out of love for all those for whom Jesus died. The Society's end is the end that Jesus had and still has today. Although religious orders and congregations do not differ so much by the end they seek as by the way they seek it, reflecting on the end helps to bring out some of the nuances in the approach of a particular group. In the *General Examen* Ignatius discusses the Society's end:

> The end of this Society is to devote itself *with God's grace* not only to the salvation and perfection of the members' own souls, but also *with that same grace* to labor strenuously *[intensamente]* in giving aid toward the salvation and perfection of the souls of their neighbors.[11]

The word *intensamente* reflects the Ignatian emphasis on *magis* (more) in the Spiritual Exercises, the call to be outstanding *(insignis)* in the following of Christ. The underlined words were added at the suggestion of Alfonso Salmerón, one of the First Companions, at the gathering of the fathers who pondered the Ignatian drafts of the *General Examen* and the *Constitutions* in 1551–52.[12] That God is the one who brings the work of the Society to fruition is a theme that was deep in the hearts of all of the First Companions.

The all-embracing end of the Society reaches out to include not only God but everyone on the face of the earth: heretics, non-believers, self, and everyone else—all in perfect love of God and neighbor and the practice of all the virtues. To fulfill that end demands the fullest application of the spirit of service and requires an immense range in the variety of works.

Exhortations in Spain

"Exhort. 1554 hisp." (*CommInst* 38–53, no. 9–34)

Nadal comments on this brief statement in the *Constitutions* over and over again. As we noted in our second chapter, during Nadal's first

---

[10] *EpistLain* vol. 4 *passim,* esp. 579; *CommInst* 57 f.

[11] *ConsCN, C: 3* (p. 24), emphasis added.

[12] *Constitutiones* 1:391, no. 1.

visit to Spain in 1554 he begins his first exhortation by reflecting on the nature of religion and religious orders. When he comes to the Society, he reflects, first of all, on Ignatius: how God called him when he was convalescing, "giving him above all to desire with great devotion the greater honor and glory of the Divine Majesty" (*CommInst* 38, no. 9). He notes that Ignatius uses the latter phrase repeatedly in the *Constitutions,* and concludes that all in the Society should commit themselves "to internalize this spirit of seeking and procuring the greater service and glory of God our Lord, whether lecturing or preaching or eating or whatever we are doing" (39, no. 9). From the Spiritual Exercises he received at Manresa, Ignatius understood his purpose or end in life to which he should devote all his energy, "and that is now the purpose of the Society" (40, no. 3). In the second exhortation he asks what the end of the Society is; replying to his own question, the reflective theologian breaks out and says even more than Ignatius explicitly said in the General Examen:

> The greatest of all: the salvation and perfection of souls *for the greater glory of God.* For this is our end toward which we strive, imitating Christ, not only through prayer but through work, using whatever is seen to help for that purpose, and we do this out of divine love. This constitutes the essence of the Society, and so Father Ignatius says that we should attend to the salvation and progress of souls "strenuously." (52 f., no. 3, with Nadal's addition italicized)

In comparing and contrasting the members of the Society with Christ, Nadal stumbles a bit in expressing himself, noting that Christ labored for us rather than for himself, while "we, on the other hand, seek first our own salvation and perfection and then the salvation and perfection of our neighbor" (53, no. 3). His words suggest a temporal sequence or a priority of self over neighbor, but a moment later any sense of priority disappears:

> Father Ignatius says "strenuously," that is, with fervor. Note the way of seeking the end, not remissly, but with a lively and strong desire even of dying for our neighbor, after the example of Christ, to the glory of God, and let this be our consolation. Wherefore, brothers, let us strive toward this end by every way that divine love can serve, and it should move us in such a way that we always seem to have accomplished little. We ought to feel this way, that we cannot bear not to have used every means possible for the salvation of the neighbor for whom Christ died. (53, no. 4)

In another exhortation given during his 1554 trip to Spain, Nadal draws some consequences for prayer that suggest the need to be contemplative even in the midst of action:

> All must try hard in the Lord, walking the path of prayer and the spiritual life, to find God in all their occupations and ministries, walking the way of the spirit only, habituating themselves to stir their hearts and find devotion

in all things, and to make use of the treasury of thoughts, of prayer, and of the habit of prayer in all their ministries, as much as the fragility of our nature will allow.[13]

In this way one familiar with God must see to it that the taste for prayer does not cool him down or divert him from the fervent pursuit of the end of his vocation or the means necessary for it, such as studies or anything done under obedience. He should make his prayer and the sensible devotion arising from it extend to the ministries to which he is called, and he should enter upon them with prayer or union or the feelings that remain in him from prayer. ("Orden," 490, no. 15)

Notes on the Examen

"In exam. annot.," 1557 (*CommInst* 139–45, nos. 12–33; 199, nos. 184–89)

In 1557 Nadal finds no tension between our salvation and that of others. He suggests adding to his remarks on the end of the Society the statement in the Formula of the Institute that the Society was founded especially for the defense and the propagation of the faith and the advancement of souls. This perspective reveals that a perfect end is proposed to the Society through the grace of Jesus Christ, and this end determines the nature and perfection of the Institute (*CommInst* 139, no. 12). Like Ignatius, the whole Society repeats in all its writings, words, and actions that Jesuits are to strive for the greater glory, honor, and service of God. Everything concerning the end of the Society both in the Examen and in the Formula of the Institute relates to this principle. The vocation and special grace of the Society are not satisfied by seeking only the glory of God, but by always longing for God's greater glory, constantly striving for the perfection of divine honor and love with spiritual joy and courage in Christ Jesus (139, no. 13).

Nadal concludes that the heavenly Father has established for the Society the very same end that he prescribed for his only-begotten Son in his incarnation, life, death, and resurrection. For the greater glory of his eternal Father, the Son sought out the sheep of the house of Israel that were lost, the salvation and perfection of souls, out of the plenitude and perfection of divine love. This attention to the salvation and perfection of souls out of a certain fullness and perfection of divine love in union with Christ Jesus is the Society's end also.[14] He writes:

---

[13] "Orden de la oración," in *Regulæ Societatis Iesu,* Dionysius Fernández Zapico, S.I., ed., vol. 4 of *Constitutiones et Regulæ Societatis Iesu,* MHSI no. 71 (Rome: 1948), 490, no. 1; a note on the manuscript written in Nadal's hand reads, "An instruction that Fr. Nadal gave the first time he visited Spain."

[14] *CommInst* 139 f., nos. 14 f. Ovey Mohammed expresses this idea well in

Therefore, we do not place the perfection of our state of life in contemplation and prayer, and help our neighbor by these alone, sitting in our cells and monasteries, which monastic life has done very well. But since divine love urges us to love our neighbor as ourselves, . . . we strive for our own salvation and that of our neighbor at the same time *[simul]*, not by prayer and sacrifice alone, but by all the other ministries through which someone can be spiritually helped. (140, no. 16)

Nadal's experience in the Roman Curia at the side of Ignatius taught him that the multiplicity of neighbors requires the Society to make choices in ministry, just as Jesus made choices in ministry, choosing especially the poor, the sick, the outcast, and sinners, while not avoiding the rich, the learned, and the powerful. The Society cannot help everyone, not even everyone who asks for help.

And as we understand from the nature of mission in Part VII of the *Constitutions,* in fact from almost all the *Constitutions,* the Society particularly strives to help those people who for lack of ministers are being lost or are in danger of being lost; whence it comes about that out of the fullness and perfection of divine love this end was given to the Society by the heavenly Father. (140, no. 17)

Continuing on its original course of making decisions out of discerning love for the greater glory of God, the Society on the eve of the third millennium expressed its concern for the poor, the marginalized, the abandoned.[15]

Part VII of the *Constitutions* contains norms for discerning choices. The wider the field and the greater the zeal, the more the need for discerning in love the greater glory of God. Reflecting on the Society's mission from the Father that shares in the mission of the Son, Nadal reveals how wide the field is for Jesuits and how great the need for discerning love. He insists that Jesuits must undertake the work of salvation truly, seriously, vigorously, fervently, and in a spirit of divine love, using every skill, every device, every ministry that can help the neighbor. They should seek the salvation of souls in every spiritual ministry, especially through preaching and the explanation of Scripture and every other ministry of the divine word, through the Spiritual Exercises, through instructing children and the uninitiated in Christianity, through administering the sacraments, through reconciling those who are quarreling, through visiting those detained in prison or confined to a hospital and intervening on their behalf, not to mention working with students in the colleges. In brief, there is nothing that can help the neighbor out of love that is not proper to the Institute (*CommInst* 140 f., nos. 18–20). The Society's end

---

"Hinduism and Ignatian Spirituality," 120.

[15] *DocsGC34,* esp. 60–66 (pp. 43–45).

has no limits and demands total disponibility.[16] They cannot, however, allow what is good to impede what is greater.

The perfection of divine love demands that the Society seek not only the salvation but also the perfection of the neighbor, for the same desire, the same zeal, and the same passionate love should move its members toward their own salvation and their neighbor's (141, no. 22). Linking a Jesuit's salvation and perfection with that of the neighbor means that much of his salvation and perfection lies in helping others (142, no. 25). Thus, when superiors mission someone to a ministry, the one sent should be confident that the greatest profit will come to him through his ministry to others. This is the Society's call, and the grace of the Institute properly leads and assists one to this (143, no. 26).

When he entered the Society, Nadal recalls, Ignatius suggested that he devote himself to preaching and working for others, but he excused himself because of his sins and incompetence and unworthiness. "In this way you will progress," Ignatius remarked, "if you attend to the salvation of others" (143, no. 26). No one, relying on his own judgment that he is imperfect or inept or exposed to danger, should feel depressed or hesitate to serve his neighbor; but if, after opening his conscience to the superior, he is nevertheless missioned to a work, let him undertake it with great courage and confident hope. By the grace of Jesus Christ that he bestows on his Society, he will be in no danger, but will advance rapidly in perfection, provided he follows the Society's approach to ministry and does not fail to rekindle his ardor at the proper times through prayer (143, no. 27).

The Society uses the Latin word *intense* (strenuously), Nadal explains, for the driving force of the Society is intense and passionate zeal and love, which should always redound to the benefit of the neighbor. This is the unique mark of the Institute, the whole raison d'être of this new religious order: that its members aim at the salvation and perfection of the neighbor out of perfect divine love, with their whole heart, mind, soul, and strength, in profound joy and consolation. By reason of the Institute, not only are they concerned with prayer and sacrifices, with preaching and the sacraments, but they also enfold all works and every ministry in one huge embrace of divine love—all this with the approbation and approval of the Church (143, no. 28).

In an appendix to his 1557 notes on the *Examen,* however, Nadal suggests a tension between the greater glory of God and the salvation of souls. He identifies striving for the greater glory of God in everything as the Society's sole or unparalleled end *(finis unicus).* Flowing from the greater glory of God and subordinate to it is the salvation and perfection of souls (199, no. 184). Jesus had faced the same problem. Answering the question, "Which commandment in the law is the greatest?" Jesus replied,

---

[16] Sanz de Diego, "La novedad," 924.

" 'You shall love the Lord your God with all your heart. . . .' And a second is like it: 'You shall love your neighbor as yourself' " (Matt. 22:36–39). By naming two commandments when asked for one, Jesus indicated that to keep one meant keeping the other.

Exhortations in Coimbra

"Pláticas espirituales en Coimbra," 1561 (1ª-20ª, nos. 37–210)

Nadal sets out in the opening exhortation at Coimbra to make clear, as we have already seen in chapter 4, that in Jesuit life three principles are at work: Everything is to be done *spiritu* (in the depths of the spirit), *corde* (in the intimacy of the heart), and *practice* (in a practical manner). Even before discussing the nature and end of the Society, he has this to say regarding prayer: "Meditation and contemplation ought to be done in a practical manner *[practice]*, that is, in such a way that they expand into work and reach fruit in execution, unconcerned about purely speculative matters" (*Pláticas espirituales* 1ª, 44, no. 13). After that salvo he is willing to lay down the foundation for making it:

> It was to help our neighbor that God wanted us to be religious. It is not sufficient to help him in my room. I have to work. Can it be enough to contemplate that God came into the world to die for souls, and not help them earnestly myself? By no means, no. I ought to die in labor, and go from one place to another to hear confessions, as many of the Society would go long distances. (4ª, 75, no. 13)

As prayer leads to action, so action leads to prayer.[17] Work for God and work for neighbor are one stream. Nadal continues:

> In this way our perfection increases; no increase comes from praying without doing something more, advancing our neighbor and gaining souls that are being lost. Our perfection goes in a circle; with perfection gained in prayer and spiritual exercises to help our neighbor, and from that to gain more perfection in prayer to help our neighbor more. (4ª, 75 f., no. 14)

A tendency in Spain at this time was to look upon prayer as an end rather than a means, so that perfection did not consist in the practice of virtue but in passing long hours in prayer and penance.[18]

Despite the multiplicity of the Society's works, one of the characters in Nadal's "Dialog" maintains in a burst of enthusiasm that the Society might add still more. Ignatius, he said, right from the beginning of his call, was so inflamed with the principle of always seeking the greater service and glory of God and with the fire of divine love that he always strove to

---

[17] See Hostie, "Cycle of Activity," 153–65. See also Christian De Deckere, S.J., "Mystique trinitaire et action apostolique selon Jérôme Nadal," *Christus* 39 (1992): 102–12.

[18] Aicardo, *Comentario* 2:388.

do what was better and more perfect, no matter where the Spirit led him.[19]

Exhortations in Alcalá (1561)

CommInst 220–488

Nadal develops the idea of the circle of prayer and action more fully in exhorting his Jesuit brothers in Alcalá in 1561, but he takes his time in doing so. He first reflects on the words of the *General Examen* describing the end of the Society and concludes: "God is our end. He pours out his love upon us in order to unite us to himself. This love reveals to us our duties. The object of love is God, and our neighbor for the sake of God" (*CommInst* 306, no. 73). It is not enough, however, to work for the love of God, according to Nadal; we also need "to seek for more and reach out farther, to the greater glory of God, the greater love of God," and to do so with fervor. This *magis* is the distinctive mark of the Institute.[20]

Nadal is so clear and insistent in Alcalá in 1561 that one wonders if he is facing a community whose mentality is in need of conversion, especially one that still favored monastic practices so that the members might feel and seem to be "religious." He tells them emphatically:

> The Society was not made for itself alone: for this end there was no need of it; the Society would not have come into existence. Prayer and solitude without external means to help souls were proper for monastic orders or for hermits, but not for the Society. Whoever wants prayer and solitude all the time, whoever likes a hidden corner and getting away from human beings and from dealing with them to their profit, does not have our calling; for such a one there are the Carthusians and other orders of monks who live in their monasteries and have this end and vocation. (324, no. 83)

He insists that a life for others demands profound internal asceticism:

> Do not fool yourselves. Let no one think that in the Society God helps him for himself alone. . . . Learning, skill, virtue, talent for preaching or hearing confessions, for giving the Spiritual Exercises, for conversing, for lecturing, and other graces of God—do not take pride in these, brother. These gifts are not for yourself alone, but in order that with them you may advance the welfare of souls. It is for this end, and the end of our vocation as well, that God gives them. If you seek them for yourself alone, they will not be given to you either, for you would be failing the Institute, failing your permanent covenant with God. Thus, you should not be surprised if you should lack the helps usually given to others in the Society. You have to

---

[19] "Dialogus II, 1562–2565" (*CommInst* 662, no. 42)

[20] "Exhort. 3ᵃ" (308, no. 74). See especially a version corrected by Nadal in 1576 to put it more emphatically: "in everything to seek the greater glory and praise of God" (ibid., 309, no. 74*).

join one end with the other, your own progress with that of the neighbor, so as never to separate our two functions from each other. (326, no. 84)

He describes the experience of one called to work simultaneously for personal salvation and the neighbor's as well, reverting to the vocabulary of a former chaplain in a military camp:

So I am in the house a little, and there I help myself in prayer and other exercises belonging to the Society. Here I arm myself to go out and fight evil spirits and sins. And then I go out to talk to a student, hear a confession, preach, or perform other ministry for the benefit of other people. In this ministry I try to make progress, to move him to the love of God and to change his life. . . . And thus, since I have worked in the service of God, I am more disposed to make progress when I come to prayer, and also as regards the other exercises that are for my own advancement. From this greater profit to myself, there is born a desire to work with greater zeal, with purer intention for the glory of God our Lord, with more fruit to souls and greater love. (326–28, no. 85)

In these ideas Nadal touches on another element of Jesuit prayer. Prayer that inclines to the apostolate extends into the work itself and leads the worker back to prayer. A huge gulf between a life of prayer and a life of action is unthinkable. Prayer must close the gap to make one enveloping circle.

This is the circle in the Society's ministries that I often mention. Because you help your neighbor and thus serve God, God gives you more help at home in your prayer and other occupations, and this greater help enables you later to work for your neighbor with more zeal and with greater profit. So there is mutual help of one exercise for another. And the sum result of it is that one goes ahead from good to better in the increase of virtue, in the service of God, in seeking more every day the glory of the eternal goodness, which is the end of our vocation and Institute. May the Lord give us this grace. Amen. (328, no. 85)

In these words Nadal indicates a life that goes far beyond alternating periods of prayer and work. Mutual causality of prayer and the apostolate demands an interior penetration of work by prayer and of prayer by the needs of souls. Not only does prayer ready us for the apostolate but it drives both men and women to undertake it, and the apostolate in turn throws them to their knees; from that prayer they will rise with greater humility and with even greater zeal and love. Their work has affected their prayer; will not prayer flow through all their work?

In the next exhortation Nadal tells the community, "The Society is not looking for men of leisure with their hands in their laps, tepid, slow to achieve the purpose of their call. . . . The grace of the Lord helps us to undertake the ministries of the Society with fervor, with intense eagerness, with the vigor of love" (337, no. 97).

In the preceding year, when Nadal wrote his *Scholia* or interpretations of the *Constitutions,* he explained that the superior general (and each member of the Society, too) should be a person always united to God. Then he went on to offer the following comments:

> What is meant is not only union in prayer, which is a much inferior virtue to love; but two unions are intended here, one of love, which contains the union of faith and hope, the other of prayer, which under this one general word embraces the full realization and practice of the spiritual life, and in this state all things are known and judged in a spiritual way and brought to execution in a spiritual way *[spiritualiter]. (NadSchol* 244)

Prayer Especially for Members of the Society

"Orationis ratio," 1560s (*EpistNadal* 4:672–81)

Nadal introduces his subject by stating that the Society embraces and teaches the kind of prayer that flows from its Spiritual Exercises, which have been singularly efficacious (*EpistNadal* 4:672). One of the special graces of the Exercises is a sense of one's vocation, bringing peace and union with God in following the way one has to go to God. The beginning and the end of prayer is love of God and zeal for souls (673). In this context Nadal says: "Feelings and affections arising from prayer that incline one to unnecessary recollection and solitude do not suggest prayer proper to the Society, which rather inclines one to discharge one's vocation and ministry, and especially to perfect obedience according to our Institute" (673). Not only does prayer lead to action, it penetrates across the threshold of the apostolate and permeates the entire action. Not only is there a connection between prayer and action, but a vital union of the two, the same spirit vivifying both. Action has become a prolongation of prayer; or, to put it in another way, prayer prolongs itself in and through action.

> And thus the prayer proper to the Society is that which extends to the exercise of vocal prayer and permeates into every exercise of the ministries of the Society; so that, as far as can be obtained by the grace of Jesus Christ, the illumination of the intellect and good affection of the will and union persists in, accompanies, and guides all our operations, in such a way that God our Lord is found in everything, "and the remainders of the thought shall keep holiday to the Lord."[21]

---

[21] Nadal often refers to these words from the psalm verse in the Vulgate: "Reliquiæ cogitationis diem festum agent tibi," translated in the Douay version as "and the remainders of the thought keep holiday to thee" (Ps. 75:11). The Latin version used by Nadal is a loose but felicitous quotation from the Vulgate or a quotation from some other Latin translation, with the numbering drawn from the Septuagint. The Latin translation is far from the Hebrew reading (numbered Ps. 76:10), which is obscure and its meaning controversial, and far from contemporary English translations as well; for

Only love can extend prayer into ministry. Nadal's explanation utterly destroys another Spanish error of the times; namely, that exterior works are less reliable and meritorious than meditation, penance, and prayers; that preaching, study, and other works done for the service of God are not religious but merely profane occupations; that one should withdraw from them to the quiet of contemplation.[22] With forceful brevity Nadal sums up the whole matter in his talk on the prayer of the Society: "Action springing from love united to God is action that is perfect" (679). In "The Society's Way of Proceeding," written during this same period, Nadal states that members of the Society "should avail themselves of the divine power, always to work in the Lord, to abide in him, to move and live in the Spirit" (*EpistNadal* 4:616, no. 15). They "should never be at their ease; but when they have no spiritual occupations in their churches or houses, they should find someone to win to Jesus Christ, always keeping the end of the Society in a very dynamic way in their minds and hearts" (616, no. 17). Not an activist, Nadal proclaims a depth of spirit that is not afraid of the world. He thus concludes his remarks on the prayer of the Society: "In these ministries they should find God in peace and quiet, applying themselves interiorly, filled with light, joy and contentment, on fire with the love of God; and thus they must find the same in all other ministries, even exterior ones" (681).

"Keep holiday to the Lord" recalls Paul's admonition, "Be filled with the Spirit as you sing psalms and hymns and spiritual songs among yourselves, singing and making melody to the Lord in your hearts" (Eph. 5:18 f.). Nadal highlights the role of consolation that continues after prayer. What stays with a person after prayer should make one sing throughout the day, should accompany and guide and delight the apostle at work, so that God is found in everything. Illumined by Light and set on fire by Love, one can see beyond appearances to the reality of things in Christ: see them with the eyes of Christ, treat them with the love of Christ and in the manner of Christ, walk in the Spirit of Christ. Much later in life he wrote again in his journal: "We should renew our acts of faith, hope, and love daily, so that these three virtues together might vitalize all our actions. Through them God will place in the heart a strong and gentle light in Christ, and the power of love will prevail."[23]

---

example, "Let all who are around him bring gifts to the one who is awesome" (NRSV).

[22] Aicardo, *Comentario* 2:389.

[23] *Orat.observ* 295, no. 964.

Fifth, Sixth, and Seventh Exhortations (1573–1576)

CommInst 804–65

Nadal himself provides both summary and conclusion to his reflections on the end of the Society.[24] He insists on that marvelous blending in which concern for one's own salvation becomes one with concern for the salvation of the neighbor. Here is the heart of the matter, the point that yields the special charism of the Society, the point whose special emphasis gives the Society its characteristic and distinctive note. Addressing the passage in the General Examen on the end of the Society, Nadal writes as follows:

> In these words . . . is the whole nucleus of the Society; here all our thought should be centered, for . . . the grace of the Society and of our vocation is not only useful for our neighbor by way of example, along with prayers and sacrifices, as is true of almost all the monastic orders; but . . . all that we have received from God—grace, doctrine, spirit, faculties, virtues, skill, all our gifts, all our ministries of the Society and all its parts—have one identical end, to be useful for ourselves and for our neighbor. For all that we have received from God we have received to employ in the salvation and perfection of our neighbor; we know that the Society was instituted for no other reason. Alas, then, for us if we strive only for our own salvation! That is not our grace; that is not our vocation. It is a good occupation, indeed, but not ours" (*Orat.observ* 807 f., nos. 7 f.).

Here Nadal confuses what Jesuits do with how they do it. What he sees as distinctively Jesuit is really distinctively Christian. None of the members of the Body of Christ can be concerned only about their own salvation. Even hermits live in a constant tension between solitude and communion with others, in which solitude fosters communion and communion fosters solitude. The difference is entirely in the way Jesuits and hermits and Dominicans and Franciscans and others go about seeking their own salvation and the salvation of others.

A religious order is necessarily a way of seeking perfection; in the Society, however, personal growth is intimately bound up with assisting others to make progress. "You should not separate these two things," Nadal says, "sometimes helping your neighbor without helping yourself; for both things must be attained, and they must be done at the same time. . . . This is what we mean when we say 'with the same grace'" (*CommInst* 808, no. 8). What helps personal spiritual growth contributes also to

---

[24] Here we have a set of exhortations in Nadal's hand after he had retired: 1ᵃ–4ᵃ are missing, 5ᵃ is a long fragment (804–19), 6ᵃ is complete (820–65), 7ᵃ is a tiny fragment (865); if any others follow, they are missing. The date of composition is uncertain, possibly between 1573 and 1576; perhaps Nadal began them in Rome, but for the most part they were written during Nadal's retirement at the Jesuit college in Hall, not far from Innsbruck. See the editor's remarks in *CommInst* 801–3.

the neighbor's welfare, and what helps the neighbor contributes to personal spiritual growth. His conclusion rolls on inevitably: "Therefore, there should be nothing either interior or exterior with which we can help ourselves that we do not earnestly put to the service of our neighbor, and nothing useful for our neighbor that we do not take up eagerly" (809, no. 9). Discernment is always necessary, of course, to determine what concrete action to undertake. Engaging in exterior works, even to the neighbor's profit, can destroy the contemplative call to solitude to the detriment of the Christian and secular communities. So also Nadal warns Jesuits that if they feel some attraction to prayer or the exercise of some virtue, and "recognize that it is calling you away from the tendency to help your neighbor, judge that it is not a good spirit but alien to your vocation" (809, no. 9).

Well trained by Ignatius, Nadal is aware that excess in devotion is possible, but not excess in love. When he points out the principle of balance between prayer and the apostolate, it does not lie in favor of solitary prayer.

> From what I have said, it follows that if you sometimes feel there would be some profit in prayer or the exercise of the virtues or interior recollection, and you recognize that [this thought] withdraws you from the tendency to help your neighbor, conclude that that is not the good spirit and that it is in opposition to your vocation. . . . Our vocation is very practical; all our spiritual exercises are practical; all of them inculcate in us zeal for our neighbor, turn our thoughts to him, carry us to him; he should be our food, our spiritual drink. (809, nos. 9 f.).

In these words Nadal in no way attacks those who live a purely contemplative life. Since he addresses members of an "apostolic" order, he supposes they will respond in a particular way to Christ's death for our salvation. He is aware that others respond to the redemption in other ways. Love for Christ that does not include love of neighbor would be a strange sort of love. (Had the ideal of love of neighbor become obscured in the contemplative orders with which Nadal was familiar?) But for some of those persons not called to the Society, zeal for souls demands a deeper and deeper solitude, an almost total withdrawal from creatures to cast oneself on God in order to win through prayers and penance graces for the souls for whom Christ gave his life. Without persons like this, something would be lacking in the Mystical Body of Christ. For a Jesuit the response to the redemptive act of Christ must be a desire to labor directly in the vineyard.

In the final fragment of the final exhortation, Nadal returns to where this chapter began. He expresses the hope that his brothers have heard his message and taken it to heart, and concludes, "Our highest end is the Divinity itself, the Trinity, blessed above all. Another end follows upon this one, joining it perfectly: divine love infused into our hearts through the Holy Spirit who is given to us" (865, citing Rom. 5:5). All along he has been talking about sharing Trinitarian life. After twice saying that God sent his Son out of love for us, John remarks, "No one has ever seen God; if we love one another, God lives in us, and his love is perfected in us" (1 John 4). When the love of God for us impels us to love our neighbor, God's love is brought to perfection. Thus the perfection of self and the perfection of our neighbor converge in the Blessed Trinity.

Even so, in this period toward the end of his life, Nadal does not hesitate to chide Jesuits on falling far short of their own ideals. In his *Meditations on the Gospels* he writes:

> Don't we follow and embrace sensible things? . . . In that we seem like the Pharisees; for we receive the commands, admonitions, precepts, and government of our superiors as if they were men and had no connection with God. For we hardly ever contemplate Christ commanding and warning and governing in the superior. Pardon me? Do we not often, and even more than often, recite our office or the Our Father with our lips only, while in our hearts we are dumb or stupid or wandering? Or do we not do these things in a speculative manner only, not a practical one? And does this not happen to us when we lecture on Scripture or study theology, or when we discourse on matters divine or touching on morals and religious discipline?[25]

Conclusion

The heart of the Jesuit vocation has led to the heart of Jesuit prayer. The prayer proper to the Society focuses not on self, one's personal musings, obsessions, attractions, needs, desires for self-growth; it focuses, rather, on the salvation and perfection of others to the greater glory of God. It imitates the prayer of Christ, attends to the concerns of Christ, adopts the perspectives of Christ. It is imbued with love of Christ and with love of those for whom he died; it is action-oriented, intensely, passionately, enthusiastically. In the words of Vatican II, its "final norm" is Christ as "put before us in the Gospel." For this reason the fathers of General Congregation 34 were able to write with enthusiasm about the work that flows from prayer:

> When understood in the light of the faith which seeks justice, the criterion of "greater need" points toward places or situations of serious injustice; the criterion of "more fruitful," towards ministry which can be more effective in creating communities of solidarity; the criterion of "more universal,"

---

[25] Jerónimo Nadal, S.J., *Adnotationes et meditationes in Evangelia* . . . (Antwerp: 1594–95), 156.

towards action which contributes to structural change to create a society more based on shared responsibility.[26]

All the preceding reveals more clearly the transformation that took place in the heart of Ignatius when he interrupted his penitential pilgrimage to Jerusalem so that he could spend time in prayer at Montserrat and especially at Manresa. He left Loyola bent on a self-centered life of penance in competition with the saints. At Manresa he not only discovered his disordered affections but saw all things new, so that his desire for self-punishment changed to a desire to win souls to the love of Christ. That transformation provides a better understanding of what motivated him and the companions who joined him in Paris in the determination to make a pilgrimage to the Holy Land, and clarifies what they wanted to do there.

Although all of the chapters in this book so far have been reflecting on the role of Ignatius and his influence on the Society of Jesus, those still to come will take a closer look at how his personal experiences became the pattern for Jesuit novices (chap. 7), students (chap. 8), and those with final vows (chap. 9), all within the grander pattern of Jesus who is the "final norm" and "the supreme rule for all who are Christians."

---

[26] "Our Mission and Justice," in *DocsGC34* 71 (p. 47).

Chronicle for Chapter 7

This matter needs close attention, and if you have to send somebody here [to Spain and Portugal], . . . I doubt that there is anyone who could accomplish more, or with more commitment and freedom, than Father Nadal, who knows the temperament *[humores]* of this place, and is held in great respect and reverence.

—Bartolomé de Bustamante to Father General Laínez

Nadal's Life and Travels (1562)

1562

Jan. 3: Leaves Alcalá

Jan. 5–10: Segovia

Jan. 11–16: Avila

Jan. 17–29: Salamanca

Jan. 30–Feb. 3: Medina del Campo

Feb. 5–7: Valladolid

Feb. 9–10: Segovia

Feb. 12–March 10: At Alcalá appoints officials, buys two mules, leaves for Saragossa

March 19–April 2: At Saragossa meets Domènech; reunited with Jiménez, who had visited his family

April 6: Leaves Saragossa, comes to Ayerbe; joins with traders who have arquebuses to defend against robbers; goes to Jaca and then to Canfranc on French border

April 8: Leaves Canfranc for Olorón, where he and his companion leave the traders

April 11: Leaves for Toulouse, eats in Pau, meets heretics who threaten them, stays overnight in Tarbes

April 13–20: At Toulouse meets Jesuits expelled from Pamiers by heretics

Between April 20–29: Near Rabastens, falls into hands of armed Calvinists;

arrives at Rodez; leaves for Lyon on April 26; at Lavoutte detours to Billom

Until May 28: At Billom receives fugitives from Tournon, goes on to Moulins with Broët

May 28–June 9: Meets Laínez and Polanco, visits college, shows Laínez exhortations

June 9: Goes to San Quentin, Cambrai

June 13: Arrives at Tournai (15 days); visits college

June 28: Leaves for Antwerp, buys books for Rome

June 30: Arrives at Louvain, meets Mercurian, visits college on July 13; continues on to Cologne and Trier

August 10: days in springs at Liége

September: Mainz, Frankfurt, Mainz

Oct. 7: Wurzburg

Oct. 17: Augsburg

To Nov. 17: Ingolstadt (11 days); returns to Augsburg

Until Dec. 15: Passes through Landsberg, visits Innsbruck (20–22 days); sets out for Salzburg

Dec. 15–Feb. 10: At Trent with Laínez, Polanco, Salmerón

Chapter Seven

IGNATIUS: MODEL OF THE SOCIETY'S GRACE

> It is for the good of the Church that institutes have their own proper characters and functions. Therefore the spirit and aims of each founder should be faithfully accepted and retained, as indeed should each institute's sound traditions, for all these constitute the patrimony of an institute.
>
> Vatican II, *On the Up-to-Date Renewal of the Religious Life*

E ven though Ignatius kept polishing the *Constitutions* until the end of his life, by the time Nadal went to Spain in 1553 to promulgate it, Ignatius had given that document its basic form, expressing clearly his mind on "the spirit and aims" of the Society of Jesus. One of Nadal's tasks was to lay a foundation for developing the "Institute's sound traditions" as a "patrimony" for those who came later. In 1995 General Congregation 34, in its decree *Conclusion: Characteristics of Our Way of Proceeding,* recognized as part of that patrimony the continuity of grace that has spanned 450 years of Jesuit life:

> In remorse, gratitude, and astonishment—but above all with passionate love—first Ignatius and then every Jesuit after him has turned prayerfully to "Christ our Lord hanging on the cross before me" and has asked of himself, "What have I done for Christ? What am I doing for Christ? What must I do for Christ?" The questions well up from a heart profoundly moved by gratitude and love. This is the foundational grace that binds Jesuits to Jesus and to one another. (*DocsGC34* 538 [p. 236])

History

W hen Nadal entered the Society in 1545, Jean Codure was dead and the other Paris companions were scattered. Rodrigues was in Portugal, Xavier in India, Favre and Bobadilla in Germany, where, following the army, the latter was wounded in battle at Mühlberg. Broët was reconciling families in Faenza; Laínez and Salmerón were attending the Council of Trent; present there as well was Jay, who had declined the bishopric of Trieste, as had Bobadilla. Acceding to the benevolent request of Duke Francis Borgia, Ignatius sent two of Coimbra's graduates to Gandía, located on the

Gulf of Valencia on Spain's southeastern coast. They were Andrés de Oviedo and Francisco Onfroy, along with five scholastics from Rome, whose mission was to start a college for Jesuits and non-Jesuits alike.[1] In 1546 Francis Borgia vowed to enter the Society, a prize catch for the Ignatian fishing net; Pierre Favre, the first companion of Ignatius in Paris, died in Rome on his way to the Council of Trent, a precious loss; Ignatius made Portugal a province, naming Simón Rodrigues the first provincial in the Society's history, a sorry mistake. Picking up court gossip from Antonio Araoz that Philip II wished to make Borgia his majordomo, Ignatius obtained permission from Paul III in 1547 to profess a certain man whose name was to remain secret for three years while he settled his temporal affairs.[2] In the sweltering days of late July, Ignatius wrote to the community at Gandía inviting them to choose the one they thought most fit to be their rector; they unanimously chose Oviedo.[3] In September he named Antonio de Araoz the first provincial of Spain, the first to be professed in the Society after the original group.[4] That year Jerome Doménech, who had directed Nadal through the Exercises, died in Sicily.

As we have seen, characteristic of the new Society's way of proceeding was that its members did not chant the Divine Office in common, unlike the members of other religious orders. Crises regarding prayer, therefore, had been brewing in Spain and Portugal long before Ignatius selected Nadal to promulgate the *Constitutions* and to correct, admonish, and amend local practices that were aberrations from what Ignatius intended. At the newly erected Jesuit college in Gandía, the community meditated from 5 A.M. to 6 A.M. and from 9 P.M. to 10 P.M.[5] The combination of personalities there created an intricate tapestry of excessive prayer and penance and questionable mysticism, interwoven with complex roles and relationships, all compounded by the virtues and limitations of the principal actors.[6] The crisis reveals a tangle of tales going on simultaneously and well illustrates the confusion regarding prayer and penance in Spain and Portugal at that time. For clarity's sake, we here disentangle three distinct stories, one tale apiece for this chapter and the next two chapters.

---

[1] *PolChron* 1:164.

[2] Ibid., 250. It was Borgia on whose behalf Ignatius was requesting the permission.

[3] See *EpistIgn* 1:551–62 for the letter, and for the choice see 562 n. 14.

[4] *EpistIgn* 1:584–86 and 586–88; *Font.narr* 1:64*.

[5] *Epist.mixt* 1:437.

[6] Manuel Ruiz Jurado, S.J., gives this episode in the life of the Society a thorough treatment in "Un caso de profetismo reformista en la Compañía de Jesús— Gandía, 1547–1549," AHSI 43 (1974): 217–64.

The first of these revolves around Andrés de Oviedo, a Jesuit priest enamored of prayer and solitude, slated to become rector of the college at Gandía.[7] The second has as its protagonist Francisco Onfroy, a Jesuit scholastic about to be ordained, caught up in questionable mysticism. The third involves Francis Borgia, the duke of Gandía, about to become a Jesuit, and Antonio Araoz, about to be named Jesuit provincial of Spain, both addicted to lengthy prayers and excessive penances. Lurking in the shadows among the duke's attendants and firmly established as his spiritual confidant is Fray Juan de Tejeda, a Franciscan lay brother who longs to be a priest.[8]

Jerónimo Nadal met the Franciscan in 1546, when Tejeda came to Rome "in an attempt to obtain through the influence of the duke of Gandía . . . what he had not succeeded in obtaining from his own order: . . . to be ordained to the priesthood."[9] Nadal also noted that the duke

> thought very highly of him because of his outstanding reputation for devotion and his remarkable practice of contemplation. He exercised a great influence over Father Andrés de Oviedo and others among our men in Gandía, to the point where, through this monk's advice or example, they were spending many hours in prayer and, in order to be freer for this, eating nothing but a cheap bread soup called *gazpacho*. Duke Francis wrote letters to Ignatius recommending this man and his cause with great solicitude and urgency. . . . I took a disliking to this monk for circumventing the will of his own superiors and using the influence of outsiders.[10]

The Tale of the Reluctant Apostle

Andrés de Oviedo worked hard. He attended Eleonor, duchess of Gandía, in her long illness and heard her final confession before her death on March 27, 1546. A few weeks later he directed the duke through the Spiritual Exercises, and at the conclusion received Borgia's vow to enter the Society.[11] That spring Oviedo directed a dozen or more people through

---

[7] In a letter to Ignatius dated April 26, 1544, Araoz calls him a priest (*Epist.mixt* 1:163). According to Ruiz Jurado he was a priest when he entered the Society on June 19, 1541 ("Un caso de profetismo," 226 n. 49, citing ARSI, *Aragon. 15*, f. 22ʳ.)

[8] The Franciscan renewal, begun in the fifteenth century and intensified in the first half of the sixteenth, was centered in Tejeda's home province of Extremadura (Candido de Dalmases, S.J., *Francis Borgia, Grandee of Spain, Jesuit, Saint* [St. Louis: The Institute of Jesuit Sources, 1991], 66). Not lost upon his followers was Francis of Assisi's practice of frequently retiring to a hermitage.

[9] "Chronicon," in *EpistNadal* 1:25. For an English version of this, see Martin E. Palmer, S.J., *Studies in the Spirituality of Jesuits*, 24, no. 5 (November 1992): 44 f.

[10] Ibid. Note that Nadal employs the word "monk" loosely; strictly speaking, Franciscans are known as "friars."

[11] *Sanctus Franciscus Borgia, quartus Gandiæ dux et Societatis Iesu præpositus*

the Exercises, and took great delight in renewing his vows on the Ascension.[12] Diego Miró, former rector of Coimbra, commented, "Master Andrés is a saint."[13] But even saints can lose their balance.

Appointed rector, Oviedo reported in a series of letters to Ignatius: he was withdrawing from preaching, hearing confessions, and so on; instead, he spent more time with the community and many hours each day with Borgia. Thoughts of working with people stirred a "contrary spirit" within him. He longed to be alone in an out-of-the-way place, had enjoyed some quiet days in a hermitage, and believed that the professed should spend a month or so each year in a desert place (*Epist.mixt* 1:422–25). He and Onfroy had talked about spending seven years in the desert or some place of solitude in prayer and contemplation. St. Francis said that superiors should not deny permission to practice the eremitical life. At the end of this letter, he asked for permission (467–72), including a note from Onfroy, who admitted to an earlier desire of going to the desert. He sometimes wished that Jesuit priests had the same rhythm of prayer, solitude, and working for the neighbor as did Francis and his companions, for there was "much deception" in preaching and hearing confessions, etc. If Ignatius recognized the will of God for him in that life, he would be delighted to go to the desert (473 f.). The "contrary spirit" in Oviedo was an angel of darkness appearing as an angel of light moving him contrary to his call, and the "deception" in Onfroy was to consider his priestly work contaminating to the spirit. Both missed the full meaning of the Incarnation!

Before Ignatius replied, Borgia secretly made his solemn profession as a Jesuit (three years before ordination, the first to be solemnly professed after Araoz).[14] He was now both duke and Jesuit.

Acting on the insight that even disordered Jesuits can be instruments of order and peace to each other, Ignatius responded to Gandía's crisis brilliantly by appealing to the responsibility each one in authority

---

generalis tertius (BorgiaMon), vols. 2, 23, 35, 38, and 41 of MHSI (Madrid, 1894–1911), 2:691.

[12] Letter to Ignatius, June 8, 1546 (*Epist.mixt* 1:283–86).

[13] Letter to Jerome Doménech, September 15, 1546 (ibid., 303).

[14] *Font.narr* 1:64*; *PolChron* 1:250. Dalmases suggests some refinements to Polanco's account and opines that the reason for granting Borgia the solemn profession immediately was probably to save his vocation (*Ignatius of Loyola*, 59 f.). Philip II could hardly insist that one bound by vow to the pope should become part of his court. Borgia made his vows in the presence of the three priests in the Jesuit community, Oviedo, Onfroy, and Saboya (a Jesuit himself and tutor of the duke's children). See the letters of Oviedo to Ignatius dated January 26 and February 24, 1547 (*Epist.mixt* 1:334, 342). The ever-present Tejeda was also in attendance (*MonBorgia* 2:544 f.).

had for those under his charge, and by challenging the one in charge. In March 1548 he wrote separately to Araoz, Oviedo, and Borgia.

In the first of these letters, Ignatius alerted Araoz to Oviedo's request to offer Mass two or three times each day. Ignatius would not seek an indult; rather, he would block it. If Oviedo were at hand, he would not let him say even one Mass each day. He opposed his desire to retire to the desert with Onfroy, was displeased with their relationship with Tejeda and Tejeda's presence in the Jesuit community. To correct these and other abuses, he appointed Araoz visitor for the whole of Spain, granting him the full power possessed by the general, and told him to correct his own excesses first (*EpistIgn* 2:11–13; 43; 46 f.). Details of this will follow in the third tale.

In his second letter Ignatius urged Oviedo as rector to moderate Borgia's penances. Again, further details will appear in the third tale to follow. He had Polanco write that, regarding the spiritual exercises and studies of the scholastics, Ignatius intended to apply at Gandía what had become common in other colleges. Polanco informed Oviedo that Ignatius wished him to be in continuing touch with Araoz as his provincial. Ignatius thought that the desire for seven years of recollection and solitude was "a serious matter and a dangerous precedent for our way of proceeding."[15] Oviedo's lengthy arguments were out of place; the subject's role was not to persuade the superior but to reveal his own motives and inner feelings; otherwise it was usually a sign he was seeking his own will. Ignatius had not read that St. Francis or other saints had given permission for a hermitage experience to a religious who had not made final profession or was not well known to the superior. What was needed was genuine indifference and obedience. The rest of the letter detailed the demands of obedience (*EpistIgn* 2:54–65).

Oviedo replied that he had received the instructions of March 12, was in constant touch with Araoz and obeyed him as he would Jesus, considering that he took the place of Jesus. He had received much consolation from the negative response to his request for the desert and firmly believed that it came from our Lord. He was grateful for the remarks on obedience. If he had been deceived, as the letter to the duke suggested and a letter from Araoz affirmed, he wished to be freed from his errors and fantasies, and signed himself "Andres Publicano" (Andrés the sinner).[16]

---

[15] Young makes Ignatius tentative: "may be a dangerous precedent," and translates the next phrase, "requiere mayor prouisión," as "needs further thought" (*Letters of Ignatius,* 166), in contrast to Polanco's message to Araoz. Since more paragraphs follow on the same subject, I prefer to translate the words as "needs further specification."

[16] *Epist.mixt* 1:494–97. He began to sign himself that way on November 3, 1547,

Ignatius's third letter manifested to Borgia his concern about Oviedo, Onfroy, and Tejeda and suggested some options: send Oviedo to Rome, Onfroy to Alfonso Salmerón, who had attracted him to the Society, and Tejeda back to the Franciscans; send away one or both Jesuits; if all three stay, separate them from one another. He left much to the duke's discretion (*EpistIgn* 2:65 f.).

Borgia replied that the Franciscan General had already decreed that Tejeda would not live with the Jesuits. Oviedo had seemed indifferent regarding the desert both before and after receiving the response from Rome and was filled with so much consolation that what the evil spirit seemed to have gained he had now clearly lost. The same was true of Onfroy. These two truly merited the name of sons. No need existed to send Oviedo to Rome.[17]

In 1549 Ignatius invited Oviedo to receive his final vows, and he joined the ranks of the solemnly professed, now fourteen in number.[18] About the same time both Oviedo and Onfroy received the degree of doctor of theology.[19] But a battle won is often a war begun.

A Pause for Prayer

Christians find in Jesus both the norm and the ideal for Christian living. They find in Mary, the woman of faith, an inspiration and an example to imitate as the first disciple of Jesus. Members of religious orders discover in their founders a model of how God acts in one called to that particular way of life. The spirit of the founder attracts and captivates, stirs and spurs the religious to do now in the present moment what the founder did in a different historical moment.

> **Fifteenth Annotation: During these Spiritual Exercises when a person is seeking God's will, it is more appropriate and far better that the Creator and Lord himself should communicate himself to the devout soul, embracing it in love and praise, and disposing it for the way which will enable the soul to**

---

when he formally requested permission to go to the desert for seven years.

[17] *MonBorgia* 2:546–48.

[18] *EpistIgn* 2:300. Diego Miró, first rector of Coimbra (in 1542; *Epist.mixt* 1:106) and also of Valencia (in 1547; *Epist.mixt* 412), was professed with Oviedo in Gandía (*Epist.mixt* 2:144). Juan Alfonso de Polanco was professed in Rome that same day, as was Emmanuel Miona, former confessor to Ignatius and Nadal in Paris (*Font.narr* 1:64*).

[19] Letter of Diego Miró from Gandía to Miguel de Torres, March 11, 1549 (*Epist.mixt* 2:126 f.).

serve him better in the future. Accordingly, the one giving the Exercises ought not to lean or incline in either direction but rather . . . to allow the Creator to deal immediately with the creature and the creature with its Creator and Lord (*SpEx* 15 [pp. 25 f.]).

We pray once more for the grace that the Holy Spirit might stir each of us, according to his or her own vocation, after the manner in which the Spirit stirred Ignatius. In the reality that we know as the communion of saints, all the members of the heavenly court are praying for all of us at this moment that we might follow that particular model with which God has gifted us.

The Grace of Ignatius

The preceding chapters reflected on various ways of discovering the special grace proper to the Society of Jesus: finding its model in the life of the primitive Church, probing the images found in the *Spiritual Exercises*, and reflecting on the intensity with which it seeks its end. For Nadal, however, the primary way of coming to know the Society's special grace is through the life of Ignatius the pilgrim, who is the one through whom God communicates that grace.

First Exhortation in Spain, 1554

"Exhort. 1554 hisp." (*CommInst* 37–41, nos. 4–18)

Nadal reminded his audience that in the Society of Jesus God had created something new to serve the Church in a particular way by communicating a particular grace to Ignatius, and to his followers through him, thus distinguishing the Society from other religious orders (*CommInst* 37, no. 4 f.). To give flesh and bones to this new spirituality within the broader stream of Christian spirituality, Nadal briefly narrated the story of Ignatius, or better, the story of God acting in Ignatius:

Seeking, then, someone to serve him in this manner, God called Ignatius in his sickness, gifting him especially to desire with felt intensity the greater honor and glory of his Divine Majesty. Just as he longed for heroic deeds as a worldling, when he gave himself to the service of God he was not content with little, but intensely desired and strove to please in every way he could. . . . Wherefore, all the members of the Society should with deep feeling keep this same thing in mind, and we should internalize this spirit of seeking and procuring in all things the greater service and glory of God

our Lord, whether we are lecturing or preaching or eating or doing something else, doing everything for the glory of God. (38 f., no. 9)

Driven by these great desires and God's movements within him,
Ignatius began to do penance, thinking to please God in accordance with
Christ's injunction, "Do penance" (Matt. 4:17). From this experience he
came to a clear knowledge of what those who follow this spiritual path
should do. He went to extremes of penance and prayer, for example, not
eating or drinking for a week, and learned by his mistakes to avoid
extremes. He clothed himself in burlap and became "a knight of Christ."
Moreover,

> under our Lord's guidance he began to pay attention to his inner life and
> the movements of the spirits within him, and through this experience the
> Lord gave him great knowledge and a vivid sense of the mysteries of God
> and the Church. . . . Here our Lord communicated the Exercises to him,
> guiding him to give himself completely to the service of God and the
> salvation of souls; . . . especially in the exercises on the King and the Two
> Standards. Here he grasped his purpose in life . . . which is now the
> purpose of the Society. (39 f., nos. 10–13)

Recognizing the need to study in order to carry out this purpose,
Ignatius began studying in Spain and later in Paris. He recruited companions (1529–34) who, after preaching and other good works, gathered
together in Rome and worked out a way of living that was embodied in a
papal bull of confirmation issued in 1540 (40 f., no. 14). Elsewhere Nadal
indicates that Ignatius went to the Holy Land in 1523, and that the other
companions wanted to but were unable to do so. "For us that means that
we are supposed to go to Jerusalem, not physically but spiritually, and we
do this by meditating on the life of Christ."[20]

Even at this early date, the major lines of Nadal's thinking were
beginning to emerge, but he had not yet organized them into an orderly
and coherent system. They developed steadily as years of experience and
years of reflection matured his thought.

Reflections Shortly after the Death of Ignatius

Ignatius died on July 31, 1556. Nadal returned from Spain to Rome,
arriving on December 10. Laínez, the vicar-general, made him superintendent of the Roman College and invited him to address the Jesuits in Rome
"on the spirit and aims of the Society." In spite of Nadal's grief at the loss
of his "father" and friend, the death of Ignatius was a profoundly freeing
experience for him. No longer need he restrain himself in talking about

---

[20] ARSI, *Instit. 18a*, fol. 430ʳ, placed in "Exhort. 1554 hisp." See *CommInst* 40 n.
14, where this text appears as a marginal insert.

Ignatius and the way God worked in him and through him. On January 2 and 4 he addressed all the Jesuits gathered at the Roman College. He was addressing men who mourned the loss of their founder, who were confused by their now friendly, now unfriendly relationship with Paul IV; men who were finding it impossible to organize a general congregation because of antagonistic pressures from King Philip in Spain and Paul IV in Rome, who were at war with each other. They were afraid that the Pope would interfere if they did convene a general congregation, yet only a congregation could approve the Constitutions. They were at a vulnerable moment. The founder was gone. Suspicions of their new order continued, with the new pope showing himself as one of the main critics. They longed for assurance and inspiration.

A nameless note taker at the Roman College has provided only a compendium of what Nadal said, but from the comments afterward, Nadal knew that the talks went well. The note taker was more explicit: "Outstanding," he wrote of the first, "absolutely wonderful and stupendous," of the second.[21] Nadal's great love for Ignatius shines through every line.

Exhortation in the Roman College, January 2, 1557

"AdhortRom" (*Font.narr* 2:3–7, nos. 1–18)

Nadal began as usual by locating the Society's spirituality within that of the Church:

> Our Lord and Savior Jesus Christ, wishing to liberate the world from the tyranny of the evil one, who kept proposing the pursuit of nothing but riches, honors, easy living, and frivolous nonsense, willed the exact opposite to be the norms for all those to be saved. . . . This is the first and common grace, common to us along with all Christians, and we ought always to be extremely grateful for it. (*Font.narr* 3, no. 4)

Beyond this grace common to all Christians, the Society received a special grace common to religious orders as well as graces peculiar to the Society. To explore those special graces Nadal proposed taking a look at Ignatius and the whole Society that flows from him (4, no. 5–7).

The Society is like other religious orders in having divinely inspired founders, being approved by the Holy See, and managing to grow in numbers and produce abundant fruit. For the Society of Jesus, a special grace shines forth in obedience and in the peculiar energy and grace of preaching and teaching and similar activities that others cannot help but admire (4, no. 7).

Nadal told the story of Ignatius, as always, with an eye to divine providence. At the very time that Luther was doing the greatest damage to

---

[21] *Font.narr* 2:1 f.

the Church, Ignatius was a military leader (*dux exercitus*—hardly a general, more like a gallant officer), a firebrand seeking worldly honor; "but in this matter he was prevented by the will of God" when he was wounded and found himself at death's door. "(*Ecce primam gratiam* [Behold the first grace])" which anyone can experience in his own conversion, and so with all the other graces, if he makes a comparison)" (5, no. 8).

"If he makes a comparison" leap out as key words. Nadal did not suggest that every Christian or every Jesuit encounters a cannonball, but he did imply that something at the heart of Ignatius's experience repeated itself in every member of his audience. Nadal had asked Ignatius to tell "how the Lord had directed him from the beginning of his conversion so that the exposition could stand as a testament for us, a paternal instruction."[22] In his so-called autobiography (*A Pilgrim's Testament*), Ignatius explains how God taught him discernment. One who makes a comparison, Nadal said, will find that God is doing the same thing in his own life.[23] The vocation and graces of Ignatius illustrate the vocation and graces of his followers. Ignatius is not so much a model as a norm to help a Jesuit discern and interpret what God is doing in his own life.

Narrating the life of Ignatius, Nadal introduced a continuous chant: "Behold another grace." Ignatius read the *Life of Christ* and the *Lives of the Saints*, experienced the various spirits pulling him in opposite directions, came to an understanding of the discernment of spirits and committed his life to the service of God. "(*Ecce 2.*ᵃᵐ *gratiam spiritualem* [Behold a second spiritual grace])." He decided that his concern would always be the greater service of God, which has become the foundation and norm of the whole Society, the measure for all the Constitutions and for every action of the Society (5, nos. 9 f.).

At Manresa Ignatius did penance, was too severe on himself, came to the balance later found in the Constitutions. "(*Ecce gratiam aliam* [Behold another grace])." Through prayer and contemplation he also came to a remarkable clarity of mind regarding things divine, especially in an illumination in prayer he received at the river Cardonner, to which he referred for the rest of his life. "(*Ecce gratiam aliam* [Behold another grace])" (5 f., nos. 11 f.).

The experience of Ignatius brought him to an insatiable longing to help his neighbor. "(*Ecce gratiam novam* [Behold a new grace])." Seeing, however, the danger of leading people into error, under the impulse of the Holy Spirit Ignatius decided to study and to find companions of the same mind. "(*Ecce et hic peculiarem Societatis gratiam* [Behold here a special

---

[22] "Præfatio Patris Natalis in acta Patris Ignatii" (ibid., 1:356 f.).

[23] See the excellent article by Leonardo R. Silos, S.J., "Cardoner in the Life of Saint Ignatius of Loyola," *AHSI* 33 (1964): 3–43, especially pp. 6–15.

grace of the Society])." He finally went to Paris and there he found companions. "(*Ecce et hic peculiare donum* [Behold here also a special gift])." Eventually the companions chose to seek approbation as a group from the Pope, and the group received approbation time and again—the least of all in its own estimate, but with its own members, its own special vocation, and its own graces. They established their own membership norms and ways of supporting the studies that they undertook. "(*Ecce et hic peculiarem Dei gratiam* [Behold here also a special grace of God])" (6f., nos. 13–17).

Finally, Nadal summarized for his audience at the Roman College what it meant to imitate the true spirit of the Society as realized in Ignatius:

> Abandoning all worldly aspirations, we should put the service of God before all that belongs to the world; in the service of God, we should always seek what is most for the glory of God; we should be mindful of penance, give ourselves to prayer, thirst for the salvation of our neighbor, and embrace study diligently for that purpose; we should forge an indissoluble bond of love with our brothers; and referring all things to the disposition of our superiors, who stand in the place of Christ, we should always give thanks to God that he has wished us to be members of this holy Society and strive earnestly to live worthily in our vocation until death, to his eternal glory and praise who is blessed forever, Jesus Christ our Lord, our leader and our commander. Amen. (7, no. 18)

This summary for the Society is obviously a summary of the major graces in the life of Ignatius from the time of his conversion up until his death. Thus Jesuit prayer is somehow prefigured in that of Ignatius. Even years later, Nadal himself longed and pleaded for prayer like that of Ignatius. That was the only kind of prayer he wanted.[24]

Exhortation in the Roman College, January 4, 1557

"AdhortRom" (*Font.narr* 2:8–10f., nos. 20–25)

In this instruction, after a brief summary Nadal underscored the Society's commitment to prayer and things of the spirit, so as to be drawn quickly into a great thirst for helping the neighbor;[25] "otherwise devotion without that desire would be dangerous in our Society, even though it is good in itself." Ignatius was especially intent upon helping those who could become companions in this work, so that they would in turn become a help to others. He achieved his goal when he found men who shared his desires, "and we should earnestly imitate him in doing the same" (*Font.-narr* 8, no. 21).

---

[24] *Orat.observ* 291, no. 948 (date uncertain; 1574?); See also *EpistNadal* 4:725.

[25] Much of the text of this exhortation is missing from the manuscript (*Font.narr* 2:1, editor's preface).

In the twentieth century the decree on the union of minds and hearts of General Congregation 32 emphasizes that Jesuits are companions in mission with one another, and General Congregation 34's decree on cooperation with the laity stresses creativity in being companions in mission with others as well. General Congregation 34 states clearly, "Vocation promotion simply means helping young people hear and respond to the stirrings of the Spirit in their hearts." This does not necessarily mean that they have a vocation to the Society of Jesus, and "we must carefully respect the particular way in which the Spirit calls each person." The congregation concludes: "At the same time, young people can only choose what they know and love. Every Jesuit and every Jesuit community must do everything possible actively to present the Society of Jesus to others in such a way that those whom God calls will know and appreciate who and what we are" (*DocsGC34* 293 [p. 141]).

Once again Nadal told his fellow Jesuits that the path of the Society follows the life of Ignatius. After his death they had found a passage in his spiritual diary in which he wrote of an intense experience of the presence of Jesus and judged it to be in some way the work of the Holy Trinity; it reminded him, Ignatius wrote, of the time that "the Father had placed me with the Son," referring to the vision he had experienced at La Storta in which he experienced the Father placing him at the side of the Son carrying his cross.[26] Nadal concluded:

> From this we gather that the foundation of our Society is Jesus Christ crucified, so that just as he redeemed the human race by means of the Cross and daily endures the greatest afflictions and crosses in his Mystical Body, which is the Church, so also one who belongs to our Society can propose to himself nothing else than, following Christ through many trials, to work together with Christ for the salvation of souls since, though redeemed by the Blood of Christ, they are perishing miserably. (*Font.narr* 9 f., no. 22–24)

Was he being prophetic? Nadal had entered Rome in the December of 1556, during a truce in the war between Spain and the Holy See. On January 19, two weeks after Nadal's exhortations to his Roman brethren, Pope Paul IV resumed the fighting, charging King Philip with treason. The King retaliated by decreeing that no Spaniard could reside in Rome and commanding the Spaniards living there to leave within three months.

---

[26] "Spiritual Diary," in *Ignatius of Loyola: The Spiritual Exercises and Selected Works*, ed. George E. Ganss, S.J. (New York: Paulist Press, 1991), notes for February 24, 1544, pp. 248 f., no. 67. See also Peter-Hans Kolvenbach, S.J., "Language and Anthropology: The *Spiritual Diary* of St. Ignatius," *CIS* 22, no. 2 (1991): 9–19; Maurice-Marie Martin, S.J., "The Mysticism of St. Ignatius: A Study of the Gift of Tears in the *Spiritual Diary*," ibid., 21–82; Simon Decloux, S.J., *Commentaries on the Letters and Spiritual Diary of St. Ignatius Loyola,* 2nd ed. (Rome: CIS, 1982).

Laínez had already delayed the First General Congregation, and now the delegates from Spain could not come to Rome. In late April or May he asked if the Society could hold its congregation in Spain. In June Pope Paul said no. He reminded Laínez that any actions of the congregation would have to be approved by the present pope regardless of what earlier popes had approved. A few days later he ordered Laínez as vicar-general to deliver a copy of the *Constitutions* to one of the cardinals, as well as all papal bulls and other documents; he also demanded a list of Jesuits living in Rome; moreover, he forbade the General to allow any Jesuit to leave Rome.

Eventually the war ended but, as we mentioned earlier, Bobadilla launched an internal war. He declared the Constitutions inoperative because a general congregation had not approved them, and the office of vicar-general nonexistent, in that it appeared only in the Constitutions and not in the papal bulls of approval. The original founding companions, therefore, should govern the Society. Having made Nadal one of his advisors in preparing for the congregation, Laínez now asked him for help in refuting Bobadilla. The battle was a bitter one, but Nadal prevailed.[27] He had spoken truly that the Society would follow the path of Jesus. How often, through good men and bad, the evil spirit tries to impede the work the Holy Spirit calls the Society to do!

Ignatius as Model for Novices

Since the vocation and graces of Ignatius illustrate the vocation and graces of his followers, this chapter reflects on how these affect the formation of novices, and the next two chapters examine how they affect the formation of Jesuit students and the "formed" members.

In chapter 4 we quoted Nadal's statement that the Society embraces a twofold life, both active and contemplative, one that strives for a higher action that attempts to bring about the salvation of others and enables others to become active or contemplative or engage in that same higher action for the salvation of others. To the Jesuits in Coimbra in 1561 he puts the question, "What life does the Society lead, the active or the contemplative?" (*CommInst* 361, no. 127). He replies by first defining the lives themselves, enabling each reader to name the life to which Christ calls him or her and to determine to some extent how the reader is living that life now. "There is in the Church the active life and the contemplative life. The active life is concerned with works of penance, with mortifying and ordering the passions, and with practicing the other active virtues; the one who devotes himself more to this leads the active life, although he also practices some contemplation" (362, no. 127). This definition sur-

---

[27] Details of this paragraph are drawn from Bangert, *Jerome Nadal,* 173–92.

prises those unaware of the history of Christian terminology. Today the active life is defined as external activity touching other people, ranging from preaching the Gospel to the corporal works of mercy; the contemplative life, on the other hand, includes solitude and silence and prayer. The active life must be a prayerful life, of course, and the contemplative includes manual or intellectual work of some kind, and perhaps some contemplative presence to others.

Patristic and monastic writers, however, and even some of the medieval Scholastics, use "active" to refer to the exercise of the virtues and ascetic practices aimed at the personal growth of the person practicing them. Some emphasize ascetical practices; others add the corporal works of mercy, like feeding the hungry or clothing the naked; still others include some spiritual works of mercy, like instructing the ignorant. St. Thomas embraces both views, sometimes seeing the active life in terms of ascetical practices, sometimes as the performance of works of mercy. For Nadal the active life means both taming the passions and performing works of mercy. Martha ministering to Jesus is an example of the active life, but she can move on to another kind of life: "The contemplative life has for its principal object the consideration of truths about God and other truths connected with God; the more perfect the object it considers, the loftier the contemplation" (362, no. 127). Martha's sister Mary at the feet of Jesus is the classic example of the contemplative life. Nadal now launches into territory often called "the mixed life":

> There is another life that is called loftier [superior] that belongs to those who foster these lives in others, and this is proper to prelates of the Church, to bishops and pastors. They have to be accomplished in both the one and the other. One leading the active life needs a little contemplation, enough to support and balance the works of mortification and penance and the practice of virtue. A contemplative needs a little action, for there is no one who does not need penance: "The just man falls seven times a day, but rises again." But the one who lives this loftier life, having to instruct others, needs plenty of both. (362, no. 127)

The mention of bishops should surprise no one. When St. Thomas Aquinas describes what he calls "the mixed life," he has in mind bishops as well, for those who live that sort of life share in some of the activities in which bishops and pastors normally engage. Nadal continues:

> If you look at the whole Society, it embraces all of them, but if you look at its primary members, the professed, it leads that life that we call loftier. In the beginning a novice is more engaged in the active life, doing penance for his sins, ridding himself of the bad habits of his former life; along with that he spends time in prayer, but makes no attempt to be of profit to his neighbor in exterior ministries, helping others only through good desires and prayers. (362, no. 128)

Limited external ministries were, indeed, part of a novice's life, but undertaken for the sake of the novice rather than the profit of others. Ironically, today such ministries might be described as the "active life" and the novice's interior work of asceticism and prayer as the "contemplative life." For Nadal, both were purifying acts of asceticism, the heart of the "active life."

In the early days Jesuit novices were not housed separately, but lived with those working in various apostolates or in a *collegio,* a residence for those attending a university. In 1549 Nadal suggested housing the novices in Messina in a separate building. Since Ignatius had previously recommended such a novitiate to Simón Rodrigues in Portugal, he responded enthusiastically.[28]

Even though, in Nadal's terms, the novices were engaged in the active life of ridding themselves of vices and acquiring virtues, still, in the middle of an exhortation on prayer in 1553, delivered during his first visit to Spain on commission from Ignatius, Nadal linked prayer with all the activities of the novitiate:

> Notice the way the Society has of making progress in prayer through the grace of our Lord:
>
> First of all, the Society gives the Spiritual Exercises with all exactitude to those it admits, to start them in prayer and advance in it, *and to experiment and test whether they are capable of prayer in terms of what we are looking for.*
>
> Next, in the customary two years of probation, the Society takes care through various experiments and exercises that [the novices] *achieve habitual facility not only in prayer but in its perfection and that of all the virtues.*
>
> And [the Society takes care] that [the novices] are penetrated to the depths with the fire of love and zeal for souls . . . the end of the Society.[29]

---

[28] Nadal to Ignatius, July 1, 1549 (*EpistNadal* 1:61–64, no. 4); speedy reply from Polanco (written under instructions from Ignatius) to Nadal, July 6, 1549 (*EpistIgn* 2:462–64, no. 6); Polanco (written for Ignatius) to Rodrigues, October 1547 (*EpistIgn* 1:603–6. A separate house would be less expensive, for it could have an income; it would be quieter without the comings and goings in a college or professed house and could accept persons for retreats; the advantage for the college or professed house would be less confusion, for all would be committed; they could go about their work more easily without a lot of untried novices underfoot, and no one would be harmed by mixing weeds with the wheat. General Congregation 2 decreed that each province should house novices separately (*EpistNadal* 1:61–62 n. 5).

[29] "Ord. oración," in *Regulæ Societatis Iesu,* vol. 4 of *Constitutiones,* 489 f. (emphases added). Nadal developed these points in more detail in 1561 in his "Exhort. 8ª en Alcalá" (*CommInst* 380, no. 152 f.; 382, no. 155).

This startling way of viewing the six novitiate experiments as ways of advancing in prayer even as they root out vices and promote virtues is foundational and affords a profound insight into the kind of prayer the Society expects. The testing is important, Nadal said, "since we have to make every effort to walk in the Spirit."[30] During some experiments the novices live outside the novitiate, even outside a Jesuit residence. They need to learn to trust in God and to rely on the inner resources God has given them.

Notice the similarity to the pattern of Ignatius's own conversion experience. The *Spiritual Exercises* state as their purpose: "to overcome oneself, and to order one's life, without reaching a decision through some disordered affection" (*SpEx* 21 [p. 31]). They are an instrument for a radical critique of the dominant culture and the radical conversion of persons living in and addicted to the blandishments of that culture.[31] Taming the passions looks to personal transformation and personal transformation looks to cultural transformation.

Praying their way through the Spiritual Exercises as their first experiment, the novices acquire a sense of being redeemed sinners called by Love to the service of Christ. They are challenged to rid themselves of all that blocks the free flow of Christ's love in them: "not only to reject faults and their roots, and insofar as they can to rid themselves of them in Christ Jesus, but also to abandon any approach to life or any custom contrary to the Institute of the Society, or different from it, even though it might be good."[32] This final point provides a key element in discerning a vocation to the Society and the authenticity of desires within the Society.

In their prayer, novices participate in some way in the contemplative life, but the primary role of contemplation is to support them in the active life of growing in virtue. Although in the active life of purgation a person needs only a little prayer "to sustain him in his works of mortification and penance and other virtues and to keep them well-ordered," novices are also preparing themselves for the ministries of the Society, and therefore spend much time in prayer.[33] "The life of a novice resembles paradise: . . . nothing to do but attend to himself . . . more prayer, more time and disposition for mortifying himself, no speculative studies; every-

---

[30] "Exhort. 1554 hisp." (*CommInst* 73, no. 86).

[31] See Gerald G. May, M.D., *Addiction and Grace* (San Francisco: Harper & Row, 1988), 14 f.

[32] "In exam. annot." (*CommInst* 191, no. 161); see also "Exhort 8ª en Alcalá" (ibid., 365, no. 131).

[33] "Exhort. 6ª en Alcalá" (ibid., 362, no. 127).

thing contributes to his own growth, to increasing in virtue."[34] Elsewhere he writes, "With the grace of God each one also draws from the Exercises a very special grace for understanding and appreciating his special vocation, and with this grace he gains a special tranquillity and union with God."[35]

The other experiments test whether the novice has received that special grace. Does he grasp that prayer bears not on self alone but on helping the neighbor? How passionately does he desire? Serving in a hospital, he has an opportunity for many charitable acts. Can he immerse himself in external works and keep alive the thoughts and feelings gained in prayer? Can he pray about his neighbor's needs? "When we see that a novice working in a hospital does not lose his sense of commitment, is not disturbed or distressed but goes about cheerfully and with joy, we have proved that the desires and fervor he had on leaving the Exercises were for real."[36]

But can the novice flourish when on his own? Even a sixteenth-century hospital provided a supportive environment.

> Because in the hospital someone supplied [the novice] with food, a bed, and everything else he needed, he is therefore sent on a pilgrimage as a third experiment, in order to learn poverty by experiencing it, and trust in God alone by begging in his name. Let him be tried in enduring insults hurled at him, and other hardships that usually distress one who is imperfect. He needs to learn to edify his neighbor in everything, to be upset by nothing.[37]

Jesuits must be ready, Nadal points out, to go to any part of the world to be of service to people. The pilgrimage tests a man's virtue and the solidity of his desires: "He sees himself poor, alone, without the help or consolation of other human beings, without money for the journey. Here they do not welcome him; there they abuse him verbally. In these and like circumstances, let him be tested on his need to seek God alone and to place his confidence in him alone."[38]

The Society next tries the novice in his own religious house in what the sixteenth century called "lowly ministries, for example, in the kitchen, the dining room, and so forth, in which a test is made of his humility, patience, and other virtues."[39] The third millennium does not deem man-

---

[34] "Exhort. 6ª en Alcalá" (ibid., 366, no. 133).

[35] "Orationis ratio" (*EpistNadal* 4:673).

[36] "Exhort. 8ª en Alcalá" (*CommInst* 381, no. 154).

[37] "Exhort. 1554 hisp." (ibid., 74, no. 88).

[38] "Exhort. 8ª en Alcalá" (ibid., 383, no. 157).

[39] "Exhort. 1554 hisp." (ibid., 74, no. 89).

ual tasks as "lowly" as did those living in Nadal's day. Today the Society tests the novice's capacity for loving service as much as his humility. "He is under observation most of the time and has to obey others besides the superior, for example, the sacristan . . . the cook . . . the buyer. . . . His virtue is thoroughly put to the proof: whether he is tempted, whether he shows signs of impatience, whether he goes about happy and joyful."[40] Does he love working for others?

Does he also have skills needed for the Society's ministries? For a lengthy period he teaches Christian doctrine to children and others ignorant of Christian teaching. Thus he gives proof of "(1) his character and ability, (2) his zeal for souls, (3) the care he takes and patience he shows."[41] Here Nadal reflects the mind and heart of Ignatius, to whom teaching Christian doctrine was so dear that one of a Jesuit's final vows bind those who pronounce them to "care for the instruction of children"; for he says, "Although this ministry is great and very important, it does not appear so, and therefore this exercise reveals how inclined and committed a person is, and how much love he has for the ministries of the Society."[42]

A novice who is an ordained priest "is ordered by way of a test to minister in whatever way God has gifted him, to lecture if he is learned, to hear confessions, to direct the Exercises. These clarify the areas where he might be most useful."[43] Like the rest, this final experiment is designed to test the inner virtue of the novice more than to minister to those with whom he deals.

All the experiments point to the ministries of the Society. They also invite the novice into a new way of praying: the prayer of the Society is not the prayer of a solitary praying for others, but apostolic praying that leads to ministering to others. As Nadal wrote to Cardinal Borromeo about the training of novices, "Other orders may train novices for choir and other ceremonies, but the Society trains its novices in the ministries proper to the Society for the salvation of souls."[44]

The experiments test both the virtues and the skills the novice has for the ministries of the Society, and also test his ability to pray. Do people find him patient or impatient, cheerful or glum, docile and willing to change or like a brick wall? Does prayer orient him toward others? Is he moving along a track that associates him with Christ's mission from the Father? Does he experience himself placed at the side of Christ carrying

---

[40] "Exhort. 8ª en Alcalá" (ibid., 384 f., no. 159).

[41] "Exhort. 1554 hisp." (ibid., 75, no. 90).

[42] "Exhort. 8ª en Alcalá" (ibid., 385, no. 160).

[43] "Exhort. 1554 hisp." (ibid., 75, no. 91).

[44] "De professione et choro" (*EpistNadal* 4:174 f.).

his cross in his Mystical Body, the Church? Is he becoming mindful that at the side of Christ he walks in a world marked by the sign of the cross, in which every death he experiences is an opportunity to enter into new life? Does he, like Jesus, consciously live and move and have his being in the Father's love? In union with Christ, the Father's only begotten Son, does he breathe forth the Holy Spirit on other people?

A novice engages primarily in the hard work of purgation, an excellent example of the active life. He tastes the illuminative life as he comes to know Christ better, and the unitive as he begins to form habits that will make him one with Jesus. He participates to some extent in the contemplative life. His prayer evolves as he learns more about the Society's ministries and tastes them experientially. He begins to be more caught up in others than in himself. He embarks on the way toward that more holistic active life that will enable him to help some people choose the active life, others the contemplative, and still others that more holistic active life characteristic of the Society. Nadal ends his remarks on prayer and the novitiate experiments with these words: "Therefore all should make every effort in the Lord, moving along the path of prayer and the spiritual life, to find God in all their ministries and activities, *walking in the Spirit,* habitually arousing spiritual fervor in all things."[45]

In the novitiate the Society expects that the novices need to be purged of sin and worldly attachments and need to spend much time in prayer. By the end of the novitiate, however, they should have made much progress both in the active life of purgation and the acquisition of virtue and in the contemplative life of prayer:

> Reflect that the active life and the contemplative life should always travel together. But the period of rigorous probation brings it about that the active comes to some perfection, and by this time the contemplative dominates and guides and governs peacefully and with enlightenment in the Lord, and in this way one comes to the higher active life which presupposes the active and the contemplative, and has the power to seal everyone with the mark of active or contemplative in accordance with the greater service of God. To be concise: the action of love united to God is perfect action.[46]

Philip Endean translates the passage to mean that the active life comes to a certain perfection and then dominates the contemplative, regulates it, and governs it.[47] Is it not more likely that the rigorous probation is designed to produce novices who are so saturated with prayer while trying to rid themselves of sin and acquire virtue, that by the time they have made

---

[45] "Ord. oración," *Constitutiones* 4:490, no. 12 (emphasis added).

[46] "Orationis ratio (*EpistNadal* 4:679).

[47] Endean, *Rahner and Ignatian Spirituality,* 72.

real progress in that difficult arena of the active life, the contemplative life takes over and governs everything? In other words, the contemplative experience of the Spiritual Exercises throughout those two years eventually becomes the dominant experience that guides all that they do.

It is also likely that in this passage Nadal uses the term "probation" loosely. Formation is not a matter of mastering an obstacle course, but a lengthy process of personal development. After the novitiate the new members are called *approved* scholastics. Although not on probation, they are being tested in one particular aspect of the higher active life, learning. The paragraph quoted above, which seems to be about novices and fits them well, should fit Jesuit students even better when they have completed their studies. They have gradually grown into the life of the Society.

Conclusion

The Society's unique training of novices bases itself on Ignatius's own experience and the way he prepared his followers. Ignatius guided the companions he found in Paris through the Spiritual Exercises. They all committed themselves to the pilgrimage to the Holy Land. When he left Paris for Spain, he said he would meet them in Venice. Months later they set out on a dangerous pilgrimage through a France at war with Spain to the shrine of Our Lady of Loreto. Along the way they disputed with "heretics" over matters of faith. Stopping in Venice, they went to work in the hospitals, taking care of the most hopeless cases. After Loreto and a visit to Rome, they returned to Venice to continue their work in the hospitals, also spending time in retreat and preaching in the surrounding cities. They asked and received papal approval of their way of life.

Ignatius and his companions left all, including their inordinate attachments to self and the world, to follow Christ; similarly, the novitiate begins to purge the novice of his own lack of freedom. Ignatius was always trying to discern the greater good, and the novice is schooled to discern how he needs to grow in virtue. At Manresa Ignatius attained great clarity regarding the things of God, and the novitiate immerses the novice in prayer and the actions of the Spirit within him.

To understand a seed, look at the tree or the flower from which it came and which it is destined one day to become. On his pilgrimage to Jerusalem, Ignatius stopped at Manresa, talking to people, living in a hospital and caring for its inmates; he begged for himself and them. Preaching, healing, and concern for the poor also marked the path of his companions on their pilgrimage to Loreto. Making the Exercises, going on pilgrimage, and showing concern for the marginalized, the little ones of God—thus pass the days of the novice in the Society as well, following the spirit and aims of Ignatius and sharing the patrimony of the Society. They too can say what countless Jesuits have said down the centuries:

In remorse, gratitude, and astonishment—but above all with passionate love—first Ignatius and then every Jesuit after him has turned prayerfully to "Christ our Lord hanging on the cross before me" and has asked of himself, "What have I done for Christ? What am I doing for Christ? What must I do for Christ?" The questions well up from a heart profoundly moved by gratitude and love. This is the foundational grace that binds Jesuits to Jesus and to one another. (*DocsGC34* 538 [p. 236])

Now we go on to consider the next step along the path toward becoming a full member of the Society, that of the scholastic or brother in studies, and examine how that step, too, imitates in its own way the path Ignatius followed.

Chronicle for Chapter 8

I hold it for certain that there is no master who teaches so convincingly, and with so much force and vigor and irresistible power, what is in practice the prayer proper to the Society, as the great Father Jerónimo Nadal.

—Jerónimo Seisdedos Sanz, S.J., *Principios fundamentales de la mística*

Nadal's Life and Travels (1563)

1563

Feb. 13–after Mar. 8: At Innsbruck; meets Canisius

Until April 19: At Vienna; exhortations

April 20: Tyrnau; returns to Vienna about May 5

Mid-May: Leaves Vienna for Prague

May 18ff.: At Prague (1+ months); returns to Vienna

After Sept. 4: Leaves Vienna

Sept. 15: Arrives at Munich; visits college

Until mid-Oct.: Innsbruck

Oct. 20–about Nov. 20: Dillingen

Until Dec. 7: Ingolstadt, Munich, Innsbruck, Trent

Dec. 10: Leaves for Venice, Padua, Rome (Jan. 12)

Chapter Eight

PRAYER PROPER TO THE SOCIETY OF JESUS

All institutes should share in the life of the Church. They should make their own and should foster to the best of their ability, in a manner consonant with their own natures, its initiatives and undertakings in biblical, liturgical, dogmatic, pastoral, ecumenical, missionary, and social matters.

—Vatican II, *On the Up-to-Date Renewal of the Religious Life*

When the Franciscans in charge of the shrines in the Holy Land told Ignatius that he could not stay there and do what he had planned to do, he did not question the decision, nor did he break with ecclesiastical authority in order to accomplish what he felt God was calling him to do. He desired to "share in the life of the Church" to the fullest extent. His conclusion, rather, was that God did not want him to stay in Jerusalem. After seriously pondering his situation, he decided "to study for some time so that he would be able to help souls"; accordingly, he went to Barcelona and then to Alcalá.[1] At this time he apparently began to think about the priesthood. He also began to seek out companions, apparently reasoning that if he and his companions were properly trained, they would be able to work for others in the Holy Land according to the desire that God had given him. He could not imagine life apart from the Church, and so he made his own "its initiatives and undertakings" in every area of study.

Just as the experiences of Ignatius set a pattern for the training of novices, so also the experiences of Ignatius during his time of studies established some norms for those in studies. In Barcelona he found that prayer distracted him from study. In Paris he found that begging distracted him from study, as did poor health. He insisted, therefore, that any member who was sick should report his indisposition to the superior; he provided income for the colleges where students pursued their studies; he cautioned against spending too much time in prayer.

---

[1] "Acta P. Ignatii" (*Font.narr* 1:430–450; see Sanz de Diego, "Loyola en Alcalá, in Plazaola," *Ignacio y su tiempo*, 883–900.

As he matured in his studies, prayer, and apostolic activities, it became clear to him that none of these stand in opposition to one another. They feed each other and feed on each other. What is important is union with God, doing at all times what God calls us to do. General Congregation 31 said the same about work and prayer:

> [I]ntimacy with Christ forges a union of our life of prayer and our life of apostolic work. Far from living two separate lives, we are strengthened and guided towards action in our prayer while our action in turn urges us to pray. Bringing salvation to men in word and deed through faith, hope, and love, we pray as we work and are invited to formal prayer that we may toil as true servants of God. In this interplay, praise, petition, thanksgiving, self-offering, spiritual joy, and peace join prayer and work to bring a fundamental unity into our lives. (*DocsGC3132* 213 (pp. 138 f.)

Ignatius did not always find it easy to convince his followers of this truth. This chapter considers the task the Society's students face in integrating prayer and study.

History

In 1545 Ignatius dismissed from the Society a brilliant but eccentric Frenchman, William Postel, filled with prophecies, whom Ignatius and others deemed filled with errors instead.[2] He was the heir of a long line. Joachim of Fiore in the twelfth century and his followers in the thirteenth and fourteenth dreamed of a more spiritual Church and looked to an "angelic pope" who would bring about the renewal. The writings of João da Silva e Menezes in the middle of the fifteenth century abounded in prophecies and errors. At the end of the fifteenth century, Savanarola also prophesied renewal through Papa Angelico. After all, the need was there. In Urbino an unknown proclaimed himself "Pope Clement XV" and gathered cardinals and other followers around him. In Spoleto and Calabria a friar claimed to be Papa Angelico and set his election for May 1549. The Society did not need the trouble the Inquisition caused Postel after he left the Society (*LainMon* 8:638–40).

A Pause for Prayer

John, the beloved disciple, once wrote, "Beloved, do not believe every spirit, but test the spirits to see whether they are from God; for many false prophets have gone out into the world" (I John 4:1 [NRSV]).

---

[2] *EpistIgn* 1:344; *PolChron* 1:148 f. See Georges Weill, *De Gulielmi Postelli vita et indole* (Geneva: Slatkine Reprints, 1969). On pp. 81–97 Weill has a chapter on Postel's "dream" for humanity. For further information and a bibliography on Postel, see *Font.narr* 3:753–65.

After testing the spirits, Ignatius deemed that Onfroy walked with false prophets.

> **Discernment of Spirits:** "It is characteristic of the evil angel, who takes on the appearance of an angel of light, to enter by going along the same way as the devout soul and then to exit by his own way. . . . he brings good and holy thoughts . . . and then strives little by little to get his own way, by enticing the soul over to his own hidden deceits and evil intentions" (*SpEx* 332 [pp. 126 f.]).

At this point we ask again for what we want. We pray, then, for the grace of that kind of prayer appropriate to our state of life, the kind of prayer to which the Father calls us, the kind of prayer that the Spirit desires to pray within us, so that we may be transformed into the likeness of the Son, walk in the Spirit of love, and bring to fulfillment the life of Jesus on earth.

The Tale of the Misguided Zealot

In 1549 the Jesuit community in Gandía was of special concern to Ignatius, not only because of its penchant for long prayers and extended solitude, which interfered with the work of the community, but also because of talk of Francis Borgia as "Papa Angelico" and because of a negative and twisted interpretation of Jesuit history.

Francisco Onfroy tended to run ahead of the Spirit. A graduate of Coimbra like Oviedo, Onfroy was a scholastic when Ignatius missioned him to Gandía in 1545.[3] When classes started in October 1546, Onfroy, who was well-versed in philosophy, put on a one-man show for two days, publicly defending theses in logic, physics, morality, metaphysics, and theology in the presence of the duke, a bishop, and many learned townspeople. In the months that followed, he taught the arts and was ordained the following spring.[4] In a letter to Ignatius, Oviedo described Onfroy as "a native of Normandy, tall and thin, well-proportioned, good looking, pleasant, not over serious, twenty-five or twenty-six years of age, healthy,

---

[3] Onfroy was also known as "Gallo" because he was from France (*EpistIgn* 12:635 n. 8; 142; 239 n. 3; 249, etc.).

[4] Letters of Oviedo to Ignatius, October 13, 1546, and January 26, 1547 (*Epist.mixt* 1:315, 332); letters of February 20 and 24, 1547, to Ignatius (ibid., 340, 342). Oviedo writes that Onfroy is going to be ordained, and in a letter of March 20, 1547, Oviedo calls Onfroy a priest, though he has not yet said Mass (ibid., 348).

of good parentage."[5] He was of a lively disposition, well-spoken (though he did not speak Spanish well), of a speculative bent, although somewhat confused, not especially prudent but enough so for hearing confessions, eager to advance in virtue and a lover of prayer and meditation, inclined to be impatient, though he has been much more gentle since ordination.[6]

Our last chapter (see p. 143) stated that Oviedo and Onfroy had spoken about spending seven years in the desert. Onfroy must have written other letters to Rome that are no longer extant, for Ignatius had convened a group of experts to consider the spirituality of Onfroy and Oviedo and the influence Tejeda exerted upon them. At the end of July Ignatius sent Borgia a lengthy document and a brief letter stating that Oviedo and Onfroy had found the desert they were looking for and would find a greater one if they did not humbly accept the guidance of obedience, for they were deceived by the father of lies.[7]

The lengthy document was entitled "On Certain Illusions Accepted as Revelations."[8] Written by order of Ignatius and corrected by him, the document began with references to the prophecies mentioned above. Most of the document concerned Onfroy, but some criticisms were directed toward Oviedo.[9] It stated that neither the General in Rome nor the provincial in Spain found Onfroy credible. He was not the sort or person who was a fit subject for prophecies, for his mind was confused, as Oviedo had indicated. Elements contributing to his deception were the practice of long prayers lacking direction or purpose and mental exercises coupled with bodily mortifications. Word had come to Rome that he was coughing up blood. The commission found unlikely his prediction that the Pope would persecute the Society or his denunciation of the Society for having become less fervent during the last three years as its membership increased; on the contrary, the commission insisted, all the evidence indicated that fervor was growing. Onfroy maintained that the Society was not well instituted and would be better instituted in spirit; he made no suggestions for reform and thought that Oviedo alone was capable of prophecy.

The commission wondered why, if Tejeda was to be an instrument for the reform of the Franciscans, he failed in obedience. For Onfroy to compare Tejeda with St. Francis was rash; he perhaps knew great things about Tejeda but he did not know everything about Francis. From the point of view of the commission, it was easy to determine which of the two had accomplished more. Furthermore, to identify Francis Borgia as the

---

[5] Ibid., 1:430.

[6] Ibid., 430 f.

[7] *EpistIgn* 2:494 f.

[8] Ibid., 12:632–54.

[9] Ibid., 12:632–52 are primarily about Onfroy; pp. 653 f. are about Oviedo.

expected "angelic pope" could, of course, later prove to be the case, but it was better to leave such things in the hands of God.

The commission examined Onfroy's assertion that no religious order had less prayer than the Society, and that any prayer lasting less than an hour or two was no prayer at all. The document dryly commented that Jesus prayed for the apostles briefly at the Last Supper and three times in the garden during his agony, that the Our Father took less than two hours, as did a psalm, or a portion of the Divine Office, or an ejaculation. The commissioners went on to argue that one could serve God in other ways than by prayer; otherwise everyone should spend twenty-four hours each day occupied with it.

Oviedo had been too gullible regarding Tejeda: considering his very words as supernatural events, believing that he lived constantly in the presence of God, that talking to him was like talking to God, that he had once been in a state of rapture for four months. Rome instead concluded that he confused people.[10]

In November Borgia replied to Ignatius that his immediate experience of Oviedo and Onfroy was far removed from the impression they had created in Rome: one of the blessings in his life was Oviedo, to whom he owed much and whom he greatly loved. Oviedo was filled with consolation and was doing well at his studies. Borgia suggested that Ignatius write to Oviedo consoling him and rejoicing with him over Borgia's report, for he was a true son of the Society despite his innocent desire to be "like a lonely bird on the housetop."[11] Borgia made no mention of Onfroy, for he knew that Ignatius was aware that Onfroy was no longer in Gandía. Trusting Borgia's knowledge of men and his immediate presence on the scene, Ignatius followed his advice and wrote to Oviedo, who kept kissing the name and signature of Ignatius and started talking in a new way.[12]

Likely enough, Rome's displeasure was not communicated to Onfroy, whose penitential excesses had caught up with him. During the summer Onfroy went to Valencia for a change of air, only to die there of tuberculosis in June of the following year.[13]

As for the "lonely bird on the housetop," Ignatius gave him the task of establishing a college in Naples, and in 1553 recommended him for an ill-fated mission to Ethiopia.[14] In 1555 he and a companion, Juan Nuñez

---

[10] Ibid., 12:653 f.

[11] *BorgMon* 2:566, citing Ps. 102:8.

[12] *EpistIgn* 2:650 f. Letter from Borgia to Ignatius, March 31, 1550 (*BorgMon* 2:568).

[13] *Epist.mixt* 2:278. Ibid., 293 n. 6; Dalmases, *Loyola: Founder of the Jesuits,* 68.

[14] *PolChron* 2:173. Letter of December 28, 1553 (*EpistIgn* 6:100).

Barreto, were the first Jesuits consecrated bishops, Oviedo as bishop of Hierapolis and his companion as patriarch of Ethiopia. Oviedo tried to renounce the title because he could not actually live in Hierapolis, and to rid himself of episcopal signet-rings, surplice, and the prescribed companion, all of which he regarded as violations of poverty. When he began to inflict excessive punishment on his body and to eat only lettuce for supper, the patriarch admonished him, but Oviedo replied that in personal matters he owed obedience only to the pope.[15] When the patriarch died in 1562, Oviedo succeeded to the patriarchate and ended his days, not in seven years in the desert, but in twice-seven years of utter poverty and solitude in a tiny village in Ethiopia in the service of some Portuguese families. Today the "saint" is recognized as Venerable Andrés de Oviedo.[16] Did he always walk in the Spirit?

The Special Prayer of the Society

This chapter reflects further on the prayer to which the members of the Society are called.[17] It flows from their way of living, the prayer of those who are on the way toward or already fully living that more holistic active life which presupposes a life of self-abnegation and of being so steeped in prayer as to be able to assist others in choosing and leading their own way of life.

The grace proper to an institute, the special grace God grants to that particular institute, shapes and gives direction to the prayer practiced in that institute. The proper prayer of an institute is that which is suitable to its special grace, even necessary to it to achieve its special way of serving God. The prayer of Benedictines is not different from that of Jesuits simply because they are more deeply immersed in the exterior forms of the liturgy. It is different because their grace is different, and they are more immersed in the exterior forms of the liturgy because their grace is different. Union with God is central to both, for all prayer tends toward absorption in God. How it tends and how that absorption is expressed is the question. In sum, the tone given to the prayer life of an institute by the spirit of that institute is central. The spirit of every institute reflects in one way or another the perennial search for God and attachment to Jesus

---

[15] *PolChron* 5:609–11.

[16] For an account of his life, see Joseph N. Tylenda, S.J., *Jesuit Saints and Martyrs*, 2nd ed. (Chicago: Loyola, 1998), 193 f.

[17] For a good summary of Nadal's position on prayer, see Josef Stierli, S.J., "Jérôme Nadal (1507–1580): Le bras droit du Fondateur," *Cahiers de spiritualité ignatienne* 15 (1991): 39–47, which is an excerpt from the French edition of Stierli's book, *Chercher Dieu en toutes choses: Vie au coeur du monde et prière ignatienne*, trans. Pierre Emonet (Paris: Centurion, 1985; German original, 1981).

crucified and risen. The full meaning of that search and of that attachment becomes apparent only in the fullness of the life revealed in making the search.

In this chapter Nadal sets the stage for what is to come. Just as in the early exhortations in Spain in 1554 he hints at the nature of the grace proper to the Society (see chapter 2 above), so also he points toward the kind of prayer he is convinced is proper to the Society. He does so in an atmosphere that is welcoming, hopeful, expectant, but also troubled. He is addressing a Society consisting mostly of scholastics in studies, rapidly growing without many experienced veterans to guide it. Addressing the scholastics, he speaks to the whole Society, instructing their superiors, not just the new members.

In the course of time, Nadal developed his thinking regarding scholastics, or preferably, Jesuit students, for today the coadjutor brothers take the same courses as the scholastics. He describes them as men who in the eyes of the Society seem capable of studies, yet are still on the way to the fullness of the Society, men who have already acquired some perfection in the virtues and who try to augment and increase it by joining it to study.[18] They are not in a state of probation regarding membership; "but they are being tested regarding their intellectual ability and capacity for learning," "and now are giving themselves to the study of all those things that are necessary or will prove useful for attaining the end of the Institute."[19] They have potential but have not yet fully realized it.

Ignatius had concluded his 1547 letter to Coimbra, mentioned in chapter 2 above, by urging the many ways in which studies can help the neighbor. Preparing to serve, acquiring virtue, and giving good example are all ways of serving, and "the fourth way . . . consists in holy desires and prayers. Although study does not grant you time for long prayers, desires can compensate for time in one who makes continual prayer out of all his tasks by undertaking them only for the service of God."[20] Some Jesuits found it difficult to hear and embrace this position.

Recall, if you will, the remark Nadal made to Borromeo: "The active life in the Society is multiplex. It consists primarily in the more excellent action of preaching, lecturing, and other spiritual ministries proper to simple priests, *and of studying for scholastics,* and secondarily in the ministry of the corporal works of mercy" (*EpistNadal* 4:174, emphasis added).

---

[18] "In exam. annot." (*CommInst* 181, no. 136). "Plática 10ᵃ en Coimbra" (*Pláticas espirituales*) 122 f., no. 37.

[19] "Exhort. 8ᵃ en Alcalá" (*CommInst* 388, no. 165). "Dialogus II" (ibid., 672, no. 51).

[20] Letter of May 7, 1547 (*EpistIgn* 1:509).

Recall as well the passage suggesting that after the rigorous probation of the novitiate, the contemplative life should guide everything:

> Reflect that the active life and the contemplative life should always travel together. But the period of rigorous probation brings it about that the active comes to some perfection, and by this time the contemplative dominates and guides and governs peacefully and with enlightenment in the Lord; and in this way one comes to the higher active life, which presupposes the active and the contemplative and has the power to seal everyone with the mark of active or contemplative in accordance with the greater service of God. To be concise: the action of love united to God is perfect action.[21]

It is by integrating prayer and study that Jesuit students gradually move into the higher active life.

Norms for Prayer—1554

"Orden de la oración" (*Constitutiones* 4:487–91, nos. 1–18)

Chapter 3 reviewed what Nadal taught about the prayer of students, especially during his 1554 visit to Spain. On this occasion, his special concern was to teach the novices and students how to prepare themselves to live the full life of the Society; and in so doing he enlightened a good many of the veterans who had not been particularly well grounded in the Jesuit way of living. Here are some ideas from another discourse on prayer that he delivered in Spain at the same time. He devoted the first half of it to a discussion of the amount of time given to prayer in the Society, and spent the second half examining the quality of that prayer.

Time for Prayer

Constitutiones 4:487–89, nos. 1–9

Five paragraphs concern students (not much time for prayer), one is about novices (more time), one deals with the fully formed (more freedom), and two apply to all the members of the Society. Nadal begins by summarizing what the *Constitutions* have to say regarding students. Although we considered this material to some extent in chapter 3, a little review will show better how Nadal expects the young Jesuit to grow in his ability to walk in the Spirit as he strives to bring prayer and study together into one integrated life. Before Nadal's summary is the text itself of the *Constitutions*. The editorial differences in the paragraph on the prayer of scholastics in the 1550, 1556, and the present-day editions of the *Constitutions* are so minuscule that all three paragraphs can be translated in the same way. The official English translation of 1995 reads as follows:

---

[21] "Orationis ratio" (*EpistNadal* 4:679).

Consequently, in addition to confession and Communion every eight days and daily Mass, they will have one hour, during which they will recite the Hours of Our Lady, examine their consciences twice each day, and add other prayers according to each one's devotion to fill out the rest of the aforesaid hour. They will do all this according to the order and judgment of their superiors, whom they oblige themselves to obey in place of Christ our Lord.[22]

Nadal summarizes these lines by describing how the student's life can be filled with prayer that surpasses the limits set down in the Constitutions:

The meditation and prayer of a student beyond the ordinary, which is the Mass and the daily prayer available for it, the examen, confession, and Communion, can be by carrying out the purpose of his studies, which is that of the Society, the exercise of obedience—even of the intellect—the actual respect shown to the superior as to Christ our Lord, to the fathers as to the apostles, to the brothers as to the disciples of the Lord; by stirring up in one the presence of God in everything; namely, by offering his studies to God and all the work they involve, by postponing the delights of prayer in order to serve in some way by preaching or in the dining room, etc. (*Constitutiones* 4:487, no. 1)

Ignatius urges the free use of imagination in prayer to lead to insight and love, for example, imagining Christ present and eating with his disciples. Seeing Christ in the superior is not a function of the imagination but of a living faith; the priests in the community *do* carry on the work of the apostles; the brothers *are* followers of Jesus. Nadal envisions the scholastic as fully conscious that all his companions are wholly and lovingly engaged in the mission of Christ. That religious orders look upon themselves as "apostolic," re-creating in the present the world of the primitive Church, is not fantasy: in the world of faith there is nothing more real. To live in this realm of faith is "to raise one's mind and heart to God," to breathe prayer all day long.

Just as offering one's studies to God is a prayerful act, rising like incense in God's sight, so also the awareness that one is preparing to carry on the mission of the Son and the Spirit in ministry to God's people is raising the mind and heart to God, all through God's initiative and in union with God. Willingly forgoing the delights of prayer to minister to God's people is raising the mind and heart to God, for ministering to people is ministering to Christ, whether it is preaching or waiting on table or visiting the sick or organizing a picnic. To minister is to surrender as Mary did in going to visit Elizabeth, to make oneself completely available to God and others. This is how Ignatius differs from other founders. The one who studies, the one who preaches, the one who serves—all participate in the mission of the Word spoken and sent by the Father, the Son

---

[22] *ConsCN* 342 (p. 142).

who has come to serve and not to be served. This self-surrender is prayer, a prayer that continues even if awareness fails.

Although the principles governing the lives of Jesuit students were established early, they were not established universally. The oldest extant norms governing student life in Padua in 1545–46 indicate that beyond weekly confession and Communion and whatever the Church obliges them to do, Jesuit students should do no more meditation or contemplation or prayer or penance than the superior allows them.[23] These norms, however, had not spread to Spain and Portugal.

Because common expectation demanded that the prayer of religious should be lengthy, the norms that Jesuit communities on the Iberian Peninsula established for themselves are not surprising. In 1547 Diego Miró wrote to Ignatius that in Valencia someone awakened the community a little before five and they gathered in the dark to meditate for an hour on the life of Christ. At eight o'clock at night they met for another hour of prayer, generally the examination of conscience, along with meditation on God's blessings and on the passion of Christ.[24] As we saw in chapter 3, similar systems still prevailed in 1553 and 1554. They had much to learn yet about prayer proper to the Society of Jesus, but they did reflect their own Spanish heritage.[25]

In the earliest form of the *Constitutions* in 1547, known as α, Ignatius recognized that "mortification plays a greater role in the time of probation [novitiate], as do meditations and longer prayers," and explained why:

> For students who persist in moving along [who walk in the Spirit] wholly focused on their studies, whatsoever they may be, with a pure intention of seeking only the service of God our Lord and the aid of their neighbor are blessed with mortification and meditation and genuine prayer in the studies themselves and are very pleasing to his Divine Majesty.

He saw the demands of study itself as a form of mortification. He modified the norms of Padua to allow "no more than an hour for meditation or spiritual reading or mental or vocal prayer," and underlined the role of the superior.[26] The emphasis in the early version of the *Constitutions* was on the positive role of study in the spiritual life if approached properly. Later versions added emphasis on the examen, a method of interior asceticism and prayer enormously useful for purging the heart and promoting purity of intention.

---

[23] *Epist.mixt* 1:591 f.

[24] Ibid., 415.

[25] For prayer as actually practiced in the early Society, see Ignacio Iparraguirre, S.J., "La oración en la Compañía naciente," *AHSI* 25 (1956): 455–87.

[26] *Constitutiones* 2:177 f.

Quality of Prayer

Constitutiones 4:489–91, no. 10–18.

Nadal begins to discuss the quality of the prayer by this reminder: "Notice the way the Society has of advancing in prayer through the grace of the Lord" (*Constitutiones* 4:489, nos. 10). He next explains the purpose of the Exercises in the Society in contrast to the way of giving them to others:

> First of all, the Society gives the Spiritual Exercises in their fullness to those it receives: not only to help them attain the principles and the method of finding prayer and advancing in it, *but the Exercises are given as an experiment and trial to see if they are apt for prayer in the way that we desire* (489 f., no. 11, emphasis added).

When others come for the Exercises, he is saying, the Society adopts an attitude of openness to whatever the Holy Spirit might do in those persons; but with those who come with a desire to become Jesuits, the openness incorporates attention to whether these persons are apt for the kind of prayer to which the Holy Spirit has called members of the Society.

Afterwards, he continues, in two years of ordinary probation, through various experiments the Society sees to it that the aspiring Jesuits make progress in the habit and facility not only in prayer but in moving toward its perfection and toward perfection in all the virtues, and that they are profoundly imbued with a passionate love and zeal for souls (489 f., nos. 12 f.). In this context he writes:

> All should strive in the Lord, walking in the way of prayer and the spiritual life, to find God in all their works and ministries, walking only in the way of the spirit, habituating themselves to arouse the spirit and devotion in all things, and in all their ministries to exploit whatever insights and feelings linger *[reliquias de la cogitatión],* as well as prayer and the habit of prayer, as far as the fragility of our nature allows.[27]

"Walking only in the way of the spirit," as seen earlier, refers to that deepest realm of the human person that goes beyond "mind" or "soul," where one is most vulnerable and open to the transcendent, the point where the Holy Spirit is most active in the human person, where "that very Spirit intercedes with sighs too deep for words" (Rom. 8:26). To walk in the spirit is to walk in the Spirit. The Society's prayer disposes one for the gift of discerning wisdom and of knowing how to apply it, to finding

---

[27] On the need for finding God in all things in contemporary society, see Mario da França Miranda, S.J., " 'Trouver Dieu en toutes choses' dans la société moderne," *Cahiers de spiritualité ignatienne* 14 (1990): 407–18.

God in all things, that is to say.[28] In the next paragraph Nadal draws this conclusion:

> In this way, one who has developed a habit of this in the Lord has to be alert so that the taste for prayer does not cool his fervor or divert his energy from pursuing the purpose of his vocation or from using the means necessary for that end, such as studies and everything undertaken under obedience; he should therefore let prayer and its fervor permeate all the activities of his calling, and enter into these things with prayer or in a prayerful mood and atmosphere or with its afterglow in the Lord. (*Constitutiones* 4:490, no. 15)

From this he concludes:

> Hence, it is clear why the Society does not allow students much time for retired prayer in view of the perfection that the Society seeks, judging it an imperfection to have to retire much to find prayer after so many exercises and trials, primarily in view of the abundant grace and influence of the Lord on the members of the Society who follow him with all their heart and strength, with great faith and confidence in his divine mercy and goodness, in the spirit and Constitutions and the Society's entire manner of living. (490 f., no. 16)

Study in the Society is more than an intellectual probe into the mystery of the universe; study is surrender to the mission of the Son sent by the Father. Illumined by love and a desire to serve, study pierces the Trinitarian presence at the heart of reality. To be saturated in that mystery is to be saturated in prayer.

Some years earlier Favre had gone right to the heart of the matter. "In your passion [*spiritu*] for knowing [*saber*]," he wrote to the scholastics in Paris in 1540,

> do not extinguish your passion for graced perceiving [*santo sentir*]. You will fulfill my desire . . . provided your principal teacher and the one who ultimately imprints learning deep within you is always the one who repeats the material with you again and again, the Holy Spirit, in whom all that is learned is well learned, and without whom whoever knows anything at all, has not come to know it yet as he ought to know it. . . . Seek the Spirit who makes letters live. (*FabMon* 102, 105)

In his own spiritual diary, Nadal wrote, "In created things themselves the power of God is to be experienced, so that he wishes to be known and contemplated and loved and adored by reason of experiencing the creature itself" (*Orat.observ* 62, no. 134). Walking in the Spirit is the same for Ignatius as finding God in all things.

---

[28] Joseph Veale, S.J., "Life of the Spirit (II): Ignatian Contemplation," *The Furrow* 28 (1977): 72 f., esp. p. 78.

Finding God in all things gradually transforms the circle of work and prayer that Nadal talks about into a circle of prayer. Commentators express the Ignatian insight in a variety of ways. Raymond Hostie underlines the rhythms in Nadal, the rhythm of meditation and contemplation, the rhythm of contemplation and action, the rhythm of divine activity and human cooperation. Thomas Clarke proposes contemplation and decision, with contemplation leading to decision and decision to further contemplation. For Michel Certeau mystique and mission tend to become one. Peter-Hans Kolvenbach stresses the harmonious compenetration of prayer and action so that "the human action is that of God with us." For Pierre Emonet action itself becomes prayer to the extent that it is the place where one encounters God. Herbert Alphonso remarks that prayer is not primarily an act but an attitude, not a specific exercise but a spirit, an atmosphere, a climate of soul enveloping the whole person; at prayer or in action, the person is united with God.[29]

In fact, the Constitutions urge the novices to take care that they reverence all creatures, and especially one another, as the First Principle and Foundation of the Spiritual Exercises demands. To pay attention means to be fully aware, to be wide awake, to act with deliberate intention. Reverence is awe in the presence of the sacred. Awe in the Society leads to a desire for mission. The Constitutions tell the novices to look upon all others as if they were their superiors, "so that by consideration of one another they may thus *grow in devotion* and praise God our Lord, whom each one should strive to recognize in the other as in his image" (*ConsCN* 250[v.5] [p. 112]). The italics are meant to highlight that Ignatius used the same words about himself in what were close to his final remarks when dictating his life to da Câmara, indicating that he "was always *increasing in devotion,* more now than in his whole life" (*Font.narr* 1:504, no. 99). Like Benedict, Ignatius did not talk much about sanctity; a word he did use, however, was "devotion"; and in this passage he makes clear what he means by it: "facility in finding God"; to this he added, "Whenever he wanted to find God, he found him." As Stierli points out, "In place of choir as the essential expression of contemplation, [Ignatius] presented

---

[29] Raymond Hostie, S.J., "Méditation et contemplation d'après le Père Jérôme Nadal," *Revue d'ascétique et de mystique,* 32 (1956): 397–419, esp. n. 59. See also his chapter "The Cycle of Activity and Prayer," in *Finding God in All Things,* 153–65; Thomas E. Clarke, S.J., "The Ignatian Exercises: Contemplation and Discernment," *Review for Religious* 31, no. 1 (1972): 62–69; Certeau, "L'universalisme ignatien," 173–83; Peter-Hans Kolvenbach, S.J., "Ponencia de clausura," in *Ejercicios espirituales y mundo de hoy,* 360; Pierre Emonet, S.J., "Faire de toute sa vie une prière continuelle," *Christus* 37 (1990): 466–76, esp. p. 469, and id., " 'Faire de toutes ses actions une prière continuelle': La prière de ceux qui n'ont pas beaucoup de temps pour faire oraison," *Cahiers de spiritualité ignatienne* 16 (1992): 45–60; Alphonso, "Vida diaria," 266; Ovey Mohammed, "Hinduism," 117–19.

a new religious ideal, 'Seeking God in all things.'"[30] The finding is in the seeking, as the Gospel promises (Luke 11:9). Novices begin to find God in all things by reverencing one another. Students continue by reverencing and respecting all that they encounter in their time of studies, seeing everything and everyone as a gift from God.

Jesuit Student Participation in the More Holistic Active Life

This section will look at some later development in Nadal's thought and reflect a little on the contemporary scene.

Nadal tells the Jesuit students in Coimbra in 1561: "The reason why Our Father gave little time to the students for prayer is that they are assumed to be so advanced and habituated to making [the Exercises] that there will be more need to restrain them lest they give too much time to prayer, rather than to have to urge them to it."[31] In the transition from the novitiate to studies, the Society's expectations change. Certainly the hard work of the active life is not over (nor will it ever be in this life).

The Society's Students and Studies

Twelfth Exhortation at Alcalá, 1561 (*CommInst* 447–54, nos. 228–37)

Nadal briefly outlines the new expectations, explaining the prominence of studies in the Society. True to the climate of the times, he sees studies as a powerful instrument for overcoming heresy; however, he admits that apart from combating heresy, study is crucial for carrying on ministries (*CommInst* 447–49, nos. 228 f.). "It is necessary to join the practical with the speculative, that is, to join the spiritual life . . . with knowledge and theology." Without that union something fundamental is lacking, but "when the spiritual life is united with learning, it is singularly efficacious and very fruitful" (450, no. 230). He describes graphically the transition from the novitiate to studies:

A scholastic [or brother] comes to studies from a house of probation where he has been trying to live the religious life and acquire virtue. He has to bring along the humility that he has gained, the patience, the simplicity, his dedication to prayer and mortification and all the other virtues . . . [a]nd on top of that he has to adorn himself with studies and attend to them. He goes, then, . . . to study, which is to go to acquire the instruments *[arma]* that he needs to help people. These instruments have to be cleaned and polished to be effective against the enemy; and, with this as his purpose,

---

[30] Stierli, "Ignatian Prayer," 136.

[31] "Plática 18ª en Coimbra" (*Pláticas espirituales*, 185, no. 21).

study is a work of special merit, for thereby he is preparing himself in love to work for the benefit of other people, which is the driving force behind studies in the Society. (450 f., no. 231)

Preparing to help other people purifies and benefits the student himself, for it forces one to seek the truth rather than self-glorification. "How will the student himself grow?" Nadal asks; his reply:

> Cling to a right intention. What am I seeking in my studies? Where am I going?—To God by the road that he has set out for me through my vocation. I want to tell you that the end of our studies has to be the end that the Society has in mind, the greater service of God, the greater profit of oneself and one's neighbors, and therefore I have to motivate myself powerfully for study. Desire for the advancement of others, zeal for the honor and service of God our Lord, have to be the principle directing our studies. (451, no. 233)

In learning, a student finds a powerful instrument for bringing the Good News to God's people, and in study, a means for discovering the instruments he can wield most effectively for others. Study prepares nature to be an instrument of grace, aims at releasing all that grace has stored. Study bridges the active life of rooting out vices and acquiring virtues and the life of contemplation, for study is extremely purgative as well as contemplative.

Nadal situates study very carefully, placing it alongside spiritual ministries. Students do not address the full gamut of "more excellent action," but learning, as a work done out of love, is a bridge to the more holistic active life characteristic of the Society.[32] Study provides an inchoate form of that life gradually unfolding and taking shape. A Jesuit student stands at the threshold of the full life of the Society. He prepares to instruct others to become active or contemplative, or to become teachers of those called to the kind of life proper to the Society. Through study he gathers and "cleans and polishes the tools" for his future ministry. Facing the task of integrating many activities into a life of prayer, he begins by integrating one activity, study. Nadal's challenge over four hundred years ago is today's challenge as well:

> The Society wants men accomplished in all that can assist its end, as far as this is possible. Can he be a good logician?—let him be one. A good theologian?—let him be one. And a good humanist—and so of all the other areas that can serve our Institute; let a man be whatever he can according to his own talent, and may he not be content with mediocrity in any of these areas. (452, no. 234)

---

[32] "De professione et choro" (*EpistNadal* 4:174).

Nadal's words echo the Kingdom and the Two Standards, challenging students, even now in studies, to service, not to glory. No room remains for ambition, pride, self-satisfaction, the desire to be honored and esteemed. Walking this path requires great interior mortification. Relying on one's own ability has to go; humility has to take its place. Empty curiosity and concern for the frivolous are of no value. Students should see themselves as helpers of those who have succeeded the apostles and disciples, carrying on the same work of saving souls. In study Christ teaches the student; in a lecture Christ teaches the student through the lecturer. A student does not need what is barren and worthless; a student needs, rather, the gifts of the Holy Spirit: the student needs purity of heart (451–54, nos. 233–37). To avoid ambition and worldly success, to rely on God rather than oneself, to seek only knowledge that is useful for the Kingdom of Christ, to experience partaking in the mission of the apostles, to find Christ in teachers and books, and to be open to the gifts of the Holy Spirit mean constant daily and all-day-long discernment.

Nadal sees Martha as an example "of laborious meditation on the mysteries that usually leads to the lifting of the mind and the contemplation of divine things."[33] In study Mary comes to her rescue, opening her mind to delight in mystery, "putting aside the confusing concern about many things, Mary comes to Martha's assistance and is united with her in our Lord."[34] A student's life contains a strong purgative element in the demanding discipline of study itself, but it is primarily illuminative, integrating the solid pursuit of learning into his life of following Christ. Henceforth, even when he is following his heart, he will have the tools with which to analyze and evaluate a situation, will know what he is getting into, will understand why he is doing what he is doing. "Hence," says Nadal,

> it is clear why the Society does not give more time to its students for private prayer, viewing the perfection to which the Society aspires, judging it an imperfection to have to withdraw much to find prayer . . . looking principally at the grace and abundant influence of the Lord . . . with great faith and confidence in his divine mercy and goodness manifest in the spirit and Constitutions and whole manner of living of the Society.[35]

---

[33] "Ad. ev., feria II maj. hebd." (*Adnotationes et meditationes in Evangelia,* 220).

[34] "Orationis ratio" (*EpistNadal* 4:674).

[35] "Orden de la oración" (*Constitutiones* 4:490 f., no. 16); also in *EpistNadal* 4:671, with minor variations.

Continuity with the New Millennium

The continuity between Nadal's approach to studies and the needs of the new millennium is striking. He follows a Christian tradition beginning with Origen and Augustine and running through the Middle Ages, which came to be known as "despoiling the Egyptians" after the manner of the Israelites immediately before the Exodus (Exod. 12:35–36). It was understood to mean the use of pagan cultural values for proclaiming the Gospel and developing a sound ethics. Thus, the first Jesuit schools, in the context of the humanism of the sixteenth century, plundered the classical pagan literature of the Golden and Silver Ages for positive cultural values. Just as St. Paul had done (see 1 Cor. 9:22), they adapted themselves to the needs of the times and the people in order to carry out the apostolic mission of saving souls. Ricci applied these principles in China, and de Nobili in India.[36] The challenge for the new millennium is clear. In its 1991 document on studies in the American Assistancy, the Society of Jesus expressed in contemporary terms what it means today for Jesuits to live out the more holistic active life that is characteristic of the Society:

> The primary apostolate of a Jesuit in this period of formation is the integration of humanistic, philosophical and theological studies so that he can participate in the Society's ecclesial mission to the contemporary world. His humanistic studies take account not only of those realities which have made culture beautiful and good but also of those realities which cause injustice, pain, and destruction. His philosophical studies develop those attitudes and critical tools whereby he can reflect systematically on the contemporary situation, analyze it, and ultimately help to develop alternatives to structures that erode justice, peace, and Christian belief. His theological studies lay a solid academic foundation for a growing understanding and appreciation of faith and its content. This will assist his own spiritual life and provide an intelligent basis for developing a Christian perspective on the world in which he lives.[37]

The evolution and development of the arts and humanities into distinct disciplines, the growth in awareness of the evolution and breakdown of differing cultures around the world, the growing international impact of local political positions, the gradual globalization of the economic order—all suggest the need for those preparing to minister in the

---

[36] Mario Fois, S.J., "La giustificazione cristiana degli studi umanistici da parte de Ignazio di Loyola e le sue conseguenze nei gesuiti posteriori," in Plazaola, *Ignacio y su tiempo*, 405–40.

[37] *Regional Order of Studies*, U.S. Assistancy (1991 proposed revision of 1983 text), no. 26.

Church to have a ready grasp of social theory as well as of philosophy and theology.

In urging scholastics to embrace studies with enthusiasm, Nadal had warned them of heresies that gnawed at the vitals of the Church and of the need to prepare for ministry. On the brink of the new millennium, a contemporary theologian addressing Jesuit scholastics and brothers in the American Assistancy who were engaged in "first studies" warned of obstacles to intellectual growth existing in American culture:

> [T]he age is very complex, the issues we face very urgent, the state of our culture in many ways disturbing, and the Church we serve—at least in its institutional aspect—in rapidly advancing disarray.
>
> Meanwhile, in a culture as anti-intellectual as our own, it's hard to have a serious intellectual life at all. It requires real virtue, rare maturity . . . and a very disciplined interior life to resist the pressures from all around us that trivialize sustained inquiry and careful reading and thoughtful conversation. (p. 1)
>
> The problem that occupied me as a young man, and which followed me into the Society . . . was a series of perplexing disconnections . . . a disconnection between the intellectual life as it was usually practiced and intelligent attention to human feelings, to the heart . . . a disconnection among the disciplines of the academy, as if [one] had nothing to do with [another; (4)] . . . and most baffling and disheartening, . . . a disconnection between the serious life of the mind and the practical affairs of life, . . . a split between theory and practice . . . as though an evil genie had devised a plan to syphon off the energies of the brightest members of every generation and set them to embittered arguing about the fine details of conflicting interpretations of various commentaries on the major commentaries written on the works of isolated geniuses, while the decisions about the great forces determining the quality of life each day for the vast majority of people were handed over to those people who never much read or thought or wondered about anything. (5)[38]

In its 1991 report the American Assistancy, at least in theory, espouses a program of studies enabling a Jesuit student to face our contemporary age. Like Nadal, it aims at developing, not primarily a philoso-

---

[38] Robert J. Egan, S.J., "To Think What We Are Doing: Intellectual Formation for Jesuit Mission," keynote address delivered at the Conference on Collegiate Studies, Jesuit Formation, and Apostolic Mission, sponsored by St. Michael's Institute, Jepson Center Auditorium, Gonzaga University, Spokane, Washington, November 1996. The talk was designed to provoke thought. Trying to fathom in faith the meaning and function of "disarray" in an organization whose life breath is the Holy Spirit is as daunting as confronting the problem of evil.

pher or theologian or social scientist, but a minister of God's Word who has passionate concern for the world in which he lives. It should produce what Egan calls "passionate intelligence and intelligent passion."[39] As Nadal cautioned, unless studies are connected with the life of the spirit, they can be an occasion of harm for many. No little vigilance must be exercised so that while the intellect flourishes the affect does not perish or suffer harm. Studies are to serve the spirit, not destroy it.[40] The union is a marriage of tension, but tension is capable of bearing great fruit.

The continuity between Nadal and the present continues in a contemporary philosopher's comment on the connection between the novitiate and first studies; in effect, this comment underlines the contemporary theologian's point:

> In the novitiate the young Jesuit learns how to discern the various spirits operative in his own soul. In first studies, the Jesuit should learn how to discern the various spirits at work within the communities and the larger culture he is drawn into and called to serve. As he learns the discipline of prayer and the cultivation of the spiritual virtues of faith, hope and love in the novitiate, in first studies he should learn the discipline of historically informed, critical reflection, the art of articulate dialogue and the analytical and organizational skills necessary to build, sustain and critique institutional loci of meaning and agency in the places he will later be sent to minister. . . . At the same time, first studies should also lead to a more radical, and more critical, self-understanding, for in studying the spirits at work in the communities he feels drawn to serve and in his wider culture, he is also studying the forces which have shaped his own identity and which continue to inspire him.[41]

Everything in the novitiate, even the intellect, had as its aim to stir up the affections. Studies obviously occupy the intellect: challenging, stimulating, sometimes overwhelming it; and the challenge for a student is to approach studies in such a way that through them he not only maintains but even increases the commitment and fervor he acquired through the novitiate and its experiments.[42] No wonder Nadal insisted that students observe obedience carefully. It protects them in Christ so that what can easily happen will not happen: studies will not inappropriately insert some

---

[39] Ibid., 5.

[40] "Exhort. 1554 hisp." (*CommInst* 64, no. 61).

[41] Timothy R. Clancy, S.J., "Teaching Jesuits Philosophy: A Rationale for the First Studies Program in the American Assistancy," paper presented before the Jesuit Philosophical Association in Pittsburgh, Pa., March 28, 1998.

[42] "In exam. annot." (*CommInst* 178, no. 124).

of the student's own will or judgment into the picture and obscure the end in view, the greater service of God and the salvation of souls (182, no. 40). Just as the task of the novitiate was all absorbing, so

> students should be totally immersed in their studies, provided they preserve their fervor and commitment. If they can help someone incidentally, they should do so, for it is proper to help their fellow students; . . . they should not, however, be allowed other ministries on behalf of their neighbor unless it is clear that these would not only not interrupt the studies but would even help them. (192, no. 167)

The Society's approach to students is very different from its approach to novices. Its emphasis moves from the heart to the head without denying or neglecting the heart. Studies should not get in the way of the heart, but if they do, the Society can make sure the student receives nourishment for the heart. "Nevertheless," Nadal stated, "the proper fruit of the Spirit in students comes from the studies themselves directed toward the end of the Society. For our end, situated as it is in the fire of divine love, ought to inflame all studies. Hence, the exercise of study should release an enormous thrust toward our salvation and perfection."[43] Nadal's thoughts here are key: relating studies to the end of the Society can only be a source of life and of love, and seeing studies in relation to God and salvation history is the raising of the mind and heart to God. A pilgrim to a sacred shrine has already grasped in his heart the object of his quest.

To reach the goal, to achieve in studies themselves the end of the Society, how should the Society proceed in the new millennium? The contemporary philosopher quoted above suggests a clear and simple outline:

> Our first studies programs aspire to triangulate the three disciplines of philosophy, theology and social theory. Each can be seen as informing and bounding what of the others is most important for this period of study. That is to say, the kind of philosophy scholastics should study ought to be the kind that illumines and underlies the practice of contemporary theology and social theory. Similarly the kind of theology appropriate for this stage of formation ought to be those areas and schools of theology that most rely on, inspire and critique contemporary philosophy and social theory. Finally the kind of social theory we ought to teach is that kind which is theologi-

---

[43] "Exhort. 5ᵃ" (ibid., 806, no. 4).

cally and philosophically informed and that is most insightful and provocative for the philosophical and theological questions of today.[44]

The contemporary theologian quoted above puts the matter this way:

The kind of intellectual formation we need will . . . continue to have certain characteristics: it should be rooted in our spirituality, oriented to the promotion of justice, informed by intelligent theology, discerning about important currents of our culture, interdisciplinary in its range, shared in honest conversations and committed friendships, arising from and flowing back into our action, our collaborative apostolic venture.[45]

As he progresses, the student will find that entering more and more into the ministerial works of the Society will assist study and ground it in reality. As Nadal wrote to Cardinal Borromeo in 1572, the Society is not monastic in nature, nor should it be judged in terms of other orders, but only in terms of its own and the means necessary to that end. He concluded thus:

Hence (since the nature of our religious order is this broad, and our ministries this multiple, difficult, and laborious), it follows that our testing periods or novitiate should be extremely painstaking and lengthy, the nature of our obedience demanding, and every practice of the religious life as perfect as it can be. . . . We also take care that those who are professed not only are tested in living as religious, but are sufficiently practiced in those ministries that they must undertake by reason of their profession. Whence it follows that they should be priests before they are professed.[46]

One trained for ministry needs to be so profoundly grounded in prayer that the ministry itself becomes prayer. Nadal, indeed, alleges the example of Ignatius, who put as much energy into resisting prayer that interfered with legitimate business as others put into entering into prayer. "Thus he was always lifted up and engaged in this kind of prayer we have been discussing." Nadal also presents Francis Xavier as an example, and concludes with a Trinitarian formula: "From all this it is clear how great a facility, with the grace of God, the Society has in prayer if one cooperates with the Spirit, whom God abundantly communicates."[47]

Nadal devoted much effort to preparing his *Evangelicæ historiæ imagines* (Gospel illustrations) and *Adnotationes in evangelia* (Gospel

---

[44] Clancy, "Teaching Jesuits Philosophy," 5.

[45] Egan, "To Think What We Are Doing," 9.

[46] "De professione et choro" (*EpistNadal* 4:174 f.).

[47] "Exhort. 1554 hisp." (*CommInst* 97 f., no. 163).

notes), which were images and meditations for Jesuit students published only after his death. Jiménez, Nadal's former socius, wrote in the introduction addressed to the Pope:

> The founder of our Society said one day, most Holy Father, to Jerónimo Nadal, one of his first companions, that he would value very highly the man who, for the benefit of the scholastics of the same Society, would put into permanent and ready form for prayer and meditation the Gospels which are read at Mass during Lent and on Sundays; he wanted it, furthermore, annotated and illustrated with suitable pictures. [Nadal] did what he knew Ignatius desired very much.[48]

At least one-third of the meditations make mention of the Trinity, looking either at the inner operations of Trinitarian life or at the mysteries of Christ's life from a Trinitarian viewpoint.[49] Nadal aims to develop a Trinitarian atmosphere for the whole of life, an awareness in faith of the Trinitarian significance of all Christian truth. He expects a Jesuit student's prayer life to be rich, as he had made clear in his teaching on prayer proper to the Society summarized above.

Conclusion

Nadal's exhortation on prayer delivered in Spain in 1554 concludes that finding God in all things, extending prayer to every aspect of our vocation and linking it with everything we do, "is not difficult but very easy through the grace of God, if we will. For if a man easily thinks of some end he wants to attain, like riches or honor or the like, what is so amazing if we can always be thinking about God, since that is the work of a human being precisely as human?" (*CommInst* 97, no. 162). Human beings are

---

[48] *Adnot. in evangelia,* †2. For the reproduction of the images only, see Joseph F. MacDonnell, S.J., *Gospel Illustrations: A Reproduction of the 153 Images taken from Jerome Nadal's 1595 book* "Adnotationes et Meditationes in Evangelia" (Fairfield: Fairfield Jesuit Community, 1998), and *The Illustrated Spiritual Exercises: Edited by Jerome Nadal, Aide to Ignatius Loyola* (Scranton: University of Scranton Press, 2001), which gives at the bottom of the title page the original Latin title of the 1593 Plantin edition in Antwerp: *Evangelicæ historiæ imagines: ex ordine Euangeliorum quæ toto anno in Missæ sacrificio recitantur, in ordine temporis vitæ Christi digestæ.* At first the meditations and the illustrations were published separately, but the edition to which the present author has access published the illustrations first and then the meditations. The University of St. Joseph in Philadelphia plans to publish selections from the meditations beginning in 2003.

[49] Hervé Gaulin, S.J., "La Vocation apostolique de la Compagnie de Jésus dans les écrits du Père Jérôme Nadal, S.J." (unpublished doctoral dissertation prepared for the Pontifical Gregorian University in Rome, 1952), 113 f.

called to serve God in all things: to serve is to obey, to serve is to love. Service is union with God. Obedience is union with God. Love is union with God. Prayer is union with God. To find God in all things is to serve God in all things. The call is to constant awareness of human partnership with God in history, constant attention to what God as creator asks of a human creature's love. The link between obedience and prayer and love is profound. Basic to created reality is the response to obey God in everything and to praise God with passionate love in everything. The Benedictine ideal *"Ora et labora"* (Pray and work) becomes transformed. The reality is the same, but the Jesuit expression of it has a different tone, a different look.

General Congregation 31 expressed that tone well in the paragraph quoted near the beginning of this chapter:

> Intimacy with Christ forges a union of our life of prayer and our life of apostolic work. Far from living two separate lives, we are strengthened and guided towards action in our prayer while our action in turn urges us to pray. Bringing salvation to men in word and deed through faith, hope, and love, we pray as we work and are invited to formal prayer that we may toil as true servants of God. In this interplay, praise, petition, thanksgiving, self-offering, spiritual joy, and peace join prayer and work to bring a fundamental unity into our lives. (*DocsGC3132* 213 (pp. 138 f.)

This is how Jesuit students are called to respond to the challenge of Vatican II stating that all institutes "should share in the life of the Church," entering into "its initiatives and undertakings in biblical, liturgical, dogmatic, pastoral, ecumenical, missionary, and social matters."

Our next chapter looks at those who have final vows in the Society and reflects on the prayer one might expect from a Jesuit after he has moved into the broad field of engagement demanded by the higher active life that is characteristic of the Society.

Chronicle for Chapter Nine

[Ignatius] instructed [Jerónimo Nadal] thoroughly in the manner of prayer, in the understanding of the Institute, the Constitutions, and the manner of governing [of the Society of Jesus]. Couple that with his great genius and natural talent, and he turned out . . . thoroughly in tune with the heart of Ignatius.

—Diego Jiménez, S.J., "Commentarium"

Nadal's Life and Travels (1564–1566)

1564

Rome: Assistant for Austria, Lower Germany; Perugia, visits college; Rome

1565

Rome: Laínez dies; Borgia elected general; Nadal refused permission to join anti-Turk armada

1566

Rome

Jan.: Named theologian to papal legate at Augsburg

Feb.: Named visitor to Germany, Austria, Rheinland

Feb. 6: Leaves Rome for Florence, Bologna, Trent, Innsbruck

March 6–April 15: Augsburg

April 16–23: Dillingen

April 24 till end of Diet: Augsburg

June 1–16: Munich

June 16ff.: Ingolstadt, Augsburg, Dillingen

July 20–24: By Danube for Vienna, dangerous storms

July 27: Arrives at Vienna (16 days)

Aug. 13: To Tyrnau, visits college (5 days)

Aug. 19–29: At Olmutz (Olomouc), founds college

Sept. 2–19: At Prague, visits college

Sept. 19–Oct. 3: To Innsbruck via Casanova, Trebon, Salzburg

Oct. 3–21: At Innsbruck, visits college; sees Canisius

Oct. 25–30: Munich

Oct. 30–Nov. 19: Ingolstadt, Augsburg, Dillingen

Nov. 19–23: Travels to Wurzburg

Nov. 24–Dec. 5: Wurzburg, Aschaffenburg

Dec. 5–7: To Heidelberg and Speyer

Dec. 7–16: At Speyer, founds college

Dec. 17–Feb. 20: Mainz

Chapter Nine

SINNERS CALLED TO BE COMPANIONS

Institutes should see to it that their members have a proper understanding of men [and women], of the conditions of the times and of
the needs of the Church, this to the end that, making wise judgments about the contemporary world in the light of faith, and
burning with apostolic zeal, they may be able to help men [and
women] more effectively.

—Vatican II, *On the Up-to-Date Renewal of the Religious Life*

One of Nadal's more gratifying experiences in Spain in 1554 was a
short side trip to Loyola. His diary indicates, however, that he
found it disgraceful that the room in which Ignatius had been
born had been turned into a kitchen. He noted that he had completed his
commission to promulgate the *Constitutions* and set sail for Genoa. His
diary recounts the dangers he endured both on land and on sea, the great
danger from pirates, the lesser danger but greater fear he experienced
while crossing mountainous territory to reach Barcelona; he writes of the
danger of falling into the sea while embarking, of a storm that scattered
the triremes, and of such horror and fear that he simply wanted to be
clear of the ship (*EpistNadal* 2:28–31). Little did he realize that his days of
traveling were just beginning, and that the storms in his life were about to
take a different form.

He arrived in Rome on October 18, 1554, having learned much
about "the proper understanding of men," and even of women, but he had
much more to learn.[1] He had learned much as well about "the conditions
of the times and the needs of the Church." He was about to learn still
more from Ignatius and from the responsibilities that Ignatius would
entrust to him. He needed to experience deeply in his own flesh what the
fathers of General Congregation 34 would express centuries later in these
words:

The mission of the Society derives from our continuing experience of
the Crucified and Risen Christ who invites us to join him in preparing the
world to become the completed Kingdom of God. . . . He calls us "to help

---

[1] Da Câmara, "Acta P. Ignatii," author's preface (*Font.narr* 1:360, no. 3*).

men and women disengage themselves from the tarnished and confused image that they have of themselves in order to discover that they are, in God's light, completely like Christ." And so we undertake all our ministries with a confidence that the Lord takes us, as he did Ignatius, as his servants—not because we are strong, but because he says to us, as he said to St. Paul, "My grace is sufficient for you, for my power is made perfect in weakness" (2 Cor. 12:9). (*DocsGC34* 31 (p. 30)

This chapter studies those with final vows, good men all of them, yet flawed men. Their task is to integrate not only prayer and study, like the students, but prayer and every apostolic work, indeed every activity whatsoever, in which they are engaged; and they must learn to do so in cooperation with and as "friends in the Lord" with other good yet flawed men called to be absorbed only in God. As Nadal said to the community in Alcalá in 1561,

> Fervor without gentleness, kindness, and meekness, harshness that irritates, zeal coupled with arrogance and indiscretion—these are alien to our way of proceeding. The spirit of God is tranquil, and with tranquillity God directs his affairs even in the turbulence of activity. If the movement comes from God, if the grace of our vocation is at work, the action does not come from us.
>
> You do not want an attitude that is harsh, difficult, intractable, in a word, zeal without enlightenment [Rom. 10:2]; rather you want your zeal conformed to the rule we have proposed: seeking always the greater glory of God.
>
> To develop the proper attitude requires mortification, cutting out the evil inside oneself, what is native to yourself, and you want to put this at the service of God. Have you not seen good men, difficult to work with, who mortified themselves and with the grace of God became so gentle and mild that their words pierce hearts and set them on fire without harshness or severity? Our vocation looks for workers like that. (*CommInst* 310, 312, no. 77)

History

The year is again 1548, a quiet year except for those areas annexed by Charles V. Ignatius wrote to Laínez offering to yield the office of general to him if the rest of the Society agreed.[2] Charles V issued the decree *Interim* on the religious situation in the Empire, and exiled Bobadilla from the countries of the Empire for criticizing the decree. Pope Paul III approved the book of the *Spiritual Exercises* in the last year of his pontificate. Ignatius appointed Nadal rector of the new college in Messina. A future general, Everard Mercurian, entered the Society.

---

[2] *EpistIgn* 12:228 f.

Not all was quiet, however, in Gandía or in the heart of Father General Ignatius. All that year he was working with good men who were limited in their vision and their understanding of the spirit of the Society. How could he affirm them, correct them, get the best out of them for the sake of the Church and the Society? Perhaps from this situation he learned much about how to deal with Nadal and others, all good men, all limited in strikingly different ways.

A Pause for Prayer

At the beginning of the *Spiritual Exercises* Ignatius writes, "It should be presupposed that every good Christian ought to be more eager to put a good interpretation on a neighbor's statement than to condemn it" (*SpEx* 22$^{vv.2-3}$ [p. 31]). Nonetheless, this simple presupposition is difficult to put into practice, and Christians place many an obstacle to the spreading of the Gospel by refusing to get along with one another.

> **Sixteenth Annotation: For this purpose—namely, that the Creator and Lord may with greater certainty be the one working in his creature—if by chance the exercitant feels an affection or inclination to something in a disordered way, it is profitable for that person to strive with all possible effort to come over to the opposite of that to which he or she is wrongly attached** (*SpEx* 16$^{vv.2-3}$ [p. 26])

> We pray that we may be wholly open to one another, so that we can see God at work in the ones we disagree with as well as the ones whose opinions are in harmony with ours, so that we may learn from one another and go forward together in God's service for the greater glory of God and the life of the world.

The Tale of Two Extremists

In March, with the screams of peacocks owned by unfriendly neighbors coming through the window, Ignatius concentrated on affairs in faraway Spain. The great-grandson of Pope Alexander VI and King Ferdinand the Catholic and a favorite of Emperor Charles V and Empress Isabella, Francis Borgia had been placed in charge of the imperial household at the age of twenty. He had been shocked when, in the course of carrying out his duties, he had beheld the Empress's deteriorating corpse only two weeks after her death in 1539. Named the fourth duke of Gandia in 1543 and secretly a Jesuit since 1547, Borgia was excessively penitential, prayerful, and devout, dedicated to God and Prince Philip, efficient in administration, on easy terms with many in high places, and eager to serve the eternal King in every way. Ignatius urged Gandía's youthful rector, Andrés Oviedo, to moderate the penitential excesses of Jesuit Francis Borgia and redirect his eagerness, giving Oviedo an opportunity to reflect on the difference between being outstanding and going to excess (*EpistIgn* 2:17).

Perhaps Oviedo reminded Borgia of the words in the *Exercises:* "When we abstain from the superfluous in things delicate and soft, this is not penance. But we do practice penance when we deprive ourselves of what is ordinarily suitable; and the more we do so deprive ourselves, the better is the penance, provided we do not harm ourselves or weaken our constitutions" (*SpEx* 84$^{vv.1-3}$ [p. 50]).

Excess had captivated Spain's provincial, Antonio de Araoz. Related by marriage to Ignatius (his aunt married Ignatius's older brother), he was intelligent, hardworking, prayerful, inclined to penance, and jealous of boundaries. Easy access to life at court was less a blessing than a drain on his spirit. Ignatius informed him that he did not approve of devoting eight hours to prayer daily, the practice obtaining at that time in Gandía and Valencia (irrespective of whether this practice stemmed from Tejeda's influence or some other source). Araoz should ask all his subjects to give an account of their schedule and their devotions and reduce them to something reasonable. He should begin with himself, reducing the three hours he spent in prayer to one or less, as his spiritual director may advise, discontinue flagellations until Ignatius advised otherwise, thereby offering good example to others (*EpistIgn* 2:46 f.). As to his "eating, drinking, clothing, sleeping, penances, and prayers," he should accept Juan Queralt as his teacher when he was nearby; and if he went to Gandía, he should take Francis Saboya as his mentor (ibid., 2:217).

Oviedo had been less successful in his mission to moderate Borgia's excesses than Borgia in his mission to Oviedo. Ignatius attacked Borgia's problem himself:

> Regarding the hours given to spiritual exercises, both interior and exterior, I think they should be reduced by half; . . . I think it would be better that half of your time be spent in study (since not only infused but also acquired knowledge will be necessary for the future), in governing your estate, and in spiritual converse, seeking always to have your soul in peace and quiet and ready for whatever the Lord may wish to work in it; for without a doubt there is more virtue and more grace in being able to rejoice in the Lord in a variety of duties and places, rather than in one only, for which we should depend much on the divine goodness. (ibid., 2:234)

A year later Ignatius and Polanco discussed the letters received from others detailing the poor health of the provincial of Spain (*Epist.mixt* 2, *passim*). Polanco wrote to Borgia:

It would be good to assign a teacher for [Araoz] who would have the authority to come to an agreement regarding his bodily regimen if his usual fervor causes him to stray in that regard. And so Our Father has charged me to ask you on his behalf to assign someone (*although he thinks that at times you have the same need*) (*EpistIgn* 2:493, italics added).

In August 1550 Borgia received the degree of doctor of theology at the hands of Oviedo (*BorgMon* 2:704); subsequently, they set out together for Rome with Araoz, Miró, and others to attend the conference that Ignatius called to discuss the newly completed *Constitutions* and other matters (*PolChron* 2:10, no. 16). After three months Borgia returned to Spain and was ordained a priest during Pentecost week in 1551 (*Epist.mixt* 2:552). His son, Juan, however, who made the journey with him, informed Ignatius in April that Francis and Araoz were again mistreating themselves, taking little care of their health and allowing no one else to moderate their eating, sleeping, and praying (*BorgMon* 1:631). Ignatius replied that he was taking the proper steps: he instructed Araoz to follow the doctor's advice on eating and sleeping and forbade him to preach for three months, so that he could care for his health (*EpistIgn* 3:531, 534).

Ignatius must have wondered, even as Jesus wondered aloud to his disciples, "Do you not yet understand?" (Mark 8:21).

Professed and Formed Coadjutors

When Nadal failed to curb Borgia in 1556 and withdrew from that effort, he did not fail in creativity; for he saw in his forced leisure an opportunity, a gift of God's providence, a chance to reflect more deeply on some of the ideas he had presented in Spain in 1554, and a welcome opportunity to write. His "Annotationes in Constitutiones" (Notes on the *Constitutions*) is a valuable work, in which he began to expand on earlier ideas that he continued to develop in later works. He took up once more, for example, the important topic of the nature of religion and of the vocation to the religious life. The writer is flawed, the readers too, but the call to holiness is real.

Notes on the *Constitutions,* 1556

CommInst 108–30, nos. 1–64

The desert purifies those who find themselves utterly powerless and vulnerable. The Borgian desert purified Nadal. Frustrated by Francis Borgia's ignorance of the Constitutions and apparently cavalier attitude toward them, humiliated by his own weakness, and weary of carrying the cross, Jerónimo Nadal sits down to write "under the guidance of Christ Jesus, who has been made wisdom for us by God. . . . Pardon me, I beseech you, . . . for I am inept, abject, nothing, and pray for me; and if I write something that sheds light on our Institute, know that it descends from the Father of lights through your prayers and sacrifices in Christ Jesus" (*ConsInst* 108 f., no. 1).

Aware that all people are called to the service of God, Nadal declares that Jesus has endowed his Church with a wide variety of gifts, including the religious life. Jesus himself has lived life to the full, and he also called the apostles to do the same (111, no. 7). The cry of Nadal's own frustrated heart is discernible in these words: "Jesus calls no one to whom he does not promise and grant the grace appropriate to the call," and again in the words that follow: "These calls are above and beyond nature, and the providence and mercy of God is such as to grant to the person chosen for any divine task the power to carry it out in proper fashion. . . . God the all-powerful did not wish the plans of his Son Christ Jesus to be worthless and without fruit" (116, nos. 19–21).

Prayerfully reflecting on the vocation to the Society, Nadal turns to God and then to his brothers in the Society; and his words reflect once more his experiences with Ignatius and Borgia and Araoz and Estrada. Call whomsoever you will to the Society, Nadal begs the all merciful Lord; send those whom you will send. We are obviously useless and unskilled. By reason of our ineptitude, our mistakes, our negligence, our sin, our misery, all we do is impede and spoil what you have decided to do by your grace and mercy (129, no. 58). Turning to his brothers, he proclaims vigorously that the grace of this least Society is immense: It brings divine help that extends to all virtues, exercises, ministries, and works, to the governance and direction of the whole Society and anyone admitted to it, so that we can courageously undertake and effectively carry out the end that God has set before us (129, no. 59). Whence comes the power through which Father Ignatius (as the one through whom God one and triune wished to establish the Society) holds within himself all that belongs to the Society, and by this power all those who are admitted into the Society receive the whole Institute of the Society in spirit, so that those who hold the office of superiors can govern others (130, no. 62). We cannot experience our own special grace if we do not hold in high esteem the grace of religion itself and every form of the monastic call (130, no. 64).

Frustrated he may have been, but he was still convinced that God was present and acting in spite of all his Jesuit brethren's human limitations. When Nadal returned to the same topics in later years, he again recognized the simultaneity of human weakness and the powerful grace of Christ. Centuries later General Congregation 32 would, in a similar recognition, coin the expression "What is it to be a Jesuit? It is to know that one is a sinner, yet called to be a companion of Jesus, as Ignatius was."[3] Nadal himself was searching for a formula like that for his own day. In his "Notes on the Constitutions," he wrote that he "both rashly and carefully" tried to express "even in awkward terms" what "he saw in his heart" regarding what it means to be a Jesuit; but he finally concluded: "In a word, if I say nothing, I have said everything. That grace cannot be expressed, but it can be experienced, and it can be fulfilled in the doing" (130, no. 63).

The Nature of the Society

Notes on the General Examen, 1557
CommInst 134–205, nos. 1–203

The war between Pope Paul IV and Philip II of Spain delayed and twice postponed the First General Congregation, whose duty it would be to elect a new general after the death of Ignatius. Nadal was not idle. He began working again on notes he had made in 1553–54 on his first trip to Portugal and Spain. In sharp contrast to the Constitutions, which progress from the "lowest" (novices) to the "highest" (the professed), the General Examen moves from the professed, to coadjutors, to scholastics, and finally to novices.

From the earliest paragraphs an outline emerges of the spirituality expected of followers of Jesus who have prayed long over the Call of the King and the Two Standards. Nadal does not gently invite his readers to progress from the less perfect to the more perfect, but challenges them to follow Jesus to the utmost. Commenting on the opening words, "This least [*mínima*] congregation," he plays on the word's Latin root, *grex, gregis* (meaning *flock,* as in a flock of sheep), and says: "It was necessary at first to refer to a congregation rather than a society, to indicate a kind of genus. Congregation, nevertheless, does suggest a sense of obedience, the kind sought in the Society: we are a flock who are led by a superior like sheep not opening the mouth of our will and judgment" (*CommInst* 134f., no. 1).

The image is not of dumb, stupid beasts, but of the Suffering Servant in Second Isaiah, who is like a lamb not opening his mouth as he is led to the slaughter (Isa. 53:7). The lowly aspect of the Suffering Servant is reflected still more in his comment on "least":

"Minima" suggests a desire and a sense of humility, so that we may experience our Society as the least and the last, and so that everyone in it may place himself lower than all the lowliest and most abject persons, the servant of all in the Lord; thus we are able to launch our boat out into the

---

[3] *DocsGC3132* 36 (p. 33).

deep, that is, to bring ourselves to profound humility and obedience, and
there to let down our nets for a catch in the name of Christ Jesus. (135,
no. 2)

Ignatius expects profound humility of those with final vows, and humility
is a challenge to accept God's love, for "the Society owes its origin to
divine inspiration" (136, no. 5). Nadal confirms that the Society and its
name come from God by appealing to Ignatius at La Storta, where "Christ
Jesus carrying his cross appeared to him, and he heard God the Father
deep within himself and experienced that the Father attached him to
Christ and claimed him for his service and following *[in illius servitutem et
sequelam assereret];* and then he said, 'I shall be propitious to you'" (137,
no. 7).

Nadal's vocabulary is striking. *Asserere* means "to join some person
or thing to oneself." *Asserere in servitutem* is juridical jargon for "to claim
someone as a slave."[4] Ignatius and the Society are not only in the service
of Christ carrying his cross, but they belong to him totally and are wholly
at his disposal, like Mary when she called herself the Lord's handmaid or
slave. The words reveal the fruit of reflection on the relationship that da
Câmara put more simply, "[He] saw so clearly that God the Father placed
him with Christ his Son."[5] Slavery in this context means radical fidelity.
Hence, to embrace "slavery" freely out of love eclipses juridical jargon
suggesting locks and chains; the words recall that beautiful image of God
holding Israel as a father holds a child in his arms, teaching him to walk,
leading his people "with cords of human kindness, with bands of love,"
lifting them like infants to his cheek (Hos. 11:1–4). Nadal continues:

> We are companions, therefore, of Christ Jesus by reason of an incredible
> and extraordinary kindness and grace shown to us. We follow Jesus carry-
> ing on his campaign, waging battle, carrying his cross even now in his
> Mystical Body, which is the Church; and so we ought to fill up those things
> that are wanting in the passion of Christ. Let us imitate Christ, therefore,
> brothers, as closely as we can with his grace; let us not want for anything
> in this life except what Christ Jesus wanted. Ours it is to be poor, chaste,
> obedient, humble; ours it is to endure contempt, insults, insolence for the
> sake of his name; ours it is to think, do, or suffer anything to win the
> salvation of souls. Christ Jesus has called us to a great work, most dear
> brothers, with great signs and wonders. Let us follow, then, with a great
> heart, great faith, great liveliness and joyfulness of mind and heart, in
> humility of heart in spirit and truth in Christ. (137 f., no. 10)

Although some months before the event at La Storta the companions had
already determined to identify themselves by the name of Jesus, thus
proclaiming that he alone was their head, Ignatius's experience of God the

---

[4] *Harper's Latin Dictionary,* s.v. "assero."

[5] "Acta P. Ignatii" (*Font.narr* 1:496 f., no. 96); *PilgTest* 96 (p. 139).

Father placing him at the side of the Son confirmed that name for him against all challenges.[6] That God the Father placed Ignatius at the side of the Son meant that the Society was the work of the whole Trinity. What may appear to be solely Christocentric spirituality is always fully Trinitarian: working at the side of Christ is always to be in the service of the Father.

Serving the Father demands that if a Jesuit begins his vowed life as a student trying to integrate learning with spirituality, study with prayer, he must end by integrating prayer with all the ministries he performs in the service of God's people. Returning to the more holistic life of the formed Jesuit, Nadal writes as follows:

> From the nature of the end [of the Society], we also understand this, that the Society embraces each life, both the contemplative and active [tum contemplativam, tum activam particularem], for in our lives we practice each of them, more especially the contemplative, and, to speak clearly, we should primarily, and almost solely [primarie . . . et quasi unice], be contemplative and given over to prayer. This is not, however, what characterizes our vocation and Institute, which is that we live the life that is called a more complete active life in which we receive power from Christ and work in Christ so that we are able to assist our neighbors, helping one to live the active life and another to live the contemplative life. (144, no. 31)

To be consistent with his remarks in 1556, he should have added to the final sentence, "and still another to live that more complete active life." We need to pay attention to various points:

• At the beginning of the paragraph Nadal emphasized the contemplative life by placing it before the active life [tum contemplativam, tum activam particularem]. He did the same in his final word on the subject in 1572, when he prepared the letter for Cardinal Borromeo, explaining why the Society should not have to chant the office together in choir or make final profession until some time after ordination. (See the prolog above.)

The two passages (in the "Notes on the Examen" and the letter to Borromeo) complement and illumine each other. Each stresses contemplation by placing it first.

• "Notes on the Examen" says that the Society "embraces each life, both the contemplative and active [tum contemplativam, tum activam particularem]" since "we practice each of them, more especially the contemplative." And then Nadal emphatically states, "[T]o speak clearly, we should primarily, and almost solely [primarie . . . et quasi unice], be contemplative and given over to prayer." "Primarily and solely contemplative" is strong language. It does not sound like, "now this, now that." "As it were" suggests the words lack precision but need proper understanding.

---

[6] Polanco, "De vita P. Ignatii et Societatis Jesu initiis" (*PolChron* 1:72–74).

These words convey the sense that one leading the more holistic life must be profoundly contemplative; indeed, contemplation should so saturate his life that he can help others to become whatever God calls them to be. Certainly the concluding paragraph in the passage from the letter to Borromeo suggests that more is demanded of Jesuits than proficiency in works. To fulfill the demands on their lives, they must be praying in all that they are doing, for they are carrying on Christ's mission:

> Because of these things (that our way of living is so broad, our ministries so multiple, so difficult, and so exhausting), it follows that our times of probation, or novitiate, should be very lengthy and carefully done, our obedience most demanding, and every aspect of the religious life perfect as far as possible. Then also, since we have so many difficult and necessary occupations, mind you, lest souls be lost for whom Christ Jesus was crucified and died, we judge that certain rituals are not proper for us since they can impede our ministries, just as certain things are suitable for other religious orders and other things are not. Besides, we also take care that those to be professed have not only been proved in the practice of living after the manner of religious, but have also been sufficiently trained in the ministries that they have to undertake. Whence it follows that they should first be priests before they are professed. Other religious orders train their novices in choir and in other ceremonies; we train ours in the ministries proper to our Institute, which prepare our men to undertake those ministries of the Society for the salvation of souls. (*EpistNadal* 4:174 f.)

This paragraph explains the multiple experiments of the novitiate, the long grounding in prayer, the need to integrate prayer and study, and especially to integrate prayer with all the works in which Jesuits engage. Recall that Nadal had written earlier in the letter to Borromeo: "The active life in the Society is multiplex. It consists primarily in the more excellent action *[actione excellentiori]* of preaching, lecturing, and other spiritual ministries proper to simple priests, and of studying for scholastics, and secondarily in the ministry of the corporal works of mercy" (ibid., 174).

Mary, the Mother of Jesus, who "pondered . . . in her heart," joined the active and the contemplative lives in such a way as to achieve the more excellent action of the higher active life. In his meditation on the Assumption of Mary, Nadal says that she lived the active life by giving birth to the Son of God, nourishing him as he grew, ministering to him as a child and as an adult:

> This action, highly exalted in itself, also led to the praiseworthy and fruitful practice of other virtues. The Martha at work in the Virgin Mary was solicitous, but peaceful and delightful; engaged in many activities, she was quiet, focused, unruffled, charming; her ministry was never ending, but it sprang from a sublime and constantly tranquil movement of the spirit. For the Virgin Mary was not active the way Martha was or others usually are, where the active life dominates and the contemplation of and taste for

divine things is an added tidbit; her spirit was not debilitated but enlarged, and blossomed forth into fully excellent action.[7]

Mary's loving example helped prepare Jesus for ministry.

Nadal's division into spiritual ministries and works of charity comes from the *Formula of the Institute* and is to be interpreted through that document. *Regimini militantis ecclesiæ* (1540) placed side by side "the ministry of the word, spiritual exercises, and works of charity." *Exposcit debitum* (1550), the version ruling the Society today, spells out in greater detail the ministry of the word, adding the phrase "and no less," followed by a more detailed list of works of charity. The norm of choice is "the glory of God and the common good."

Contemporary Jesuits meeting the needs of the marginal people they serve understand that norm. Especially since General Congregations 32, 33, and 34, they struggle in a holistic manner to raise people's consciousness to the injustices that spawn their immediate needs, and to empower the marginalized themselves to change the social structures dehumanizing them.

In theory, at least, preaching the Gospel is a loftier action than sweeping the floor, but the glory of God and the common good might require sweeping the floor and remaining quiet about the Gospel. Moreover, the way one sweeps the floor may be far loftier than the way another preaches the Gospel, and the life of the sweeper may be far more exalted than the life of the preacher, and the sweeping may impact the neighbor far more powerfully and effectively than the preaching. What is important is the love in the heart of the one who performs the action. The Society is called to engage in actions lofty and lowly, both in a lofty manner.

What is superior or loftier about this life, higher or better, more holistic, more integrated, more complete, more advanced, or more comprehensive, is not that the person living it moves from the concern for personal growth to concern for the growth of others, but that the person takes action beyond prayer and good example to bring about that growth, and brings it about in such a way that some of those acted upon act upon others. The action is efficacious, generative; it multiplies its effect and is satisfied when the good produces more good.

Chapter 8 demonstrated that Nadal had insisted with students that through obedience, love, and a right intention all their study could be prayer. This is what he says in "Notes on the Examen" to those with final vows regarding prayer and the sacred works in which they were engaged:

---

[7] "Ad. ev. 'Transitus Matris Dei'" (*Adnotationes et meditationes in Evangelia*), 583 f.

One thing is sure: prayer is a big part of a religious institute, a prime necessity. I mean that prayer of which Paul says, "I will pray with the spirit, but I will pray with the mind also" [1 Cor. 14:15], which covers every bit of spiritual endeavor, purgative, illuminative, and unitive. The Society embraces all these diligently with great eagerness and spiritual delight in Christ Jesus. (*CommInst* 161, no. 79])

He illustrates the purgative through the meditations of the First Week of the Exercises, which aims to strip off the "old man," and then refers to the contemplations on all the mysteries of Christ, concluding:

Finally, we rest in love, so that we place our end in the source from which prayer should flow, in love, the greatest and most divine virtue, so that from the fire of its zeal we go out to our ministries in joy and humility, courageously in Christ Jesus. This is the pattern that we gather from the book of the *Exercises*. (161 f., no. 79)

Although he has hitherto said nothing about Ignatius as our model, at this point, as though bursting with thoughts that will no longer remain silent, he describes the prayer of Ignatius as fulfilling completely the Jesuit ideal. That remarkable outburst is reserved for the next chapter.

New Mission to Spain and Portugal, 1560

On July 2, 1558, the First General Congregation elected Diego Laínez successor to Ignatius as general of the Society. Meeting from June 19 until September 10, the congregation also approved the *Constitutions* Ignatius had written. After some time in office Laínez became aware of disagreements between Borgia and Araoz, so in 1560 he appointed Nadal commissary general with full powers over Spain and Portugal, and sent him to visit the Iberian Peninsula once more. Araoz, the provincial of Castile, and Borgia, the delegate of the General, differed on matters of policy, resulting in divisions among the Jesuits, some backing Araoz and others backing Borgia. In 1559, moreover, a book claiming Francis Borgia as its author (even though he had written only one short article in it) was placed on the Index of Forbidden Books by the Inquisition; and to add to the ferment, toward the end of 1559 gossip was rampant in the court to the effect that while Philip had been in England with Mary Tudor, Borgia had been living in concubinage with Philip's sister, Juana, regent in the King's absence. Ironically, he was in fact her spiritual director and she, with the permission of Ignatius, had secretly been received into the Society with the vows of a scholastic, remaining a Jesuit to the day of her death.[8] Asked by Cardinal Henrique, regent of Portugal, to advise him on certain matters,

---

[8] For the story of Juana and the correspondence involved, see Hugo Rahner, S.J., *Saint Ignatius Loyola: Letters to Women* (New York: Herder and Herder, 1960), 52–67.

Borgia slipped across the Portuguese border in early December to visit the cardinal in Évora. Rumors spread that he was running away.

A month later in Alcalá, Nadal encountered Araoz, who received him coolly. Nadal wrote to Borgia in Oporto, Portugal, not commanding him but urging him to return to Spain to refute the charges of heresy and sexual misconduct. Later he came upon Borgia in Oporto, and found him deeply confused about whether he should return to Spain to clear his name or press on to Rome to become assistant to Laínez, as the General had requested, with the concurrence of the Pope. In this perplexed state Borgia surreptitiously crossed the frontier and attempted to flee across Spain and through France on his way to Rome, but before long ill health compelled him to return to Spain. He and Nadal came to no agreement as to whether he should remain in Spain or go to Rome. One thing was certain: the Spanish court was not pleased.[9]

And then, Nadal had to face the problems of Bartolomé de Bustamente, the provincial of Andalusia. For some time now prominent men in his province had accused Bustamente of coercing them along paths that were appropriate for other religious orders but not for the Society. They reprehended him for showing excessive severity in his manner of governing, introducing choir and litanies in common, talking about cells and cloister, enforcing rigidity in daily order, thereby depriving the faithful of Masses and confession, among other charges.[10] His rectors had called a meeting to discuss how they should counter their provincial's severity. Bustamente had protested to Laínez and then gone off to Oporto to seek Borgia's advice; now he was debating whether to accompany Borgia to Rome. Laínez wrote, charging Nadal to deal with the problem locally and not permit Bustamente to leave Spain. Nadal must have heaved a weary sigh: during his first visit to Spain, he had spent much time and energy in explaining the unique character of the Society; yet now a man who had been considered apt to serve as provincial had missed much of his message.

In these troubled circumstances Nadal undertook to give some exhortations to the Jesuits in Coimbra. In the third exhortation he returned to the theme of discovering the grace of the Society in the life of Ignatius. Gradually Nadal's vision of Ignatius had changed from a more external model to a model for the interior life. Five years of reflection after his friend's death helped him grasp more profoundly and express more precisely the inner dynamic of the life of Ignatius as a model of discern-

---

[9] To fill out the details of these paragraphs, see Bangert, *Jerome Nadal,* 219–37.

[10] Letter of Juan Suarez to Father General Laínez, January 6, 1560 (*LainMon* 4:603–9).

ment for Jesuits, especially for those with final vows. What follows is half translation and half summary of the third exhortation in Coimbra.[11]

The Grace of Ignatius

Third Exhortation in Coimbra, Spring 1561
Pláticas espirituales, 62–70, nos. 1–25

Nadal began with the freedom of God, who is always full of surprises, who sets aside human standards and calls each of us according to his own will. God chooses whomsoever he wishes, and who can contradict God? Because of his sinfulness Ignatius did not deserve to be chosen; his natural virtues, although helpful, were not enough. God chose him even so and began to do in him what Ignatius would then have to put into practice in the Society (*Pláticas* 62 f., nos. 2 f.).

Wounded in battle, Ignatius wanted to pass the time reading and asked for worldly *[profanos]* books, shoddy and worthless stories *[de historias perjudiciales y malas]*—Amadis of Gaul and the like. He was handed instead the *Lives of the Saints* and the *Life of Christ.* "In them," said Nadal,

> he discovers two spirits, one to serve the world and to perform great secular tasks in its service, and another to do great deeds like the founders of religious orders, St. Francis and St. Dominic. As it turned out, the thoughts of vain things left him sad and upset, and the other thoughts left him feeling good and peaceful. From this early experience he realized that the ones that led him to serve God were good. And so he said to himself: I want to follow these but not the others, and so he made this his determination. (63, no. 4)

Nadal concluded that from this experience of Ignatius came the rules for making an election or choice as practiced in the Society, "since each one from the beginning reflects on the consolation that moves him in order to name it: this gives me light, this gives me hope, and so I follow this and not that" (63 f., no. 5).

Once Ignatius had given himself to God's service, God gave him "the grace to develop all his natural talents quietly and gradually." Nadal added:

> We, too, should come to a better knowledge of ourselves, direct everything to the greater service of God, be generous after his example, not trusting in ourselves but aware that with God's grace we can do anything. The one who can preach should preach, the one who can lecture should lecture, and so of all other things. (64, no. 6)

---

[11] Also found in *Font.narr* 2:148–57, nos. 1–25.

Ignatius's experience with penance is another example of discernment. He wants to serve God as best he can, "looks around for something 'better' to do, and the first thing that comes to mind is penance." After performing every penance that suggested itself to him, "[b]efore he received greater grace and clarity, he experienced profound interior distress, although some consolation as well. He hallucinated, and the devil tried to deceive him through something that gave him great delight." Grace came to his aid; he understood the experience and overcame it. He had "terrible scruples and wild imaginings," but "God freed him from these things, even though he had little understanding of spiritual things. . . . To rid himself of the scruples, he went for a week without eating or drinking. He told everything to his confessor, both the good and the bad; when the confessor told him to eat, he did so, and he was rid of the scruples" (64 f., nos. 7 f.).

"In imitation of this we begin immediately with penance in the First Week of the Exercises." Then he explained that when Ignatius came to greater clarity, he had no illusions or desires for "penance that was going to ruin him"; he realized that he would have to restrain himself, and so also he desired that "no one would do penance without his confessor's or his superior's knowing it." Thus, the grace of Ignatius became the grace of the follower of Ignatius. This purgative way, Nadal concluded, is the path to the illuminative way which itself leads to the unitive way (65, no. 9).

God taught Ignatius the way a teacher does a child, gradually illuminating his mind "to such a degree that he came to a profound knowledge of all the mysteries of the Catholic faith and especially of the Most Holy Trinity" (65, no. 10). He had a special illumination one day by the river Cardoner in which he "understood all things in a clear and very sudden light. . . . Thus he experienced himself moved to contemplation and union with God, so that he felt devotion in everything everywhere very easily" (65 f., nos. 10 f.). Nadal continued, "In imitating him, then, we do penance to prepare ourselves for contemplation and devotion and union of our wills with God our Lord." Each one should proceed according to the graces that God bestows on him, denying himself so that God may communicate himself. "No one should question that God will give us this grace if we act in this manner, and more will be given to the one who humbles himself the more and who is more obedient, following the path that God our Lord has shown us" (66, no. 12).

Nadal concluded by saying that Ignatius applied himself to penance and to prayer and thus "became intent on helping his neighbor. From this we gather that our prayer should immediately incline us toward the practical, according to the end of our Institute, to help souls that are being lost and for whom God gave his life, just as the Father [Ignatius] conducted himself" (66, no. 13).

Up to this point, Nadal said, everything reflects the Exercises that Ignatius made and that the Society uses. Now he adds that one can also learn much from the experiments common in the Society (66, no. 13). The pilgrimage experiment reflects the pilgrimage of Ignatius to Jerusalem "in the utmost poverty," following his example.[12] "He visits the hospitals with much consolation and comfort in the Lord," thus giving rise to the hospital experiment (66 f., no. 14). Returning from the Holy Land, Ignatius discerned that he must study in order to help his neighbor. "From this experience we come to undertake studies in order to achieve the help God has placed in the Church" (67, no. 16). In studies Ignatius ran into three problems: consolation in prayer that interfered with his studies, poverty, and sickness. "From this experience," said Nadal, "it was decided that in the Society prayer would be linked with study but directed along with study toward the same end. So that need would not become a problem, the colleges can have an income; and so that sickness would not be a problem, all are to inform the superior as soon as they are unwell" (67 f., nos. 17–21).

Because he could not achieve all that God had communicated to him, Ignatius sought companions in his enterprise, but the would-be pilgrims were unable to go to the Holy Land as they desired (69, no. 22). They presented themselves to the Pope to give him an account of their way of living. Seeking the greater glory of God, they linked the priesthood to the "monastic" (religious) life:

> But why should the Society exist, since there are many other excellent religious orders? (I think highly of them all—to do otherwise is a sign that one has little understanding of one's own institute.) True enough, they were sufficient; but we will be of assistance in what is left over, for all those who labor for the Church of God, bishops, priests, and religious, always have something left over because they cannot attend to it and are cut off from it, or for some other good reason. We take on ourselves in general what is left over, especially those people and nonbelievers who have the greater need, such as heretics, or a city that is depraved, if there

---

[12] The pilgrimage of Ignatius shares much with other pilgrimages of his time, but differs in many ways. Here we summarize Michel Mollat du Jourdin's writing on the subject: Pilgrimage assumes effort, a desire for adventure, an appetite for the unknown, a thirst for new experiences, a willingness to break out of old categories, an interior conversion and surrender and search for God in poverty and humility, humiliation, and anonymity. Finding at the end that Jerusalem was not his goal, Ignatius became a "pilgrim of the absolute" ("Saint Ignace et les pèlerinages de son temps," in Plazaola, *Ignacio y su tiempo*, 161–78). For the characteristics and meaning of Ignatian pilgrimage, see Kolvenbach, "Certain Pathway to God," *cis* 22 (1991): 25–45.

is such a place, and so on. Because we are the last, we take on the last and the hindmost in order to help. (69, no. 23)

It follows from this that Jesuits do not work with those who already have someone to help them. They seek none but the lost, and so Father Ignatius established missions, as is clear in the fourth vow made to the pope. In all they do Jesuits bind themselves closely to the pope, for as universal superior he has charge over what everyone else fails to do (69 f., no. 24). Nadal emphasized this same idea in talks in Alcalá that same year, that it is appropriate to regard the Society like another Ruth, who followed the reapers and gleaned the grain they left behind. It is a special grace for the Society to bring up the rear, doing what others leave undone.[13]

Nadal concluded by saying,

Let us now recapitulate: what is the Society? I recognize that God saw what I now see and also what lies hidden from my eyes: great edification for many people, the reform of many, and what is to come will be much more, as Our Father [Ignatius] used to say for we are starting out and those who will come later will have an advantage over us. For if God, seeing all this, chose to establish this way of life, it should be held a great grace from him. The Society, then, is the communication of this grace, for the Holy Father has conceded the exercise of all those ministries to its members so that they might cooperate more fully with what God wants for his greater glory" (70, no. 25).

Ignatius as Model in the Life of the Formed Jesuit

God communicates the grace of the Society in such a manner that Jesuit novices are formed through experiences similar to those that Ignatius had in the early days after his conversion (chapter 7); and the way of study and prayer of Jesuits in their student years is modeled on the experiences of Ignatius himself (chapter 8). Ignatius is also a model for the lives of those admitted into the full life of the Society.

---

[13] "Exhort. 2ª en Alcalá," 1561 (CommInst 262, no. 32). Note the alternate reading for lines 71–76, and similar language about Ruth in "Exhort. 12ª" (ibid., 442, no. 224), which itself offers an alternate reading for lines 58–61. Simón Rodrigues used this same image when writing to Father General Mercurian on July 25, 1577, discussing the origins of the Society. God established the Society, he said, "so that the sons of this Society, like Ruth the faithful Moabitess, in the spirit of humble solicitude might follow in the footsteps of earlier harvesters and gather from the harvest field of the Lord the ears of grain that escaped their hands [Ruth 2:2 f.]" (Fontes. narr 3:10, no. 2).

On Prayer, Especially for Jesuits

"Orationis ratio" (*EpistNadal* 4:672–81)

Ignatius wanted the Exercises to be the normal source of spiritual nourishment in the Society not only from the beginning but constantly.[14] In an undated manuscript, Nadal tells his Jesuit audience:

> What is of most value in our Lord in the Exercises and in every kind of prayer is great generosity, surrendering to God all our capacities and all that we do and all that we are, with his grace not failing to cooperate with all our might along the path to perfection, always hoping and intensely desiring and asking that God may accomplish in them and in everything else what is more for his glory and praise.[15]

After explaining that one grounded in the Exercises daily practices the purgative way through self abnegation and obedience and the illuminative and unitive ways in the various ways in which they pray, he comments:

> The felt experience in prayer and the desire for it that inclines one to recollection and unnecessary solitude does not seem to be prayer proper for the Society; rather, it is the prayer that inclines one to carry out his calling and ministry, and especially perfect obedience according to our Institute. (*EpistNadal* 4:673)

He repeats this to make sure they understand:

> And therefore prayer proper to the Society is the kind that extends to vocal prayer and to all the ministries of the Society, and in which, as far as the grace of Jesus Christ can bring it about, the illumination of the intellect, and the good affect of the will, and union itself persevere through, accompany, and guide all our operations in such a way that God our Lord is found in all things. (673 f.)

No matter how much effort this must take, the initiative is God's: illumination of the mind, good affect of the will, union—all are gifts from God. Nadal continues:

> This is the proper orientation for prayer: it should bring to fullness and direct and give spiritual relish to the activities we undertake, extending its strength and power to them in the Lord; and the activities should bring prayer to its fullness and bestow on it both power and joy. In this way, joined like Martha and Mary and assisting one another, we do not embrace just one part, even though the better part, of the Christian life; but setting

---

[14] "Exhort. 6ᵃ" (*CommInst* 845 f., no. 41). Also in *EpistNadal* 4:669, with slightly different orthography.

[15] In *EpistNadal* 4:672 f. The text is in the hand of Jiménez with emendations by Nadal. Since Jiménez was Nadal's companion and secretary from 1560 to 1562, it is reasonable to date the manuscript within that period.

aside the troublesome worries about many things, Mary and Martha help one another and are united in the Lord. (674)

The Exercises enable us to live to the full this more holistic life characteristic of the Society: "Briefly, in all the exercises they should find peace and quiet and devotion; for all should be directed towards the fire of love and zeal for souls, lest they be lost. In everything, then, one should find God our Lord and his own way of praying" (675).

Later we encounter a passage familiar by now:

Reflect that the active life and the contemplative life should always travel together. But the period of rigorous probation brings it about that the active comes to some perfection, and by this time the contemplative dominates and guides and governs peacefully and with enlightenment in the Lord, and in this way one comes to the higher active life that presupposes the active and the contemplative, and has the power to seal everyone with the mark of active or contemplative in accordance with the greater service of God. To be concise: the action of love united to God is perfect action. (679)

The final paragraph of this instruction summarizes and makes explicit all that Nadal has been at pains to say:

The Society's prayer and contemplation demand that each one extend them to the activities that he engages in, all of which are spiritual: preaching, lecturing on Scripture, teaching Christian doctrine, giving the Exercises, hearing confessions, administering the Most Blessed Sacrament, and attending to other good works. In these ministries one should find God in peace and tranquillity, embracing them interiorly in light, joy, and contentment, with the fire of God's love; and in this way one should seek the same thing in all his other ministries, even exterior ones. (681)

Nadal's remarks provide the context for finding God in all things. He is addressing men who lead a life of continued application of the Exercises, which aim at wiping out all inordinate affections in order to seek God's will alone (*SpEx* 1 [p. 21]). To find God in everything, they immerse themselves in both the service of Christ and the work of bringing the grace of Christ to God's people. Thus their prayer runs through the day, directing every action, and every action is prayerful.

That twofold vision seems to be the quiet assumption of Ignatius in his comments in the *Constitutions* where he makes it abundantly clear that the wisdom and prudence of love rather than rules should be the norm for the professed and formed coadjutors. He could easily have prefaced his remarks with a summary of his own life, such as Nadal has given above:

Given the length of time and approbation of their life which are required before admission into the Society among the professed and also the formed coadjutors, it is presupposed that those so admitted will be men who are spiritual and sufficiently advanced that they will run in the path of

Christ our Lord to the extent that their bodily strength and the exterior occupations undertaken through charity and obedience allow. Therefore, in what pertains to prayer, meditation, and study, as also in regard to the bodily practices of fasts, vigils, and other austerities or penances, it does not seem proper to give them any other rule than that which discreet charity dictates to them, provided that the confessor always be informed, and also, when a doubt about advisability arises, the superior. Only this will be said in general: On the one hand, they should take care that the excessive use of these practices not weaken their bodily strength and . . . take up so much time that they are rendered incapable of helping the neighbor spiritually according to our Institute; on the other hand, they should be vigilant that these practices not be relaxed to such an extent that the spirit grows cold and the human and lower passions grow warm.[16]

In an instruction he gave at about this time, Nadal told the coadjutor brothers, who are mostly busy like Martha about temporal affairs, that they could draw much fruit from constant meditation on the things they were doing; "and if some distraction or anxiety comes along, pay little attention to it, for solicitude is not condemned in Martha but simply joined to her state in life; . . . wherefore Mary should companion Martha so that the solicitude will do no harm" (*EpistNadal* 4:453). The prayer of one who leaves himself open to the Society's grace becomes increasingly more integrated, more concrete, more adapted to the times and the circumstances in which he lives, more clearly Christocentric and Trinitarian: toward the Father, through the Son, in the Spirit.

Conclusion

The heart of the Society's prayer is love: love of God and love of neighbor. The Jesuit of fable is a gross caricature: a man of cold, calculating reason, a dialectical genius. True, the Jesuit is a man of reason enlightened by faith, but Ignatius wrote the *Constitutions* for men of passionate faith whom superiors have to restrain rather than exhort. More striking than Ignatius's genius for organization is his complete immersion in God, his awareness of the diaphanous nature of reality, and especially his presence to reality. At Manresa, "all things appeared new to him."

Nadal makes awe and wonder the ideal for every Jesuit: to look upon and be present to all things as new, completely changed, profounder in meaning, richer in significance, more luxuriantly present, because experienced in the fullness of their reality as creatures issuing from the triune God. To see everything as new demands contemplation of the Trinity, but perhaps even more it demands profound penetration of creatures themselves, being present to them in awe. Penetration results from prayer but especially while working with those same creatures. Faith,

---

[16] *ConsCN* 582 (p. 254).

piercing through their natural appearances and outward environment, sets them in the fullness of the context of a world created and redeemed by the triune God, and at this point love takes charge.

All Christian contemplation centers on the Trinity, and the more deeply one enters into that mystery and becomes present to it, or the more deeply that mystery enters into the pray-er and becomes present to the one praying, the more perfect the pray-er's contemplation becomes. One who does not know the Father and the Holy Spirit does not really know the Son, for Christ himself is the revelation to the world of the Trinity. Only in the light of the three divine Persons does one genuinely grasp the meaning of life and death, of creatures, of hell and heaven.

To insist on a Trinitarian orientation to prayer does not set limits on prayer but gives it a field of play broader than all creation. At the same time, fully Trinitarian prayer plants one's feet squarely on the earth. If a Jesuit grasps a Trinity-pervaded universe, then that grasp generates not merely a vision, a wonderment, an overwhelming gasp at the beauty and grandeur of it all; it initiates an immensely practical surging forward to meet and tangle with a world in revolt against that beauty and grandeur and love. Love born out of love moves to love.

When Nadal describes the vision of La Storta to the brethren at Coimbra and recounts how the Father placed Ignatius with Christ carrying his cross, he adds, "Great consolation, then, for me and for each one, that God has done the same to me in his person [Ignatius, that is]."[17] Placed by the Father at the side of Christ, the Jesuit can only respond in love that labors at the side of Christ.

Because Jesus obeys the Father in love, a Jesuit finds that obedience is a way of loving the Father. Because Jesus lovingly chooses the poverty of God's abandoned poor, a Jesuit chooses poverty with love. Because he finds Christ in everyone, he wears himself out in labor. A heart bursting with love must express that love and carry on the work of love. To find Christ is to plunge into prayer: contemplation of the Trinity and the love of God's people meet and express themselves in action; labor for others is at once an expression of love and a visible outpouring of prayer to the Father. Obedience, poverty, suffering—these, after all, in their profoundest meaning are nothing else but the prayer and love of Christ. The folly and fullness of love have brought the Jesuit to a knowledge and profound contemplation of the living Christ, the ever present Christ, Christ suffering in his members. At the time of Ignatius, this included the street children, the orphans, the starving and the freezing in the Roman winter of 1538–39, the prostitutes, the Jews; and today it comprises those in refugee camps, in AIDS hospitals, in prisons, in dysfunctional families; it embraces

---

[17] "Plática 4ª en Coimbra" (*Pláticas espirituales,* 72, no. 4). Also found in *Font.narr* 2:159, no. 4, with slightly different orthography.

the mentally ill, the poor, the outcast, and the marginalized. This contemplation moves the Jesuit to a deeper love.

La Storta means, says Nadal, that "God has chosen us to be companions of Jesus and grants this special grace to the Society."[18] Special grace implies a special prayer, a prayer like Christ's, whose perfection will be found in the contemplation of the Trinity and in the love and union of charity that extend beyond Father, Son, and Holy Spirit through the works of the ministry to all who are beloved of those Three. The works of the ministry may demand the sacrifice of the sweetness of prayer; they do not demand the sacrifice of prayer itself.

This orientation to prayer marks a new turn in the history of religious institutes. Like the prayer of Ignatius, it is utterly absorbed in the work of the all-holy Three. So too, says Nadal, is the prayer of his followers necessary for the work that they have been called to do; "and we are confident that the grace of that prayer and contemplation has been prepared in the Society for all of us, and we maintain that it is linked with our vocation."[19]

That vocation, like all vocations, demands, as Vatican II says, "a proper understanding of men [and women], of the conditions of the times and of the needs of the Church." With that gift of prayer one can make "wise judgments about the contemporary world in the light of faith." Accompanying that gift to the Society is a gift to the whole Church. Through it Jesuits will "be able to help men [and women] more effectively" in accordance with the statement of General Congregation 34:

> The mission of the Society derives from our continuing experience of the Crucified and Risen Christ who invites us to join him in preparing the world to become the completed Kingdom of God. . . . He calls us "to help men and women disengage themselves from the tarnished and confused image that they have of themselves in order to discover that they are, in God's light, completely like Christ." And so we undertake all our ministries with a confidence that the Lord takes us, as he did Ignatius, as his servants—not because we are strong, but because he says to us, as he said to St. Paul, "My grace is sufficient for you, for my power is made perfect in weakness." (2 Cor. 12:9).[20]

---

[18] "Exhort. 1554 hisp." (*CommInst* 51 f., no. 29). Also in *Font.narr* 1:313 f., no. 16, with slightly different orthography.

[19] "In exam. annot." (*CommInst* 163, no. 82).

[20] *DocsGC34* 31 (p. 30). The internal quotation is from "Discourse to General Congregation 34," by Peter-Hans Kolvenbach, S.J., January 6, 1995 (ibid., p. 266).

This chapter has considered the prayer of the Jesuit with final vows. Our next chapter looks more closely at the grace of Trinitarian prayer granted to Ignatius, "the grace of that prayer and contemplation . . . prepared in the Society for all of us, . . . and linked with our vocation." As a grace flowing from the side of Christ, it is linked in some way with every Christian vocation.

Chronicle for Chapter Ten

His Paternity [Francis Borgia], . . . because his sickness does not allow him . . . to govern the Society as he should, has confirmed Fr. Nadal as his vicar-general, and has entrusted him with carrying out this office in all the provinces of our Society with the same authority that the superior general has.

—Polanco, to the provincials of Spain

Nadal's Life and Travels (1567–1568)

1567

Jan. 20: Interrupts stay at Mainz to visit Aschaffenburg (13 days)

Feb. 2–20: Frankfurt (2 days), Mainz

Feb. 24–April 2: At Cologne, exhortations

April 2–6: To Trier via Koblenz

April 6–May 9: At Trier, visits college

May 9–June 15: Saint Vith, Liege, Brussels

June 15–end Sept.: Louvain (Spa, St. Omer, Courtrai, Liege, Namur, Dinant while there)

Oct. 1–11: Antwerp

Oct. 12–27: Brussels, Ghent, Tournai, St. Omer

Oct. 27–Nov. 6: St. Omer; to Tournai

Nov. 7–end of year: Cambrai

1568

Jan. 1–Feb. 3: Cambrai

Feb. 8–mid March: Louvain; before March 25: Antwerp

April 11–18: Brussels; returns to Louvain

April 28–June 7: Louvain (Antwerp, Brussels)

June 7–15: To Paris via Brussels (one day)

June 15–July 15: At Paris, visits college

July 15–20: To Verdun

July 20–26: At Verdun, visits college

July 26–Aug. 6: To Chambery via Lorraine (Toul) and Burgundy (direct route through Lyons unsafe)

Aug. 6–16: Chambery

Aug. 17–ca. 29: At Lyons attends provincial congregation, visits college

Aug. 31: Chambery; told to return to Rome if French roads unsafe

Sept. 1–22: Journeys to Rome

Oct. 9: Named assistant for Spain

Chapter Ten

TRINITARIAN PRAYER OF IGNATIUS

Before all else, religious life is ordered to the following of Christ by its members, and to their becoming united with God by the profession of the evangelical counsels. For this reason, it must be seriously and carefully considered that even the best-contrived adaptations to the needs of our time will be of no avail unless they are animated by a spiritual renewal, which must always be assigned primary importance even in the active ministry.

—Vatican II, *On the Up-to-Date Renewal of the Religious Life*

T he following of Christ" implies sharing his life received from the Father, a life of being sent, so that in, with, and through the Son we participate in his mission of salvation, and in union with the Father and the Son breathe forth the Holy Spirit in his mission of sanctification, and thus participate in the mission of the Holy Spirit as well. General Congregation 33 has said that

[o]nly to the extent that he is united to God so that he be "led gladly by the divine hand," is a Jesuit "a man on a mission." In this way, he will learn to find God in all things, the God who is present in this world and its struggle between good and evil, between faith and unbelief, between the yearning for justice and peace and the growing reality of injustice and strife. But we cannot achieve this familiarity with God unless we set aside a regular time for personal prayer.[1]

History

When Ignatius, a layman at the time, began to talk to people about spiritual things, Church officials, fearing heresy, cross-examined him.[2] They always found him to be orthodox, but occasionally they forbade him to

---

[1] *Documents of the 33rd General Congregation of the Society of Jesus (DocsGC33)* (St. Louis: The Institute of Jesuit Sources, 1984), d. 1, pt. 1B, no. 12 (p. 46). The first internal quotation is from *ConsCN* 813$^{v.2}$ (p. 400).

[2] This section draws on Kamen, *Spanish Inquisition,* especially chaps. 5–6; Bangert, *Jerome Nadal,* chap. 14; De Guibert, *Spiritual Doctrine,* chap. 5; O'Malley, "Early Jesuit Spirituality," 3–26.

continue the work in which he was engaged. As noted earlier, Melchor Cano likened the Society to the *alumbrados,* and de Pedroche charged that the *Spiritual Exercises* were tinged with the errors of this group, who emphasized the role of the Holy Spirit but ignored the work of the Holy Spirit—the Church itself. The Spanish Inquisition, initially concerned principally with the sincerity of the *conversos,* Jews who had become Christians, also feared the possible inroads of heresy. In its concern to keep heresy out of Spain, the Inquisition not only banned certain books from coming into Spain but also, fearing the influence of the *alumbrados,* forbade some works written in Spain and some devotional manuscripts as well. The Spanish *Index of Forbidden Books* of 1559 banned a book by the *converso* Juan de Ávila (a friend of the Society and now a canonized saint). That same year Cano influenced the banning of a book by fellow Dominican Fray Luis de Granada, and of another published under the name of Francis Borgia, a work compiled by a printer from the writings of various authors, including a leaflet by Borgia. The Jesuit rector in Seville inquired of the Inquisitors whether the ban included manuscript copies of the *Spiritual Exercises* that the novices used. On receiving an affirmative reply, he handed over the copies, went to bed, and stayed there. Mysticism was suspect. In the 1570s the Society became concerned about the emphasis on the role of affectivity in the unpublished works of Antonio Cordeses, the provincial of Aragón, and in the teaching of Baltasar Álvarez, for a time the confessor of Teresa of Ávila.

During Everard Mercurian's generalate (1573–80), a list of books was drawn up in 1580 containing what was deemed appropriate reading for Jesuits. The only Jesuit writings included were letters from the Indies and the *Vita* of St. Ignatius. An earlier list in 1575 had indicated that, in addition to those already on Gregory XIII's list of forbidden books, there were others seemingly inappropriate for Jesuits. One forbidden author was Johannes Tauler, a fourteenth-century Dominican, who was a favorite of the Lutherans. Paradoxically, in 1543 Peter Canisius had published an edition of Tauler's *Sermons* and *Institutions* that appeared a month after Canisius himself entered the Society. Another author on Mercurian's "prohibited" list was Hendrik Herp, a fifteenth-century Franciscan. Paradoxically enough, the Carthusian Bruno Loher had dedicated a new edition of Herp's work to Ignatius and all his Jesuit sons because of their total commitment to both contemplation and action.[3] Other distinguished authors banned included Jan van Ruysbroeck, Blessed Henry Suso, Blessed Ramón Lull, St. Gertrude, and St. Mechtilde. The long-term consequence of these decisions was an overemphasis on method in prayer rather than on openness to the Spirit's creative and impelling activity. That overemphasis, along with suspicion of the mystical (attitudes espoused by some

---

[3] The preface is found in *Font.narr* 1:755–61.

Jesuits at that time), prevailed even after the middle of the twentieth century; indeed, it lingers in the minds of many to the present day.

A Pause for Prayer

With Germanic boldness Karl Rahner says, "[T]he innermost determination of the world is that it is the 'surrounding world' or the 'living space' for God Himself who 'becomes' in the world." From this he concludes, "Therefore, the ultimate reason why every man exists is that, by his life and existence with the Incarnate Word, he might make it possible for God to undertake the adventure of his love outside of himself."[4] Our whole task as human beings is to open ourselves freely and joyfully to our relationship with the Incarnate Word, who is madly in love with us.

> **Contemplation to Attain Love: "Love ought to manifest itself more by deeds than by words"** (*SpEx* 230[v.2] [p. 94]).
>
> We ask once more for what we desire, which here is to welcome into our lives freely and joyfully the presence and activity of the three Divine Persons (as Ignatius did), to relate freely and joyfully to Father, Son, and Holy Spirit, to seek Trinitarian prayer such as Ignatius had, which is to say: to allow the Son freely and joyfully to pray within us the way he wishes to pray and the way the Holy Spirit wishes us to pray, without fear and without seeking what is beyond what the Spirit wishes to give, confident that the Spirit will satisfy our deepest yearnings: "Take, Lord, and receive all my liberty. . . . Give me love of yourself along with your grace, for that is enough for me" (*SpEx* 234[v.5] [p. 95]).

Background Reflections on the Religious Life

Previous chapters showed how Nadal insisted that the life of Ignatius was a model for all the members of the Society, and that the unique graces of Ignatius were also the particular graces and character of the Society of Jesus. The inner, mystical life of Ignatius, his union with God that overflowed into service, and the greater glory of God were also unique features meant for every Jesuit's life. This chapter considers Nadal's fuller development of Ignatius's Trinitarian prayer and explores how this prayer should

---

[4] Karl Rahner, S.J., *Spiritual Exercises,* trans. Kenneth Baker, S.J. (New York: Herder and Herder, 1965), 114.

characterize the prayer of the Society and of each Jesuit. Many other writers have addressed this topic since my earlier work in 1957, *Contemplation in Action*.[5]

Notes on the Examen ("In examen annotationes"), 1557

CommInst 134–205, nos. 1–203

Nadal leads into the Trinitarian prayer of Ignatius inadvertently by outlining the history of the relationship between the priesthood and the religious life. In his "Notes on the Examen," he comments on the now famous passage in the *General Examen* in which Ignatius describes the exterior manner of living in the Society as ordinary, without regular obligatory penances and austerities. Each member may, with the superior's approval, practice those penances that he finds helpful for his spiritual progress or that the superior may impose upon him for the same purpose.[6] Ordinary *[communis]*, he explains, does not mean either the ordinary life of people in secular society or the ordinary life of monks, who undertake certain penances as part of their rule.[7] Monks originally were likened to others who lived in solitude: they could not preach or teach or receive holy orders. In the feudal hierarchy the monastic was inferior to the sacerdotal; perfection for the most part was found in the priesthood. In the early centuries the relation between a bishop and his priests constituted something like a religious order. Monks helped priests by their prayers and fasting, and were satisfied with what St. Jerome called "holy rusticity."[8]

Times changed, Nadal continues. Either because of the influx of wealth and the negligence of those in charge, or because fewer entered religious institutes whose members were not clerics, priests and clerics became more remiss in their mode of living, less likely to give good example to others; and so through divine providence monks came to accept ordination. Where ordinary priests had failed, ordained monks became the reforming element and the bishops' main workforce, assisting the hierarchy to shepherd their flocks. Through the providence of God, the Church saw to it that the contemplative life was not lacking in the Church, so that those who were active were helped by contemplatives quietly

---

[5] For additional material on Ignatian prayer and spirituality see appendix 3, pp. 273 f. below.

[6] "Examen" (*Constitutiones* 2:9a, no. 4 [Text B, ca. 1556]).

[7] In a later work Nadal indicates that *communis* refers to the ordinary life of secular priests (*NadSchol* 3).

[8] *CommInst* 156 f., no. 61–63. "Epist. 3" (ad Paulinum), no. 3 (*Corpus scriptorum ecclesiasticorum latinorum* CSEL [Vienna: Hoelder-Pichler-Tempsky, 1866–], 54:447); *Patrologiæ cursus completus: Series Latina*, ed. Jacques-Paul Migne (Paris, 1844–91), 22:542.

serving Christ Jesus their spouse in simple ways *[familiariter]*. Thus it followed that those who were active engaged in their spiritual activities sedately and peacefully, as it were, through the prayer of the contemplatives joining contemplation with action in Christ (157 f., nos. 64–66).

To unfold the layers of meaning that Nadal explores here, we must examine the stratified meaning of the Latin word *familiariter*. Although *familiariter* means first of all, "by families," and secondly, "familiarly" or "intimately," the basic meaning of *familiaris* as an adjective is "of or pertaining to a servant," and as a noun it simply means "servant." Its second meaning is "of or belonging to a household or family," and its transferred meaning is "familiar, intimate, friendly." The passage suggests that the contemplative serves Christ in a loving and familiar manner, but it also strongly suggests the picture of the contemplative as servant in the house of the Lord, performing the simple tasks of the household. The prayer life of a monk, true enough, consists in contemplation, but just as much so in simple daily menial tasks that become contemplation. In like manner, the person engaged in ministry is free from hurry and flurry, rush and distraction. Where harmony prevails, Christ works and prays in peace and tranquillity.

In this summary of the evolution of the priesthood and the religious life, Nadal manifests a striking vision and experience of the Communion of Saints, the cooperation of contemplatives with those engaged in active ministry, all through the providence of God. This cooperation in ministry, through the prayer of contemplatives on the one hand and the prayerful activity of the Church's ministers on the other, although it is by no means foreign to the Jesuit experience, does not adequately express Nadal's vision of Jesuit prayer, as will soon become clear.

Some monks, Nadal continues, with great fruit take on sacerdotal ministries, such as teaching and administering sacraments, not by reason of their institute but by way of exception. All monks, however, are called to the monastic life, to vigils, fasting, chanting the office, wearing the cowl, to solitude, to sitting in their cell or going about in silence. Not all take on the ministry of the word or the sacraments, but only those who seem fit for the ministry (157, no. 67). The Order of Preachers, of course, by its very institute, engages in the ministry of preaching. The call and status of the Society of Jesus, however, is not to be monks but, for most of its membership, to be priests or be preparing for the priesthood. Fundamental to the Society is every priestly ministry, not only the celebration of Mass but the ministry of word and sacraments. With the Holy See's approval, the Society takes from every ecclesiastical state whatever is helpful to the end proposed (158, no. 68).

The Society has embraced especially the pursuit of the virtues in their perfection, and the greatest of these is love (158, nos. 69 f.). "On this alone let us put our effort; where it leads, let us strive for that" (158 f., no.

70). To do so does not mean ignoring the other virtues, for the Society seeks the perfect observance of all the virtues, not only the more important ones (159, no. 73). Nadal enumerates some of the virtues; as was the case in chapter 6, he again proceeds from love of God to obedience. Speaking for a moment about obedience, he suddenly finds himself talking about prayer. It is important to see how his mind jumped from one to the other.

Obedience

A rich and remarkable vocabulary clothes the first sentence of three brief paragraphs on obedience: "We especially strive carefully for the perfection of obedience in the quiet joy of our hearts" (160, no. 76). Obedience is a response of love that fills the heart with joy. Nadal's fundamental supposition is that through obedience one shares in the mission of the Son from the Father. Jesus' attitude toward the Father models the Jesuit's attitude toward the superior.

In this view, the willing execution of a command even though one may disagree with it does not satisfy the perfection of obedience. The Institute demands uniting obedience of judgment with willingness and execution: not only should one carry out the command and do it willingly with steadfast heart, but he should also judge and consider it right and good and to be carried out exactly and promptly. Doing so entails contemplating and reverencing in the superior the presence, actions, words, will, and judgment of Christ, recognizing in faith and love that Jesus chooses (astonishingly) to deal with each person intimately through superiors (160 f., no. 76).

Nadal, who repeatedly said no to Ignatius before the Society was founded, cannot get over the gift of his vocation to the Society, a lovely gift from a loving God. He is astonished, even confused. He expects the same reaction from every Jesuit. In the Spiritual Exercises the *confusion* Ignatius asks the exercitant to pray for in the meditation on sin comes from the realization of God's enormous unconditional love and forgiveness in spite of the enormity of one's sins: It's crazy! one cries. Obedience in the Society, as a willing and loving surrender to a loving God, is clearly a form of prayer, of contemplation, joyful, enduring, penetrating and pervading other actions and attitudes, a way of living.

The next paragraph is about that strange phenomenon called "blind obedience." The loving conviction that Jesus is present in the person and actions of the superior, "dispelling our darkness," explains the possibility of blind obedience, otherwise totally nonsensical:

> We therefore embrace what we call blind obedience, as though we are deprived of our own judgment by reason of the splendor of holy obedience and the contemplation of the presence of Jesus Christ in our superiors. Should we be surprised that the presence of divine light should dispel our

darkness, that is, absorb our will and judgment so that we will and judge in Christ and through Christ? (161, no. 77)

The obedient Jesuit might expect to be astonished, even confused by God's enormous unconditional love.

The third paragraph states that, by reason of one's vocation and by reason of the vow of obedience, this kind of obedience can be practiced "easily and with complete dedication in the quiet joy of our hearts" (161, no. 78). Nadal had earlier spoken of poverty as "liberty of spirit in the face of the persistent solicitation of things" (147, no. 39). Obedience is clearly liberty of spirit in the face of one's own will. Chastity, too, is liberty of spirit in the face of the attractiveness of others.

In that contemplative mode, reflecting on the presence of Christ in the superior calling each one to complete Christ's mission from the Father, Nadal launches into some remarks that changed Jesuit terminology about prayer when they were discovered in more recent times, as we shall see below.

Prayer

Nadal accepts as certain the need for prayer in a religious institute, a prayer

> that embraces all divisions of spiritual effort, purgative, illuminative, and unitive. The Society diligently and with great eagerness embraces this kind of prayer, tasting its sweetness in Christ Jesus. She exercises all her members first of all in those meditations touching on repentance and the stripping-off of the old man, and then in the contemplation of all the mysteries of Christ, in which we desire to obtain an experience of the way, the truth, and the life. Finally we rest in love, so that we place our end in that from which prayer ought to take its source; namely, in charity, the most divine virtue, so that with it and its fervor and zeal we go forth to our ministries in cheerfulness of spirit and humility of heart, with devotion and courage in Christ Jesus.[9]

Although there are distinctions between active prayer (what a person does) and passive or mystical prayer (what God does in the person), the beginning of all prayer is passive and a mystical experience: God calls each one and moves each one to pray. Prayer is response to God's initiative. In the course of time God's activity should increase and the person's decrease (perhaps with little consciousness) until the person and God are united in love. The call to prayer is not for Jesuits alone, nor for religious alone, but for all Christians, all human beings: God calls all to

---

[9] 161 f., no. 79. For the Spiritual Exercises as a school of prayer, see appendix 4, p. 274 below.

surrender totally to God in a love from and into the heart of God and toward other people.

The Prayer of Ignatius

Freely admitting that his remarks on prayer were somewhat out of place from a logical point of view, Nadal nonetheless hastened to add to his comments on the Spiritual Exercises by touching on the prayer of Ignatius:

> But there is one thing I shall not omit (even though this is not the proper place to speak of prayer, but elsewhere): we know that Father Ignatius received from God the singular grace to enjoy freely the contemplation of the Trinity and to rest in it. One day the grace would lead him to contemplate the whole Trinity, to be drawn to it and be completely united to it in great devotion and consolation. At another time he contemplated the Father, at another the Son or the Holy Spirit. He enjoyed this contemplation frequently at other times, but especially (almost as his only prayer) during the last days of his life.
>
> Father Ignatius received this kind of prayer by reason of a great privilege and in a most extraordinary way; and this besides: so that in everything, in actions and in conversations, he was wholly caught up in the presence of God and the love of things spiritual—contemplative also in the midst of action [simul in actione contemplativus] (which he used to express in this way: God is to be found in everything).
>
> We have seen that grace and interior light break forth on his shining countenance and in the clarity and precision of his actions in Christ, much to the wonderment and consolation of all of us; and we have felt something of that grace channeled, as it were, to the rest of us. The same privilege, therefore, that we understand was granted to Father Ignatius we believe has been conceded to the whole Society, and we are confident that the grace of that prayer and contemplation has been prepared in the Society for all of us, and we maintain that it is linked with our vocation.
>
> Therefore, let us also place the perfection of our prayer in the contemplation of the Trinity, and in the love and union of charity, extended, indeed, to our neighbor through the ministries of our vocation, which, to be sure, we easily prefer to the taste and sweetness of prayer. (162f., nos. 80–83)

Accordingly, we see that the prayer of Ignatius is

- Trinitarian
- a great privilege
- a gift that includes finding God in all things
- a gift prepared for the whole Society

These points deserve consideration one at a time, slowly and deliberately; for as Father Arrupe said when he was general of the Society,

Neither the Society's way of proceeding nor its radical charism can be adequately understood and appreciated unless we mount up to the very top, to the Trinity. In the return to the sources that Vatican II called for, the Society cannot stop without going all that distance. Only in the light of Ignatius's Trinitarian intimacy can we Jesuits understand, accept and live the Society's charism.[10]

Each paragraph deserves repetition and comment:

Trinitarian

To repeat what we have just seen:

But there is one thing I shall not omit (even though this is not the proper place to speak of prayer, but elsewhere): we know that Father Ignatius received from God the singular grace to enjoy freely the contemplation of the Trinity and to rest in it. One day the grace would lead him to contemplate the whole Trinity, to be drawn to it and be completely united to it in great devotion and consolation. At another time he contemplated the Father, at another the Son or the Holy Spirit. He enjoyed this contemplation frequently at other times, but especially (almost as his only prayer) during the last days of his life.[11]

Hugo Rahner points out that from the very first days at Manresa to the end of his life, the characteristic of Ignatius's mysticism was its Trinitarian orientation.[12] In Manresa Ignatius enjoyed his first vision of the three Divine Persons, which so impressed him that for the rest of his life he felt great devotion in praying to the Trinity. In his autobiography, referring to himself in the third person, Ignatius says:

One day while saying the Office of Our Lady on the steps of the same monastery, his understanding began to be elevated so that he saw the Most Holy Trinity in the form of three musical keys. This brought on so many

---

[10] Pedro Arrupe, S.J., "The Trinitarian Inspiration of the Ignatian Charism," *Studies in the Spirituality of Jesuits* 33, no. 3 (May 2001): 3 (originally published in CIS 13, no. 1 [1982]: 12).

[11] "Illud vero non omittam (etiamsi proprius hic locus non est, ut de oratione dicam, sed alius): Patrem Ignatium scimus singularem gratiam accepisse a Domino, ut in contemplatione Sanctissimæ Trinitatis exerceretur libere ac conquiesceret; nunc quidem gratia contemplandæ totius Trinitatis ducebatur, in illam ferebatur, in illam uniebatur toto corde, magno sensu devotionis atque spiritualis gustus; nunc Patrem contemplabatur, nunc Filium, nunc Spiritum Sanctum. Et hujus quidem contemplationem accepit, cum alias frequenter, tum vero (quasi si unice dicas) ad annos suae peregrinationis ultimos" ("In exam. annot." [*CommInst* 162, no. 80]; also in *EpistNadal* 4:651, with slightly different orthography).

[12] Hugo Rahner, S.J., "Die Mystik des hl. Ignatius und der Inhalt der Vision von La Storta," *Zeitschrift für Aszese und Mystik* 10 (1935): 202; for an English version see *The Vision of St. Ignatius in the Chapel of La Storta*, 2nd ed. (Rome: CIS, 1979), 5–132, esp. p. 70.

tears and so much sobbing that he could not control himself. That morning, while going in a procession that set out from there, he could not hold back his tears until dinnertime; nor after eating could he stop talking about the Most Holy Trinity, using many comparisons in great variety and with much joy and consolation. As a result, the effect has remained with him throughout his life of experiencing great devotion while praying to the Most Holy Trinity.[13]

Ignatius further reports that on another occasion "the manner in which God had created the world was presented to his understanding with great spiritual joy. He seemed to see something white, from which some rays were coming, and God made light from this."[14] On yet another day he experienced a great illumination:

> Once he was going out of devotion to a church situated a little more than a mile from Manresa; I believe it is called St. Paul's, and the road goes by the river. As he went along occupied with his devotions, he sat down for a little while with his face toward the river, which ran down below. While he was seated there, the eyes of his understanding began to be opened; not that he saw any vision, but he understood and learnt many things, both spiritual matters and matters of faith and of scholarship, and this with so great an enlightenment that everything seemed new to him.
>
> The details that he understood then, though there were many, cannot be stated, but only that he experienced a great clarity in his understanding. This was such that in the whole course of his life, after completing sixty-two years, even if he gathered up all the various helps he may have had from God and all the various things he has known, even adding them all together, he does not think that he had got as much as he had at that one time.[15]

Nadal remarks that the illumination left Ignatius with a dynamic experience of contemplation and union with God, so that he easily felt devotion in everything and everywhere.[16] Hugo Rahner sums up the experience by saying that Ignatius saw everything, all the mysteries of faith and the entirety of creation, as coming from and returning to the triune God.[17]

The *Spiritual Diary,* which Ignatius wrote in February and March of 1544, during some weeks of discernment over poverty, supplies numerous examples. He approaches the Father through the mediation of the Mother

---

[13] "Acta P. Ignatii" (*Font.narr* 1:402, no. 28); For an English version see *PilgTest* 28 (p. 40).

[14] "Acta P. Ignatii," 402, no. 29; *PilgTest* 40 (p. 41).

[15] "Acta P. Ignatii," 404, no. 30; *PilgTest* 30 (p. 42 f.).

[16] "Plática 3ª en Coimbra" (*Pláticas espirituales* 66, no. 11); also in *Font.narr* 2:158, no. 2, with slightly different orthography.

[17] Rahner, *Mystik,* 205; for an English version, see id., *Vision of St. Ignatius,* 77.

and the Son. He speaks with the Holy Spirit and seems to see him in a flame of fire. Through our Lady and the Son he asks the Father to send him the Holy Spirit. He sees "how the Son first sent the apostles to preach in poverty; and then how the Holy Spirit, by communicating himself and the gift of tongues, confirmed them; and how thus, when the Father and the Son sent the Holy Spirit, all three Persons confirmed that mission."[18] He offers his decision to the Father. He feels intense devotion and perceives the Holy Spirit interiorly. He gives thanks to the Divine Persons. He repeats the previous offering out of devotion to the Holy Trinity.

Feeling sluggish, he has no confidence in finding grace in the Most Holy Trinity. He asks our Lady and her Son to be intercessors with the Holy Trinity. He asks the Eternal Father, the Eternal Son, and the Eternal Holy Spirit to confirm him. Then the Holy Trinity absorbs him and he is bathed in peaceful tears. He addresses each Person, or the three in their unity. In speaking to one he finds the other two. Over and over again he experiences devotion, joy, intense sobbing, a flood of tears. Sometimes his devotion terminates in Jesus, sometimes in the Father, sometimes in the Trinity, sometimes in the Trinity and Jesus, or in the Name and Essence of the Holy Trinity. In all these experiences he is absorbed in the salvific activity of the three Divine Persons. Reading the *Spiritual Diary* opens all the implications in Nadal's remark that Ignatius "was lifted up by anything whatsoever, as happened, for example, one day when they were in the garden, and looking at the leaf of an orange tree, he went into a lofty, elevated discourse about the Trinity."[19]

In his own spiritual diary Nadal recalls that Laínez had this to say of Ignatius:

> "He is on extraordinarily close terms with God, for he has already passed beyond all sensible visions, like seeing Christ present or the Virgin, and those that are seen through forms and figures, and now enjoys purely spiritual ones in the unity of God." Afterwards I learned from Father Ignatius himself that he holds intercourse with the Divine Persons and finds a variety of distinct gifts from the distinct Persons, as though the Father would communicate his grace through the channel of his Son. In this contemplation, however, he finds greater gifts in the person of the Holy Spirit.[20] I also learned from Father Ignatius himself that in contemplation

---

[18] *Obras completas de S. Ignacio de Loyola,* ed. Ignacio Iparraguirre, S.I., 322, no. 15; for an English version see "The *Spiritual Diary,*" in Ganss, *Ignatius of Loyola: The Spiritual Exercises and Selected Works,* 241, no. 15. See Noëlle Hausman, S.C.M., "Ignatius Loyola and the Mission of the Holy Spirit: An Interpretation of the Spiritual Diary (1544–1545)," *CIS* 20, nos. 1–2 (1990): 39–59.

[19] "Plática 4ª en Coimbra" (*Pláticas espirituales* 71, no. 2); also in *Font.narr* 2:158, no. 2, with slightly different orthography.

[20] For a study of the role of the Holy Spirit in the spirituality of Ignatius, see Manuel Ruiz Jurado, S.J., "El Espíritu Santo en la espiritualidad ignaciana," *Manresa* 70

he finds God, being itself and the source of being, as often as he gives himself to prayer, without regard to order or method, but that God is to be sought in a variety of ways.[21]

Ignatius is a model, not by reason of the visions that Laínez describes, but by reason of his familiarity with the Divine Persons, as it was depicted by Nadal.

Some years later, addressing the Jesuits in Coimbra, Nadal warned that seeking visions, revelations, and other extraordinary gifts was vanity and the way to deceptions and illusions.[22] The antidote Ignatius found for illusion was keeping his feet firmly planted on the ground of the Incarnation. He sought the place where Jesus walked. He delayed his first Mass for eighteen months, hoping to offer it in Bethlehem; but at length he settled for the chapel in St. Mary Major in Rome where pious belief said the crib was preserved. Teresa of Avila also grounded herself on the Incarnation and saw the possibility of illusion in visions and other extraordinary experiences. The goal is union and familiarity with God. Extraordinary gifts, given for others, are gifts only when shared in concrete activities.

Ignatius's Great Privilege

"Father Ignatius received this kind of prayer by reason of a great privilege and in a most extraordinary way—"[23] He received [concepit] this kind of prayer as a gift; he conceived within himself this kind of prayer, was pregnant with it so that it bore fruit.[24]

That this grace granted to Ignatius was a great privilege is beyond doubt. That it was a privilege having personal characteristics that can be called proper to Ignatius, distinguishing him from the founders of other religious institutes, is also beyond cavil. The mysticism of Ignatius, a loving service of the Trinity at the side of the Savior carrying his cross, produced an order so revolutionary that even other religious attacked it vigorously as undermining the very essentials of religion. An urgency of love surging from a realistic grasp of the loving action of the Trinity in the lives of ordinary human beings shaped Ignatius's Institute in almost ruthless

---

(1998): 217–30.

[21] *Orat.observ.* (1545), 33, no. 8; also in *Font.narr* 2:315 f. and *EpistNadal* 4:645, with slightly different orthography.

[22] Fourteenth Exhortation in Alcalá (*CommInst* 481, no. 280).

[23] "Hanc rationem orationis concepit Pater Ignatius magno privilegio, selectissime" ("In exam. annot." [*CommInst* 162, no. 81]).

[24] In his "Vida diaria," Herbert Alphonso, translates the Latin *concepit* into the Spanish *consideró* (considered). I think that *concepit* describes a passive rather than an active experience of Ignatius.

fashion and trimmed practices hallowed by centuries of saints. The urgent love of the Trinity had created the universe, had clothed one person in Flesh and sent another to sanctify the world in Spirit; Ignatius could take no other standard: he must imitate love incarnate.

Finding God in All Things

After interrupting the first sentence of no. 81 in midcourse, as we did above, let us now quote it in full in order to supply the proper context:

> Father Ignatius received this kind of prayer by reason of a great privilege and in a most extraordinary way; and this besides: so that in everything, in actions, and in conversations, he was wholly caught up in the presence of God and the love of all things spiritual: contemplative also in the midst of action (which he used to express in this way: God is to be found in every-thing).[25]

The contemplation of Ignatius bore fruit: it replicated itself in action. "And this besides [tum illud præterea]" indicates the fruit of that kind of prayer: that he felt [sentiret] the presence of God and contemplated it [contem-plaretur]. He experienced the presence of God passionately, was absorbed in it, riveted by it, enraptured by it. Furthermore, he felt [sentiret] a surge of love for the whole spiritual realm and was bathed in it [contemplaretur] as well. He was caught up in the love of God and in the love of God's creatures as well; and this was not just for a moment but in everything—in every action, in every conversation—seeing everything, as Daniélou says, from the point of view of the Trinity, grasping the relationship of each creature to the three Divine Persons as their source and as the goal to which each returns.[26]

What more can Nadal say? At this moment he tosses off the phrase that adds nothing but serves as a climax and captures it all: "simul in actione contemplativus" (contemplative also in the midst of action). In uninterrupted, seamless contemplation, contemplative in prayer and

---

[25] "Hanc rationem orationis concepit Pater Ignatius magno privilegio, selectissi-me; tum illud præterea: in omnibus rebus, actionibus, colloquiis, ut Dei præsentiam rerumque spiritualium affectum sentiret atque contemplaretur, simul in actione contem-plativus (quod ita solebat explicare: Deum esse in omnibus rebus inveniendum)" ("In exam. annot." [CommInst 162, no. 81]). It can also be found in EpistNadal 4:651, with slightly different orthography. See comments of Emerich Coreth, S.J., "In actione contemplativus," Zeitschrift für katholische Theologie 76 (1954): 55–82; for an English version see "Contemplation in Action," in Contemporary Spirituality, ed. Robert W. Gleason, S.J. (New York: Macmillan, 1968), 184–211; Fernand Lévesque. S.J., "Contem-plation et action chez saint Ignace," Cahiers de spiritualité ignatienne 3 (1979): 23–29; Lopez Tejada, "Paz interior," 475–504.

[26] Jean Danielou, S.J., "La spiritualité trinitaire de Saint Ignace," Christus 3 (1956): 354–72.

contemplative in action, Ignatius found God in prayer and in everything else as well.[27]

Præterea (besides) is not a superfluous word, nor is *simul* (at the same time, likewise, also). *Præterea* functions in the same way as the words of Jesus "and the second is like to this," when he links love of God with love of neighbor (Mark 12:31). *Præterea* ties the gift of Trinitarian contemplation to the gift of finding God in all things, and *simul* asserts that in finding God in all things Ignatius is as contemplative in action as he is in contemplating and being absorbed in the Father, Son, and Holy Spirit. *Simul* may very well suggest the unity and simultaneity of two aspects of one and the same gift of prayer, contemplation and action—that the contemplation is taking place at the very same moment that the action is taking place; but its main function is to unite the contemplation of the Trinity with finding God in all things. Both *præterea* and *simul* distinguish and unite two aspects of one and the same gift of prayer: (1) Ignatius is contemplative in praying to the Persons of the Trinity; (2) besides that *[præterea]*, he is at the same time *[simul]* contemplative in finding God in all things.

Certainly Nadal is drawing a contrast between Ignatius's contemplation of the Trinity on the one hand and his engagement in various activities on the other. The point he is making is that Ignatius is contemplative in his actions and not only in his prayer. The manuscript reveals that he first attempted to express himself by writing the words "simul in actione contemplationis" (at the same time as in the action of contemplation). Does he mean (1) an action that contemplation itself performs or produces or (2) the action of contemplating that Ignatius is performing?

Regarding this first option, note that contemplation is an action that has its own impact on others apart from an intervening action like preaching. The presence and contemplation of contemplatives impacts the people in their neighborhood and throughout the world. Thérèse of Lisieux was active in and through contemplation *(in contemplatione activus)*, to such an extent that Pius XI named her patroness of foreign missions along with Francis Xavier, who affected people not only through his contemplation but also through preaching, baptizing, and many other activities that flowed from his contemplation.[28] Nadal does not dwell on the impact that contemplation has on others. He seems to think of contemplatives as centered on their own sanctification without concern for others. Perhaps that was true of his day; it certainly does not accord with the experience

---

[27] François Charmont, S.J., *L'Union au Christ dans l'action selon saint Ignace* (Paris: Bonne Presse, 1959), 114.

[28] See Hans Urs von Balthasar, *Thérèse of Lisieux: The Story of a Mission*, trans. Donald Nicholl (New York: Sheed and Ward, 1954), 93–147, esp. p. 136.

of many contemplatives in the present age. One thing is very clear to Nadal: such self-centered spirituality has no place in the life of a Jesuit!

Nadal consistently maintains that contemplation should lead to action: to preaching or hearing confessions or feeding the poor, for example. This sounds very much like the position of St. Thomas Aquinas that the "mixed life," which consists of both action and contemplation, is better than either the active life or the contemplative life; for the one leading the mixed life both contemplates and communicates to others what he or she has contemplated. St. Thomas, however, is talking about communicating through preaching or teaching, whereas Ignatius and Nadal include many other activities as well.

With regard to the second option, that *in actione contemplationis* means "in the action of contemplation" (that is to say, in the action of contemplation in which Ignatius is engaged), it could refer to an extension of the same act of contemplating the Trinity when he moves from prayer to action. Or it could mean that when Ignatius became engaged in activity after contemplating the Trinity, he found another fertile field for contemplation in the actions and activities themselves. The text states clearly that in everything, in all his actions and conversations, Ignatius "was wholly caught up in the presence of God and the love of all things spiritual." Nadal does not deny that Ignatius is communicating to others the fruit of his contemplation; in fact, he rather implies it. He does say, however, that in doing so he is once more caught up in the presence of God. Since God is active in creation, the text suggests that Ignatius is caught up in the presence and activity of God, the presence and activity of Father, Son, and Holy Spirit in all those actions and conversations and everything else, and sees all those actions and persons and everything else as filled and saturated with God.

Adrien Demoustier sees the Trinitarian contemplation of Ignatius as a gift received from God that moved him toward God and rendered him capable of performing an action that expressed the gift received. This seems to mean that the very gift of contemplating the salvific activity of the Trinity drew Ignatius to participate in the saving action of the Divine Persons by bringing it to others through his preaching, conversation, or whatever else he did, fully aware that through him the Divine Persons were doing in others what they were doing in him.[29] Demoustier's argument is rather subtle; but he seems to be saying that the actions of Ignatius would be the equivalent of "to contemplate, and to communicate to others the fruit of contemplation"; extending the activity beyond preaching to feeding the poor, teaching Christian doctrine to street children, establishing three homes to accommodate wayward women, orphans, and

---

[29] Adrien Demoustier, S.J., " 'Contemplatif en action': Essai sur une formule de Jérôme Nadal," *Christus* 38 (1991): 470–478.

Jewish converts respectively, and so on. Demoustier, however, goes beyond the actions to the prayer that accompanies those actions; for Nadal is talking about the prayer of Ignatius during his actions, not about the actions themselves.

Nadal might just as easily have written *simul in actionis contemplatione* (likewise in contemplation of the action), referring to Ignatius's awareness of God in all that he did. In any event, and perhaps to avoid ambiguity, Nadal crossed out *contemplationis* and wrote *contemplativus* instead: just as Ignatius was contemplative in his Trinity-centered prayer, so likewise was he contemplative in everything he did; and this is what Ignatius meant by "finding God in all things."

Both Francis Xavier and Thérèse, like the monks and nuns of old, sought God in prayer and found God as well in all that they did, and the contemplatives of today do the same. The actions of Thérèse and the monks were different from the actions of Francis and Ignatius, but they had the same salvific effect upon others. It seems that when Nadal coined the phrase "contemplative also in the midst of action," he had in mind, not just any action, but the kinds of actions in which Jesuits are called upon to engage—actions that enable others to embrace lives of asceticism or contemplation, or apostolic activity that helps other people to change their lives. Nonetheless, all are called to be contemplative in one degree or another, and all are called to be contemplative to some degree in all their actions, whatever those actions may be—preaching or cooking, chanting psalms or selling merchandise, digging in the garden or changing diapers; for God is present and deserves our surrender in all of these.

As Miguel Nicolau points out succinctly, if Nadal's formula "simul in actione contemplativus" is compared with the Thomistic formula "contemplata aliis tradere" (to pass on to others the fruit of contemplation), it is clear that the latter speaks of contemplation previous to the action of passing on its fruit (the contemplation of a preacher before he preaches), whereas Nadal's formula speaks of contemplation simultaneous with the action itself, suggesting that union with God is not lost in the external activities of the apostolate.[30]

The formulas seem to capture and express the special grace of each religious order—the special grace of preaching in the Order of Preachers and the special grace of being involved in numerous apostolates in the Society of Jesus. Each is a gift to the other and to the whole Church. The Thomistic formula invites Jesuits and all others engaged in preaching to be aware of and to respond to the grace and call to contemplate what they preach before they preach. The Nadalian formula invites Dominicans and all others to contemplate while they preach, and when engaged in any

---

[30] Miguel Nicolau, S.J., "La oración de San Ignacio: Formulas que la expresan," *Manresa* 28 (1956): 91–104, esp. p. 97.

external apostolates to be aware of and to respond to the grace and call to be united with God not only in prayer but in the midst of any action whatsoever.

There is no evidence that Nadal thought he had created a phrase that captured the prayer of Ignatius perfectly. Whether "contemplative also in the midst of action" was in his mind a "throw-away phrase," as one is tempted to call it, or whether Nadal—to use that awful phrase of American public-relations officers—had "run it up the flagpole to see if anyone saluted," there is no way to know. Twentieth-century Jesuits have, indeed, saluted; but one wonders how many, if any, sixteenth-century Jesuits saw or heard the phrase. There is no evidence that the "Annotationes in examen" in which it appears was published. It may have been copied and sent around to various communities, and it may or may not have made an impression.

The expression as Nadal used it does, indeed, go beyond the Thomistic formula. Had Nadal meant the same as Thomas, he could have used the words of Thomas. Both were concerned about prayer and action, but they were not trying to make the same point. Explaining the difference between the "contemplative life" and the "mixed life," the Angelic Doctor wrote that in the first, one contemplates, whereas in the second, one not only contemplates but communicates to others the fruit of that contemplation; probably he had in mind preaching and teaching. Had he intended to discuss the full "prayer life" of the person who lived the "mixed life," he might well have included expressions similar to those Nadal used of Ignatius. Nadal goes beyond Thomas on two counts: (1) after describing Ignatius's contemplation of the Trinity, he includes many more ways of acting and relating to people than preaching and teaching; and (2) he includes the prayer experience of Ignatius during his activities and while relating to others: "in everything, in actions, and in conversations, he was wholly caught up in the presence of God and the love of all things spiritual."

Perhaps Nadal hardly noticed the phrase he used, but the idea is certainly not foreign to his way of thinking. Just as he systematically talked about the "active life," the "contemplative life," and the "higher active life," he frequently and systematically talked about contemplation that should lead to action and used various ways of saying that the two should join together so that everything should become prayer. Even in explaining the three lives, he insists that Jesuits should be "primarily and, as it were, uniquely contemplative"—simply another way of saying, "contemplative in prayer and contemplative in action as well."

Gilles Cusson comments that according to Nadal Ignatius would not have been caught in the conflict between action and contemplation, and von Balthasar says equivalently the same of Thérèse. Both wedded the two. Ignatius did not speak of contemplation in the sense of the contemplative life, nor of action as a way of life opposed to a way consecrated to prayer. That is why Nadal substitutes the adjective *contemplativus* for the noun *contemplationis*. The adjective expresses an attitude, a *tone* of being. For Ignatius, one does not give oneself to contemplation as to a distinct activity, but one is contemplative at the very core of one's being; one is contemplative in *everything* and not just in the "prayer of contemplation." Moreover, in this context the word *action* is surprisingly broad, encompassing not only St. Benedict's *work* and St. Thomas's *charitable action,* but EVERYTHING: living, acting, walking, eating, sleeping. Even *prayer* is one action among many as far as Ignatius is concerned. To be contemplative in every action is to find God in all things, to praise, reverence, and serve him in everything—in a word, to worship and be united with God in everything at the very depths of one's being.[31] No wonder that in the Jewish tradition there is a blessing for everything, and in the Roman Catholic *Book of Rites* blessings are found for airplanes and crops and everything in between; and in the cult of saints a patron or patroness can be found for doctors and nurses, for farmers and pilots and seamstresses, and so on, ad infinitum.

Cusson's remarks awakened the present author and explained to me why, between 1957 and the present, I had become incresingly uncomfortable with terms like "contemplation in action," "a contemplative in action," and "contemplatives in action." It was not simply because some used the terms to avoid the call to become contemplative in prayer. Rather, in the phrase *simul in actione contemplativus,* the word *contemplativus* was not a noun but an adjective; that fact was beginning to rise from the subconscious to an active level of awareness. It refers, not to a person who lives a certain way of life, but to a way or tone of being or doing, an attitude: eating, singing, playing, praying *in a contemplative manner.*[32] A contemplative in action is a Carmelite sweeping the floor or a Carthusian tending the garden, not a Jesuit teaching a class or feeding the poor; but the Carmelite, the Carthusian, and the Jesuit should all be *contemplative* in whatever action they are doing. Nuances in explaining the phrase differ from those of forty-five years ago.

Simul, Cusson adds in the same passage, means "at the same time as the action," not in spite of the action, but in, along with, and across the action. Teresa of Avila spoke of the union she experienced with God

---

[31] Gilles Cusson, S.J., "Les Exercices spirituels, école de contemplation," *Cahiers de spiritualité ignatienne* 17 (1993): 245–52, esp. p. 247. Finding God in all things is also thoroughly Jewish: see Moore, "Ignatian Perspective," containing references to Heschel and Buber.

[32] In his "The Formation of Contemplatives in Action" (*Review for Religious* 33 (1974): 1031–52), Ladislas Orsy, S.J., obviously uses the term "contemplatives in action," and no one can fault him for it; but what he is addressing is how to form persons to be *contemplative* in their actions.

"despite the trials she underwent and the business affairs she had to attend to," but complained of "in a certain way, a division in her soul."[33] Jacques Lewis comments that in Teresa there was simultaneity of action and contemplation, but apparently not continuity and identity, a division between the contemplative life deep in her soul and the activities required for her apostolate. In Ignatian spirituality, however, the Jesuit should be contemplative *in* the action and find God *in* everything.[34] One action that was especially dear to Ignatius was the liturgical action of the Eucharist.[35] There he experienced the Son fulfilling his mission from the Father. The action itself revealed God and all other actions revealed God as well, for he directed all to the service of God and the salvation of others. He found God in the action, not in spite of the action.

Commentators pay little attention to *simul*. One of those, however, who do pay attention is the Spanish Jesuit Rodrigo Mejía, who stresses the simultaneity of the two aspects of the great privilege Ignatius enjoyed of finding the triune God in prayer and also in all that he did.[36] Another who takes *simul* seriously is Peter-Hans Kolvenbach. He thinks Nadal would find it strange to see us commenting on this phrase as though it were something extraordinary. For Nadal it summarizes his whole experience of Ignatius.

> Faithful to the anthropology of his times, Jerónimo Nadal wanted to include "all our activity in Christ" in a cyclical movement that passes from the spirit to the heart and from the heart to praxis, so as to return from praxis to the heart and from the heart to the spirit—*spiritu, corde, practice*—in a vibrating movement that "simul" explicitates in the formula "simul in actione contemplativus."[37]

Kolvenbach's comments are important; for some authors seem to suggest that Jesuit prayer consists solely in contemplating while acting and that there is no need for contemplative prayer leading to contemplative action. Such an interpretation yields highly delusional results and is not at all Ignatian.

---

[33] "The Interior Castle," VII. 1. 10, in *The Collected Works of Teresa of Avila*, trans. Kieran Kavanaugh, O.C.D., and Otilio Rodriguez, O.C.D. (Washington, D.C.: Institute of Carmelite Studies, 1980), 2:431.

[34] Jacques Lewis, S.J., "L'Oraison ignatienne," *Cahiers de spiritualité ignatienne* 13 (1989), 100.

[35] Lévesque, "Contemplation," 27.

[36] Rodrigo Mejía Saldarriaga, S.J., *La dinámica de la Integración Espiritual: Buscar y hallar a Dios en todas las cosas* (Rome: CIS, 1980), 459–61. He points out that authors who use the phrase invariably omit *simul*, thereby creating a false impression.

[37] Peter-Hans Kolvenbach, S.J., "Ponencia de clausura," in *Ejercicios espirituales y mundo de hoy*, Congreso Internacional de Ejercicios, Loyola, 20–26 septiembre de 1991, ed. Juan Manuel Garcia-Lomas (Bilbao: Mensajero, 1991), 359.

The prayer of Ignatius ends in action in which he finds God as much as he does in prayer. Nowhere do we find Ignatius absorbed in contemplating eternal processions within the Godhead, the immanent activities of the three Divine Persons; rather his prayer concerns the real situations that he faces, so that he is riveted by the operations in time of the all-holy Three, the Divine Persons acting in creation.[38] He contemplates and does spontaneously what God shows him, contemplative in prayer and contemplative likewise in action.[39] God is not a thing but the source of all things. To find God operating in the world about us and to find God in all things are one and the same. The prayer does not begin with God and end with things or begin with things and end with God; rather, the prayer embraces God and things (the world already sacred because God acts upon it). God and things cannot be separated.

In Messina Nadal had said that prayer is to issue in affect (setting one on fire) and in action (moving one to do God's holy will).[40] In Spain in 1554 he emphasized that prayer does not suffice for a Jesuit; it must be joined with action for the neighbor. Prayer leads to action, and prayer-filled actions are performed with gusto. He comments that Ignatius called this "walking in the spirit" *(ambulare in spiritu)*. The Society finds prayer and God and devotion in everything.[41]

Nadal found it helpful to begin his prayer from the last grace received in prayer, what he called the leftovers of meditation *(reliquiæ cogitationum)*. Ignatius did not condemn the method, but said it was the mark of a beginner;[42] he himself found devotion wherever and in whatever manner he pleased.[43] Contemplation and action for the neighbor are not opposites but a continuum. Rather than ceasing one pursuit to perform the other, Ignatius glided from one to the other and back again, contemplative all the way. To find God in prayer in any way whatsoever and to find God in action no matter what the circumstances are very much the same thing. The unity is found in the love springing from the experience of the triune God creating all things. At Manresa "everything appeared to him to be new," because he saw all things for the first time the way they really are, coming from God and returning to God. All things, thereafter, spoke to him of the Trinity. No wonder he found facility in prayer!

---

[38] Lafrance, "Nota," 174.

[39] Bottereau, "La Prière," *Nouvelle revue théologique,* 403.

[40] *"De oratione,"* 1551 *(CommInst* 29, no. 7).

[41] "Exhort. 1554 Hisp." (ibid., 74, no. 87; 92, no. 145; 97, no. 161).

[42] "Orat.observ." (1545), 33, no. 8; also in *Font.narr* 2:316 and in *EpistNadal* 4:645, with slightly different orthography.

[43] "Acta quædam nostri P. Ignatii" *(Font.narr* 2:122, no. 6).

This grasp of all things from the viewpoint of the Trinity, Hugo Rahner insists, pervades the Exercises, beginning with the Foundation and its view of all creation. In the Second Week Ignatius presents Christ as the King of the whole world leading all to his Father. The Father is the end of all things, and Christ the Leader and Way who grips the souls of human beings in the Holy Spirit to take them with him to the Father. The path he follows is that of the cross. And so the cross stands in its Trinitarian context: Christ must suffer and so lead all things to the Father. Ignatius asks the exercitant to join Christ in poverty and humiliation and suffering in carrying out this Trinitarian plan that embraces the universe.

The vision at La Storta exemplifies in a striking manner the significance of all this to Ignatius and to the Society. Rahner has submitted the early accounts of the vision to minute examination to determine its exact content. For the present purpose it is enough to make use of one of Nadal's accounts containing all the essential elements Rahner has pointed out.

Nadal states that

> when Ignatius first came to Rome, before anything was done about the confirmation of the Society, and was praying on the way, Christ Jesus appeared to him carrying his cross. In his soul he heard God the Father, and he experienced that he placed him beside Christ and dedicated him to Christ's service, and said, "I shall be propitious to you [plural]."[44]

The Trinitarian orientation is clear. So is the inclusion of the companions in the experience. The Father places Ignatius with the Son, the Father dedicates him, the Father speaks to him. The Ignatian ideal in the Exercises is to be accepted by the Father in the service of the Son bearing his cross. To him the whole meaning of La Storta sums itself up in being placed by the Father in the service of the Son: "One day, a few miles before reaching Rome, he was at prayer in a church and experienced such a change in his soul and saw so clearly that God the Father placed him with Christ his Son that he would not dare doubt it—that God the Father had placed him with his Son."[45]

To be placed by the Father in the service of the Trinity with Christ bearing the cross had been Ignatius's prayer ever since Manresa. Now he was so placed. This felt realization animated him on reaching Rome. The Father had accepted him and the whole Society in the service of Christ in the Trinitarian plan to redeem. Moreover, all things coming from the creative power of God held a place in that redemptive plan. Only the overabundance of love that flowed from the realization that he had an

---

[44] "In exam. annot." (*CommInst* 136 f.); also in *EpistNadal* 4:649, with slightly different orthography.

[45] Da Câmara, "Acta P. Ignatii" (*Font.narr* 1:496–98, no. 96). For an English translation, see *PilgTest* 139.96.

active part with Christ in that plan can explain his boundless energy and activity in working for the marginalized people of Rome: street urchins, prostitutes, orphans, beggars, and the Jews, who were objects of discrimination. He found in the poor and the outcast Christ suffering; in the sinners he loved, Christ being sinned against; in the orphans, Christ's "little ones," who must be brought to him. Everything clamored about redemption. He gave the Exercises to win apostles for Christ and taught catechism in the streets that Christ's Blood might not be shed in vain. All this activity did not take him from the Trinity, for his work was always the work of the Trinity.

The greatest task of Ignatius in Rome, however, was organizing that group of men to whom, with him, God the Father had promised to be propitious. After the Society's confirmation, he devoted much of his energy to writing the *Constitutions*. From his diary we know that while vesting for Mass and celebrating the Holy Sacrifice, he frequently experienced visions of the Most Blessed Trinity.[46] Ignatius was seeking light and guidance. He wanted to do God's will; he wanted to serve. His heart overflowed with consolation and his eyes with tears. Thinking of our Lord, he felt great devotion, and this remained with him as he went about the streets of Rome to consult various officials.[47] He found God easily in prayer; he found him in action as well. There are two ways in which we can view his prayer, but it is the same gift of prayer. As Joseph de Guibert says very well, Ignatius's contemplation of the Trinity is not speculative but intensely practical.[48] His gift is practical mysticism, what Harvey Egan calls "loving service mysticism."[49] For Ignatius the burning love he conceives in his meditations on the Trinity finds its outlet in acts of love. One of those Persons of the Trinity had become man and died for the human race, and he, too, must give his life in labor. The prayer life of Ignatius, therefore, is a unity with the double aspects of profound contemplation of the Trinity and absorbing action for the neighbor in which he readily finds the presence and love of Father, Son, and Holy Spirit.

De Guibert has indicated that Ignatius's encounters with the Trinity show no trace of the nuptial imagery usual in many of the great mystics; instead, they manifest a mysticism of service. On the other hand, Karl Truhlar has commented that a mysticism of service should not be opposed

---

[46] "Ephemeris S. P. N. Ignatii" (*Constitutiones* 1:86–158); for an English version see *The Spiritual Journal of St. Ignatius Loyola,* trans. William J. Young, S.J. (Woodstock, Md.: Woodstock College Press, 1958; reprinted Jersey City, N.J., 1971), 19 f., no. 26; or Ganss, "The *Spiritual Diary,*" in *Ignatius of Loyola,* nos. 82–87 (pp. 251 f.).

[47] "Ephemeris S. P. N. Ignatii," 106.

[48] de Guibert, *Spiritual Doctrine,* 137–39; id., *Spiritualité,* 126 f.).

[49] Harvey D. Egan, S.J., *Christian Mysticism: The Future of a Tradition* (New York: Pueblo, 1984), 41, 199 f.

to a mysticism of union, but rather supposes it; and Donatien Mollat has further noted that the foundation and explanation of a mysticism of service is the mystery of the nuptial union of Christ and the Church. Maurice Giuliani has shown that union accompanies service; and in pointing that out Maurice-Marie Martin has summarized the matter well: "Service and union are not in opposition, nor are we saying that service has priority over union: service and union are in reciprocal priority. Service is true when it is in union with God, and union with God is only realized in service." Michael Buckley has reflected on the hints in Ignatius that suggest a mysticism of union beyond de Guibert's mysticism of service. Ignatius, Buckley points out, refers to the Church as the spouse of Christ in the Exercises (*SpEx* 353, 365 [pp. 133, 135]), and each member of the Church shares in that mysterious relationship. Ignatius hints at the spousal relationship in the fifteenth annotation, describing God as "embracing the soul with love" (15 [p. 25]). Ignatius writes in his *Spiritual Diary* of the Trinity's "embracing" him (*Constitutiones* 1:98) and hopes that Borgia will be "embraced and united."[50]

Commentators do well to see beyond de Guibert's assumptions about an Ignatian mysticism of service to a mysticism of union that stresses intimacy and passionate love. It is worthy of note, moreover, that in each of these mysticism-of-union passages there is also some reference to service. Ignatius is eager to serve in love the one who loves him.

Without using the terminology, Pedro Arrupe was asking for a mysticism of service from the alumni of Jesuit schools in his address "Men for Others."[51] Whether the Jesuits murdered in El Salvador in 1989 talked about the mysticism of service or not is irrelevant; they lived the reality, and they wrote about the reality.[52] They were also very much in love with

---

[50] *EpistIgn* 2:236. Here follow the sources for the quotations in this paragraph: Joseph de Guibert, S.J., "Mystique Ignatienne: A propos du 'Journal Spirituel' de Saint Ignace de Loyola," *Revue d'ascétique et de mystique* 19 (1938): 120; id., *Spiritual Doctrine,* 55; Carolus Truhlar, S.J., *De experientia mystica* (Rome: Univ. Gregoriana, 1951), 50; Donatien Mollat, S.J., "Le Christ dans l'expérience spirituelle de Saint Ignace," *Christus* 1 (1954): 43; Maurice Giuliani, S.J., "Finding God in All Things," in *Finding God in All Things: Essays in Ignatian Spirituality Selected from Christus,*" trans. William J. Young, S.J. (Chicago: Henry Regnery Co., 1958; originally in *Christus* 6 (1955): 172–94); Maurice-Marie Martin, S.J., "The Mysticism of St. Ignatius: A Study of the Gift of Tears in the Spiritual Diary," *CIS* 22 (1991): 22–86; Michael J. Buckley, S.J., "Ecclesial Mysticism in the *Spiritual Exercises* of Ignatius," *Theological Studies* 56 (1995): 441–63. See also Arrupe, "Trinitarian," 42; De Deckere, "Mystique," 108–10.

[51] Pedro Arrupe, S.J., "Men for Others: Training Agents of Change for the Promotion of Justice," in *Justice with Faith Today: Selected Letters and Addresses-II,* ed. Jerome Aixala, S.J. (St. Louis: The Institute of Jesuit Sources, 1980), 123–38.

[52] John Hassett and Hugh Lacey, eds., *Towards a Society That Serves Its People: The Intellectual Contribution of El Salvador's Murdered Jesuits* (Washington, D.C.: Georgetown University Press, 1991).

and committed to serving the oppressed people of El Salvador, in whom they saw the face of the suffering Christ.

Privilege of Members

At this point Nadal draws a conclusion regarding those called to the Society of Jesus:

> We have seen that grace and interior light break forth on [Father Ignatius's] shining countenance and in the clarity and precision of his actions in Christ, much to the wonderment and consolation of all of us; and we have felt something of that grace channeled, as it were, to the rest of us.[53]

The end of the sentence in no. 82 is deliberately vague: "We have the sense that something (*nescio quid* [I don't know what]) of that grace has, as it were *[quasi]*, been diverted to us." It is a bold statement, not boldly stated. Jesuits share in the grace of Ignatius somehow, somewhat. Visions, ecstasies, and similar phenomena are not at stake; they do not mark the essence of Ignatius's prayer. The writer then gets bolder:

> The same privilege, therefore, that we understand was granted to Father Ignatius we believe has been conceded to the whole Society, and we are confident that the grace of that prayer and contemplation has been prepared in the Society for all of us, and we maintain that it is linked with our vocation.[54]

Nicolau wonders whether Nadal thinks that God has prepared gifts of infused prayer in the strict sense of the word for every Jesuit—mystical in the full sense, or mystical gifts in a wider sense: simply a facility of being in the presence of God and speaking to him familiarly. He is of the opinion that Nadal means to indicate for the members of the Society a vocation to extraordinary and infused gifts, one that it more or less proximate and more or less vague; his opinion is worth considering. He argues from Nadal's solemn way of speaking, the gravity with which his hope is expressed, his calling it the same privilege as that of Ignatius, whose extraordinary contemplation of the Trinity he has just treated. All these factors, to his mind, seem to indicate that Nadal is speaking of

---

[53] "Hanc vero gratiam ac lucem animæ suæ, quodam quasi splendore vultus, claritate ac certitudine actionum suarum in Christo explicari vidimus, magna nostra omnium admiratione, et magna cordis nostri consolatione; et quasi derivatum in nos nescio quid illius gratiæ sensimus" ("In exam. annot." [*CommInst* 162 f., no. 82]). Also found in *EpistNadal* 4:651 f., with slightly different orthography.

[54] "Quod igitur privilegium Patri Ignatio factum intelligimus, idem toti Societati concessum esse credimus, et gratiam orationis illius et contemplationis in Societate omnibus nobis paratam esse confidimus, eamque cum vocatione nostra coniunctam esse confitemur" ("In exam. annot.," 163, no. 82). Also found in *EpistNadal* 4:652, with slightly different orthography.)

infused gifts, and this he believes is confirmed by the final sentence (above) of this part of the passage. This sentence, Nicolau maintains, in view of its contextual link with Ignatius's contemplation, can easily be understood of a degree of infused prayer, mystical in the full sense of the word "to which Nadal exhorted . . . insofar as one can exhort to phenomena which are more a matter of passive reception than of persevering effort and activity" (Nicolau, *Jerónimo Nadal,* 256). The terminology is Nicolau's, not Nadal's. I prefer to avoid the question of extraordinary and infused prayer, lest we bog down in unnecessary and unfruitful controversy. Nicolau softens his opinion somewhat to "seems to suggest (though not exclusively or necessarily) an *infused and mystical* contemplation" in "What Nadal Meant by 'In Actione Contemplativus,'" *CIS* 8 (1977): 7–16. I like the clarity and directness of the down-to-earth mysticism of John R. Sachs, S.J.: "In grace, we are not only drawn into God's love and life, we are drawn into God's *action* in this world. Or, we could say, it is precisely in and through our action, when we open ourselves up to God, that God as Spirit is at work in the world" ("Ignatian Mysticism," *The Way,* Supplement no. 82 (1995): 77).

Jesuits are like Ignatius: sharing in his vocation, they share in his grace of prayer. He is not a model external to the Jesuit experience, but the primary example of that experience. How Jesuits participate in the Christian pattern of prayer becomes clearer as they reflect on the experience and prayer of Ignatius. If the grace of Ignatius is the grace of the Society, then the prayer of Ignatius will be found incarnated in as many ways as there are Jesuits who pray. Since growth in prayer is a *process,* they will all be at different stages and in them at different times, some more aware of their own efforts in turning toward the Divine Persons, some more aware of being gifted in their relations to Father, Son, and Spirit. It behooves each one to recognize the pattern taking shape in his own life. Nadal wrote of his own prayer life:

> No one should desire to imitate the saints in those privileges with which Christ adorns them in this life; that imitation is genuine and profitable that imitates the means that disposed them to attain these gifts. This comforted me when I desired to imitate the contemplation of Father Ignatius and his sense of divine things.[55]

Kolvenbach makes the point that the circle of prayer and action keeps on compressing until the two components of prayer and action interpenetrate each other so harmoniously that the human action is God's action with us. He cites Nadal's remark to himself in his spiritual journal:

---

[55] *Orat.observ* 127, no. 326.

"You cherish through his will, remember through his memory; all that you are, is and lives and acts, not in yourself, but in Christ."[56]

Nadal explains that Ignatius's prayer, which he enjoyed by reason of a great privilege, had a twofold aspect: he was intimately familiar with the Trinity and at the same time contemplative in action, finding God in all things. Nadal believes that this kind of prayer is offered to all members of the Society. The conclusion is explicit: "Therefore, let us also place the perfection of our prayer in the contemplation of the Trinity, and in the love and union of charity, extended, indeed, to our neighbor through the ministries of our vocation, which, to be sure, we easily prefer to the taste and sweetness of prayer."[57] Preferring ministry to the taste and sweetness of prayer differs profoundly from preferring ministry to contemplation, for contemplation in prayer continues in contemplation in ministry. Preferring ministry over sweetness underscores self-abnegation and continual mortification, as Ignatius puts it to Francis Borgia, "going out of oneself and entering into one's Creator and Lord, [recognizing] that our whole eternal welfare abides in all created things, making them be and conserving them in existence by infinite being and presence," and therefore, as the *Constitutions* state: "loving him in all creatures and all creatures in him."[58]

The final sentence in Nadal's text (above) makes clear that Ignatius enjoyed one gift of prayer: familiarity with the Trinity and finding God in all things, one privilege with two aspects complementing and demanding one another.[59] If a Jesuit is to be like Ignatius, it is not sufficient for him

---

[56] Kolvenbach, "Ponencia de clausura," 360, citing Nadal, *EpistNadal* 4:697 (also see *Orat.observ* 122, no. 308).

[57] "Hæc cum ita sint, et perfectionem nostræ orationis constituamus in contemplatione Trinitatis, in charitatis amore atque unione, extensa quidem in proximum per nostræ vocationis ministeria, quæ quidem gustui ac suavitati orationis facile præferimus" (*CommInst* 163, no. 83). Unfortunately *EpistNadal* 4 omitted this sentence, causing some problems of interpretation. In 1949 Nicolau supplied the sentence in *Jerónimo Nadal,* 256, citing the manuscript in Instit. 186a, fol. 40v., preserved in the Roman Archives of the Society of Jesus.

[58] *EpistIgn* 1:339, citing *ConsCN* 288[v.3] (p. 124). For a lengthy reflection on Ignatius's words to Borgia and their relevance to "contemplative in action," see Aurora Royo Millán, R.J.M., "'Contemplativo en la acción': Semblanza espiritual de San Ignacio," *Teología espiritual: Revista cuatrimestral de los Estudios Generales Dominicanos de España* 17 (1973): 327–66.

[59] When Louis Verny published his excellent analysis of "contemplative in action" ("In actione contemplativus," *Revue d' Ascétique et de Mystique* 26 [1950]: 60–78), he was working with a text that did not contain the above sentence. Unaware, therefore, of Nadal's final conclusion about Trinitarian prayer, Verny read the text to mean that Ignatius had two privileges, lofty prayer to the Trinity and the gift of finding God in all things. He concluded that Jesuits are called to share with Ignatius the second of the two privileges. This understanding, however, would be a truncated version of Jesuit prayer. Putting the stress on the second aspect of Ignatius's prayer has this

to be either contemplative in his prayer or contemplative in action. If Ignatius enjoyed the contemplation of the persons of the Trinity, so should the Jesuit, and if besides that *[tum illud præterea]* his prayer was such that *[ut]* he was contemplative also in action, that he found God in all things, so also should the Jesuit be at one and the same time contemplative in prayer and contemplative also in action. It would not do to say that one can hardly be contemplative in action without *first* being contemplative in prayer—one must be careful not to split Jesuit prayer in two—but it is safe to say that one who is not contemplative in prayer can hardly be contemplative while in action.

Perhaps this is belaboring the issue, but the emphasis seems necessary since some writers and speakers, when referring to this passage in Nadal, *seem* to suggest that the whole prayer of Jesuits is summed up in being contemplative in action, as though Jesuits have no share in Ignatius's gift of contemplating the three Divine Persons in their creative and salvific activity. In like manner, Rodrigo Mejía Saldarriaga discusses the pastoral problems that can and do arise with Nadal's spontaneous throwaway phrase (if one may call it that), especially when *simul* is omitted.[60]

Ignatius's contemplation of the Divine Persons in their work of saving the human race contained the seed of action; action was its natural fruit, already contained in it in some way. His action was what we might call "contemplative action," action aware of its full atmosphere and purpose. The pattern of his life shows how God develops in someone Ignatius's kind of prayer and Ignatius's kind of action. If Jesuits are to be like Ignatius, they are not to be carbon copies; but his grace is *somehow* theirs, they share in what belongs to him; but, more important, living within the charism of the Society and drawing on its power, they enjoy the grace of their own unique relationship with the Trinity and capacity to find God in all things.

Adrien Demoustier says that Ignatius went from prayer to service (action) to the union of the two, and because Nadal describes the gift of Ignatius as "singular," Demoustier suggests that the followers of Ignatius are to move in reverse fashion from service to prayer to the union of the two.[61] The prayer of Ignatius may, indeed, be "singular," but that does not mean that Jesuits do not share in it in some way. Before being trained in service, they are first grounded in prayer, in the Trinitarian scheme of the incarnation, and they steep themselves in the activities of one of the Trinity, namely, Jesus. One would think, therefore, that if they are to

---

advantage, however: finding God in all things unlocks the depths and heights of Trinitarian prayer and all that it implies. Verny's task would have been made easier had he had the full text at hand.

[60] Mejía, *La dinámica,* 461–66.

[61] Demoustier, "Contemplatif," 472.

become contemplative in their prayer and in their action as well, they would do well to seek the Father, Son, and Holy Spirit both in their prayer and in their action.

Conclusion

Perfectæ Caritatis, Vatican II's decree on the up-to-date renewal of the religious life, urged all religious to rediscover and return to the original charism of the community, to the spirit and aims of the founder(s). The Spirit's effort to respond in the Society of Jesus has led the Society from a rationalistic to a more affective understanding of the Spiritual Exercises, one that emphasizes the discernment of spirits. The Spirit had guided the Society from group retreats, where the director gave the same "points" to a large audience, to privately directed retreats that see the Holy Spirit actively engaged with each exercitant; from eight-day retreats for religious to thirty-day retreats for everybody or retreats in everyday life lasting perhaps nine months. The Society has moved from a dry and legalistic *Epitome* to an exploration of the *Constitutions* that is just beginning to discover the inner force and persuasiveness of Ignatian legislation, from a spirit of "managing people" to a spirit of "managing *with* people," a spirit that cherishes the Ignatian insistence that the superior should know each person well whom he governs. In the spirit of the first Jesuits, who worked in hospitals and prisons and fed the poor and taught street gamins, Jesuits are becoming more profoundly aware that the faith that does justice is at the heart of every one of the Society's works. With Pedro Arrupe Jesuits have caught some of the vision of La Storta: the Father placing us at the side of Christ carrying his cross. With Peter-Hans Kolvenbach Jesuits are trying to carry that cross as a sign of reconciliation: to differing cultures, religions, and forms of Christianity; to the marginalized of the world, the poor, the refugees, the abandoned; to women and co-workers; to all those of goodwill. The Society has been humbled; the Society has been blessed. Jesuits reach out to others because the Father has reached out to them in the Son through the Spirit, "refounding" the Society day by day in the present moment, or as Kolvenbach prefers, confronting the experience of Ignatius with "creative fidelity."[62]

Earlier in this chapter Nadal's opening remarks on prayer concerned the prayer Jesuits learn through the Spiritual Exercises, and his passage on the prayer of Ignatius presented Ignatius as the exemplar of prayer in the Society. Each passage concluded in substantially the same way:

---

[62] See the author's article "A Foundational Experience," *CIS* 31, no. 1 (2000): 23–35, and also Peter-Hans Kolvenbach, S.J., "Creative Fidelity in Mission," ibid., 31, no. 3 (2000): 25–40.

Prayer of the Spiritual Exercises	**Prayer of Ignatius**
Finally we rest in love, so that we place our end in that from which prayer ought to take its source, namely, in charity, the most divine virtue, so that with it and its fervor and zeal we go forth to our ministries in cheerfulness of spirit and humility of heart, with devotion and courage in Christ Jesus.	Therefore, let us also place the perfection of our prayer in the contemplation of the Trinity, and in the love and union of charity, extended, indeed, to our neighbor through the ministries of our vocation, which, to be sure, we easily prefer to the taste and sweetness of prayer.

An almost perfect balance exists in the conclusions of the two passages. In the opening passage the Exercises form a Jesuit's prayer into contemplation ending in love that moves to apostolic labor. In the second passage the prayer of Ignatius is loving contemplation of the Trinity that extends to finding God in the midst of apostolic action, whence the Jesuit's contemplation should be of the Trinity, extending itself to the apostolate out of love. The only difference is the explicitly Trinitarian element in the second column. The fact that prayer in its perfection is explicitly described as Trinitarian does not take away from the Trinitarian orientation of ordinary prayer in the Society. Nonetheless, the sentence in the second column provides the key to understanding the entire text: like the prayer of Ignatius, the prayer of the members of the Society has a double aspect, contemplation of the Trinity and union in apostolic love.

When one views the passage in its whole context, it seems rather obvious that Nadal does not intend to indicate here two privileges granted to Ignatius. Contemplation and action are united in the love of the Trinity. Robert Browning's oft-quoted line: "God's in his heaven, all's right with the world," makes sense only because God is not only in heaven but is in the world as well. For Ignatius, familiarity with God demands as a natural complement the facility of finding God in all, which extends into action the love of the Trinity conceived in contemplation.

In the life of the Society, prayer and action tend to lose their separate identities in love. Or perhaps it would be better to say that in the Society, when prayer reaches its perfection in love, it is wedded to action; "and they become one flesh" (Gen. 2:24). Hence, finding God in everything has two aspects: finding God in prayer and finding God in action, at the base of which can only be love. In one way or another God calls all men, women, and children of every time and place to such prayer according to the unique vocation of each. All are called to pray; all are called to prayerful action. Prayer is more than an action; it is a process, and it begins and ends with God.

Traditionally, it is only in the unitive stage that the two dimensions of the same gift come together: Trinitarian union joined with familiarity and mysticism of service. The search for God or enlightenment is a process. The prayer journey is like a pilgrimage: the sacred goal is already present within the pilgrim at the beginning of the pilgrimage, becoming more present each step along the way. Pilgrims are not so concerned about where they are in the journey as in the origins and destiny of the journey offered to them.

At the beginning of this chapter we read the statement from Vatican II, "Before all else, religious life is ordered to the following of Christ by its members, and to their becoming united with God by the profession of the evangelical counsels," insisting that "even the best-contrived adaptations to the needs of our time will be of no avail unless they are animated by a spiritual renewal, which must always be assigned primary importance even in the active ministry." We also quoted General Congregation 33:

> Only to the extent that he is united to God so that he be "led gladly by the divine hand," is a Jesuit "a man on a mission." In this way, he will learn to find God in all things, the God who is present in this world and its struggle between good and evil, between faith and unbelief, between the yearning for justice and peace and the growing reality of injustice and strife. But we cannot achieve this familiarity with God unless we set aside a regular time for personal prayer. (*DocsGC33* 12 [p. 46])

The Church, in whose life we share, is that visible institution that symbolizes both the beginning and the end, the profoundly spiritual, participating in the life of God, and the profoundly earthly, rooted in time but equally at home in eternity; it is the Communion of Saints, all one in our pilgrim journey to God. As T. S. Eliot puts it in "Little Gidding," echoing Dante and the mystic Julian of Norwich,

> We shall not cease from exploration
> And the end of all our exploring
> Will be to arrive where we started
> And know the place for the first time. . . .
> And all shall be well and
> All manner of thing shall be well
> When the tongues of flame are in-folded
> Into the crowned knot of fire
> And the fire and the rose are one.[63]

This chapter has been on the Trinitarian prayer of Ignatius, a grace shared with the rest of the Society. The final chapter will look at the grace proper to the Society of Jesus as it reaches full maturity in the elderly Jesuit who can no longer engage in all the activities of his earlier years. It studies how the tongues of flame are ultimately in-folded.

---

[63] T. S. Eliot, *The Complete Poems and Plays: 1909–1950* (New York: Harcourt, Brace & World, 1971), 145.

Chronicle for Chapter Eleven

What many in Germany have been longing for, that Fr. Jerónimo Nadal would come to Germany, he has finally prevailed upon me to grant, and I was not able not to send him, both because of his wish and inclination that have always drawn him to the Germans, and because of the good that his presence will bring to ours.

Father General Mercurian, to the provincial of Germany

Nadal's Life and Travels (1569–1580)

1569–72: At Rome, assistant for Spain

1571: Named vicar-general

1572: Pope Pius V dies, Borgia dies; Polanco vicar-general. Everard Mercurian elected general

1573

April 12–June 16: At Rome, assists at GC 3; given various tasks; (Everard Mercurian elected general)

July 18: At Tivoli, retired

1574

April 15: Fr. General Mercurian sends him to Hall.

May 25: Arrives in Bologna, goes to Padua on 27th

June 13–15: Innsbruck

June 15: At Hall, works on meditations and images

1575

After Aug. 15: To Augsburg via Munich

Oct. 1: Still in Augsburg, plans to go to Hall on Oct. 4 or 5

Oct. 5: At Hall, working on his writings

1576

Jan. 12ff.: At Innsbruck, assists at provincial congregation; catches bad cold, returns to Hall; until end of year, at Hall, working on his writings

1577

Jan.-April: At Hall, working on writings

April 28: Writes from Innsbruck

June-July: Writes from Hall

Aug. 31: Leaves Innsbruck by litter for Venice via Verona, Padua

Sept. 13: Arrives at Venice

1578

Returns to Rome, stays at novitiate on Quirinal

1579

Still at the novitiate

1580

April 3–Easter Sunday: Dies, full of days, in Rome

Chapter Eleven

ON THE WAY IN: PRAYING FOR THE CHURCH AND THE SOCIETY

The manner of life, of prayer, and of work should be in harmony with the present-day physical and psychological condition of the members. It should also be in harmony with the needs of the apostolate, in the measure that the nature of each institute requires, with the requirements of culture and with social and economic circumstances. . . . Effective renewal and adaptation cannot be achieved save with the cooperation of all the members of an institute. . . . The members of each institute should recall, first of all, that when they made professions of the evangelical counsels they were responding to a divine call, to the end that . . . they might live for God alone. They have dedicated their whole lives to his service. . . . Since this gift of themselves has been accepted by the Church, they should be aware that they are dedicated to its service also.

—Vatican II, *On the Up-to-Date Renewal of the Religious Life*

T he Jesuit Constitutions insist on living in the world of the present moment, on learning the language of the people, on eating their food, on dreaming their dreams—not nostalgic dreams of the past, but dreams for the present and for what is to come. Legislating in the *Constitutions* for those who are sent to work somewhere, Ignatius talks about going there on foot or perhaps on horseback. Should a Jesuit go in the manner of the poor or in some other manner? The norm, he says, is need, decorum, *not* ostentation: what is necessary, what is fitting, what is proper. The norm is still good in the age of jet travel; it will still be good when Jesuits go beyond the stars.

"Effective renewal and adaptation cannot be achieved save with the cooperation of all the members of an institute," including the elderly, maybe especially the elderly. Perhaps the essence of old age is attempting to live "in harmony with" the disharmonious, "in harmony with one's present-day physical and psychological condition," with all its limitations and disharmonies, and at the same time and especially "in harmony with" the ultimate harmony, the *perichoresis:* the inner dance of the Father, Son, and Holy Spirit that out of love freely creates the outer dance of harmony. Creation sometimes experiences the loss of harmony, the longing for harmony, for integration, for wholeness. God's response to the world's disharmony is the Trinitarian dance called Incarnation, sweeping up all of creation into its rhythm. "Responding to a divine call . . . dedicated to his service," those who have made a "gift of themselves" are aware that they are "dedicated" to the service of the Church as well, to one another, and to the whole world, to the dance of all God's holy people. This is the human story.

In 1977 Father General Pedro Arrupe called upon all students and graduates of Jesuit schools throughout the world to be men and women for others: gifts given to be given. In the same way, General Congregation 34 said bluntly to the whole Society:

> [The Jesuit] does not build his own business or his own career, because he does not build his own home and family. His chastity has made it possible for him to grow in his poverty. At the end of his life, through his vow of chastity, he will have become poor in a way that his previous talents and energy and education made impossible. . . . He has built up nothing for himself, and looks to God for the definition of his life. This poverty that flows from his chastity is not the destruction of his Jesuit life; in many ways it is its completion and fulfillment. (*DocsGC34* 243 [p. 118])

This chapter is about the completion and fulfillment of a Jesuit's life.

History

Diego de Hozes of Málaga, who joined the companions in Venice in 1537, died in 1538 before the Society was officially recognized, a young man of uncertain age. Jean Codure, the first "Jesuit" to die, was thirty-three. Pierre Favre died at forty, Xavier at forty-six, Jay at forty-eight, Laínez at fifty-three, Broët at sixty-two, Ignatius at sixty-five, Rodrigues at sixty-nine, Salmerón at seventy, and Bobadilla at eighty-one. Of the second generation, Nadal lived to be seventy-two and Peter Canisius seventy-six, confined to his room only during the last nine months of his life; Pedro Ribadeneira survived until eighty-five and Miguel de Torres until he was eighty-six; but they were exceptions among men who tended to die in their fifties and sixties or even earlier.

Nadal and Xavier, Favre and Bobadilla, and many others traveled by foot or by horseback thousands of miles and back again. They sailed in ships that took forever. Walking was good, healthy exercise. No one who walked from Rome to Portugal suffered from jet lag, but walking could exhaust a man who caught a cold or, worse, was exposed to the plague. No one had to get there overnight and then fly to Los Angeles the next weekend. Walking was peaceful, far more relaxing than jumping into a car or hopping a plane, a good break from lecturing or preaching or teaching catechism or working at a desk. Above all, walking was a good way to pray. Some say the early general congregations were fruitful because the only ones who attended them were those able and fit to walk to Rome.

In the new millennium instant communication exists, jet lag exists, space travel is on the way; and for twenty million dollars a rich man can enjoy a week's vacation on a satellite in space. How are Jesuits to live in the present and, especially, in the future that is to come some day, when instant communication will no longer be possible, and a radio message from interstellar space will take many more years in transit than a letter from Ignatius in Rome to Xavier in India?

In 1552 Ignatius wrote a letter to those sent on mission. Take care of yourself. Take care of your health, and take care that in attending to the needs of others you do not forget to take care of yourself. Take time for prayer, for examining your conscience, for the sacraments. Take time for yourself or you will not be able to give time to others. When you cannot do everything, make sure that you first do the work you have been missioned to do. Prioritize everything else. Prefer the spiritual to the corporal, the more urgent to the less urgent, the more universal to the particular, the lasting to the transient if you cannot do both. See to it that the effects are lasting. Do what is needed and what you are good at doing. Be humble enough to start from the bottom and work your way up rather than trying to start at the top. Respect the Society and its head. Preserve its good name. Attract good men to carry on the work (*EpistIgn* 12:251–53).

Good advice for anyone suffering from jet lag; good advice for the space traveler and the time traveler. Bodies and the mystery of the Incarnation still have their own inevitable time. Human beings need quiet—to be alone at times, to pray, to play, to read, to rest, to sleep, simply to be. If ever there has been need for a Jesuit, a Christian, a human, to be countercultural, it is now. No one can afford to succumb to the contemporary fear of silence, solitude, and peace.

A Pause for Prayer

Contemplation to Attain Love: "Love consists in a mutual communication between the two persons. That is, the one who loves gives and communicates to the beloved what he or she has, or a part of what one has or can have; and the beloved in return does the same to the lover" (*SpEx* 231 [p. 94]).

We ask for what we desire, that we may learn from the past and be unafraid of the future, welcoming it with open arms and open hearts. "For all that has been, 'Thanks'; for all that will be, 'Yes'" (Dag Hammarskjöld).

The Future in the Present Moment

How does one live in this new era of cyberspace and outer space, of interplanetary space and interstellar space, in the reality of this world that includes virtual reality: virtual supermarkets, virtual libraries, virtual gold, virtual sex? How does one pray? How does one evangelize?

The present is the future of the past. How does one live in that future when there is little time left? That is how to live in the new millennium.

The Navaho poem quoted above in the preface continues:

> In old age wandering on a trail of beauty,
> Lively, may I walk;
> In old age wandering on a trail of beauty,
> Living again, may I walk.
> It is finished in beauty.[1]

Those with the best sense of being near the finish, of having reached the future of their past, are those with the longest past, those who have lived through the time of their dreams, dreams that exceeded reality, and dreams that fell far short of reality. Time and again the basic documents of both the Church and the Society present the final days of one's life (the future of one's past) as illuminating the future yet to come or, better, illuminating the present we confront. Consider some basic documents demanding attitudes of mind and heart required for living:

Scripture: *Openness to the Spirit*

The old man, Simeon, filled with the Spirit, was ready to depart in peace once he held in the flesh the hope of Israel. The old woman, Anna, who lived in the temple serving God with fastings and prayers night and day, had become a living prayer. They were like Abraham, the father of us all, who was not afraid at seventy-five to leave everything at the call of God and to start a new life he knew not where; and he was ready to start all over again when God tested him, apparently asking for the sacrifice of his son. To follow the Holy Spirit wherever he leads demands the ability to find God wherever he appears, on the loftiest mountain or in the lowliest babe.

---

[1] Hillerman, *Pocket Prayers.*

Spiritual Exercises: *Indifference*

At the beginning of the *Exercises,* in the First Principle and Foundation, Ignatius insists on making oneself indifferent to all created things so as not, among other things, to prefer health to sickness or a long life to a short life. The elderly have already been gifted with a long life; the infirm have already been gifted with sickness. Even so, the elderly still need to be ready for a longer life or a shorter life, and the infirm must be ready to recover their health or live a longer or shorter time in sickness. Both elderly and infirm Jesuits need to be contemplative in the living moment, to find God in their actual situation and be ready to meet him wherever he may be in the future. Their acceptance of their vulnerability and woundedness, their openness to whatever may come, model the manner in which the Society of Jesus must accept the brokenness of its own members, facing whatever future lies ahead for both the Society and for each individual Jesuit—as Christians, as human persons, as pilgrims on the way to one knows not where.

Decision making involves peripheral vision. Jesuits have to look beyond their own immediate needs and desires to the common good of the Society, the Church, and the world. Many years ago, whenever the Oregon Province was strapped financially, the procurator would gather what money he could and send it to the missions; it returned a hundredfold.

Clarity of Vision, Freedom

In the *Spiritual Exercises* (186 [p. 79]), Ignatius invites the exercitant to imagine the future in order to confront the present, to put oneself at death's door in order to make a life-changing decision. Why? Certainly not to frighten someone into a life-giving decision. Rather, on one's deathbed one sees clearly; inordinate affections dissolve and disappear; one is free. As someone wrote recently, it is easy to give up possessions after death.

"Dying is safe. You are safe. Your loved one is safe."[2] On one's deathbed one is safe. The invitation in the Exercises is to surrender in all respects safety into the hands of the one who loves as no other loves. That is how choices in the new millennium need to be made. Observe the elderly, especially the infirm. The elderly deceive themselves if they avoid the thought of death, whether sobering or reassuring. Death stalks them; are they frightened? Death beckons them; are they excited about the new adventure? Are they both frightened and excited? They are free, they are safe. They find themselves like those in Scripture who are called by God to a special task, like Abraham, like Mary the Mother of Jesus. "Do not be

---

[2] Kathleen Dowling Singh, *The Grace in Dying: How We Are Transformed Spiritually As We Die* (New York: HarperCollins, 2000), 1.

afraid," God says to them; "I shall be with you." Do not be afraid of the unknown; do not be afraid of what you cannot control. Henri Bergson wrote, "The shortest, the swiftest, and the surest way to plumb Truth is through a mortal leap into the Unknown."[3]

Surrender

In the Rules for the Discernment of Spirits (322 [pp. 126 f.]), Ignatius indicates that the experience of desolation can teach one that all is from God, all is gift, and no one should claim as one's own what belongs to God. At the end of the Exercises, in the Suscipe (234 [p. 95]), the exercitant surrenders everything to God. For the elderly and the infirm there is nothing theoretical about this surrender. To surrender to God is the demand of every moment. "When you were younger," Jesus said to Peter, "you used to fasten your own belt and to go wherever you wished. But when you grow old, you will stretch out your hands, and someone else will fasten a belt around you and take you where you do not wish to go" (John 21:18). The call of the elderly and infirm is to profound contemplation in the midst of diminishing action, diminishing until the only action is being, surrendering to God each day some aspect of their lives that will never return. This contemplation enters into and joins the action of God's very self and moves *in* to the mystery of creation transparent to its creator. The past will never return; one cannot cling to it just as Magdalen could not cling to Jesus (John 20:17). One enters healthily into the world of the future by surrendering ahead of time to each surprise the future brings. For God eternally makes all things new even as they grow old and wear down, moving each person toward new beginnings: a future out of this world. The world one leaves is ever new, full of surprises, unpredictable, always changing, renewing itself, eroding mountains, beaches, plains, creating others; the world beyond, St. Paul says, is even more surprising.

General Examen and Constitutions: *Interiority*

For Ignatius, the *Constitutions* were open-ended, constantly in process of revision as experience dictated. He knew novices, scholastics, coadjutors, and the professed from experience; he knew the sick and the dying from experience. He legislated for all of them. He knew no elderly; there were none to know except himself, the senior citizen, and he made no mention of them beyond the comment that some members might be "weaker because of age" (*ConsCN* 303 [p. 127]).

Today Jesuits live into their seventies, eighties, nineties, and a few surpass one hundred years of age. They verge on infirmity, but need not be infirm. They can be "weaker because of age," but actively engaged in

---

[3] Ibid., 3.

apostolic work. Even so, there comes a moment when most agree with Bobadilla, who quotes the psalmist that after eighty aches and pains increase.[4] What happens to their prayer? Is there some moment along the line when the Jesuit, "contemplative, and contemplative also in action," enters upon a new stage in his life not clearly included in Nadal's division of "active life, contemplative life, and more holistic active life"? When he is on the way down physically, is he also on the way down spiritually and apostolically? What happens when the catalog describes him as "pastoral minister," but *orat pro Soc.* (praying for the Church and the Society) would actually be more accurate? What happens when he reaches that final stage? How does he live and pray while dying? Since he is now in what was once his future, his experience of that future points the way to how the rest of the Society should strive to live in the future.

Recently someone asked a wise elder, who was obviously beginning to deteriorate physically, whether he experienced himself as a person and as a Jesuit to be living more or less fully than before, to be on the way up as he grew older or on the way down. Without hesitation he replied, "I find myself on the way *in.* My interior life is richer. I have more insights than before." Sounding a bit like St. Ignatius, he commented, "It's wonderful to find God in prayer whenever I want."

Nadal took a countercultural stance against a multitude of preconceptions and prejudices regarding the nature of religious life. He had to convince Jesuits that in this radically new and different religious order, growth meant a journey *out* rather than a journey *in,* that in the Society one journeys in only by journeying out. Over against the third millennium's frantic activity, both young and old have to see to it that they are on the *way in* even as they go out.

As the Trinity fills and regulates a Jesuit's prayer, so also it fills and regulates the ups and downs of the whole course of his days, attuning his life and death to the life and death of one of the Trinity who became human for us. For flesh to walk in the Spirit is not easy. Years ago an elderly Jesuit was assigned to the infirmary. He could barely limp around the house and grounds, but was willing to pass the time of day with scholastics. Day after day he made but one request: "Pray for my perseverance." The test of the Constitutions of the Society of Jesus is in the living, and the biggest test and the brightest witness is old age. Have the Constitutions so entered into a man's being that he lives in them as in his natural habitat? All Jesuits need to live in that habitat.

---

[4] August 11, 1589, letter of the eighty-year-old Bobadilla to Father General Claude Aquaviva (*Font.narr* 3:321), alluding to Ps. 90:10.

Being for Others

Every decision the Society makes in the future and every decision any one makes will be imperfect, for imperfection is a part of life and will involve both a death and new life: new limitations, new liabilities, new obstacles to overcome, new possibilities, new opportunities, new openings for creative activity and creative responses to the new liabilities. The General Examen and the Constitutions view sickness as a part of life. What they prescribe for the sick always harmonizes with what they prescribe for everyone.

Thus, in the *General Examen* an applicant to the Society is advised, "[O]ne who is sick should, by showing his great humility and patience, try to give no less edification in time of illness to those who visit him and converse and deal with him, than he does in time of full health, for the greater glory of God" (89$^{v.3}$ [p. 42]). Similar words appear in the *Constitutions,* which bid those who are sick to draw fruit from the sickness not only for themselves "but for the edification of others, . . . employing good and edifying words which show they accept the sickness as a gift from the hand of our Creator and Lord, since it is a gift no less than is health" (272$^{v.2}$ [p. 120]). Ignatius knew well from personal experience what a gift sickness can be: total self-transformation—and from a cannonball!

His words about the sick harmonize with the words in the *Constitutions* about workers in the vineyard of the Lord: those who are "missioned" to reside somewhere rather than to travel are told that the first way they can be of help to their neighbor "is by giving the good example of a thoroughly upright life and of Christian virtue, striving to edify those with whom one deals no less, but rather even more, by good deeds than by words" (637 [p. 294]).

Staying home serves the Lord as well as traveling. Sickness (and old age) serve the neighbor as much as good health. Dwindling faculties and diminishing numbers in the Society—both are gifts. Sickness and old age demand creativity; so do diminishing numbers. The openness of the old and the genuine Ignatian indifference of the sick model how to live in the bewildering world of the ever changing future. Handing on to others the work one does demands creativity; moving into new fields of endeavor untouched by others also demands all the creativity daily practiced by the sick and the old who still wish to be for others. To be for others—that is the key.

The wise elder mentioned earlier gave a talk not long ago to a large group of Jesuit Volunteers. One of the volunteers asked him, "What do you do?" He replied, "I live on a reservation with Native Americans. What do I do? I love the people, that's what I do. Oh, I also listen to 'Step Fives' in Alcoholics Anonymous, visit the sick, anoint, converse with people, and other parish activities. But what do I do? I love the people and they love me." Love is "the way in."

Even dying is working in the vineyard of the Lord. Ignatius offers this advice:

> As during his whole life, so also and even more at the time of his death, each member of the Society ought to strive earnestly that through him God our Lord may be glorified and served and his neighbors may be edified, at least by the example of his patience and fortitude along with his living faith, hope, and love." (595[2,3] [p. 266])

If dying is one's future and if dying is both a way of living and a way of working, then in the future one should live as dying. If one listens and gives credence to the dire predictions of drought and famine, of pestilence, epidemics, and violent changes in the weather that lie in the very near future, and if we expect to survive and help others to survive, it will be crucial to have the patience and fortitude, the living faith, hope, and love that the dying possess.

Complementary Norms

In providing norms complementing and updating the *Constitutions,* the members of General Congregation 34 embraced the present and the future of the contemporary world, rich with senior citizens, some strong and vigorous, others weak and failing. The congregation did not hesitate to do what Ignatius could not do, work out norms regarding the elderly.

Servants, Now and Forever

Stating that the elderly and the infirm "continue to be apostolically fruitful," the congregation included them as workers in the vineyard of the Lord, adding significantly that they "make others sharers in their own wisdom, acquired by the experience of serving our mission" (*ConsCN CN:* 244, §1 [p. 267]). For Ignatius, service is not so much "action" as it is the giving of one's self.[5] If a zitherist learns to zither by zithering and a runner learns to run by running, then a servant learns to give himself by serving others. After years of service the elderly finally learn that servants serve others and not themselves. They are not climbing any ladders, nor are they "in charge" of any offices. They are clearly "extra hands," servants, and they are content to be servants; for servants, they discover, are free, free to serve wherever anyone is in need.

In the local "retirement" community where I have my office, elderly Jesuits sing together at daily Mass, though they clearly lack the timbre of days gone by. Their conversation at meals, lively at times, is interspersed with silence. They are comfortable together, help each other in their

---

[5] Cusson, "Exercises spirituels," 249.

physical disabilities, are welcoming to visitors and friendly to guests. Not all their time is spent in visiting doctors: each has a variety of tasks, quiet, hidden, performed without fanfare. They visit the sick, celebrate liturgies, lead marriage encounters, hear confessions, counsel, attend the dying, and engage in a hundred other priestly offices. Scratch the surface and you might find that one of them has met the liturgical needs of four different communities before lunch! They are happy, joyful, vocally grateful to God and to the Society, in sheer wonderment at the grace of their vocation. Two of them might be sitting peacefully at ten in the morning, chatting together in the most relaxed way, two human beings present to each other and therefore to God, a symbol of God's dream for the whole human race.

All the ideals and dreams and aspirations expressed in the quotations from Vatican II and the general congregations find concrete expression in the simple service of their lives. Although memories, like Nadal's "leftovers from prayer," stir hearts and shape lives, the elderly share their wisdom more in the way they serve (by work or by prayer) than by narrating tales of days gone by, unless those tales reveal wisdom to be imitated or foolishness to be avoided, rather than fruitless longing for what is no more. In the service they provide, they often smile as they experience themselves as "unprofitable servants" (Luke 17:10 [NAB]), or bow their heads gratefully for the opportunity to sow and to reap a harvest no matter how small. After all, life is not a self-service department store. In the end, it's all God; memory proclaims, "All is grace."[6]

Is it only at the end that one arrives where one should have been from the beginning? Thomas Merton has written (so a friend asserts):

> We need to live at the center of our being which is untouched by sin and by illusion, a point of pure truth. A point or spark that belongs entirely to God, which is never at our *disposal*, from which God *disposes* our lives, which is inaccessible to the **fantasies of our own mind** or the **brutalities of our will.**

Those who have freely chosen to enter a retirement community, or have come guided by the gentle hand of obedience, have experienced a moment of pure truth in which they have acknowledged that their lives are wholly at the disposal of God, that their own fantasies are not in charge, and certainly not their own brutal wills. They choose because God has chosen. That is the way choices should be made.

Confidence in God

Addressing the elderly and infirm, General Congregation 34 emphasized that they "ought to take care that others are encouraged by the

---

[6] Georges Bernanos, *The Diary of a Country Priest* (Toronto: Macmillan, 1937), 255 (the final page in any edition).

example of their filial and confident dedication to God in sickness and failing strength" (*ConsCN CN:* 244, §1 [p. 267]). Elderly Jesuits, especially those confined to an infirmary or a nursing home, often experience the loss of friends, loss of vigor, loss of health; they go shuffling from one doctor to another and from one surgery to another. They long for better days. They mirror, in fact, their healthier brothers who mourn the loss of numbers, the lack of manpower and money and other resources. For both, the challenge is to discover in some new way that "less is more." Death itself—death of a person, death of a project, death of an institution—while deserving to be mourned, nonetheless opens up countless possibilities. Accepting death in any form is countercultural these days. Need the Society pay the cost of maintaining in existence something that is peacefully slipping away? As old ways disappear and as trying to make old ways appear relevant becomes fruitless, filial confidence in God may be the only foundation for evangelization. Experience has shown time and again that when all human ingenuity runs out, we are where we want to be. That moment when "the earth is void and empty" is the moment for God to stir the waters and bring forth a fresh creation.

The special trials and temptations of the elderly illumine the temptations of the twenty-first century. The fear of being a burden on the community reflects the sin of evaluating people for their productivity, as does the discouraging thought that can thrust its way into our mind: After all these years, what have I achieved? Temptations, of course, contain an element of truth. Work accomplishes something, but being can accomplish even more. The "work" has changed, yet remains profoundly part of that more holistic active life characteristic of the Society.

The most recent crop of new novices in the Oregon Province consists of a medical doctor from Central America, a graduate of one of the province's universities with a degree in Latin-American studies, a Vietnamese-American who is a licensed machinist, and a Mexican with degrees from two universities who has been working in management. When they begin to move about the province, marvelous chemistry will develop between novices and infirmary-bound Jesuits, between novices and adventuresome elderly who welcome them into the community. Ignatius was intensely aware of the conflicts that can exist between those of differing nationalities and cultures. Differences also make for opportunities. In the new millennium not every choice should confirm the blandness of uniformity.

Extending the Horizons of Prayer

After affirming that all the members of the Society, especially superiors, should have a particular care for the elderly and infirm (244, §2 [p. 267]), the *Complementary Norms* states: "Major superiors should give to our elderly and infirm members a special mission to pray for the Church and the Society and to unite their personal suffering and limitations to the worldwide salvific ministry of the Church and the Society" (ibid., §3). The Mystical Body of Christ is wondrously efficient. Even the "personal sufferings and limitations" become part of the *ministry* of the Church and the Society. *Nothing* is lost. *All* is grace.

The above norm also is in harmony with the statement in the *Constitutions* addressed to workers in the vineyard of the Lord that a second way of helping the neighbor is "by desires in the presence of the Lord and by prayers for the whole Church, especially for those persons in it who are of greater importance for the common good" ($638^{vv.1,2}$ [p. 294]). Explicitly named are "friends and benefactors, living and dead," as well as "those for whose particular benefit they and the other members of the Society are working in diverse places. . . . ecclesiastical and secular princes, and other persons who have great power to promote or *impede* the good of souls and the divine service" (638 f. [p. 294], italics added). Praying for the Society echoes the insistence in the *Constitutions* that all members should pray for the Society ($812^{v.4}$ [p. 400]). There comes a time when all other apostolates dissolve and a man's whole energy is spent in praying for the Church and the Society (and the world). That man is, indeed, *on the way in.*

The striking aspect of this norm directed at major superiors is that it complements a passage in the *Constitutions* indicating the help that can be given to dying members of the Society (596 [p. 266]). The practice of missioning the elderly and infirm to pray for the Church and the Society (and the world) demonstrates that such a missioning truly is a *help* to the elderly and the infirm, for which they are deeply grateful. To feel missioned is to feel sent by God. In all decision making it is imperative that each one acts like "a man sent from God" (John 1:6), for no one is here to fulfill his own desires, but rather to fulfill the mission of Jesus.

To be infirm or to be elderly (one gradually approaching infirmity) is not to withdraw from the vineyard of the Lord. The work is different or gradually becoming different. One dying Jesuit's only concern before he died, his nurse said, was wondering who would take his place in praying for the community. The work is prayer alone, or gradually becoming nothing but prayer. If their superior seriously missions the elderly and the infirm to pray for the Church and the Society and if they seriously accept that mission, they find their horizons opening up, broadening, embracing more and more. Gradually letting go of the particular works that have engaged them over the years, they find themselves facing a larger world, a more sinful world, a larger Church and a larger Society, a Church and a Society profoundly in need, suffering, groping in darkness, engaging new problems, starting new initiatives, entertaining new hopes, new plans, and new desires. Their prayer is likely to expand, likely to become more radically passive, allowing them to receive a new way of acting based on the gifts of God and not on human gifts.[7] They are on their way in, into a more profound interior life; into a more silent, more thoughtful, more reflective life; into a deeper way of living the apostolic life. They are not regressing from the Jesuit ideal, but bringing it to completion. One day an elderly Jesuit was asked, "How's your prayer life these days?" "Not very good," he replied; "I have a hard time praying, except for all the time." In the world of the twenty-first century, Jesuits will need more than ever before the ability to be like the elderly, on the way in at all times.

The Final Days of Jerómino Nadal

In 1573 at the age of sixty-six, as Nadal foresaw the beginning of the end, he asked to be relieved of responsibilities in the government of the Society. For three more years he worked on his writings in the town of Hall in Austria. Even as he modeled in a positive way the union of learning and spirituality, by 1575 he was also modeling in a negative way the weakness and vulnerability of Jesus in his passion. The melancholy and depression of his first years as a priest descended upon him once more, and he became a difficult member of the community. It is even said that his unreasonable behavior drove his superior out of the Society. Even that experience was not without fruit. It seems likely that an entry in his diary belongs to this time:

> The hidden root of pride and ambition is uprooted, and indeed by God's good gift, if something happens that makes it clear to you that you have been rejected by everyone, for by reason of it a tremendous light bursts forth accompanied by great consolation, profound tranquillity and peace of mind, genuine spiritual poverty in Christ, so that then for the first time it is possible to see that all things have been left behind and have been consumed in this experience of genuine renunciation. (*Orat.observ* 296, no. 968)

The elderly are no longer concerned about leaving all and following Jesus as though making a generous choice; in them there is only an awareness that the choice has been made much more profoundly within them by God.

To become cranky or crotchety is generally a free choice, a free refusal to accept the changes in one's own life and in the surrounding world, and often reflects other free choices made along the way; to be cheerful in spite of pain and exhaustion is also a free choice, a free surrender to a gift; to be depressed is often a clinical condition requiring medical attention. To divest oneself of self-love means to surrender to the consuming fire of divine love.

"You find by experience," Nadal wrote in his journal, "that if you ask God for better health . . . God will not grant it, but rather something

---

[7] Demoustier, "Contemplatif en action," 475.

else that pertains to the soul's health" (*Orat.observ* 297, no. 970). At the end of 1576 Nadal's free choice, more reflective of earlier free choices, was to ask to spend the rest of his life in prayer and preparing to die, or go to Venice and keep busy hearing confessions (*EpistNadal* 3:731). Early in 1577 he wrote to Father General Mercurian that he had finished much of his writing: the exhortations, instructions, scholia, images, notes, and meditations. He still had a few more to complete, but lacked the energy for study and writing. Perhaps he could hear confessions in Venice and direct the Exercises. "I am an old man, Father, and I am sick and run down, but my heart is more high-spirited than ever through the Lord's grace" (ibid., 735 f.).

He went by litter to Verona and then to Venice for a few months before moving on to Rome, where he died in 1580 on Easter Sunday at the age of seventy-two.

In so far as we can determine, the last words he wrote at Hall were "What a gift! God wants to talk to me, and wants me to talk to him" (ibid., 301, no. 980).

Conclusion

In the Jesuit commitment to mission, perhaps Jesuits have clung too fiercely to the mission and not sufficiently to the God who has missioned. Jesuits can learn from hermits, who have little grip on the world, and from Jesuit elderly, who are gradually losing their grip on what has been their small part of the world. As it slips out of their grasp, their hands become more able in their weakness to hold and sustain the whole world the way hermits do. They become capable of holding anything their major superiors mission them to hold in prayer. They are undistracted by particularities or closeness. They need no longer "sweat the small stuff," for nothing is any longer small for one who works in silent concert with him who "holds the whole world in his hands." Their "manner of life, of prayer, and of work" is more in harmony with their "physical and psychological condition," and also with "the needs of the apostolate." They are contemplative, contemplative in prayer and contemplative also in action, the only action they now have that means anything to them, to pray for the Church and the Society, for the whole world, in all that they do: breathing, eating, sleeping, brushing their teeth, reading when possible, watching TV, extending hospitality to their visitors, quietly accepting the gift of each moment, "walking in the Spirit," quietly surrendering all that they are each moment to God whom they find in all things in a brand-new way. They now "live for God alone." They have discovered the truth of General Congregation 34's claim:

[The Jesuit] does not build his own business or his own career, because he does not build his own home and family. His chastity has made it possible for him to grow in his poverty. At the end of his life, through his vow of chastity, he will have become poor in a way that his previous talents and energy and education made impossible. . . . He has . . . built up nothing for himself, and looks to God for the definition of his life. This poverty that flows from his chastity is not the destruction of his Jesuit life; in many ways it is its completion and fulfillment. (*DocsGC34* 243 [p. 115])

The same is true of every hermit, of every religious solitary. Is it not also true in every convent, in every monastery as well? And in every nursing home, in every church and many a private home, where little old ladies and little old men seek God with or without their beads every day. Is it not true that in the new poverty of their aloneness they find a new richness that stems from the love that has filled their lives? God's is the initiative, as it was in the beginning, is now, and ever shall be. "See, I am making all things new" (Rev. 21:5).

Epilog

W riting this book has taught its author much about the differences in Christian spiritualities. Much I learned from my association, lasting almost thirty years, with Cecilia Wilms, a multi-talented hermit in the Cistercian tradition and my co-worker for over fifteen years. An emphasis on different aspects of our relation to Christ produces a distinct "spirit" in our ways of following the same Lord. Jesuits and hermits are far apart in their service of God—or are they?

Bruno, the founder of the Carthusians, hermits who live in community, was a schoolman who gave up teaching to go to the desert. Ignatius was a country nobleman who gave up the arts of war and peace to go to the big cities, where, among other things, he established schools. He was profoundly drawn to the Carthusians and, as Jean Beyer says, the *Soli Deo* (God alone) of the Carthusians dominated his whole life, so much so that he remained a Carthusian at heart.[1] He is, notwithstanding, a Jesuit, and there is a difference. As Michael Buckley has affirmed, "the Jesuit was to be the Carthusian become apostolic."[2]

At Manresa the great hero of Ignatius was St. Humphrey, a desert solitary. The older and more infirm a Jesuit becomes, the more his prayer verges on that of a hermit, the prayer of one distant from the community yet living at the heart of the community, prayer filled with the pain, the hopes, the longings of the world. That is why it is important that a major superior *mission* an elderly or infirm Jesuit to pray for the Church and the Society. Prayer is his work done on behalf of his neighbor. Nevertheless, although somewhat the same, the prayer for others of the hermit and the prayer for others of the infirm Jesuit will be different; for one proceeds from the fullness of contemplation and communion arising out of solitude, and the other proceeds from the fullness of contemplation and communion arising out of action on behalf of others. The Jesuit's prayer is neither "reduced" nor "elevated" to the prayer of a hermit, but flows from the Kingdom, the Two Standards, and the end of the Society, endowed with a

---

[1] Jean Beyer, S.J., "Saint Ignace de Loyola chartreux . . . ," *Nouvelle revue theologique* 78 (1956): 938.

[2] Michael J. Buckley, S.J., "Mission in Companionship: Of Jesuit Community and Communion," *Studies in the Spirituality of Jesuits*, 11, no. 4 (1979): 13.

shape and a flavor distinct from the prayer that flows from solitude and "the barren advantages of the desert."[3] The hermit, the contemplative, participates in the priestly mission of the Son to intercede before the Father at all times for all creatures on the face of the earth. The Jesuit, indeed, is called to pray for the flock committed to his care, but he participates more in the prophetic mission of the Son to proclaim the Good News and bring the Good News by word and deed to every creature on the face of the earth. Every Jesuit in the twenty-first century needs to move toward that experience.

In comparing one form of Christian spirituality with another, one can easily confuse the part emphasized with the totality. On his first trip to Spain, Nadal compared the Carthusian absorbed in prayer with the Jesuit absorbed in the service of God and neighbor:

> What suffices for a Carthusian, even a holy one, is not enough for us, for God calls us to another end, namely, to the fullness of divine love. Since this embraces the neighbor also, the fullness of love means availing of every useful means possible to achieve the perfection of our neighbor also. We not only pray for our neighbor but work at whatever can bring him some good.[4]

Indeed, Jesuits do, but God calls the Carthusian (and all others as well) to the fullness of divine love—the Carthusian by praying more profoundly, the Jesuit by serving more zealously, and others by doing to the full whatever God has called them to do. What is important for each is responding to the call of Christ. Do not confuse the fullness of charity with the fullness of works.

Jesuits and hermits alike are called to walk in the Spirit. (Is there anyone not so called?) Walking in the Spirit, of course, is another way of saying walking in solitude, which is the ambience of the hermit, and walking immersed in the world through obedience, which is the heart of Jesuit life. To return to the words of Karl Rahner quoted above in chapter 10, "[B]y [their] life and existence with the Incarnate Word, [they] . . . make it possible for God to undertake the adventure of his love outside of himself." Both are called to be contemplative in all that they do. The hermit, as well as the Jesuit, "sets out to find prayer and God and devotion in everything. The Society, however, does not practice prayer in a solitary fashion after the manner of a hermit, but extends it and joins it to the actual ministry of our calling and of obedience" (ibid., 97, no 161).

Both hermits and Jesuits are called to love. The difference is not that hermits love God and Jesuits love people; both hermits and Jesuits

---

[3] Phrase taken from the life of St. Bruno, *Vita antiquior,* in Migne, *Series Latina,* 152, 485A. Also see Conwell, *Impelling Spirit,* 368.

[4] "Exhort. 1554 hisp." (*CommInst* 53, no. 33).

live at the heart of the Church and the world, loving both God and God's people. The difference lies more in the ambience of each, in the solitude of one and the immersion in the world through obedience of the other. Jesuits live and thrive and survive on solitude as well as hermits, but not all the time, not even most of the time. The hermit, too, lives in obedience—in obedience to God found in the hermit's heart and the needs of the world and proper authority—but proper authority speaks to a hermit in a far more general way than to a Jesuit.

Both hermits and Jesuits find God in solitude and obedience, but in very different ways. The prayer of both hermits and Jesuits is people oriented, embracing the whole world, so that the hermit faces the whole world in solitude and prayer, and the Jesuit faces the whole world in obedience, in the ministry in which he is engaged. The hermit who lives life to the full in solitude in one small part of the world is not likely to be prey to distractions from the whole world for which the hermit prays. The Jesuit who ministers intensely in one small part of the world must have a Trinitarian vision of all creation and not lose sight of the rest of the world. The Jesuit's prayer, Nadal says, should reach out beyond solitude to the living—out of his vocation (which is world embracing) and to obedience (the work in which he is actually engaged). Neither hermit nor Jesuit is identified by occupation, but of each is true what General Congregation 34 said: "Because we are companions of Jesus, our identity is inseparable from our mission."[5] Mission, of course, is much broader than the work a person does.

The Final Days of a Jesuit

Having escaped death on August 6, 1945, when the first atom bomb destroyed Hiroshima and took the lives of thousands, Father General Pedro Arrupe suffered a heart attack on August 6, 1981, upon his return from Bangkok to Rome. From Hiroshima on, he had faced life with luminous hope, and he did so, insofar as he could, for the rest of his days. Personally radiant, ever turning inward, he was captured by the vision of the Trinity even as he cried out for justice in the world: fashioning new priorities; seeking a Society rooted and grounded in love, intensely Eucharistic; emitting a feeling of sacredness, of the transcendent, of the Beyond. Calling all to be persons for others, he enlarged the minds and hearts not only of Jesuits but of many others as well.

To his brother Jesuits as they assembled for General Congregation 33, which would elect his successor, he addressed these words:

> More than ever, I now find myself in the hands of God.
> This is what I have wanted all my life, from my youth.

---

[5] *DocsGC34* 26 (p. 28).

> And this is still the one thing I want.
> But now there is a difference:
> the initiative is entirely with God.
> It is indeed a profound spiritual experience
> to know and feel myself so totally in his hands.[6]

Pedro Arrupe's surrender was complete. His address ends in a statement of hope followed by a prayer containing his own oblation, and a final expression of his deepest desire:

> I am full of hope, seeing the Society at the service of the one Lord and of the Church, under the Roman Pontiff, the vicar of Christ on earth. May she keep going along this path, and may God bless us with many good vocations of priests and brothers: *for this I offer to the Lord what is left of my life, my prayers, and the suffering imposed by my ailments.* For myself, all I want is to repeat from the depths of my heart:
>
> Take, O Lord, and receive: all my liberty, my memory, my understanding, and my whole will.
> All I have and all I possess—it is all yours, Lord: you gave it to me;
> I make it over to you: dispose of it entirely according to your will.
> Give me your love and your grace, and I want no more.[7]

The initiative is entirely with God—did he already realize the full truth of those words? God chose to take Arrupe's Suscipe literally—his liberty, his memory, his understanding, his entire will, as this brilliant and holy man was gradually reduced to a state resembling infancy.

The next day the members of the general congregation gathered in the chapel at La Storta, where Ignatius had experienced that "God the Father placed him with Christ his Son," and heard Arrupe's homily for the occasion read to them as he sat in the silence imposed by his condition. These are some of his words:

> How often in these eighteen years I have had proof of God's faithfulness to his promise: "I will be favorable to you in Rome."
>
> A profound experience of the loving protection of divine providence has been my strength in bearing the burden of my responsibilities and facing the challenges of our day. True, I have had my difficulties, both big and small; but never has God failed to stand by me. And now more than ever I find myself in the hands of this God who has taken hold of me.
>
> . . . Like St. Paul I can say that I am "an old man, and now also a prisoner of Christ Jesus." I had planned things differently; but it is God who disposes, and his designs are a mystery: "Who can divine the will of the Lord?" But we do know the will of the Father, that we become true images of the Son; and the Son tells us clearly in the Gospel, "Anyone who does not carry his cross and come after me cannot be my disciple."

---

[6] *DocsGC33*, p. 93, with sentences rearranged in sense lines.

[7] Ibid., pp. 94 f., italics added; with the Suscipe rearranged in sense lines.

Father Lainez, from whom we have the words of the promise "I will be favorable," proceeds to explain that Ignatius never understood them to mean that he and his companions would be free of suffering. On the contrary, he was convinced that they were called to serve Christ carrying his cross. (ibid., pp. 96f.)

While helpless as a tiny babe in his final years, Pedro Arrupe in his diminishment exerted a forceful impact upon his every visitor. In 1990, while doing research in the Jesuit archives in Rome, I could not bring myself to visit the former Father General's room (no communication was possible) for a moment of prayer. I have learned much since then about diminishment, both physical and mental, recognizing it now as part of the process of transformation that human beings go through in participating in the paschal mystery of Jesus' passover to the Father, what the medieval mystics called "transmigration." Now I would find it strengthening to visit one I loved and cherished who was going through this transitional passage through death to new life. Arrupe said both by his living and by his dying that it is fitting and right to die.

The Final Days of a Hermit

On the First Sunday of Lent, before entering the last year of her life and already plagued by ill health, Cecilia wrote in her journal (unpublished), "It is still quiet. Blessing. Deep gratitude. An invitation and challenge to live fully the present moment and let neither the past [n]or the future impinge on it."

The only moment that exists is the present, and she lived each moment fully. Since the present is pregnant with the future, to live fully in the present demands confronting the future. The only future humans know is the present, the future of the past. In the light of that "future" (known as experience), each one confronts the present moment and the future who is God.

Early in 1968 she was walking on the beach with her close friend and abbess, Myriam Dardenne, both from Belgium and founding members of Our Lady of Redwoods Abbey in Whitethorn, California. Cecilia had found the tall redwoods oppressive and was thinking about going to Spokane, Washington, for a year of therapy with a psychologist. On May 20, 1968, she recalled that day in her journal:

Feel sad today, weary. The walls are closing in again and I get frightened. Suddenly I recall an afternoon at the ocean, with Myriam, last January. I see again the wild scenery of Bear Harbor, the upcoming tide and especially that bird (a seagull?) dancing on the waves, moving with the stream, up and under, up and under and up again. I remember what I thought and said to Myriam: If I could but live like that bird, let the stream of life go through me, without rebelling, without being afraid. . . . If the bird would rebel but one instant against the wave, wouldn't it be crushed? . . . To be like the seagull dancing on the waves, to let life stream through me, to say yes to life. I want it so badly and yet feel so powerless, crushed, paralyzed. Jesus, where are you?

A prayer, a cry for help, a longing desire, straining into the future. Her journal that year is filled with the desire to say in capital letters YES to LIFE, to TRUST LIFE, to BE ME, to LET LIFE HAPPEN.

After the year of therapy and the discovery of the creative possibilities in living the monastic life alone in "the desert of the city," she spent about five years more solidifying her experiment before leaving the Cistercian Order and becoming a "consecrated virgin" in the local church. After the new canon law appeared with its categories of "consecrated virgins" and "hermits," she recognized that the life she was living was that of a consecrated virgin who was a hermit.

On September 8, 1953, she had entered the Cistercian monastery of Our Lady of Nazareth in Belgium. On the same date in 1996 she moved to a different hermitage, and it seemed fitting to leave the final pages of her journal blank and begin a new one with this new move. "God keeps faith," she wrote. "Dreams become reality and are transformed in the process."

As she began to move toward her sixty-fifth birthday, with its promise of a little extra income from Social Security, she dreamed of cutting back on the number of her working hours in order to spend the time, in her words, "entering more profoundly into the sources of the monastic tradition." A few minutes after midnight on July 1, 1997, the month in which she would turn sixty-five, she phoned from her hermitage: she was in much pain; could I take her to the emergency hospital? Thus began a two-week odyssey of visits to doctors and day-long tests providentially paid for by Medicare, which becomes effective at midnight on the first day of the month of a person's sixty-fifth birthday. The verdict at last: terminal cancer. A doctor with a vinyl folder explained her options clearly and gently: radiation therapy, chemotherapy, each with advantages and disadvantages and possible side effects. At the end, she gently and firmly shook her head, communicating her "No, thank you" to all that he had said. He sat there for a full minute in silence, then closed his folder and silently left the room. She knew, and I knew, that her cherished dream was about to be fulfilled: she was about to enter completely into the Source of all traditions.

The final entry in her journal was dated some days earlier, July 9, 1997. Poor health was now her lot, and the doctor would hospitalize her that very day. She was now in the future of her past, but she addresses the present, now, this moment:

"Wait my soul, silent for God . . ." Waiting. Trusting. Letting be. Letting go. But also an increased sense of being "under attack," attacked in and through my body, but aimed at the inner spirit. I want to let be and embrace what is, now, each moment; I don't want the evil spirit to get a stronghold or sneak in through the back porch by letting feelings of weariness and discouragement or lack of trust—in doctor and health professionals, in God's guidance, in my own sense of being and perception of what's going on within me—to creep up and distract me from living and embracing this ordeal as a hermit. *All* is mercy. All is prayer. All is gift. All is *kairos* [opportunity]. And so, "Wait my soul, silent for God."

Surrender. The bird is dancing on the waves, moving with the stream, letting life stream through her. God is faithful and has heard her prayer. She is ready to choose LIFE in death.

Note how similar her last words were to those of Pedro Arrupe, and how different. Arrupe's were about surrendering to God, Cecilia's about waiting for God in silence: active surrendering in total passivity, and active waiting in total passivity—to and for a God experienced by each of them as always faithful: two different spiritualities at work, two of many different ways God has of bringing human beings to completion.

Cecilia danced on the waves for ten more months, dying in the hermitage on May 13, 1998. She loved to dance before the Blessed Sacrament, and my own conviction is that she is still dancing, and that since her death she has been responsible for much of this book.

"Amen. *Maranatha.* Come, Lord Jesus" (Rev. 22:20).

It is the Risen Christ who is constantly active in all dimensions of the world's growth, in its diversity of cultures and its varied spiritual experience. As there is a unified goodness in God's work of creation, so in Christ's redemptive work, the fragmentation caused by sin is being healed by a single thread of grace throughout the restored creation.

—General Congregation 34, *Our Mission and Culture*

APPENDIXES

Appendix 1

Selected articles on Nadal and Jesuit prayer and published books on Jesuit spirituality

Bacht, H., S.J. "Das Ringen um die tägliche Betrachtungsstunde in der jungen Societas Jesu." *Erbe und Auftrag* 59 (1983): 15–30.

Begheyn, Paul, S.J. "The Controversies on Prayer after the Death of Ignatius and Their Effect on the Concept of Jesuit Mission." *Centrum Ignatianum Spiritualitatis (CIS)* 24 (1993): 78–93.

Cantin, Roger, S.J. "L'Élection de Jérôme Nadal: Des ténèbres jaillit la lumière." *Cahiers de spiritualité ignatienne* 4 (1980): 263–73.

Cusson, Gilles, S.J. "Les Exercices spirituels, école de contemplation." *Cahiers de spiritualité ignatienne* 17 (1993): 245–52.

Daniélou, Jean, S.J. "La Spiritualité trinitaire de saint Ignace." *Christus* 3 (1956): 354–72.

de Deckere, Christian, S.J. "Mystique trinitaire et action apostolique selon Jérôme Nadal." *Christus* 39 (1992): 102–12.

Decloux, Simon, S.J. "L'Actualité de la spiritualité ignatienne." *Nouvelle revue theologique (NRT)* 112 (1990): 641–59.

Demoustier, Adrien. "'Contemplatif en action': Essai sur une formule de Jérôme Nadal." *Christus* 38 (1991): 470–78.

Emonet, Pierre, S.J. "Faire de toutes sa vie une prière continuelle." *Christus* 37 (1990): 466–76.

———. "'Faire de toutes ses actions une prière continuelle': La prière de ceux qui n'ont pas beaucoup de temps pour faire oraison." *Cahiers de spiritualité ignatienne* 16 (1992): 45–60.

França Miranda, Mario da, S.J. "'Trouver Dieu en toutes choses' dan la société moderne." *Cahiers de spiritualité ignatienne* 14 (1990): 407–18.

Gonzalez, Luis, S.J. "Contemplativos en la acción: En la Escuela de los Ejercicios ignacianos." *Manresa* 59 (1987): 389–403.

Hennaux, Jean-Marie, S.J. "Contemplation et vie contemplative d'après les Exercises de saint Ignace." *Vie consacrée* 62 (1990): 234–46

Hostie, Raymond, S.J. "Meditation et contemplation d'après le Père Jérôme Nadal." *Revue d'ascètique et de mystique (RAM)* 32 (1956): 397–419.

Iparraguirre, Ignacio, S.J. "La oración en la Compañía naciente," *Archivum historicum Societatis Iesu (AHSI)* 25 (1956): 455–87.

Lafrance, Jean, S.J. "Nota sobre la oración trinitaria de San Ignacio." *Manresa* 53 (1981): 171–78.

Lévesque, Fernand, S.J. "Contemplation et action chez saint Ignace." *Cahiers de spiritualité ignatienne* 3 (1979): 23–29.

Lopez Tejada, Dario, S.J. "La paz interior, y el buscar y hallar a Dios en todas las cosas." *Revista de espiritualidad* 24 (1965): 475–504.

Nadal, Jerónimo. *Epistolæ et monumenta P. Hieronymi Nadal.* Edited by Miguel Nicolau, S.J. Vols. 13, 15, 21, and 27 of the series Monumenta historica Societatis Iesu (MHSI). Rome: Institutum historicum Societatis Iesu (IHSI), 1962. This source contained a number of Nadal's previously unedited or partially edited works. In this book it is abbreviated to *EpistNadal.*

———. *P. Hieronymi Nadal commentarii de instituto Societatis Iesu (CommInst).* Edited by Miguel Nicolau, S.J. *EpistNadal* vol. 5. Rome: IHSI, 1962.

———. *P. Hieronymi Nadal orationis observationes (Orat.observ).* Edited by Miguel Nicolau, S.J. Vol. 90a of MHSI. Rome: IHSI, 1962.

Nicolau, Miguel, S.J. *Jerónimo Nadal, S.I. (1507–1580): Sus obras y doctrinas espirituales.* Madrid: Consejo superior de investigaciones cientificas, 1949. This monumental work on Nadal had helped me immensely in the 1950s.

———. "La oración de san Ignacio: Fórmulas que la expresan." *Manresa* 28 (1956): 91–104.

———. "¿Cómo enseña San Ignacio la Oración?" *Manresa* 28 (1956): 169–82.

———. "'Contemplativo en la acción': una frase famosa de Nadal." CIS 25 (1977): 7–16.

———. "Jérôme Nadal (1507–1580): Le bras droit du Fondateur." *Cahiers de spiritualité ignatienne* 15 (1991): 39–47.

Pelland, Gilles, S.J. "Réflexions sur l'inspiration trinitaire du charisme ignatien.'" *Cahiers de spiritualité ignatienne* 6 (1982): 147–68.

Royo-Millán, Aurora, R.J.M. "'Contemplativo en la acción': Semblanza espiritual de San Ignacio." *Teología espiritual: Revista cuatrimestrial de los Estudio Generales Dominicanos de España* 17 (1973): 327–66.

Ruiz-Jurado, Manuel, S.J. "La perspectiva de San Ignacio en su visión del mundo y su influjo en el modo de ser de la Compañía." *Manresa* 45 (1973): 241–62.

Sheldrake, Philip, S.J., "Finding God in All Things: Ignatian Prayer and the Spiritual Exercises." *Milltown Studies* 29 (1992): 5–13.

Silos, Leonardo R., S.J. "Cardoner in the Life of Saint Ignatius of Loyola." AHSI 33 (1964): 3–43.

Sudbrack, Josef, S.J., "'Gott in allen Dingen finden': Eine ignatianische Maxime und ihr metahistorischer Hintergrund." *Geist und Leben* 65 (1992): 165–86.

Tanner, Norman P. "Medieval Crusade Decrees and Ignatius's Meditation on the Kingdom." *Heythrop Journal* 31 (1990): 505– 15.

Appendix 2

Selected material dealing with the Trinitarian foundations of Ignatian spirituality and prayer

Action and Contemplation Together: Responses to Fr. Arrupe's Letter. Rome: CIS, 1977.

Aldea, Quintin, ed. *Ignacio de Loyola en la gran crisis del siglo xvi.* Congreso internacional de historia, Madrid (19–21 noviembre de 1991). Bilbao: Mensajero, 1991).

Bangert, William V., S.J. *Jerome Nadal, S.J., 1507–1580: Tracking the First Generation of Jesuits.* Edited by Thomas M. McCoog, S.J. Chicago: Loyola University Press, 1992.

Bertrand, Dominique, S.J. *Un Corps pour l'Esprit: Essai sur l'expérience communautaire selon les Constitutions de la Compagnie de Jésus.* Paris: Desclee de Brouwer, 1974).

Decloux, Simon, S.J. *The Ignatian Way: "For the Greater Glory of God."* Translated by Cornelius M. Buckley, S.J. Chicago: Loyola University Press, 1991.

Downey, Michael. *Altogether Gift: A Trinitarian Spirituality.* Maryknoll, N.Y.: Orbis Books, 2000.

Falkner, Andreas, S.J., and Paul Imhof, S.J., eds. *Ignatius von Loyola und die Gesellschaft Jesu, 1491–1556.* Würzburg: Echter, 1990.

Lonsdale, David, S.J. *Eyes to See, Ears to Hear.* Chicago: Loyola University Press, 1990.

Mejía-Saldarriaga, Rodrigo, S.J. *La Dinámica de la Integración Espiritual: Buscar y hallar a Dios en todas las cosas.* Rome: CIS, 1980.

Plazaola, Juan. ed. *Ignacio de Loyola y su tiempo.* Congreso internacional de historia (9–13 Setiembre 1991). Bilbao: Mensajero, 1992.

Rahner, Hugo, S.J. *Ignatius the Theologian.* Translated by Michael Barry. New York: Herder and Herder, 1968.

———. *The Vision of St. Ignatius in the Chapel of La Storta.* 2nd ed. Rome: CIS, 1979.

Ravier, André, S.J. *Ignatius of Loyola and the Founding of the Society of Jesus.* San Francisco: Ignatius Press, 1987.

Sievernich, Michael, S.J., and Günter Switek, S.J., eds. *Ignatianisch: Eigenart und Methode der Gesellschaft Jesu.* Freiburg im Breisgau: Herder, 1990.

Wulf, Friedrich, S.J., ed. *Ignatius of Loyola: His Personality and Spiritual Heritage, 1556–1956.* St. Louis: The Institute of Jesuit Sources, 1977.

Young, William, S.J., trans. *Finding God in All Things: Essays in Ignatian Spirituality* Selected from Christus. Chicago: Henry Regnery Co., 1958.

Appendix 3

Additional bibliographical material on Ignatian prayer and spirituality

Arrupe, Pedro, S.J. "The Trinitarian Inspiration of the Ignatian Charism." *Studies in the Spirituality of Jesuits* 33, no. 3 (May) 2001: 1–49 (originally published in *CIS* 13, no. 1 (1982): 11–69; the entire issue was entitled *The Trinity in the Ignatian Charism.*

Bottereau, George, S.J. "La prière personnelle d'Ignace de Loyola." *NRT* 95 (1973): 393–404.

Danielou, Jean, S.J. "La spiritualité trinitaire de Saint Ignace." *Christus* 3 (1956): 354–72.

de Deckere, Christian, S.J. "Mystique trinitaire et action apostolique selon Jérôme Nadal." *Christus* 39 (1992): 102–12.

Dumeige, Gervais, S.J. "The Mystery of the Trinity in the Life of St. Ignatius" *CIS* 13, no. 1 (1982) 70–105.

Haas, Adolf, S.J. "The Foundations of Ignatian Mysticism in Loyola and Manresa," *CIS* 13, no. 1 (1982): 149–96.

Lafrance, Jean. "Nota sobre la oración trinitaria de San Ignacio." *Manresa* 53 (1981): 171–78.

Lewis, Jacques S.J. "L'Oraison ignatienne." *Cahiers de spiritualité ignatienne* 13 (1989): 31–41, 97–103, 195–203.

Lopez Tejada, Dario, S.J. "La paz interior, y el buscar y hallar a Dios en todas las cosas." *Revista de espiritualidad* 24 (1965): 475–504.

Pelland, Gilles S.J. "Réflexions sur l' 'inspiration trinitaire du charisme ignatien.'" *Cahiers de spiritualité ignatienne* 6 (1982): 147–68; in English: "Ignatius and the Trinity: Theological Insights." *CIS* 13, no. 1 (1982): 119–48.

Rasco, Emilio, S.J. "New Testament Elements in Father Arrupe's Address." *CIS* 13, no. 1 (1982): 106–18.

Silos, Leonardo R., S.J. "Cardoner in the Life of Saint Ignatius of Loyola." *AHSI* 33 (1964): 3–43.

Appendix 4

Additional material on the Spiritual Exercises as a school of prayer

Cusson, Gilles, S.J. "Les Exercices spirituels, école de contemplation." *Cahiers de spiritualité ignatienne* 17 (1993): 245-52.

Gonzalez, Luis S.J. "Contemplativos en la acción: En la Escuela de los Ejercicios ignacianos." *Manresa* 59 (1987): 389-403.

Hennaux, Jean-Marie, S.J. "Contemplation et vie contemplative d'après les Exercices de saint Ignace." *Vie consacré* 62 (1990): 234-46.

Hostie, Raymond, S.J. "Méditation et contemplation d'après le Père Jérôme Nadal." *Revue d'ascétique et de mystique (RAM)* 32 (1956): 397-419.

Lewis, Jacques, S.J. "Les Exercices spirituels, école de prière." *Cahiers de spiritualité ignatienne* 17 (1993): 235-44.

Nicolau, Miguel, S.J. "¿Cómo enseña San Ignacio la Oración?" *Manresa* 28 (1956): 169-82.

Sheldrake, Philip, S.J. "Finding God in All Things: Ignatian Prayer and the Spiritual Exercises." *Milltown Studies* 29 (1992): 5-13

Stierli, Josef S.J. "Jérôme Nadal (1507-1580): Le bras droit du Fondateur." *Cahiers de spiritualité ignatienne* 15 (1991): 139-47.

Veale, Joseph, S.J. "Life of the Spirit (II): Ignatian Contemplation." *The Furrow* 28 (1977): 72-78.

BIBLIOGRAPHY

Albert, St. *The Rule of St. Albert.* Edited by Hugh Clarke, O.Carm., and Bede Edwards, O.D.C. Aylesford and Kensington, 1973.

Alphonso, Herbert, S.J. "La vida diaria como oración." In *Ejercicios espirituales y mundo de hoy.* Congreso Internacional de Ejercicios, Loyola, 20–26 septiembre de 1991, edited by Juan Manuel Garcia-Lomas. Bilbao: Mensajero, 1991.

Arroyo, José. "La tradición orante ignaciana y su valor actual." *Confer* 23 (1984).

Arrupe, Pedro, S.J. "The Trinitarian Inspiration of the Ignatian Charism." *Studies in the Spirituality of Jesuits* 33, no. 3 (May 2001). Originally in *Centrum Ignatianum Spiritualitatis (CIS)* 13, no. 1 (1982).

———. "Men for Others: Training Agents of Change for the Promotion of Justice." In *Justice with Faith Today: Selected Letters and Addresses-II,* edited by Jerome Aixala, S.J. St. Louis: The Institute of Jesuit Sources, 1980.

Astráin, António, S.J. *Historia de la Compañía de Jesús en la Asistencia de España.* 7 vols. Madrid, 1902–25.

Augustine, St. *The Rule of Saint Augustine.* Introduction and commentary by "Tarsicius J. Van Bavel, O.S.A.; translated by Raymond Canning, O.S.A. Garden City, N.Y.: Doubleday, 1986.

Balthasar, Hans Urs von. *Thérèse of Lisieux: The Story of a Mission.* Translated by Donald Nicholl. New York: Sheed and Ward, 1954.

Bangert, William V., S.J. *Jerome Nadal, S.J., 1507–1580: Tracking the First Generation of Jesuits.* Edited by Thomas M. McCoog, S.J. Chicago: Loyola University Press, 1992.

Barber, Richard. *The Knight and Chivalry.* Rev. ed. Woodbridge: Boydell, 1995.

Begheyn, Paul, S.J. "The Controversies on Prayer after the Death of Ignatius and Their Effect on the Concept of Jesuit Mission." *CIS* 24, no. 1 (1993).

Benedict, St. *The Rule of St. Benedict.* Edited by Timothy Fry, O.S.B, et al. Collegeville, Minn.: The Liturgical Press, 1981.

Bernanos, Georges. *The Diary of a Country Priest.* Chicago: Thomas More Press, 1983.

Bertrand, Dominique, S.J. *Un Corps pour l'Esprit.* Paris: Desclée de Brouwer, 1974.

Beyer, Jean, S.J., "Saint Ignace de Loyola chartreux. . . ." *Nouvelle revue theologique (NRT)* 78 (1956).

——. "Novità della Compagnia di Gesù nelle strutture degli ordini religiosi." *Vita consacrata* 27 (1991).

Bingemer, Maria Clara. " 'Perfection in Whatever State of Life': Ignatian Spirituality and Lay Holiness." *Review of Ignatian Spirituality* 28, no. 86 (1997).

Bonaventure, St. *Meditationes vitæ Christi.* Chapter 5 of *S. Bonaventuræ Opera,* edited by A. Peltier. Paris, 1868.

Borgia, Francis, S.J. *Sanctus Franciscus Borgia, quartus Gandiæ dux et Societatis Iesu præpositus generalis tertius (EpistBorg).* Vols. 2, 23, 35, 38, and 41 of the series Monumenta historica Societatis Iesu (MHSI). Madrid, 1894–1911.

Bottereau, George, S.J. "La prière personnelle d'Ignace de Loyola." *NRT* 95 (1973).

Broët, Paschase, S.J. *Epistolæ PP. Paschasii Broëti, Claudii Jaji, Joannis Codurii, et Simonis Rodericii Societatis Iesu (EpistBroët).* Vol. 24 of MHSI. Madrid, 1903; reprinted 1971.

Cacho Blecua, Juan Manuel. "Del gentilhombre mundano al caballero 'a lo divino': Los ideales caballerescos de Ignacio de Loyola." In Plazaola, *Ignacio y su tiempo.*

Câmara, Luis Gonçalves da, S.J. "Memoriale seu diarium Patris Ludovici Gonzalez de Camara." In *Font.narr* 1:527–752.

Câmara, Luis Gonçalves da. "Acta P. Ignatii." In *Font.narr* 1:354–507.

Campbell-Johnston, Michael, S.J. "How I Pray: Being and Doing." *The Tablet* 246 (1992).

Cantin, Roger, S.J. "Le Troisieme Degré d'humilité et la gloire de Dieu." *Science Ecclésiastique* 8 (1956).

——."L'Élection de Jérôme Nadal." *Cahiers de spiritualité ignatienne* 4 (1980).

Caraman, Philip, S.J. *Ignatius Loyola: A Biography of the Founder of the Jesuits.* San Francisco: Harper and Row, 1990.

"Censura exercitiorum S. Ignatii confecta et archiepiscopo toletano oblata anno 1553." In the appendix of *PolChron* 3:503–24.

Certeau, Michel de, S.J. "L'Universalisme ignatien: Mystique et mission." *Christus* 13 (1966).

Charmont, François, S.J. *L'Union au Christ dans l'action selon saint Ignace.* Paris: Bonne Presse, 1959.

Clancy, Thomas H., S.J. "The Proper Grace of the Jesuit Vocation according to Jerome Nadal." *Woodstock Letters* 86 (1957).

——. *Introduction to Jesuit Life.* St. Louis: The Institute of Jesuit Sources, 1976.

Clarke, Thomas E., S.J. "The Ignatian Exercises: Contemplation and Discernment." *Review for Religious* 31, no. 1 (1972).

Condivi, Ascarico. *The Life of Michelangelo.* Translated by Alice Sedgwick Wohl; edited by Hellmut Wohl. 2nd ed. University Park: Pennsylvania State University Press, 1976.

Constitutiones Societatis Jesu (Constitutiones). 4 vols. Vols. 63, 64, 65, and 71 of MHSI. Rome: Institutum historicum Societatis Iesu (IHSI), 1934.

Constitutions of the Society of Jesus and Their Complementary Norms (ConsCN), The. St. Louis: The Institute of Jesuit Sources, 1996.

Contarini, Gasparo, Card. *Regesten und Briefe des Cardinals Gasparo Contarini (1483–1542)*. Compiled by Franz Dittrich. Braunsberg: 1881.

Conwell, Joseph F., S.J. *Contemplation in Action: A Study in Ignatian Prayer*. Spokane: Gonzaga University, 1957.

———. *Prayer Proper to the Society of Jesus according to Jerome Nadal, S.J. (1507–1580)*. Rome: Pontifical Gregorian University, 1957.

———. "Living and Dying in the Society of Jesus or Endeavoring to Imitate Angelic Purity." *Studies in the Spirituality of Jesuits* 12 (May 1980).

———. "A Foundational Experience." *CIS* 31, no. 1 (2000).

———. *Impelling Spirit: Revisiting a Founding Experience, 1539: Ignatius of Loyola and His Companions: An Exploration into the Spirit and Aims of the Society of Jesus as Revealed in the Founders' Proposed Papal Letter Approving the Society*. Chicago: Loyola Press, 1997.

Coreth, Emerich, S.J. "In actione contemplativus." *Zeitschrift für katholische Theologie* 76 (1954).

———. "Contemplation in Action." In *Contemporary Spirituality*, edited by Robert W. Gleason, S.J. New York: Macmillan, 1968.

Corpus scriptorum ecclesiasticorum latinorum (CSEL). Vienna: Hoelder-Pichler-Tempsky, 1866–.

Cusson, Gilles, S.J. "Les Exercices spirituels, école de contemplation." *Cahiers de spiritualité ignatienne* 17 (1993).

Dalmases, Cándido de, S.J. *Ignatius of Loyola: Founder of the Jesuits: His Life and Work*. St. Louis: The Institute of Jesuit Sources, 1985.

Daniélou, Jean, S.J., "La Vision ignatienne du monde et de l'homme." *Revue d'ascétique et de mystique (RAM)* 26 (1950).

———. "La spiritualité trinitaire de Saint Ignace." *Christus* 3 (1956).

Deckere, Christian De, S.J. "Mystique trinitaire et action apostolique selon Jérôme Nadal." *Christus* 39 (1992).

Decloux, Simon, S.J. *Commentaries on the Letters and Spiritual Diary of St. Ignatius Loyola*. 2nd ed. Rome: *CIS*, 1982.

———. "L'Actualité de la spiritualité ignatienne." *NRT* 112 (1990).

Demoustier, Adrien, S.J. "'Contemplatif en action": Essai sur une formule de Jérôme Nadal." *Christus* 38 (1991).

Dictionnaire de spiritualité ascétique et mystique (DSAM).

Digulleville, Guillaume de. In *Pèlerinage de la vie humaine, de Guillaume de Diguilleville*, by J. J. Stürzinger. London: Nichols & Sons (para el Roxburghe Club), 1893.

Documents of the 31st and 32nd General Congregations of the Society of Jesus (DocsGC3132). St. Louis: The Institute of Jesuit Sources, 1977.

Documents of the Thirty-Fourth General Congregation of the Society of Jesus (Docs-GC34). St. Louis: The Institute of Jesuit Sources, 1995.

Downey, Michael. *Altogether Gift: A Trinitarian Spirituality*. Maryknoll, N.Y.: Orbis Books, 2000.

Dumeige, Gervais, S.J. "The Grace Bestowed on the Founder—for All the Companions." *CIS* 19, no. 1 (1988).

Dunn, James D. G. *Jesus and the Spirit: A Study of the Religious and Charismatic Experience of Jesus and the First Christians as Reflected in the New Testament.* Grand Rapids: Eerdmans, 1975.

———. *Pneumatology.* Vol. 2 of *The Christ and the Spirit.* Grand Rapids: Eerdmans, 1998).

Dunn, John S., C.S.C. *The Way of All the Earth: Experiments in Truth and Religion.* Notre Dame: University of Notre Dame Press, 1978.

Dyckman, Katherine, S.N.J.M., Mary Garvin, S.N.J.M., and Elizabeth Liebert, S.N.J.M. *The Spiritual Exercises Reclaimed: Uncovering Liberating Possibilities for Women.* New York: Paulist Press, 2001.

Egan, Harvey D., S.J. *Christian Mysticism: The Future of a Tradition.* New York: Pueblo, 1984.

———. *Ignatian Spirituality and Social Justice.* Toronto: Regis College, 1991.

———. *Ignatian Spirituality: Finding God in Everything.* Toronto: Regis College, 1991.

———. *Toward a Postmodern American Catholicism: Ignatian Spirituality and the Mission of a Jesuit University Today,* lecture in the Distinguished Jesuit Lecture series at the University of San Francisco, 1999.

Egan, Robert J., S.J. "Jesus in the Heart's Imagination." *The Way,* Supplement no. 82 (1995).

Eickhoff, Georg. "Claraval, Digulleville, Loyola: La alegoría caballeresca de *El peregrino de la vida humana* en los noviciados monástico y jesuítico." In Plazaola, *Ignacio y su tiempo.*

Einem, Herbert von. *Michelangelo.* Translated by Ronald Taylor. London: Methuen, 1973.

Eliot, T. S. *The Complete Poems and Plays: 1909–1950.* New York: Harcourt, Brace & World, 1971.

Emonet, Pierre, S.J. "Faire de toute sa vie une prière continuelle." *Christus* 37 (1990).

———. " 'Faire de toutes ses actions une prière continuelle': La prière de ceux qui n'ont pas beaucoup de temps pour faire oraison." *Cahiers de spiritualité ignatienne* 16 (1992).

Endean, Philip, S.J. "The Ignatian Prayer of the Senses." *Heythrop Journal* 31 (1990).

———. *Karl Rahner and Ignatian Spirituality.* Oxford: Oxford University Press, 2001.

Epistolæ mixtæ ex variis Europæ locis ab anno 1537 ad 1556 scriptæ (Epist.mixt). 5 vols. Vols. 12, 14, 17, 18, and 20 of ᴍʜsɪ. Madrid, 1898–1901.

Esser, Cajetan, O.F.M. *Origins of the Franciscan Order.* Translated by Aedan Daly, O.F.M., and Dr. Irina Lynch. Chicago: Franciscan Herald Press, 1970.

Fabre, Pierre-Antoine. "Ignace de Loyola et Jérôme Nadal: Paternité et filiation chez les premiers jésuites." In Plazaola, *Ignacio y su tiempo.*

Farge, James K. "The University of Paris in the Time of Ignatius of Loyola." In Plazaola, *Ignacio y su tiempo*.

Favre, Pierre, S.J. *Beati Petri Fabri, primi sacerdotis e Societate Iesu epistolæ (Epist-Fab)*. Vol. 48 of MHSI. Madrid, 1914; reprinted 1972.

———. *The Spiritual Writings of Pierre Favre*. Translated by Edmund C. Murphy, S.J. St. Louis: The Institute of Jesuit Sources, 1996.

———. "The *Memoriale* of Pierre Favre." In *The Spiritual Writings of Pierre Favre*.

Fernández, Luis. "Iñigo de Loyola y los alumbrados." *Hispania sacra* 35 (1983).

Fois, Mario, S.J. "La giustificazione cristiana degli studi umanistici da parte de Ignazio di Loyola e le sue conseguenze nei gesuiti posteriori." In Plazaola, *Ignacio y su tiempo*,

Fontes narrativi de Loyola et de Societatis Iesu initiis (Font.narr). Edited by Cándido de Dalmases, 4 vols. Vols. 66, 73, 85, and 93 of MHSI. Rome: IHSI, 1943–65.

For Matters of Greater Moment: The First Thirty Jesuit General Congregations: A Brief History and a Translation of the Decrees (MattGM). Edited by John W. Padberg, S.J., Martin D. O'Keefe, S.J., John L. McCarthy, S.J. St. Louis: The Institute of Jesuit Sources, 1994.

França Miranda, Mario da, S.J. " 'Trouver Dieu en toutes choses' dans la société moderne." *Cahiers de spiritualité ignatienne* 14 (1990).

Francis and Clare: The Complete Works. Translated with introduction by Regis J. Armstrong, O.F.M. Cap., and Ignatius C. Brady, O.F.M. New York: Paulist Press, 1982.

Ganss, George E., S.J. *Saint Ignatius' Idea of a Jesuit University: A Study in the History of Catholic Education*. Milwaukee: Marquette University Press, 1954.

Garcia-Villoslada, Ricardo, S.J. *San Ignacio de Loyola: Nueva Biografía*. Madrid: Biblioteca de Autores Cristianos, 1986.

Gaulin, Hervé, S.J. "La Vocation apostolique de la Compagnie de Jésus dans les écrits du Père Jérôme Nadal, S.J." Unpublished doctoral dissertation prepared for the Pontificia Universitas Gregoriana, Rome, 1952.

Gilardi, Lorenzo M., S.J. "Autobiografie di Gesuiti in Italia (1540–1640): storia e interpretazione." *Archivum historicum Societatis Iesu (AHSI)* 64 (1995).

Giuliani, Maurice, S.J. "Finding God in All Things." In Young, *Finding God in All Things*.

Guibert, Joseph de, S.J. "En quoi diffèrent réellement les diverses écoles catholiques de spiritualité?" *Gregorianum* 19 (1938).

———. "Mystique Ignatienne: A propos du 'Journal Spirituel' de Saint Ignace de Loyola." *RAM* 19 (1938).

———. *Leçons de théologie spirituelle*. Toulouse, 1943.

———. *The Jesuits: Their Spiritual Doctrine and Practice: A Historical Study*. Translated by W. J. Young, S.J. St. Louis: The Institute of Jesuit Sources/Chicago: Loyola University Press, 1964.

Guigues I, *Coutumes de Chartreuse* (Bd de Latour-Maubourg: du Cerf, 1984),

Hamilton, Alistair. *Heresy and Mysticism in Sixteenth-Century Spain: The Alumbrados*. Toronto: University of Toronto Press, 1992.

Hamilton, Andrew, S.J. "In Sin Was I Conceived." *Review of Ignatian Spirituality* 29, no. 88 (1998).

Harter, Michael, S.J., ed. *Hearts on Fire: Praying with Jesuits.* St. Louis: The Institute of Jesuit Sources, 1993.

Hassett, John, and Hugh Lacey, eds. *Towards a Society That Serves Its People: The Intellectual Contribution of El Salvador's Murdered Jesuits.* Washington, D.C.: Georgetown University Press, 1991.

Hausman, Noëlle, S.C.M. "Ignatius Loyola and the Mission of the Holy Spirit: An Interpretation of the *Spiritual Diary* (1544–1545)." *CIS* 20, nos. 1–2 (1990).

Hillerman, Tony. "With Beauty before Me." In *Pocket Prayers,* edited by Gertrud Mueller Nelson and Christopher Witt. New York: Doubleday Books, 1995.

Hopkins, Gerard Manley, S.J. *The Poems of Gerard Manley Hopkins.* Edited by W. H. Gardner and N. H. MacKenzie. 4th ed. London: Oxford University Press, 1967.

Hostie, Raymond, S.J. "Méditation et contemplation d'après le Père Jérôme Nadal." *RAM* 32 (1956).

———. "The Cycle of Activity and Prayer according to Father Jerome Nadal." In Young, *Finding God in All Things.* Originally in *Origins* 6 (April 1955).

Houdek, Frank J., S.J. "Jesuit Prayer and Jesuit Ministry: Context and Possibilities." *Studies in the Spirituality of Jesuits* 24, no. 1 (1992).

———. "The Limitations of Ignatian Prayer." *The Way,* Supplement no. 82 (1995).

Howell, Patrick J., S.J. *As Sure as the Dawn: A Spiritguide through Times of Darkness.* Kansas City: Sheed & Ward, 1996.

Ignatius, St. *Sancti Ignatii de Loyola Societatis Iesu fundatoris epistolæ et instructiones (EpistIgn).* 12 vols. Vols. 22, 26, 28, 29, 31, 33, 34, 36, 37, 38, 40, and 42 of MHSI. Madrid, 1903–11; reprinted in Rome, 1964–68.

———. *The Spiritual Journal of St. Ignatius Loyola.* Translated by William J. Young, S.J. Woodstock, Md.: Woodstock College Press, 1958; reprinted Jersey City, N.J., 1971.

———. *Letters of St. Ignatius of Loyola.* Translated by W. J. Young. Chicago: Loyola University Press, 1959.

———. *Sancti Ignatii de Loyola Exercitia Spiritualia.* Vol. 100 of MHSI. Rome: Historical Institute of the Society of Jesus (IHSI), 1969.

———. *Saint Ignatius of Loyola: The Constitutions of the Society of Jesus (Cons.).* Translated and annotated by George E. Ganss, S.J. St. Louis: The Institute of Jesuit Sources, 1970.

———. *Obras completas de S. Ignacio de Loyola.* Edited by Ignacio Iparraguirre, S.I. Madrid: Biblioteca de Autores Cristianos, 1991.

———. *The Spiritual Exercises of Saint Ignatius (SpEx).* Trans. with commentary by George E. Ganss, S.J. St. Louis: The Institute of Jesuit Sources, 1992.

———. *A Pilgrim's Testament: The Spiritual Memoirs of St. Ignatius of Loyola (PilgTest).* Translated by Parmananda R. Divarkar, S.J. St. Louis: The Institute of Jesuit Sources, 1995.

———. "Responsio P. Manarei ad quædam Lancicii postulata." In *Scripta de Sancto Ignatio de Loyola,* 1:506–24. Vols. 20 and 21 of MHSI. Madrid: 1904.

———. "Ephemeris S. P. N. Ignatii." In *Constitutiones* 1:86–158.

———. "Spiritual Diary." In *Ignatius of Loyola: The Spiritual Exercises and Selected Works,* edited by George E. Ganss, S.J., 238–70. New York: Paulist Press, 1991.

Institutum Societatis Iesu. 3 vols. Florence: SS. Conception, 1893.

Iparraguirre, Ignacio, S.J. "La oración en la compañía naciente." *AHSI* 25 (1956).

———. *Práctica de los ejercicios de San Ignacio de Loyola en vida de su autor, 1522–1556.* Bilbao: El Mensajero del Corazó de Jesús,/Rome: Institutum Historicum Societatis Iesu, 1946.

Jesuit Ratio Studiorum: 400th Anniversary Perspective, The. Edited by Vincent J. Duminuco, S.J. New York: Fordham University Press, 2000.

Jiménez, Diego, S.J. "Commentarium de vita et virtutibus Patris Nadal." In *Epistolæ et monumenta P. Hieronymi Nadal (EpistNadal),* 1:26–46.

John of the Cross, *The Spiritual Canticle.* Any edition.

Jourdin, Michel Mollat du. "Saint Ignace et les pèlerinages de son temps." In Plazaola, *Ignacio y su tiempo.*

Julius III, Pope. *Exposcit debitum* (1550). In *Constitutiones* 1:375–83.

Kamen, Henry. *Philip of Spain.* New Haven: Yale University Press, 1997.

———. *The Spanish Inquisition: A Historical Revision.* London: Weidenfeld and Nicolson, 1997.

Kennedy, Michael, S.J. *Eyes on Jesus: a Guide for Contemplation.* New York: Crossroad, 1999.

Kolvenbach, Peter-Hans, S.J. "Language and Anthropology: The *Spiritual Diary* of St. Ignatius." *CIS* 22, no. 2 (1991).

———. "'Anguish with Christ in Anguish': Ignatian Spirituality and the Cross." *Theology Digest* 44, no. 1 (1997).

———. "Creative Fidelity in Mission." *CIS* 31, no. 3 (2000).

———. *The Road from La Storta.* St. Louis: The Institute of Jesuit Sources, 2000.

———. "Ponencia de clausura." In *Ejercicios espirituales y mundo de hoy.* Congreso Internacional de Ejercicios, Loyola, 20–26 septiembre de 1991, edited by Juan Manuel Garcia-Lomas. Bilbao: Mensajero, 1991.

———. "A Certain Pathway to God *(Via quædam ad Deum)."* In *The Road from La Storta.*

———. "'Christ . . . Descended into Hell.'" In *The Road from La Storta.*

———. "'Fools for Christ's Sake.'" In *The Road from La Storta.*

———. "Ignatius of Loyola: Experience of Christ." In *The Road from La Storta.*

Lackner, Bede K., O.Cist., trans. "Early Cistercian Documents in Translation." In *The Cistercians: Ideals and Reality,* by Louis J. Lekai, O.Cist. Kent State University Press, 1977.

Ladero Quesada, Miguel Angel. "Ecos de una educación caballeresca." In Suárez Fernández, *Ignacio en la gran crisis.*

Lafrance, Jean. "Nota sobre la oración trinitaria de San Ignacio." *Manresa* 53 (1981).

Laínez, Diego. *Lainii monumenta: Epistolæ et acta Patris Jacobi Lainii secundi præpositi generalis Societatis Iesu (EpistLain)*. 8 vols. Vols. 44, 45, 47, 50, 51, 53, and 55 of MHSI. Madrid 1912–17.

Lekai Louis J., O.Cist. *The Cistercians: Ideals and Reality*. Kent State University Press, 1977.

———. "Motives and Ideals of the Eleventh-Century Monastic Renewal." In *The Cistercian Spirit: A Symposium*, by M. Basil Pennington, O.C.S.O. Shannon: Irish University Press, 1970.

Leturia, Pedro, S.J. "La hora matutina de meditación en la Compañía naciente." *AHSI* 3 (1934).

Lévesque, Fernand, S.J. "Contemplation et action chez saint Ignace." *Cahiers de spiritualité ignatienne* 3 (1979).

Lewis, Jacques, S.J. "L'Oraison ignatienne." *Cahiers de spiritualité ignatienne* 13 (1989).

Liturgy of the Hours, The. New York: Catholic Book Publishing Co., 1975.

Llorca, Bernardino, S.J. *La inquisición española y los Alumbrados (1509–1667)*. Biblioteca Salmanticensis, Estudios no. 32. Salamanca: Universidad Pontificia, 1980.

Longhurst, John E., S.J. "Saint Ignatius at Alcalá, 1526–1527." *AHSI* 26 (1957).

Lopez Tejada, Dario. "La paz interior, y el buscar y hallar a Dios en todas las cosas." *Revista de espiritualidad* 24 (1965).

MacDonnell, Joseph F., S.J. *Gospel Illustrations: A Reproduction of the 153 Images taken from Jerome Nadal's 1595 book* "Adnotationes et meditationes in Evangelia." Fairfield: Fairfield Jesuit Community, 1998.

———. *The Illustrated Spiritual Exercises, Edited by Jerome Nadal, Aide to Ignatius Loyola*. Scranton: University of Scranton Press, 2001.

Marías, Julián. "Las generaciones en la época de San Ignacio de Loyola: El mundo de 1491." In Suárez Fernándes, *Ignacio en la gran crisis*.

Martin, Maurice-Marie, S.J. "The Mysticism of St. Ignatius: A Study of the Gift of Tears in the Spiritual Diary." *CIS* 22 (1991).

May, Gerald G., M.D. *Addiction and Grace*. San Francisco: Harper & Row, 1988.

Medina, Francisco de Borja, S.J. "Ignacio de Loyola y la 'limpieza de sangre.'" In Plazaola, *Ignacio de Loyola y su tiempo*.

Mejía Saldarriaga, Rodrigo, S.J. *La dinámica de la Integración Espiritual: Buscar y hallar a Dios en todas las cosas*. Rome: CIS, 1980.

Meures, Franz, S.J. "Jesuit Corporate Identity: Promoting Unity and Cohesion in the Society of Jesus." *Review of Ignatian Spirituality* 29, no. 3 (1998).

Michael J. Buckley, S.J. "Ecclesial Mysticism in the *Spiritual Exercises* of Ignatius." *Theological Studies* 56 (1995).

———. "Mission in Companionship: Of Jesuit Community and Communion." *Studies in the Spirituality of Jesuits* 11, no. 4 (1979).

Mohammed, Ovey N., S.J. "Hinduism and Ignatian Spirituality." *The Way,* Supplement 68 (1990).

Mollat, Donatien, S.J. "Le Christ dans l'expérience spirituelle de Saint Ignace." *Christus* 1 (1954).

Monumenta Constitutionum prævia. Vol. 1 of *Constitutiones.*

Moore, Donald, S.J. "An Ignatian Perspective on Contemporary Jewish Spirituality." *Thought* 67 (1992).

Myers, Ched. *Binding the Strong Man: A Political Reading of Mark's Story of Jesus.* Maryknoll, N.Y.: Orbis, 1988.

Nadal, Jerónimo, S.J. *Evangelicæ historiæ imagines: ex ordine Euangeliorum quae toto anno in Missæ sacrificio recitantur, in ordine temporis vitæ Christi digestæ.* Antwerp, 1593.

———. *Adnotationes et meditationes in Evangelia.* . . . Antwerp: 1594–95.

———. *Pláticas espirituales del P. Jerónimo Nadal, S.I., en Coimbra (1561).* Edited with notes by Miguel Nicolau, S.I. Granada: Facultad teológica de la Compañía de Jesús, 1845.

———. *Scholia in constitutiones et declarationes S.P. Ignatii.* Prato: Giachetti & Sons, 1883.

———. *Epistolæ et monumenta P. Hieronymi Nadal (EpistNadal).* Edited by Miguel Nicolau, S.J. Vols. 13, 15, 21, and 27 of MHSI. Rome: IHSI, 1962.

———. *P. Hieronymi Nadal commentarii de Instituto Societatis Iesu (CommInst).* Edited by Miguel Nicolau, S.J. Vol. 90 of MHSI. Rome: IHSI, 1962.

———. *P. Hieronymi Nadal orationis observationes (Orat.observ).* Edited by Michael Nicolau, S.J. Vol. 50a of MHSI. Rome: IHSI, 1964.

———. "De oratione." In *CommInst* 26–30.

———. "Exhortationes in hispania" *(Exhort. 1554 Hisp.).* In *CommInst* 75.

———. "Annotationes in Constitutiones" (1556). In *CommInst* 120f.

———. "Natalis ephemerides" *(NadEphem).* In *EpistNadal* 2:1–97.

———. "Acta quædam nostri P. Ignatii." In *Font.narr* 2.

———. "Adhortationes in Collegio Romano" *(AdhortRom),* 1557. In *Font.narr* 2.

———. "In exam. annot." In *P. Hieronymi Nadal commentarii de Instituto Societatis Iesu (CommInst).* 195, no. 175.

———. "Exhort. 4 in Alcalá" (1561). In *CommInst* 335 f.

———. "Dialogus II (1562–65)." In *CommInst.*

———. "Exhort. 1567 Colon." In *CommInst* 799.

———. "De professione et choro," in *Epistolæ et monumenta P. Hieronymi Nadal (EpistNadal).*

———. "Exhort. 2 in Alcalá." In *CommInst* 262.

———. "Exhort. 3ª & 12ª in Alcalá." In *CommInst.*

———. "Ad. ev., Transitus Matris Dei." In *Adnotationes et meditationes in Evangelia.*

———. "Ad. ev., feria II maj. hebd." In *Adnotationes et meditationes in Evangelia.* Antwerp: 1594–95.

———. "Plática 4ª en Coimbra." In *Pláticas espirituales,* 72.

———. "Capita quædam, quibus in spiritu adiuuari possumus." In *EpistNadal* 4:578–80.

———. "De ministerio verbi Dei." In *Epistolæ et monumenta P. Hieronymi Nadal (EpistNadal)* 4:663 f.

———. "De ratione instituti." In *EpistNadal* 4:514 f.

———. "Orationis ratio in Societate." In *EpistNadal* 4:670–81.

———. "Plática 11ª en Coimbra." In *Pláticas espirituales del P. Jerónimo Nadal.*

———. "Orden de la oración." In *Constitutiones et regulæ,* 486–91.

———. " 'The Chronicle: The Beginning of His Vocation.' " Translated by Martin E. Palmer, S.J. *Studies in the Spirituality of Jesuits* 24, no. 3 (1992), and 24, no. 5 (1992).

Nicolau, Miguel, S.J. *Jerónimo Nadal, S.I. (1507–1580): Sus obras y doctrinas espirituales.* Madrid: Consejo superior de investigaciones cientificas, 1949.

———. "La oración de San Ignacio: Fórmulas que la expresan." *Manresa* 28 (1956).

———. "What Nadal Meant by 'In Actione Contemplativus.' " *CIS* 8 (1977).

Nolan, Albert, O.P. *Jesus before Christianity.* New York: Orbis, 1992.

O'Collins, Gerald, S.J. "The Mission Christology of General Congregation 34." *CIS* 27, no. 3 (1996).

O'Malley, John W. *The First Jesuits.* Cambridge, Mass.: Harvard Univ. Press, 1993.

———. "Early Jesuit Spirituality: Spain and Italy." In *Religious Culture in the Sixteenth Century: Preaching, Rhetoric, Spirituality, and Reform,* by John W. O'Malley, S.J. Variorum, 1993.

O'Reilly, Terence. "Melchor Cano and the Spirituality of St. Ignatius Loyola." In Plazaola, *Ignacio y su tiempo.*

"Observata patrum." In *Constitutiones* 1:390–96.

Olivares, Estanislao, S.J. "Aportación de la Compañía de Jesús a la vida religiosa en su época." *Manresa* 56 (1984).

Orella Unzué, José Luis. "La Provincia de Guipúzcoa y el tema de los judíos en tiempos del joven Iñigo de Loiola (1492–1528)." In Plazaola, *Ignacio y su tiempo.*

Orsy, Ladislas, S.J. "The Formation of Contemplatives in Action." *Review for Religious* 33 (1974).

Pate, Dennis Edmond. "Jeronimo Nadal and the Early Development of the Society of Jesus, 1545–1573." Dissertation presented at the University of California, Los Angeles, 1980. In *Dissertation Abstracts,* A41 (1980–81).

Patrologiæ cursus completus, series Latina. Paris: Barnier.

Paul III, Pope. *Regimini militantis Ecclesiæ* (1540). In *Constitutiones* 1:14–21.

Pieris, Aloysius, S.J. "Ignatian Exercises against a Buddhist Background." *The Way,* Supplement 68 (1990).

Plazaola, Juan, ed. *Ignacio de Loyola y su tiempo.* Congreso internacional de historia, 9–13 Setiembre 1991. Bilbao: Mensajero—Universidad de Deusto, 1992.

Polanco, Juan de, S.J. *Vita Ignatii Loiolæ et rerum Societatis Iesu historia.* In *Vita Ignatii Loiolæ et rerum Societatis Iesu historia (PolChron).* 6 vols. Vols. 1, 3, 5, 7, 9, and 11 of MHSI. Rome: IHSI.

"Prima Societatis Jesu instituti summa." In *Constitutiones,* 1:14–21.

Przywara, Erich, S.J. "God in All Things." *Sursum Corda* 12 (1972).

Rahner, Hugo, S.J. "Die Mystik des hl. Ignatius und der Inhalt der Vision von La Storta." *Zeitschrift für Aszese und Mystik* 10 (1935).

———. *Saint Ignatius Loyola: Letters to Women.* New York: Herder and Herder, 1960.

———. *The Vision of St. Ignatius in the Chapel of La Storta.* 2nd ed. Rome: CIS, 1979.

Rahner, Karl, S.J. *Spiritual Exercises.* Translated by Kenneth Baker, S.J. New York: Herder and Herder, 1965.

———. "The Ignatian Mysticism of Joy in the World." In *Theological Investigations,* trans. Karl-H. and Boniface Kruger. Helicon Press, Baltimore: 1967.

Rathbone, Julian. *The Last English King.* London: Little, Brown and Co., 1997.

Ravier, André, S.J. *Les Chroniques: Saint Ignace de Loyola.* Paris: Nouvelle Librairie de France, 1973.

"Regional Order of Studies, U.S. Assistancy." 1991 proposed revision of 1983 text.

Regulæ Societatis Iesu. Edited by Dionysius Fernández Zapico, S.I. Vol. 71 of MHSI. Rome: 1948.

Reites, James W., S.J. "St. Ignatius of Loyola and the Jews." *Studies in the Spirituality of Jesuits* 13 (September 1981).

Ribadeneira, Pedro de, S.J. *Vita Ignatii Loyolæ.* In *Font.narr* 4:62–931.

———. "De prognatis genere hebræorum Societatis aditu non excludendis." In *Patris Petri de Ribadeneira Societatis Iesu sacerdotis Confessiones, epistolæ, aliaque scripta inedita,* 2 vols. Madrid, 1920–23.

———. "Hist. de la Asist. de España." Manuscript preserved in the Archivum Romanum Societatis Iesu, Hisp. 94.

Rodriguez Osorio, Hermann, S.J. "La oración en las pláticas espirituales de Jerónimo Nadal en Coimbra (1561)." *Manresa* 70 (1997).

Royce, Thomas R., S.J. "The Ignatian Vision of the Universe and of Man." *Cross Currents* 4 (1953/1954).

Royo Millán, Aurora, R. J. M., " 'Contemplativo en la acción': Semblanza espiritual de San Ignacio." *Teología espiritual: Revista cuatrimestral de los Estudios Generales Dominicanos de España* 17 (1973).

Ruiz Jurado, Manuel, S.J. "La perspectiva de San Ignacio en su visión del mundo y su influjo en el modo de ser de la Compañía." *Manresa* 45 (1973).

———. "Un caso de profetismo reformista en la Compañía de Jesús—Gandía, 1547–1549." *AHSI* 43 (1974)

———. "Cronologia de la vida del P. Jerônimo Nadal, S.I. (1507–1580). *AHSI* 48 (1979).

———. "La figura de Jerónimo Nadal en la primera crisis grave de la Compañía (1556–1557)." *Manresa* 52 (1980).

———. "El Espíritu Santo en la espiritualidad ignaciana." *Manresa* 70 (1998).

Sacchinus, Franciscus, S.J. *Historiæ Societatis Iesu pars quarta.* Rome, 1652.

Sachs, John R., S.J. "Ignatian Mysticism." *The Way,* Supplement no. 82 (1995).

Sanz de Diego, Rafael M.ª, S.J. "Ignacio de Loyola en Alcalá de Henares (1526–1527): Andanzas de un universitario atípico." In Plazaola, *Ignacio y su tiempo,*

———. "La novedad de Ignacio de Loyola ante un mundo nuevo." In Plazaola, *Ignacio y su tiempo.*

Schineller, J. Peter, S.J. "The Pilgrim Journey of Ignatius: From Soldier to Laborer in the Lord's Vineyard and Its Implications for Apostolic Lay Spirituality." *Studies in the Spirituality of Jesuits* 31, no. 4 (1999).

Schneiders, Sandra M., I.H.M. *Finding the Treasure: Locating Catholic Religious Life in a New Ecclesial and Cultural Context.* Vol. 1 of *Religious Life in a New Millennium* (New York: Paulist Press, 2000).

Schurhammer, Georg, S.J. *Francis Xavier: His Life, His Times.* Translated by M. Joseph Costelloe, S.J. 4 vols. Rome: IHSI, 1973.

Sheldrake, Philip, S.J. "Theology of the Cross and the Third Week." *The Way,* Supplement no. 58 (1987).

Silos, Leonardo R., S.J. "Cardoner in the Life of Saint Ignatius of Loyola." *AHSI* 33 (1964).

Singh, Kathleen Dowling. *The Grace in Dying: How We Are Transformed Spiritually As We Die.* New York: HarperCollins, 2000.

Solignac, Aimé. "Vie active, contemplative, mixte." In *DSAM.*

Stierli, Josef, S.J. *Ignatius von Loyola: Seine Gestalt und sein Vermächtnis.* Würzburg, 1956.

———. *Woodstock Letters* 90 (1961): 135–66. Translated by Morton J. Hill, S.J.

———. *Chercher Dieu en toutes choses: Vie au coeur du monde et prière ignatienne.* Translated by Pierre Emonet. Paris: Centurion, 1985.

———. "Jérôme Nadal (1507–1580): Le bras droit du Fondateur." *Cahiers de spiritualité ignatienne* 15 (1991).

———. "Ignatian Prayer: Seeking God in All Things." In *Ignatius of Loyola: His Personality and Spiritual Heritage 1556–1956: Studies on the 400th Anniversary of His Death,* edited by Friedrich Wulf, S.J. St. Louis: The Institute of Jesuit Sources, 1977.

Suárez Fernández, Luis. *Ignacio de Loyola en la gran crisis del siglo XVI.* Bilbao: Mensajero, 1991.

———. "El marco histórico de Iñigo López de Loyola y su educación cortesana." In Suárez Fernández, *Ignacio en la gran crisis.*

Summa theologiæ 2ª 2ᵃᵉ.

Switek, Günter, S.J. "Die Eigenart der Gesellschaft Jesu im Vergleich zu den anderen Orden in der Sicht des Ignatius und seiner ersten Gefährten." In *Ignatianisch: Eigenart und Methode der Gesellschaft Jesu.* Edited by M. Sievernich, S.J. and G. Switek, S.J. Freiburg: Herder, 1990.

Synopsis historiæ Societatis Jesu. Ratisbon: Pustet, 1914.

Tacchi Venturi, Pietro. *Storia della Compagnia di Gesù in Italia.* 2nd ed. Rome, 1950.

Tanner, Norman P. "Medieval Crusade Decrees and Ignatius's Meditation on the Kingdom." *Heythrop Journal* 31 (1990).

Teresa of Avila. *The Collected Works of Teresa of Avila.* Translated by Kieran Kavanaugh, O.C.D., and Otilio Rodriguez, O.C.D. Washington, D.C.: Institute of Carmelite Studies, 1980.

"'Tractatus de approbatione Ordinis Fratrum Prædicatorum.'" Edited by Th. Käppeli, O.P. *Fratrum Archivum Prædicatorum* 6 (1936).

Truhlar, Carolus, S.J. *De experientia mystica.* Rome: Universitas Gregoriana, 1951.

Tugwell, Simon, O.P. *The Way of the Preacher.* Appen. 2, "The Apostolic Life." Springfield: Templegate, 1979.

——, ed. *Early Dominicans: Selected Writings.* The Classics of Western Spirituality series. New York: Paulist Press, 1982.

Tylenda, Joseph N., S.J. *Jesuit Saints and Martyrs.* 2nd ed. Chicago: Loyola, 1998.

"United with Christ in Mission." In *Documents of the Thirty-Fourth General Congregation of the Society of Jesus,* 17–23.

"Up-to-Date Renewal of Religious Life, Decree on the." In *Vatican Council II: The Conciliar and Post-Conciliar Documents,* 611–23.

Vatican Council II: The Conciliar and Post-Conciliar Documents (DocsVatII). Edited by Austin Flannery, O.P. Collegeville, Minn.: The Liturgical Press, 1975.

Veale, Joseph, S.J. "Life of the Spirit (II): Ignatian Contemplation." *The Furrow* 28 (1977).

Verny, Louis. "In actione contemplativus." RAM 26 (1950).

"Vita antiquior." In *Patrologiæ cursus completus: Series Latina,* edited by Jacques-Paul Migne (Paris, 1844–91).

"Vita antiquior Brunonis." In *Patrologiæ cursus completus, series Latina.* Paris: Barnier.

Vitry, Jacques de. *Historia orientalis.* Quoted in Esser, *Origins of the Franciscan Order.*

Vries, Piet Penning de S.J. "All or Nothing: Carmelite Spirituality against an Ignatian Background." Trans. by Mrs. W. Dudok van Heel, *Spiritual Life* 17 (1971).

Wankenne, André, S.J. "Painters of the Passion." *Lumen Vitae* 9 (1954).

Weill, Georges. *De Gulielmi Postelli vita et indole.* Geneva: Slatkine Reprints, 1969.

Wilms, Cecilia W. "Thoughts in Solitude." *Raven's Bread* 1, no. 2 (1997).

Wolter, Hans, S.J. "Elements of Crusade Spirituality in St. Ignatius." In *Ignatius of Loyola: His Personality and Spiritual Heritage, 1556–1956*. St. Louis: The Institute of Jesuit Sources, 1977.

Wright, John H., S.J. "The Grace of Our Founder and the Grace of Our Vocation." *Studies in the Spirituality of Jesuits* 3 (February 1971).

Xavier, Francis, S.J. *The Letters and Instructions of Francis Xavier*. Translated with introduction by M. Joseph Costelloe, S.J. St. Louis: The Institute of Jesuit Sources, 1992.

Young, William J., S.J., ed. *Finding God in All Things: Essays in Ignatian Spirituality Selected from* Christus, translated by William J. Young, S.J. Chicago: Henry Regnery Co., 1958.

INDEX

Abraham, 3, 55, 63, 69, 250, 251
active life, 85–86, 158, 172, 199, 231
    definition of, 157–59
    higher (more holistic)
agere contra, 115
Alcalá, 9, 48, 167, 192
    exhortations in, 89ff., 113–19, 135–36
    time for prayer, 60
Alexander VI, Pope, great-grandfather of
    Francis Borgia, 193
alumbrados, 31, 48
Álvarez, Baltasar, 216
Álvarez, Juan, 104
Amadis of Gaul, 107, 118, 204
Anna the prophetess, 250
Anthony, St., 33, 124
anti-mysticism, 215–17
apostolic age, model of how to live
    Christian life, 73
apostolic life
    as imitating life of apostles, 73
    various ways of imitating apostles, 74
Aquaviva, Claude, 20, 20 n. 42
Aquinas, Thomas, St., xviii, 33, 158, 229
    his formula *contempla aliis tradere,*
    230–231
Araoz, Antonio, 81, 146, 148. *See also*
    Araoz, Antonio, offices held.
    about to become provincial, 147
    excesses in prayer and penance, 194–95
    first professed after original companions,
    146
    goes to Rome for meeting on
    Constitutions, 195
    need to correct own excesses, 149
    and Oviedo, 149
    related to Ignatius by marriage, 194
    relationship with Borgia, 79, 202
Araoz, Antonio, offices held
    first provincial of Spain, 146
    provincial of Castile, 28, 78
    visitor for whole of Spain, 149

Arendt, Hannah, 55
Arrupe, Pedro, S.J., xvii, 20 n. 42, 222,
    237, 242, 248, 269
    final years, 265–67
    his *Suscipe,* 266
    homily at La Storta, 266
Augustine, St. 33, 53, 183
Augustinians, 74, 124
Avignon, 10–11

Barcelona, 167
Baroëllo, Stephen, 71
Barreto, Juan Nuñez, first Jesuit bishop
    along with Oviedo, 171–72
Basil, St., 33
Begheyn, Paul, S.J. *See* Michael Campbell-
    Johnston, S.J.
Bellini, Isidoro, scholastic shipwrecked
    with Nadal, 109
Benedict, St., 33, 74, 77 n. 6, 124, 179,
    232
Benedictines, 172, 189
Bergson, Henri, 252
Bernard, St., 27
Bertrand, Dominique, S.J., xx
Beyer, Jean, S.J., 263
Bobadilla, Nicholás, 8, 10, 81, 111, 145,
    157, 192, 248
Bonaventure, St. (Pseudo-Bonaventure),
    xxiii
Borgia, Eleonor, duchess of Gandía, 147
Borgia, Francis, St., xxiii, 20, 20 n. 42, 53,
    67, 145, 170, 240. *See also* Borgia,
    Francis, St., difficulties experienced.
    at 20 in charge of imperial household,
    193
    about to become a Jesuit, 147
    appoints Nadal vicar-general, 214
    attends Rome meeting on *Constitutions,*
    195
    commissary general of Spain, 78
    dedicated to Prince Philip, 194

289